Communications in Computer and Information Science 559

Commenced Publication in 2007
Founding and Former Series Editors:
Alfredo Cuzzocrea, Dominik Ślęzak, and Xiaokang Yang

More information about this series at http://www.springer.com/series/7899

Jeanne Lam · Kwan Keung Ng
Simon K.S. Cheung · Tak Lam Wong
Kam Cheong Li · Fu Lee Wang (Eds.)

Technology in Education

Technology-Mediated Proactive Learning

Second International Conference, ICTE 2015
Hong Kong, China, July 2–4, 2015
Revised Selected Papers

Springer

Editors
Jeanne Lam
HKU School of Professional and Continuing Education
Pokfulam
Hong Kong

Kwan Keung Ng
Caritas Institute of Higher Education
Tseung Kwan O
Hong Kong

Simon K.S. Cheung
The Open University of Hong Kong
Homantin
Hong Kong

Tak Lam Wong
The Hong Kong Institute of Education
Tai Po
Hong Kong

Kam Cheong Li
The Open University of Hong Kong
Homantin
Hong Kong

Fu Lee Wang
Caritas Institute of Higher Education
Tseung Kwan O
Hong Kong

ISSN 1865-0929 ISSN 1865-0937 (electronic)
Communications in Computer and Information Science
ISBN 978-3-662-48977-2 ISBN 978-3-662-48978-9 (eBook)
DOI 10.1007/978-3-662-48978-9

Library of Congress Control Number: 2015954991

Springer Heidelberg New York Dordrecht London

Springer-Verlag GmbH Berlin Heidelberg is part of Springer Science+Business Media
(www.springer.com)

Preface

This edited volume consists of extended papers selected from the Second International Conference on Technology in Education (ICTE 2015), which was held at the Caritas Institute of Higher Education, Hong Kong, SAR China, during July 2–4, 2015.

Nowadays, technology has emerged in various facets of teaching and learning. In a technology-enabled learning environment, students can learn in more proactive ways. This aligns to the ideas of student-centered learning. Technology-mediated proactive learning has become an important topic for further investigation, and therefore ICTE 2015 took "Technology-Mediated Proactive Learning" as its main theme. The focus was placed on how technology can be used to enable proactive learning so as to enhance learning effectiveness and enrich learning experience. After a careful paper review process, a total of 26 papers were selected for inclusion in this volume. These papers are organized in five groups, namely, technology-enabled learning, mobile learning and ubiquitous learning, learning platforms and advising systems, open learning and online learning, and institutional strategies, policies, and practices.

Our sincere thanks go to the conference Organizing Committee for their effective administration and unfailing support. Our thanks also go to the International Program Committee. The high quality of the papers could not have been maintained without their professional comments and advice in the paper review process.

October 2015

Jeanne Lam
Kwan Keung Ng
Simon K.S. Cheung
Tak Lam Wong
Kam Cheong Li
Fu Lee Wang

Organization

Conference Chair

Reggie Kwan	Caritas Institute of Higher Education, Hong Kong

Organizing Committee

Chairs

Jeanne Lam	HKU School of Professional and Continuing Education, Hong Kong
Kwan Keung Ng	Caritas Institute of Higher Education, Hong Kong

Members

Melani Au	HKU School of Professional and Continuing Education, Hong Kong
Oliver Au	The Open University of Hong Kong, Hong Kong
Radar Chan	HKU School of Professional and Continuing Education, Hong Kong
Simon K.S. Cheung	The Open University of Hong Kong, Hong Kong
Wai Shing Ho	Caritas Institute of Higher Education, Hong Kong
Wing Leung	HKU School of Professional and Continuing Education, Hong Kong
Louise Luk	Caritas Institute of Higher Education, Hong Kong
Fu Lee Wang	Caritas Institute of Higher Education, Hong Kong
Beryl Wong	The Open University of Hong Kong, Hong Kong
Tak Lam Wong	The Hong Kong Institute of Education, Hong Kong

International Program Committee

Chairs

Simon K.S. Cheung	The Open University of Hong Kong, Hong Kong
Tak Lam Wong	The Hong Kong Institute of Education, Hong Kong

Members

Zoraini Wati Abas	Universitas Siswa Bangsa Indonesia, Jakarta
Oliver Au	The Open University of Hong Kong, Hong Kong
Ching Sing Chai	Nanyang Technological University, Singapore
Gary Cheng	The Hong Kong Institute of Education, Hong Kong
Wing Sum Cheung	Nanyang Technological University, Singapore
Daniel Churchill	The University of Hong Kong, Hong Kong

Khe Foon Hew	The University of Hong Kong, Hong Kong
Wai Shing Ho	Caritas Institute of Higher Education, Hong Kong
Kian Sam Hong	University Malaysia Sarawak, Malaysia
Gwo Jen Hwang	National University of Tainan, Taiwan
Morris Siu Yung Jong	The Chinese University of Hong Kong, Hong Kong
Kwok Wing Lai	University of Otago, New Zealand
Jeanne Lam	HKU School of Professional and Continuing Education, Hong Kong
Chwee Beng Lee	University of Western Sydney, Australia
Ji Yeon Lee	Inha University, South Korea
Kai Ming Li	The Hong Kong Institute of Education, Hong Kong
Kam Cheong Li	The Open University of Hong Kong, Hong Kong
Ping Li	The Hong Kong Institute of Education, Hong Kong
Rose Liang	National University of Singapore, Singapore
Chiu Pin Lin	National Hsin Chu University of Education, Taiwan
Will Ma	Hong Kong Shue Yan University, Hong Kong
Shaun Nykvist	Queensland University of Technology, Australia
Innwoo Park	Korea University, Korea
Choon Lang Quek	Nanyang Technological University, Singapore
Ali Simsek	Anadolu University, Turkey
Yanjie Song	The Hong Kong Institute of Education, Hong Kong
Vincent Tam	The University of Hong Kong, Hong Kong
Jeff Tang	Caritas Institute of Higher Education, Hong Kong
Fu Lee Wang	Caritas Institute of Higher Education, Hong Kong
Chun Wang Wei	Far East University, Taiwan
Su Luan Wong	University Putra Malaysia, Malaysia
Yau Yeun Yeung	The Hong Kong Institute of Education, Hong Kong
Yuen Tak Yu	City University of Hong Kong, Hong Kong

Organizers

明愛專上學院
Caritas Institute of Higher Education

HKUSPACE
香港大學專業進修學院
HKU School of Professional and Continuing Education

香港公開大學
THE OPEN UNIVERSITY OF HONG KONG

Contents

Open Learning and Online Learning

Institutional Strategies, Policies and Practices

Learning Platforms and Advising Systems

Technology-Enabled Learning

Technology-Mediated Learning: Status and Challenges in Perspective

Kam Cheong Li(✉)

University Research Centre, Open University of Hong Kong, Kowloon, Hong Kong
kcli@ouhk.edu.hk

Abstract. Technology has become virtually an integral part of all areas of educational delivery. While technology brings new means and ways of learning to students and teachers, it also poses challenges to them. This paper attempts to offer glimpses of the transformation of technology-mediated learning that are taking place, with examples in three key areas: learning spaces, learning modes, and learning materials. It highlights the pervasive permeation of technology. Noting the challenges confronting educators in the adoption of the fast changing technology, it proposes a model to systematically identify the difficulties to tackle now and in time to come. The model takes into account the general environment that the educational institution operates in, as well as the readiness of the institution, the instructor and the learner.

Keywords: Technology-mediated learning · Learning modes · Learning spaces · Learning materials

1 Introduction

In this day and age, technology has been a mainstay in the development of our world, characterized by numerous 'information societies' [16]. Technology development ramifies into every aspect of human lives. The development of technology has been bringing tremendous changes to how learners go about their learning. This short paper attempts to offer a glimpse of this development. It is summarized from part of a keynote address in the 2015 International Conference on Technology in Education.

In the next section, a spread and aftermath of technology in education will be provided, including examples of current trends and the impact of technology on higher education, which encompasses evolving learning spaces, modes and materials.

Then, some major challenges together with potential benefits are discussed in perspective with a proposed model for considering the challenges of technology for educational purposes.

2 Development of Technology Mediation for Learning

The growth of technology has penetrated into virtually all aspects of education [9]. Educational technology has been bringing a paradigm shift in all aspects of learning.

J. Lam et al. (Eds.): ICTE 2015, CCIS 559, pp. 3–9, 2015.
DOI: 10.1007/978-3-662-48978-9_1

Some key trends in adopting technology are summarized in relation to learning spaces, learning modes and learning materials here.

Learning Spaces. For many centuries, teaching was carried out in classrooms (or lecture rooms) or venues where the teacher and the learner were physically present. Nowadays, increasing number of educational institutions have set up in their campus learning spaces as rooms for class teaching and learning. Such facilities are commonly called technology-mediated (or technology enabled) active learning spaces (or environment) or future classroom. The gradual transformation of classrooms into learning spaces reflects changes taking place in our general understanding of learning — students do not automatically learn when the teacher provides instructions, but learning takes place when students are engaged in learning [5]. In the learning space, technology plays a key role in facilitating learning. Typically ample use of computer screens for sharing of information and computing facilities allow fast search and retrieval of information for maximizing benefits of face-to-face contacts through flexible grouping of learners and communications with the teacher. With technology-mediation in the learning space, teachers are no longer restricted in the front of the class. Instead, they typically talk in the middle of the room or in individual groups [17, 18].

By creating learning spaces in the virtual world, technology has also freed learning from limitations of physical facilities. An example that students have enjoyed is 'Second Life', a three-dimensional virtual world, where individuals can interact with others via voice and text chat in an immersive 3-D environment [15]. Another example is Augmented Reality (AR), which provides 'a combination of real world elements captured through a camera with multimedia elements such as text, images, video, or 3D models and animations' [6].

Learning Modes. The development of educational technology has brought about a diversity of learning modes — 'Distance learning', 'online learning', 'blended learning', and 'mobile learning' being examples. These modes of learning make it ubiquitous [2] and thus it is not necessarily a result of teaching or instruction given by a teacher any longer. Figure 1 shows the frequency of the use of relevant terms on the internet as reported in Google search. These reflect the popularity and development trends in the learning modes.

It is worth noting that the usage of all four teams has increased by leaps and bounds. In particular, the usage of the decades-old term, "distance learning", has also greatly increased, and that for the relatively new term/phenomenon of "online learning" has had exponential growth. It can also be seen that the growth substantially quickened in 2008, the year from which Massive Open Online Courses (MOOCs) gradually became popular. Also around the time, tablet computers were becoming popular and the emergence of iPads in 2010 probably relates to the growth of the learning modes in subsequent years'.

It should be safe to predict that mobile devices will play an increasingly important role in learning. In the United States, more than 90 percent of the US college students use one or more mobile devices for school work during a typical school day for academic work [12]. Evidently, mobile devices, easily portable and allowing flexibility during

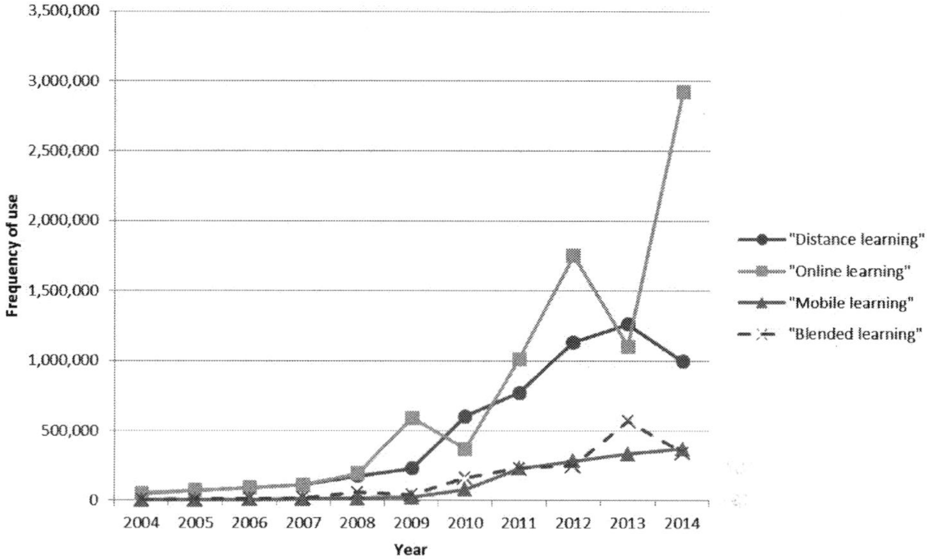

Fig. 1. Frequency of use of four learning-mode terms on Google Search from 2004 to 2014

student's learning process, have become part of university life. An increasing number of students have been encouraged to bring their own laptops, tablets, smartphones, or other mobile devices with them to the learning environment [10].

Learning Materials. A large quantity of learning materials are digitized for modern educational technology. Learning contents can be encoded, stored, transmitted and presented in various forms, such as PDF files, ePub, HTML, mobile apps, as well as audio and video files.

The volume of digitized materials has grown exponentially recently. The phenomenal growth of open educational resources (OERs) and MOOCs (in which all learning materials are digitized) is evidence of this development. The growth covers virtually all areas, including research material. For example, based on a search in PubMed Central, the growth of e-journals has been remarkable as shown in Fig. 2.

As reflected in these spaces, learning modes and learning materials, technology has permeated our education and is becoming the key driver of development. The changes have been fast, especially in the last decade, and such rapid nay frequent changes can be expected in coming decades too. Technology mediation has evidently become the key driver in development of learning. It is important to be able to properly utilize technology and overcome the challenges for implementing effective technology mediation for learning [1, 3, 4].

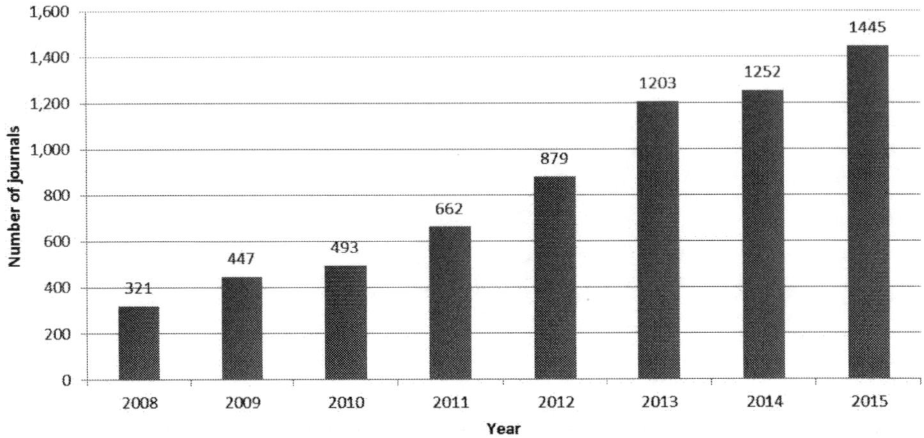

Fig. 2. The number of journals with immediate free access in the PubMed Central from 2008 to 2015 (based on data from Morrison, 2015) [7].

3 Challenges

The pervasiveness of technology in education makes it necessary that educational institutions and educators consider its adoption and customization in teaching delivery, no matter whether they are planning the curriculum, designing a learning system, preparing a lesson, or monitoring learning performance of students. Yet more often than not, there are difficulties to overcome in implementing effective technology mediation for learning.

The following model, as shown in Fig. 3, is proposed with a view to facilitating discussion and identification of challenges in the deployment of technology. There are four key areas in the model. The first is the macro-environment, which refers to the general environment where certain technology is to be adopted. It covers the availability of technology, user-friendliness, and general level of acceptance of technologies. These could pose serious challenges to adoption of technology. If a certain type of technology is not yet available, it cannot be adopted and the dilemma is whether to wait or go ahead with alternative means to satisfy the need. That the technology is available does not mean that it should be considered immediately for adoption. The extent to which it can be easily or appropriately used, and the extent to which the community expects to and accepts the use of the technology for the purposes are decisive.

The other three key areas are related to how ready they are to adopt the technology, including institutions', instructors' and learners' readiness.

At the *institutional level*, adoption of proper technology depends on foresight for development. The farsightedness of the key decision makers can facilitate or hinder the adoption of technology. The extent to which the institution can afford the technology and adapt it to its context play key roles and are also common challenges. Overcoming them is often the prerequisite for adopting the technology.

For example, the implementation of blended learning requires the provision of the core technological infrastructure for an effective course management system that is user-friendly for faculty and students [13]. The 'lack of proper acquisition of ICT' leads to

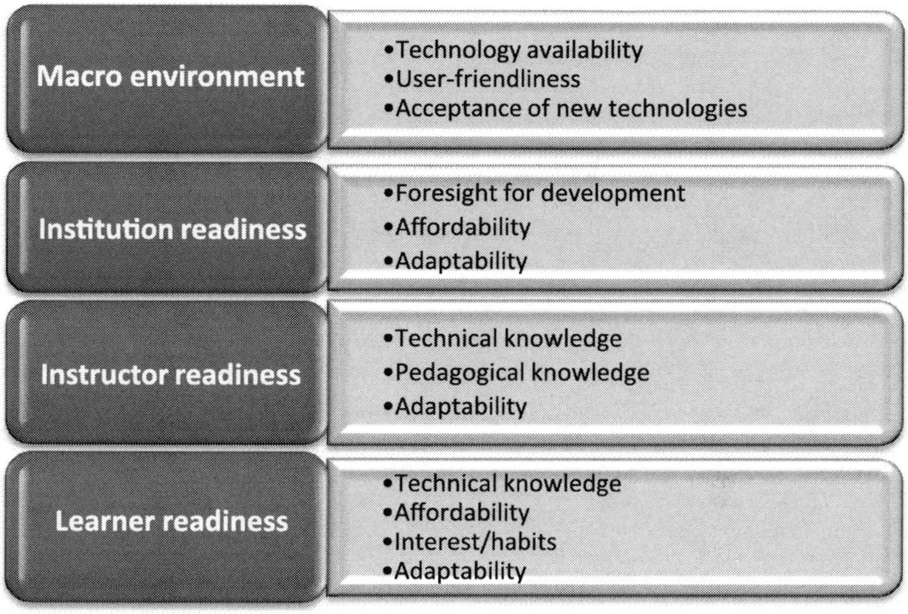

Fig. 3. Factors to consider for adopting technology for learning

'low utility, low ICT skills, inadequate supporting infrastructure and high cost of maintaining and servicing equipment' [11]. Besides, the high recurrent costs associated with the effective use of technology [8] could be barriers to implementation.

As for instructors and teachers, common key challenges include the extent to which their technical knowledge is sufficient for utilizing the available technology for effective teaching, how adequate is their pedagogical knowledge in deploying the technology for learning, and the extent to which the technology can be easily adapted or customized to the context for convenient teaching and learning. This is important. For example, Schoonenboom [14], found that the feeble intentions to use Learning Management Systems (LMS) among university instructors can be explained by low LMS ease of use as one of the factors. Their technical knowledge has a bearing on how they use educational technology, such as the LMS.

For a learner to be able to benefit from technology mediated in the learning process, they must possess the technical knowledge to use the technology. The technology must be affordable, interesting and in line with the life habit of the learner so that learning can be sustained. Also, the extent to which the technology can be tailored to suit the learning context of the learner plays a crucial role.

4 Concluding Remarks

This brief paper highlights pervasive permeation of technology in education, a phenomenon that no educator can afford to ignore. With examples in three key areas of development, learning spaces, learning modes and learning materials, it is evident that technology is bringing about a paradigm shift. Educators must master the trend and their technology relevant to their context so as to excel in their professional practices.

In the context, to properly benefit from technological mediation, it is necessary to be vigilant of a broad range of challenges. The model proposed in this paper offers a general plan to identify difficulties, which should assist educators in analysing challenges ahead in their adoption of technology.

References

1. Halimi, K., Seridi-Bouchelaghem, H., Faron-Zucker, C.: An enhanced personal learning environment using social semantic web technologies. Interact. Learn. Environ. **22**(2), 165–187 (2014). doi:10.1080/10494820.2013.788032
2. Holmes, M.R., Tracy, E.M., Painter, L.L., Oestreich, T., Park, H.: Moving from flipcharts to the flipped classroom: using technology driven teaching methods to promote active learning in foundation and advanced masters social work courses. Clin. Soc. Work J. **43**, 215–224 (2015)
3. Larsen, T.J., Sørebø, A.M., Sørebø, Ø.: The role of task-technology fit as users' motivation to continue information system use. Comput. Hum. Behav. **25**, 778–784 (2009). doi:10.1016/j.chb.2009.02.006
4. Lee, D.H., Shon, J.G., Kim, Y.: Design and implementation of OSMD based learning management system for mobile learning. Indian J. Sci. Technol. **8**(1), 154–160 (2015)
5. Li, K.C., Wang, F.L.: Student Engagement: Meanings, Approaches and Ideas for Educators Interested in ICT. In: Li, K.C., Wang, F.L., Yuen, K.S., Cheung, S.K.S., Kwan, R. (eds.) ICT 2012. CCIS, vol. 302, pp. 1–10. Springer, Heidelberg (2012)
6. Martin-Gutierrez, J., Fabiani, P., Benesova, W., Meneses, M.D., Mora, C.E.: Augmented reality to promote collaborative and autonomous learning in higher education. Comput. Hum. Behav. (2014). doi:10.1016/j.chb.2014.11.093
7. Morrison, H.: Dramatic Growth of Open Access Dataverse (2015). Accessed http://dataverse.scholarsportal.info/dvn/dv/dgoa/faces/study/StudyPage.xhtml;jsessionid=d14ffe493f807dcff317002c05a7?globalId=hdl:10864/10660&studyListingIndex=0_d14ffe493f807dcff317002c05a7
8. Nawaz, A., Zubair Khan, M.: Issues of technical support for e-Learning systems in higher education institutions. Int. J. Mod. Educ. Comput Sci. **2**, 38–44 (2012)
9. Nguyen, L., Barton, S.: iPads in Higher Education—Hype and Hope. British Journal of Educational Technology (2014). doi: http://www.researchgate.net/profile/Lemai_Nguyen/publication/260088377_iPads_in_higher_educationHype_and_hope/links/0c96053c3ea5de7b44000000.pdf
10. New Media Consortium and the EDUCAUSE Learning Initiative. The NMC Horizon Report: 2015 Higher Education Edition (2015). Accessed http://cdn.nmc.org/media/2015-nmc-horizon-report-HE-EN.pdf
11. Onyije, L.E., Opara, J.A.: Information and Communication Technologies (ICT): a panacea to achieving effective goals in institutional administration. Int. Lett. Soc. Humanistic Sci. **12**, 81–87 (2014)
12. Poll, H.: Pearson Student Mobile Device Survey 2014—National Report: College Students (2014). Accessed http://www.pearsoned.com/wp-content/uploads/Pearson-HE-Student-Mobile-Device-Survey-PUBLIC-Report-051614.pdf

13. Porter, W.W., Graham, C.R., Spring, K.A., Welch, K.R.: Blended learning in higher education: institutional adoption and implementation. Comput. Educ. **75**, 185–195 (2014)
14. Schoonenboom, J.: Using an adapted, task-level technology acceptance model to explain why instructors in higher education intend to use some learning management system tools more than others. Comput. Educ. **71**, 247–256 (2013)
15. Tugba Tokel, S., Isler, V.: Acceptance of virtual worlds as learning space. Innov. Educ. Teach. Int. **52**(3), 254–264 (2015)
16. Webster, F.: Theories of the Information Society. Routledge, New York (2014)
17. Xu, Y., Zhang J., LI, K.C.: The Transformation of Space Paradigm: From Teaching Space to Learning Space. E-Education Research. (forthcoming)
18. Zhang, J., Chen, W.: The main position of instruction: a study of the future classroom. Mod. Educ. Technol. **10**, 41–50 (2010)

Unpacking the Digital Backpack for the Adult Learner – A Universal Design for Learning Approach

Sylvia Chong(✉)

SIM University, 535A Clementi Road, Singapore 599490, Singapore
sylviachong@unisim.edu.sg

Abstract. Technology is able to overlap curriculum with learning by providing network resources, connectivity and organization. Learners can choose to move away from tangible learning resources and house them within network or cloud-based applications. The connectivity is a key advantage that provides learners easy access. The technology also allows the learner to organise and accomplish their learning tasks more efficiently. A learner's digital backpack in the practice of pedagogy is an example of such a concept. A digital backpack is exactly what it sounds like: a virtual bag with an array of digital tools, resources, and instructional materials selected to engage and support learners. This article presents the digital backpack for adult learners. The backpack is anchored on the design concepts and principles of Universal Design for Learning (UDL), an instructional design framework that supports diverse means of knowledge representation to develop learner's knowledge and understanding.

Keywords: Digital backpack · Adult learners · Universal design for learning (UDL)

1 Introduction

Today's learner requires a learning environment that is interactive as well as engaging. Higher education institutions have been exploring teaching and learning models that are both flexible and effective to provide learners with an efficient access towards quality learning. Courses vary in their use of teaching and learning resources, ranging from computers to textbooks. Technology has the ability to overlap curriculum and learning by enhancing the learning with network resources, connectivity and organization. Learners can choose to move away from tangible teaching and learning resources and organize them in network or cloud-based applications. A key advantage is in the connectivity that provides learners access to these teaching and learning materials from home, school or by mobile devices. Aside from the connectivity, the technology also allows the learner to organise and accomplish their learning tasks effectively. A learner's digital backpack in the practice of pedagogy is an example of such a concept. A digital backpack is exactly what it sounds like: a virtual bag that contains an array of digital tools, resources, and instructional materials specially selected to engage and support learners in their learning.

J. Lam et al. (Eds.): ICTE 2015, CCIS 559, pp. 10–22, 2015.
DOI: 10.1007/978-3-662-48978-9_2

This article presents the digital backpack for adult learners in SIM University, Singapore. The backpack purposefully combines technology with pedagogy to support the teaching and learning of the working adult learner enrolled in a part time degree program in SIM University. The design of this digital backpack is anchored on *Universal Design for Learning* (UDL) concepts and principles. UDL is an instructional design framework that supports diverse means of representation of knowledge with the aim to develop learner's knowledge and understanding while engaging them in learning [1, 2].

2 Relevant Studies

This literature review provides background research related to the analysis of the digital backpack for adult learners. Three key themes were reviewed.

1. The use of digital backpacks
2. UDL as an instructional design framework for learner engagement, and
3. The adult learner in higher education.

These three areas are pertinent to the development of a structure for analysing the digital backpack for the adult learner at SIM University, Singapore.

2.1 Digital Backpacks

There are not many scholarly studies on the design, development and implementation of digital backpacks. An early publication by Hoagland, Aplyn and Rice in 2001 [3] compared the digital backpack with a digital portfolio where evidence and artefacts of learner's learning are collected and presented. The importances of portability as well as the concept of a digital platform for learners to express content understanding within the digital backpack or portfolio were highlighted by Hoagland, Aplyn and Rice (2001) [3]. In another article on digital backpacks for teaching and learning, Amirian (2007) [4] explored solutions to overcome various technology integration issues. Amirian [4] suggested designing and developing a digital backpack with the necessary technological teaching tools that higher education faculty can access for their instruction.

The undergraduates' "digital backpacks" are likely to contain a range of mobile devices and technological tools [5] designed to enable the 21st century learner to stay connected and 'always on' [6]. The digital backpack does not replace teaching, instead it provides learners with a versatile and smoother platform to organize and store data more effectively and efficiently.

> "As the interactive multimedia technologies of the digital world replace the static technologies of print, a far richer palette opens up for instructional designs, and especially for designs that are flexible enough to meet the challenge of individual differences" [7].

Basham, Meyer and Perry [8] in 2010 outlined a digital backpack that is able of organizing a collection of teaching and learning materials, both software and hardware. Organizing a digital backpack allowed the learner to implement technological organization with different folders. By incorporating design aspects of technological organization, Basham, Meyer and Perry [8] highlighted 3 key types of technologies that can be found in digital backpacks - foundational technologies, modular technologies and instructional technologies.

The concept of foundational technologies within a digital backpack would be related to the technological tools that learners will require to successfully address their educational tasks. This set of tools will depend largely on the higher education institution's selected operating systems. These foundational technologies usually remain relatively constant while the learner remains enrolled with the institution. Core applications may include word processing, movie making, audio and video applications and various other desktop publishing software. Basham, Meyer and Perry's [8] study recommended that learners become familiar with the user interface as this will provide some shared commonality across a range of instructional projects.

Modular technologies consist of software that is specific to curricular or instructional needs of projects or courses. These modular technologies provide the learner with organizational planning for projects. Learners are able to complement modular technologies with foundational technologies to complete specific learning projects or assignments [8]. This suite of technological tools can also be multi-functional and versatile to be utilised across a range of modules.

The third suite of technological tools that Basham, Meyer and Perry [8] suggested that a digital backpack include is instructional support resources. These include the curricula resources that provide the structure, guidance, and specific information learners need to successfully complete their courses. These instructional support resources support the organization of learning goals, objectives, and plan of action. Much of this content is developed and tailored to needs of learners. Some content may be provided on other e-learning platforms or educational databases such as iTunes U. Digital media offers tremendous flexibility that enables teachers to differentiate their approaches in a way that is simply not feasible when restricted to traditional media such as print, speech, and images. With digital media, one piece of a curriculum can be designed with built in customization features so that it can be adapted to suit many different students [2].

2.2 UDL as an Instructional Design Framework

Universal design for learning (UDL) is a design framework that developed from the architectural universal design movement. UDL emphasizes the design and development of instructional resources with an intrinsic flexibility towards supporting diverse learners through improved access to information and [2]. UDL, defined by the Center for Applied Special Technology (CAST) in 2008, is "a framework for designing educational environments that enable all learners to gain knowledge, skills, and enthusiasm for learning… by simultaneously reducing barriers to the curriculum and providing rich supports for learning" [9]. UDL is also developed based on Vygotsky (1978)'s [10] three learning prerequisites:

- the need to recognize patterns in perceptual information,
- the need to apply strategies for acting on the perceived patterns, and
- the need to be engaged by a task.

Drawing on research in learning, cognitive and neuro sciences, UDL is a teaching and learning design approach that enhances access, participation as well as progress for a diverse range of learners [1]. The UDL design structure offers educators a framework of design of instruction and assessment that can augment the learner's knowledge, scaffold their learning as well as facilitate metacognition [11]. The underlying focus of UDL is on inclusiveness for flexibility and customization in designing curriculum for optimum content access for diverse learners [2]. The design model supports the simple access to information or activities, with a learning plan that takes into account the range of abilities [12]. UDL is anchored in three principles that address critical features of any teaching and learning environment:

Principle I: provide multiple means of representation (the what of learning);
Principle II: provide multiple means of expression (the how of learning); and
Principle III: provide multiple means of engagement (the why of learning) [11].

UDL builds upon brain research to increase accessibility on cognitive and pedagogical levels. It supports inclusion at a time when our general population is becoming more diverse Learning is distributed across three interconnected networks:

- the *recognition* networks are specialized to receive and analyse information (the "what" of learning);
- the *strategic* networks are specialized to plan and execute actions (the "how" of learning); and
- the *affective* networks are specialized to evaluate and set priorities (the "why" of learning) [13].

Multiple Means of Representation (The What of Learning). UDL's first design principle, *Multiple Means of Representation*, encourages flexible as well as multiple presentation methods that can provide learners with alternative ways to access content and information. Learners differ in the way they perceive and learn. Some may simply learn better or quicker with visual or auditory representations rather than the printed text. Teaching and learning environments that capitalizes on the flexibility of technology can offer learning opportunities through multiple means of representation. The transfer of learning takes place when multiple representations provides the platform for learners to draw connections within and between, concepts. In short, there is not one means of representation that will be optimal for all learners; providing a range of options is essential. Today's learning management systems (LMS) are able to offer varied digital means to embed hyperlinks that can support these options. Intelligent tutors and learning systems are fundamental to providing e-learning environments that meet diverse online learning needs, support metacognition, and foster interactive learning. This is an example of UDL that can maximize opportunities for learning and understanding [14].

Multiple Means for Action and Expression (The How of Learning). Diversity in learning is more pronounced today than ever before. Learning sciences research has shown that learners differ in how they perceive and navigate instructional information in a learning environment [14]. In reality, there is no single form of action and expression that is ideal for all learners. The second UDL principle, *Multiple Means for Action and Expression,* encourages educators to be conscious and mindful of learner's differences and to develop flexible and multiple opportunities for acquiring and demonstrating their knowledge [11]. Multiple means for action and expression is why the educators integrate technology with the curriculum towards authentic learning. This UDL principle also emphasizes the need to have options to scaffold practice and performance, allowing for media choices for communication. Digital and virtual content are able to remove, reduce or manage the barriers imposed on the learner by physical books, print materials, and laboratories.

Multiple Means for Engagement (The Why of Learning). Learners have varied approaches and motivations for how and why they engage in their learning. What may work for one may cause disengagement for another learner? [14]. Hu and Kuh [15] in 2002 highlighted that the "... most important factor in student learning and personal development during college is student engagement or the quality of effort students themselves devote to educationally purposeful activities that contribute directly to the desired outcomes" (p. 555). A key focus within this principle is to scaffold coping skills and strategies. The set of skills and strategies will encompass learning opportunities for developing interest, sustaining effort and persistence, and self-regulation. This includes providing for individual choice and autonomy. Learners will benefit from these strategies and supports that enhance collaboration and communication.

UDL principles provide educators with signposts to develop innovative ways to make teaching and learning more accessible and appropriate for learners [16]. The principles in UDL do not just provide access to information or activities, but rather facilitates a teaching and learning plan to be accessible to all [12]. The UDL framework encourages educators to integrate pedagogies and technologies that support learning and engagement. Rose, Meyer & Hitchcock [2] in 2006 posit that with the UDL approach "learning is supported and facilitated by the interaction between the learner and the curriculum" (p. 19). The UDL model embraces an inclusive instructional design framework that focuses on flexibility, customization, media-based instructional techniques and technologies to meet unique learning needs and by doing so, meet the needs among a wide range of learners. Emphasizing multiple means of representations, multiple means of expression, and multiple means of engagement, the UDL model focuses on providing multiple pathways to learning and instruction [2, 11, 13, 14]. The basic premise of UDL is that learning barriers happen during the interaction with curriculum rather than within the learner. Thus when learning does not take place, the delivered curriculum, not the learner, should be evaluated and revised.

2.3 The Adult Learner in Higher Education

Today, there is an increasing diversity of learners pursuing higher education [17]. A general overview of the apparent trends in learners in higher education is that about 50 percent of these learners are considered to be "traditional" learners who are between the ages of 18 to 25 years of age and are children at the tail end of the baby boomers, with the rest of the population as being considered as adult learners. Adult learners in higher education are most often described as non-traditional: over the age of 25 [18].

The influx of adult learners into higher education in Singapore cannot be ignored, more inquiries are needed. Singapore's shifting demographics is another key factor that is presenting further challenges to education [19]. Singapore demographic trends show decreasing number of young people, declining birth rates, increased life expectancy for aging generations and an increase in the number of non-Singaporean residents [20]. Demographics shifts, fuelled by increased life expectancy and a growing knowledge economy have continually emphasized the crucial role of lifelong learning. Swelling numbers of working adults will require more education and training to support today's global economy [21].

With the turn of the century, the Singapore economy is going moving from a primarily manufacturing focused economy to an information-based economy [22]. The growth of the global information-based economy has added urgency to calls to upgrade education and training as prime sources of national economic competitiveness. In August 2012, the Singapore government affirms its commitment to Continuing Education and Training (CET) sector by diversifying the University pathways [23]. SIM University (UniSIM) was identified as Singapore's 6th University. UniSIM, dedicated to working adults, has provided pathways for many to pursue lifelong learning and higher education while balancing career, family and social responsibilities [24].

Higher education adult learners have unique learning characteristics and motivation as compared with their traditional counterparts [25]. As noted by Merriam and Brockett [26] in 2007, there is an immediate need to better comprehend the adult who "opts to assume primary responsibility for planning, implementing, and evaluating his/her own learning" (p. 35). In 2010, Moore [27] observed that adult learners tend to have set preferences as to what their learning styles are and for teaching and learning to be effective, instructors must adapt their teaching to accommodate these styles.

Studies have found adult learners to be achievement oriented, motivated by prospects of career advancement, and relatively independent with requirements for flexible instructions and schedules that support their life and work commitments [25, 28]. Adult learners are self-directed in their learning; most adults have concrete immediate goals; adults may prefer to learn quickly and get on with their lives; adults enter a learning situation with a variety of life experiences; past experience becomes increasingly important; adults with a positive self-concept will find learning easier; usually adults prefer to be self-directed [29]. As self-directed adult learners, they have a need to have a sense of control over their own learning and be actively involved in the learning process [30]. Adult learners are also practical and are interested in learning that is relevant for their career growth. Based on their experience, they expect to be treated as equals and they assume that they can openly articulate their opinions [30].

A review of the literature of adult learning is not complete without a discussion of Malcolm Knowles' work on andragogy [31–33]. Knowles describes andragogy as "the science and art of educating adults" [31], distinguishing it from pedagogy, the teaching and learning with children. Samaroo, Cooper, and Green (2013) [34] state that andragogy is not intended to replace pedagogy, but to meant to parallel or complement a wide variety in educational practices. Recently, andragogy is defined as a teaching approach oriented to a specific age group towards other models that emphasize the role of the learner in the teaching process [35]. This evolved version of andragogy focuses on learner-centered teaching methods, as opposed to the instructor-centred practices associated with pedagogy [36, 37]. The growth of online education offered learning opportunities for implementing andragogy in higher education. Cercone (2008) [38] explored how online learning can facilitate aspects of learning that cater to the adult's learning preferences, such as self-directed learning, the need for applicability and relevance as well as the opportunity collaborative learning.

3 Concept and Components UniSIM Backpack

The challenge for the university in today's digital age involves developing an effective pedagogy that meets the changing needs of learners. UniSIM Backpack (Fig. 1) is an application launched by SIM University for their adult learners in their part time undergraduate programmes (http://www.unisim.edu.sg/mobile/unisim-backpack.html). UniSIM's backpack's cloud and mobile technology is designed to support the adult learners as they store and organize their learning materials, providing for learning anytime, anywhere. The social media component makes learning and "hitting the books" more engaging and interactive. UniSIM digital backpack is available in both iOS as well as Android versions.

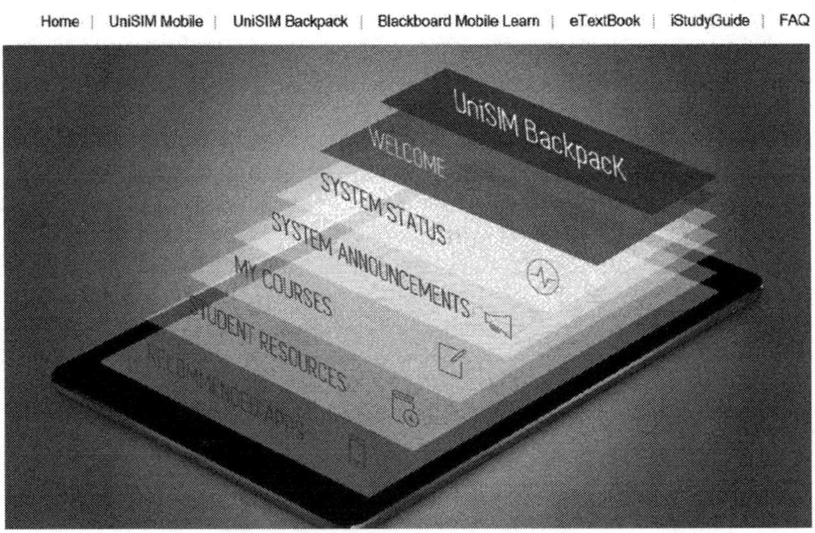

Fig. 1. UniSIM digital Backpack (http://www.unisim.edu.sg/mobile/unisim-backpack.html)

Aside from a variety of digital tools to organise, supplement or extend learning resources, the UniSIM digital backpack utilizes a palette of technological features and tools that support the inclusion of varied teaching and learning strategies such as asynchronous discussion boards, online chatrooms, interactive games, and video. Learners can also use the social media tools to share and collaborate with fellow learners or course mates. Working together to compare notes, ask questions, and to master the information. This learning environment is not only a tool that provides access to more knowledgeable others, it is also a part of a system that allows the adult learner to link their learning to their work and practice processes. UniSIM's digital backpack consists of 3 key components.

Learning Component. With this application, learners are able to access their interactive study guides, recorded lectures as well as past year exam papers organised in a form of a virtual backpack. This component consists of 2 parts: *System Status* and *My Courses.*

The *System Status* portion (Fig. 2) provides access to Blackboard, SIM University's learning management system. This infrastructure allows for teaching and learning management and distribution of course content; digital content and open educational resources and specialized social media platforms which enable interaction between the educators and learners. Course content distribution and management of class assignments with adaptive learning optimization platforms allow instructors to tailor individualized content and assignments to learner capabilities and allowing for continual assessment of learners' learning through dynamic, interactive dashboards.

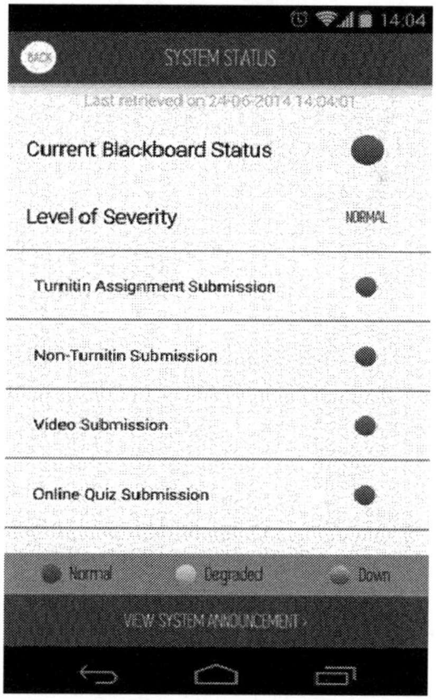

Fig. 2. System status

My Courses is the second portion in the Learning Component. A key feature of SIM University's learning experience is the used of interactive study guides (iStudy Guides) for individual modules. The Interactive Study Guide (iStudyGuide) provides learners with a single point-of-access to key learning resources. These learning activities and references are mapped to the course structure.

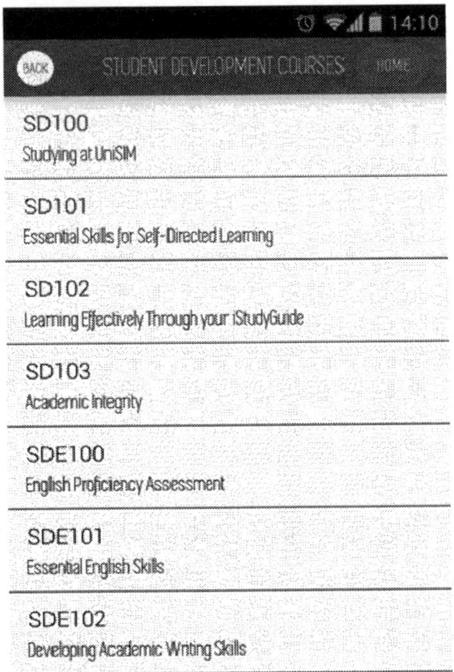

Fig. 3. Student development courses

System Announcements. The application provides a platform that enables the learners to receive important notifications from the University. General system announcements as well as announcements or notices that are specific to the different schools or courses in the University can be found. General announcements also include system status announcements of the learning management system (for example maintenance shut-downs).

Student Development Resources. The UniSIM digital backpack comes installed with useful learning resources (e.g. academic writing, essential skills etc.) to enhance their UniSIM learning experience (Fig. 3).

4 UDL Elements in UniSIM Backpack

Edyburn (2010) [39], a leading researcher in the area of accessibility and assistive technology, recognises the key role of technology in implementing UDL. Edyburn [39] noted that digital technology is highly flexible and printed or paper-based materials cannot rival the level of learning support that is viable when digital media is incorporated. The universal design for learning model (Table 1) incorporates specific research-based principles and instructional guidelines for designing flexibility and inclusive instruction for a wide range of individuals along multiple learning pathways. Some examples that are found in the UniSIM Backpack are also listed in Table 1.

Table 1. Universal design for learning model principles

UDL representation elements		
The "what" of learning	Provide multiple ways of clearly identifying and explaining (through visual or auditory means rather than printed text)	Represent key information in optional modalities; Examples: textual, visual, or auditory; media-based formats
	Provide multiple ways to teach important concepts, incorporate different teaching styles (can interact with the content using multiple senses)	Examples: highlighting, different sensory modes, digital materials, emoticons, graphics, video, charts, diagrams, interactive models, electronic reminders
UDL engagement elements		
The "how" of learning	Provide varied ways to involve learners in the learning process	Use media to provide different ways to construct knowledge and demonstrate learning
	Provide multiple means of action and expression for learners to demonstrate their learning	Examples: models, feedback, media and communication, problem-solving, practice, goal setting, monitoring progress
UDL expression elements		
The "why" of learning	Provide multiple means of engagement while maintaining learning expectations	Acknowledge of learning diversity: Examples: context, content, demonstration, alternate levels, self-reflection, visual timers, active learning, scheduling tools, collaboration, sensory stimulation
	Provide scaffolds and alternate means of collecting information	Integrate new information, categorization, advanced organizers, pre-teaching, multiple examples, emphasize relationships; scaffolds, interactive models; multiple entry points, prompts

Experts agree that help systems, multiple representations, the use of media for dual encoding, modelling, scaffolding, and collaboration contribute to improved knowledge construction, knowledge transfer, integration, and strategic learning. The theory behind universal design is to consider a wide range of possible learning abilities, design for those needs, and provide multiple pathways for learning. Three key themes on learner expectations for interactive learning: communication, control, and engagement [40] are relevant in the analysis UniSIM backpack study. The next phase will include an evaluation of the backpack as well as how strategic learning, interactive learning as well as the role of collaborative instruction support communication, control, and engagement with adult learners.

5 Conclusion - Pedagogy and Technology Must Go Hand in Hand

Based on expected growth trends among adult learners, educators and instructional designers need to use proactive approaches to create, implement, and master the use of interactive, media-based technologies that target diverse strategic learning needs. Flexible and customizable instruction is needed to meet a wider range of adults and educators need training on how to use interactive, engaging instructional tools. However as Garrison and Kanuka (2004) [41] asserted, "It is not just finding the right mix of technologies or increasing access to learning ….inherently is about rethinking and redesigning the teaching and learning relationship" (p. 99). Technologies that support the aims of multiple means of representation have the potential to meet the differing learning needs. "As the interactive multimedia technologies of the digital world replace the static technologies of print, a far richer palette opens up for instructional designs, and especially for designs that are flexible enough to meet the challenge of individual differences" [7].

Matzen and Edmunds (2007) [42] noted that "while some researchers have argued that technology can cause a shift to more constructivist instruction, others have suggested that technology can only facilitate that transition" (p. 419). In the case of the UniSIM backpack, a shift needs to occur where the pedagogy is the priority towards a goal of greater learner engagement and higher order thinking skills, while the technology is viewed as a means to that end.

When higher education educators deliberately integrate technologies within a learning experience, they aim to increase the teaching and learning engagement as well as to support learners in their understanding. Advances in technology must be matched with advances in pedagogy. Educators must balance ideas and knowledge with that of the adult learners' level of understanding and learning. Technology has shown to bring about increased levels of learning engagement however to maximise the potential, technology and pedagogy must work hand-in-hand, for without this partnership; technology serves only as the access but not the pedagogy. In implementing and improving the UniSIM digital backpack the technology-pedagogy integration should be considered along with teaching and learning issues.

There is a continuous need to address online instructional effectiveness based on: the use and design of interactive, customizable learning tools; media-based customizable instructional support systems that encourage active rather than passive learning; the integration of systems that assess strategic learning along with learning outcomes; and training in support areas for online instruction and educational technology. Future research about UD instruction and adult digital backpack should examine motivation, collaboration, and the role that customization on strategic learning components of the backpack. For the research to be impactful, it will have to address research questions of concern to a wider range of stakeholders and also employ a wider range of methodologies.

References

1. Center of Applied Special Technology CAST. Universal Design for Learning Guidelines Version 2.0. Wakefield, MA: Author (2011)
2. Rose, D.H., Meyer, A., Hitchcock, C.: The Universally Designed Classroom: Accessible Curriculum and Digital Technologies. Harvard University Press, Cambridge (2006)
3. Hoagland, C., Aplyn, E., Rice, M.: The digital backpack: issues in the development and implementation of a digital portfolio. In: Montgomerie, C., Viteli, J. (eds.) Proceedings of World Conference on Educational Multimedia, Hypermedia and Telecommunications 2001, pp. 759–761. AACE, Chesapeake (2001). http://www.editlib.org/p/8237. Accessed 17 August 2015
4. Amirian, S.: Digital backpacks: facilitating faculty implementation of technologies for teaching and learning. Comput. Sch. **24**, 5–14 (2007)
5. Millea, J., Green, I., Putland, G.: Emerging technologies: A framework for thinking. Australian Capital Territory Department of Education and Training (2005). Accessed 1 October 2005
6. Oblinger, D., Oblinger, J.: Is it age or IT: first steps toward understanding the net generation. Educ. Net Gener. **2**(1–2), 20 (2005)
7. Rose, D., Dalton, B.: Learning to read in the digital age. Mind Brain Educ. **3**(2), 74–83 (2009). Accessed http://www.wiley.com/bw/journal.asp?ref=1751-2271&site=1
8. Basham, J.D., Meyer, H., Perry, E.: The design and application of the digital backpack. J. Res. Technol. Educ. **42**(4), 339–359 (2010)
9. Center of Applied Special Technology (CAST). Universal Design for Learning Guidelines Version 1.0. Wakefield, MA: Author (2008)
10. Vygotsky, L.S.: Mind and society: The development of higher mental processes (1978)
11. Rose, D. H., Gravel, J.W.: Curricular Opportunities in the Digital Age. Students at the Centre Series: Nellie Mae Educational Foundation (2012)
12. Hitchcock, C., Meyer, A., Rose, D., Jackson, R.: Providing new access to the general curriculum universal design for learning. Counc. Except. Educ. **35**(2), 8–17 (2002)
13. Rose, D.H., Meyer, A.: Teaching Every Student in the Digital Age: Universal Design for Learning. Association for Supervision and Curriculum Development, Alexandria (2002)
14. Rose, D.H., Meyer, A.: A Practical Reader in Universal Design for Learning. Harvard Education Press, Cambridge (2006)
15. Hu, S., Kuh, G.D.: Being (dis) engaged in educationally purposeful activities: The influences of student and institutional characteristics. Res. High. Educ. **43**(5), 555–575 (2002)
16. Eagleton, M.: Universal design for learning. Research Starters (2008). www.ebscohost.com/uploads/thisTopic-dbTopic-1073.pdf Accessed 17 August 2015
17. Finn, D.: Principles of adult learning: an ESL context. J. Adult Educ. **40**, 34–39 (2011)
18. Marschall, S., Davis, C.: A Conceptual framework for teaching critical reading to adult college students. Adult Learn. **23**(2), 63–68 (2012)
19. Chong, S.N., Cheah, H.M.: Demographic trends: impact on schools. New Horiz. Educ. **58**(1), 1–15 (2010)
20. Singapore Department of Statistics: Latest Key Indicators (2013). http://www.singstat.gov.sg. Accessed 22 August 2015

21. Chong, S., Loh, W.M., Babu, M: The Millennial Learner: a new generation of adult learners in higher education. Adv. Sch. Teach. Learn. 2(2) (2015). http://tlc.unisim.edu.sg/research/AdvSoTL-3/pdf/chong_loh_babu.pdf. Accessed 31 August 2015
22. Gopinathan, S., Lee, M.H.: Challenging and co-opting globalisation: Singapore's strategies in higher education. J. High. Educ. Policy Manage. **33**(3), 287–299 (2011)
23. MOE (Ministry of Education): Report of the Committee on University Education. Pathways Beyond 2015 (CUEP). Singapore (2012)
24. SIM (2014). http://www.unisim.edu.sg/about-unisim/Overview/Pages/Facts-Figures.aspx. Accessed 17 August 2015
25. Reay, D.: Class, authenticity and the transition to higher education for mature students. Sociol. Rev. **50**(3), 398–418 (2002)
26. Merriam, S.B., Brockett, R.G.: The Profession and Practice of Adult Education: An Introduction. Wiley, San Francisco (2007)
27. Moore, K.: The three-part harmony of adult learning, critical thinking, and decision making. J. Adult Educ. **39**(1), 1–10 (2010)
28. Clemente, K.A.: Experiences of Adult Students in Multi-Generational Community College Classrooms (Unpublished doctoral dissertation). Pennsylvania State University, University Park (2010)
29. Cranton, P.: Teaching for transformation. New Dir. Adult Continuing Educ. **2002**(93), 63–72 (2002)
30. Bash, L.: Adult Learners in the Academy. Anker Publishing Company Inc., Bolton (2003)
31. Knowles, M.S.: The Modern Practice of Adult Education, vol. 41. Association Press, New York (1970)
32. Knowles, M.S.: The Adult Learn. A Negl. Species. American Society for Training and Development, Madison (1973)
33. Knowles, M.S.: Andragogy in Action. Jossey-Bass, San Francisco (1990)
34. Samaroo, S., Cooper, E., Green, T.: Pedandragogy: A way forward to self-engaged learning. New Horiz. Adult Educ. Hum. Res. Dev. **25**(3), 76–90 (2013)
35. Henschke, J.A.: Considerations regarding the future of andragogy. Adult Learn. **22**(1), 34–37 (2011)
36. Halx, M.D.: Re-conceptualizing college and university teaching through the lens of adult education: regarding undergraduates as adults. Teach. High. Educ. **15**(5), 519–530 (2010)
37. Taylor, B., Kroth, M.: Andragogy's transition into the future: Meta-analysis of andragogy and its search for a measurable instrument. J. Adult Educ. **38**(1), 1–11 (2009)
38. Cercone, K.: Characteristics of adult learners with implications for online learning design. AACE J. **16**(2), 137–159 (2008)
39. Edyburn, D.L.: Would you recognize universal design for learning if you saw it? Ten propositions for new directions for the second decade of UDL. Learn. Disabil. Q. **33**(1), 33–41 (2010)
40. Sims, R.: Beyond instructional design: making learning design a reality. J. Learn. Des. **1**(2), 1–7 (2006)
41. Garrison, D.R., Kanuka, H.: Blended learning: uncovering its transformative potential in higher education. Internet High. Educ. **7**(2), 95–105 (2004)
42. Matzen, N.J., Edmunds, J.A.: Technology as a catalyst for change: the role of professional development. J. Res. Technol. Educ. **39**(4), 417–443 (2007)

Utilization of COCA by Japanese Students

Yoko Hirata[1(✉)] and Yoshihiro Hirata[2]

[1] Hokkai-Gakuen University, 1-40, Asahimachi 4 chome, Toyohiraku, Sapporo, Japan
hira@eli.hokkai-s-u.ac.jp

[2] Hokkai-Gakuen University, 1-1, S26 W11, Chuo-kuraku, Sapporo, Japan
hirata@hgu.jp

Abstract. Recently it has become evident that the utilization of corpora (large searchable catalogues of native language text) assist students in fostering better understandings of collocations, grammar patterns, and other lexical patterns. However, in Japanese educational settings, there are comparatively fewer reports of success. How Japanese students specifically may best utilize corpora in their language learning is not yet well understood. This study looks at the outcomes for Japanese university students who were instructed in the use of the Corpus of Contemporary American English (COCA) as part of a communicative language course. It also presents students' opinions with regards to the use the corpus; how useful they felt it was, and whether or not they felt it helped them achieve success in the course. Some important implications are explored and suggestions are made for future attempts at utilizing open language resources in tertiary educational settings.

Keywords: Corpora · Open language resources · Blended learning · Japanese educational institutions

1 Introduction

Recently, there has been a shift in focus on language study away from employing traditional materials such as vocabulary lists and phrase books, to utilizing *corpora*: large searchable catalogues of native language texts from a wide range of sources. Among many corpora, the Corpus of Contemporary American English (COCA) and The British National Corpus (BNC) are now two major ones available online, free of charge. Using corpora, or corpus in the singular, we can identify lexical, grammatical and discourse patterns frequently used in authentic contexts. The first large-scale corpus-based dictionary is *Collins COBUILD (Collins Birmingham University International Language Database)*. Before corpora were developed, dictionaries and grammar books were created using linguists' intuitions [26]. However, corpora provide valuable information even for linguists, such that they might answer questions which are difficult to sort out from their intuitions alone. Research has indicated corpora have contributed to language teaching in many different ways [2, 10, 12, 31, 32]. For example, textbook and teaching material writers have utilized corpora to present current lexical and grammatical information to students. These students' materials include corpus-informed textbooks, such as *Touchstone* [25], and learning

J. Lam et al. (Eds.): ICTE 2015, CCIS 559, pp. 23–31, 2015.
DOI: 10.1007/978-3-662-48978-9_3

materials, such as *Collins COBUILD Concordance Samplers* [16]. In addition, dictionaries based on corpora have been compiled such as the *Cambridge Advanced Learner's Dictionary*, the *Oxford Dictionary of English,* and the *Longman Language Activator.* Furthermore, various corpus-designed activities have been developed in order to assist students in analyzing language patterns through co-occurring words [5]. Research has shown that students can learn to recognize lexical and grammatical patterns, collocations, and connotations and become more aware of language use and patterns of various forms without necessarily relying on dictionaries and phrase books [4, 6, 17, 33]. This approach is called Data-Driven Learning (DDL), a term coined by Johns [19]. Studies have also shown that DDL approaches have played an important role in the recent developments in language teaching methodologies in different contexts for different purposes [1, 11, 13, 14, 20–23, 27, 30].

On the other hand, despite these benefits, not enough empirical studies have been conducted to prove that DDL approaches are more effective than conventional teaching practices. For example, DDL has mostly been used within the confines of writing courses and little research has been done to examine the feasibility of teaching communicative functions using DDL. In addition, the majority of studies have so far indicated that DDL is only suitable for advanced students [3, 29].

For Japanese students who do not have many opportunities to be exposed to vast amounts of authentic English information in everyday contexts, online corpora are readily available and full of valuable linguistic information. Despite the rapid growth of these corpora, however, there is still a general lack of research concerning how they can best be presented to students of varying proficiencies. It is also important for instructors to be able to determine how students, who are likely to have never consulted corpora before, should be guided into the use of corpora such that they might discover their own learning strategies and be left with a continued desire to consult corpora independently as necessary.

2 The Corpus of Contemporary American English

Among free online corpora, COCA, which is accessible on online [http://corpus.byu.edu/coca/], contains 450 million words and is the only large corpus of American English [15]. Compared with BNC, this corpus is approximately four times larger and "attempts to capture a snapshot of English as it is used in the United States" [24]. COCA has a number of advantages over the other corpora for students, especially for Japanese students of English, in various ways. Firstly, it is equally balanced in terms of types of content being used: spoken English (20 %), fiction (20 %), popular magazines (20 %), newspapers (20 %), and academic journals (20 %). The spoken texts include transcripts of broadcast interviews, and conversations taken from different types of TV and radio programs [24]. The written texts are derived from "the web and other electronic sources" under license [24]. Secondly, the corpus data has been updated every six to nine months with the most recent texts available in the United States [24]. Thirdly, as Japanese students learn only North American English in secondary school, the language provided by this corpus is appropriate and familiar to students. In addition, COCA is a 'stable, fast and reliable' language resource which doesn't require any 'substantial training' [8]. Lastly and most importantly, according to the findings of the investigation of how Japanese undergraduate students assess COCA and BNC, compared with BNC, COCA is highly appreciated by students for its well-organized, useful language examples as well as various functions [18]. Their study has also revealed that students appreciate the simplicity and user-friendliness of its interface, which is easy for those unfamiliar with corpora to use to search for collocations and co-occurring words.

3 Purpose of the Study

The purpose of this study is to examine Japanese undergraduate students' opinions with regards to the use of COCA as part of a communicative language course. The focus is placed on determining how the corpus can be incorporated into the classroom.

Research questions

1. How do students perceive COCA and how useful do they feel it is?
2. Do students feel COCA helped them to achieve success in the course?

4 Methodology

4.1 The Setting and Student Profiles

Twenty Japanese university students aged 18 to 20 years in two different classes participated in this study. These students included those who studied economics, law, humanities and engineering. The objective of the course was to help students develop their communication skills. They had learned English for six years and had attained at least a lower-intermediate level of English proficiency. They were accustomed to teacher-centered language learning in a large lecture-type classroom. Their English experiences in the secondary school were all examination-oriented. These classes were offered weekly for ninety minutes. Although students were highly motivated to improve their English proficiency levels, they needed tremendous support to find out how they could best improve their English skills.

4.2 Procedures

The course focused on common lexical phrases people use in their daily lives. Students were required to become familiar with various notions such as *time*, *direction*, *size*, *frequency* as well as communicative functions such as *describing what people look like*, *describing number and length of times*, *giving directions* and *making polite requests*. Sociolinguistic and contextual meaning was of high importance in order for students to come to be able to understand how real conversations flow. In order to help students to become more competent at both communicating and analyzing the language, DDL activities using analytic approaches were introduced into the classroom. The purpose of these activities was to assist students in understanding the meanings of utterances by deriving meaning more from context than from the words and sentences in isolation. The language data used for the creation of the activities was COCA and the lines for the activities were carefully selected in order to help students learn how the target words or expressions are used, while avoiding offensive or inappropriate words.

The activities in the course aimed to teach students how to describe things they do on a regular basis using the words and phrases listed in the textbook. The example phrases focused in the course include: *do homework*, *do the dishes*, *do the laundry*, *get dressed*, *get up*, *make lunch*, *make the bed*, *take a bath* and *take a nap*.

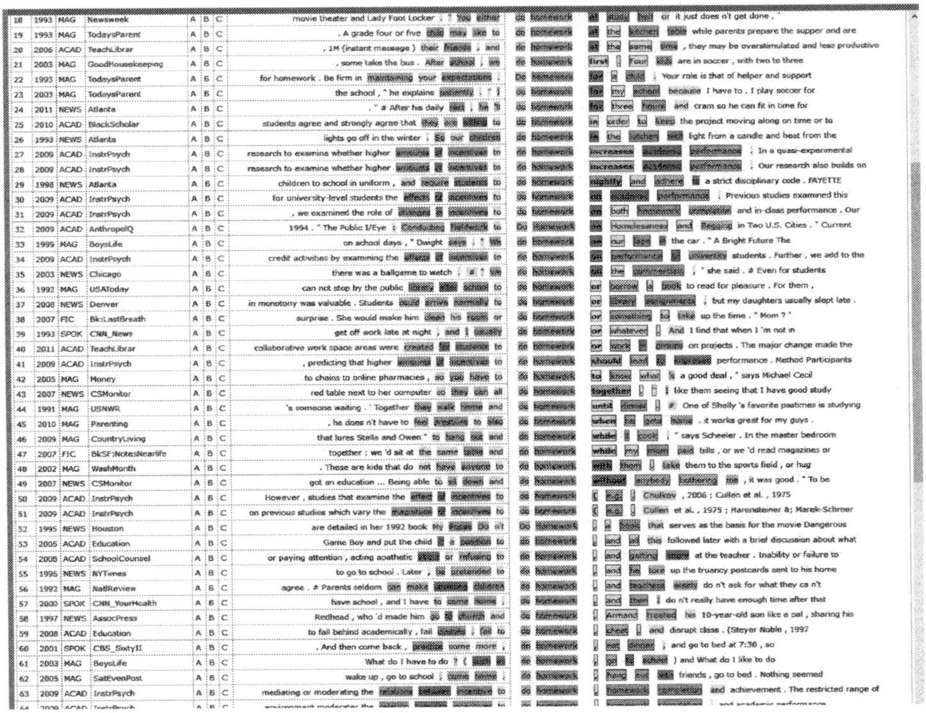

Fig. 1. Search results including *do homework* in COCA

Students worked in groups, and were asked to find how these phrasal verbs are used in daily contexts. Students learned these basic phrases in secondary school but, since there were many more usages to learn, it was worth introducing DDL activities at this stage. Then students were encouraged to identify what kinds of words are used with the phrases as well as the context associated with them. Using the lexical patterns in the concordance lines students described their daily lives. Figure 1 indicates that the phrase *do homework* is closely associated with time phrases such as *four hours a day* and things children often do routinely such as *hang out with friends* and *go to school*. Similarly, the phrase *do the laundry* is often used with phrases indicating location such as *in the basement* and expressions describing other common housework routine such as *cook*, *take care of the kids*, and *fix dinner* as seen in Fig. 2.

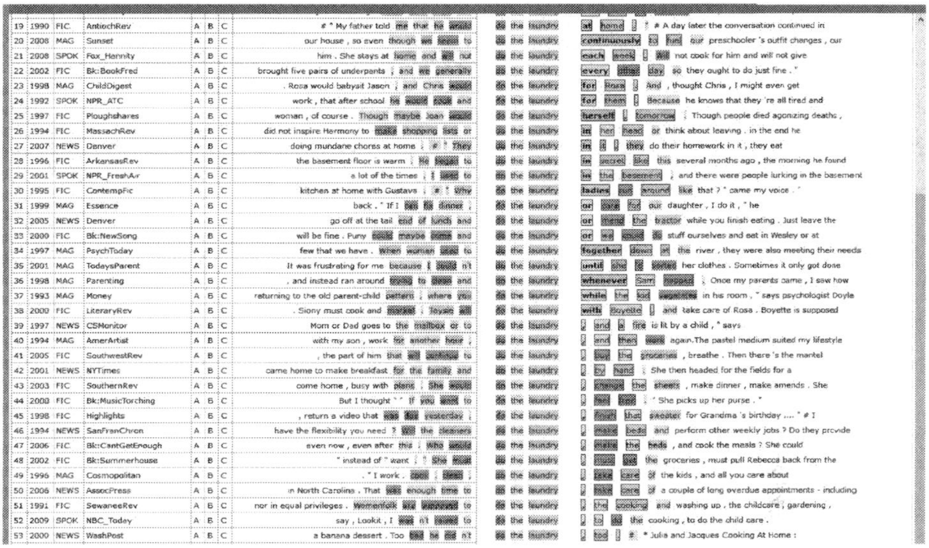

Fig. 2. Search results including *do the laundry* in COCA

Students also made dialogues with the help of concordance examples in order to learn how the words and patterns they had acquired fit into every dialogue. Cultural awareness was also promoted by asking students to compare and contrast the language and social routines in Japan with those of English speaking countries. For example, although the expression *make the bed* isn't a common household routine in Japan, with

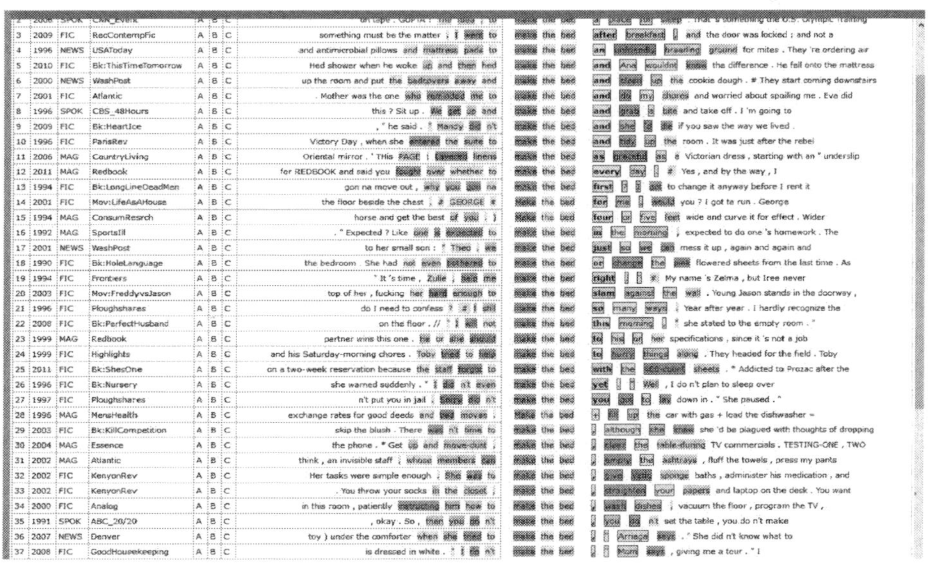

Fig. 3. Search results including *make the bed* in COCA

words and phrases provided by examples shown in Fig. 3, students were easily able to come to understand that many people in English speaking cultures *make the bed* in the morning as part of their morning ritual.

Students then improvised sentences using the concordance lines that were presented to them. Students in groups of three or four competed with each other to create as many sentences as possible.

5 Findings

5.1 Students' Thought About Using COCA for Their Language Activities

At the beginning of the course, few students used COCA resources when creating dialogues. Some students thought it was difficult to use them for their study. However, as time passed, there were some students, not all, who came to understood the benefits of the lines and thought the patterns and expressions they learned from them were useful for their communication. This is in accordance with the findings of Boulton and Tyne [9] who point out that "different students react to corpora differently" and therefore individualized treatment is required.

As the lessons progressed, all the students referred to the corpus data. They didn't consult other resources such as electronic pocket dictionaries or textbooks either. It's clear that, after sufficient exposure, students come to understand the benefits of the lines and thought the patterns and expressions they learned from the corpus were useful for making dialogues and communicating with each other. When students didn't know how to connect a specific word with other words they went back to the data to find out how they could use them.

5.2 Challenges of Referring to Corpus

The students' feedback indicates that there were some drawbacks to using the corpus for their language studies. Firstly, as Boulton and Tyne [9] claim, many students pointed out the fact that each line wasn't a complete sentence and that that made it difficult for them to understand the meaning of the lines the keywords were included in. It was difficult for them to understand in what kind of context they can be used. These students were uncomfortable with reading incomplete sentences. Each line looks like just one long sentence without any break. Students weren't familiar with reading incomplete sentences without a period at the end of each. However, some advanced students claimed that because the concordance lines were so neatly arranged, they could understand what words or expressions they should focus on. Unfortunately, the number of those students was quite small.

Secondly, there were students who thought it was better to have Japanese translations of the lines. The advanced students tended to appreciate the benefits of concordance lines, but even some of them felt they needed the Japanese. Thirdly, many students thought textbooks and dictionaries were more reliable resources to refer to than the materials based on the corpus. Although the instructor strongly emphasized the need to refer to the corpus data, many students, at the beginning of the course, consulted their electronic pocket dictionaries or textbooks exclusively. Lastly, students have never experienced creating dialogues, even in Japanese. They cannot create simple, everyday dialogues even using their own native language. What you can do is closely connected with what you have experienced so far. Therefore, although they can communicate without any problems using their native language, the assignment was so difficult for the students that they couldn't concentrate on using concordance lines as a reference tool.

Despite students' generally negative perceptions of the concordance lines at the beginning of the course, many of their opinions changed as lessons progressed. Many students found the DDL activities to be valuable largely in how they provided uniquely accessible language data, noticeably authentic compared to traditional textbook examples. With the implementation of revised activities as the course progressed, students increasingly recognized how the lines could be of benefit in helping them to understand how key words and expressions were to be used in different contexts. None of them needed Japanese translations of the lines. Students thought, compared with the textbook, the corpus materials had a greater influence on how they created sentences. Overall, the concordance lines which had been employed in the course provided students with considerable exposure to English.

6 Discussion and Conclusions

The Findings from this study have indicated that DDL activities are feasible for Japanese students, and DDL was found to have become an effective tool. However, there are several tips future DDL instructors should be aware of to increase their chances of successfully implementing DDL. Firstly, instructors should be aware that students' educational backgrounds strongly affect their ability to appreciate and adopt DDL. It is important for instructors to understand that since students may possess ingrained dispositions toward the traditional passive ways of learning English, they should be introduced to DDL learning methods with plenty of help and direction, so that they can take full advantage of this new form of language investigation. Secondly, having students come to appreciate the benefits of DDL takes time. In order for students to adjust themselves to this new teaching approach, instructors need to revise their teaching methods constantly, based on the continual feedback from their students. Careful selection of concordance lines is also important, especially for students with lower levels of proficiency [7]. Furthermore, it is important for instructors to teach students how to approach their reading of the lines, such as reading from the center of each line, rather than from left to right [28]. With revisions to approaches, DDL will help students become more engaged in language activities and enhance their English skills. Above all, encouraging students to actually use the patterns they've seen in the corpus and integrating these with their own previous experiences and everyday lives, is the key to achieving success with DDL activities.

References

1. Al-Lawati, N.: Learning strategies used and observations made by EFL Arab students while working on concordance-based grammar activities. Arab World English J. **2**(4), 302–322 (2011)
2. Atkins, D., Brown, J.S., Hammond, A.L.: A Review of the Open Educational Resources. (OER) Movement: Achievements, Challenges, and New Opportunities. Report for the William and Flora Hewlett Foundation (2007). http://www.hewlett.org/programs/education-program/open-educational-resources, 27 February 2014
3. Aston, G.: Corpora in language pedagogy: matching theory and practice. In: Cook, G., Seidlhofer, B. (eds.) Principle & Practice in Applied Linguistics. Studies in Honour of H. G. Widdowson, pp. 301–312. Oxford University Press, Oxford (1995)
4. Barlow, M.: Software for corpus access and analysis. In: Sinclair, J.M. (ed.) How to Use Corpora in Language Teaching, pp. 205–221. John Benjamins, Amsterdam (2004)
5. Bennett, G.: Using Corpora in the Language Classroom: Corpus Linguistics for Teachers. University of Michigan Press, Ann Arbor (2010)
6. Boulton, A.: DDL is in the details … and in the big themes. In: Davis, M., Rayson, P., Hunston, S., Danielsson, P. (eds.) Proceedings of the Corpus Linguistics Conference: CL 2007 (2007). http://hal.archives-ouvertes.fr/docs/00/32/69/94/PDF/2007_boulton_CL_big_themes.pdf#search='DDL+is+in+the+details+%E2%80%A6+and+in+the+big+themes'
7. Boulton, A.: Testing the limits of data-driven learning: language proficiency and training. ReCALL **21**(1), 37–54 (2009)
8. Boulton, A.: Hands-on/hands-off: alternative approaches to data-driven learning. In: Thomas, J., Boulton, A. (eds.) Input, Process and Product. Developments in Teaching and Language Corpora, pp. 152–168. Masaryk University Press, Brno (2012)
9. Boulton, A., Tyne, H.: Corpus-based study of language and teacher education. In: Bigelow, M., Ennser-Kananen, J. (eds.) The Routledge Handbook of Educational Linguistics, pp. 301–312. Routledge, New York (2015)
10. Borthwick, K., Dickens, A.: One size doesn't fit all: contrasting approaches to building communities of OER users amongst the language teaching community. The EUROCALL Proceedings. Research-publishing.net (2012). http://research-publishing.net/publication/chapters/978-1-908416-03-2/Borthwick_Dickens_21.pdf, 27 February 2014
11. Chambers, A.: Integrating corpus consultation in language studies. Lang. Learn. Technol. **9**(2), 111–125 (2005)
12. Comas-Quinn, A., Beaven, M., Pleines, C., Pulker, H., de los Arcos, B.: Languages open resources online (LORO): fostering a culture of collaboration and sharing. EUROCALL Rev. (18) (2011). http://www.eurocall-languages.org/wordpress/wp-content/uploads/2014/01/review18.pdf, 27 February 2014
13. Conroy, M.: Internet tools for language learning: University students taking control of their writing. Australas. J. Educ. Technol. **26**(2), 861–882 (2010)
14. Curado Fuentes, A.: A corpus-based assessment of reading comprehension in English for tourism studies. In: Hidalgo, E., Quereda, L., Santana, J. (eds.) Corpora in the Foreign Language Classroom: Selected Papers from the Sixth International Conference on Teaching and Language Corpora (TaLC 6). University of Granada, Spain, 4–7 July, 2004 (Language & Computers), pp. 309–326. Editions Rodopi B.V., Amsterdam (2007)
15. Davies, M.: The 385 + million word corpus of contemporary American English (1990–2008 +): design, architecture, and linguistic insights. Int. J. Corpus Linguis. **14**, 159–190 (2009)

16. Goodale, M.: Collins COBUILD Concordance Samplers. HarperCollins Publishers, London (1995)
17. Granger, S., Paquot, M.: Lexical verbs in academic discourse: a corpus-driven study of learner use. In: Charles, M., Pecorari, D., Hunston, S. (eds.) Academic writing: At the interface of corpus and discourse, pp. 193–214. Continuum International Publishing Group, London (2009)
18. Hirata, Y., Hirata, Y.: Web-based corpora for open and flexible language learning: Japanese students' needs and preferences. In: Li, K.C., Yuen, K.S. (eds.) Emerging Modes and Approaches in Open and Flexible Education, pp. 308–325. Open University of Hong Kong Press, Hong Kong (2014)
19. Johns, T.: Should you be persuaded: two samples of data-driven learning materials. In: Johns, T., King, P. (eds.) Classroom Concordancing. English Language Research Journal 4, 1–16 (1991)
20. Kaur, J., Hegelheimer, V.: ESL students' use of concordance in the transfer of academic word knowledge: An exploratory study. Comput. Assist. Lang. Learn. **18**(4), 287–310 (2005)
21. Kennedy, C., Miceli, T.: Corpus-assisted creative writing: Introducing intermediate Italian learners to a corpus as a reference resource. Lang. Learn. Technol. **14**(1), 28–44 (2010)
22. Kettemann, B.: Tracing the emo side of life: using a corpus of an alternative youth couture discourse to teach cultural studies. In: Frankenberg-Garcia, A., Flowerdew, L., Aston, G. (eds.) New Trends in Corpora and Language Learning, pp. 44–61. Continuum, London (2011)
23. Liu, D., Jiang, P.: Using a corpus-based lexicogrammatical approach to grammar instruction in EFL and ESL contexts. Mod. Lang. J. **93**(1), 61–78 (2009)
24. Lee, D.Y.W.: What corpora are available?. In: O'Keeffe, A., McCarthy, M. (Eds.) The Routledge Handbook of Corpus Linguistics, pp. 107–121. Routledge, Longman; New York, NY (2010)
25. McCarthy, M., McCarten, J., Sandiford, H.: Touchstone. Cambridge University Press, Cambridge (2014)
26. Newmeyer, F.J.: Grammar is grammar and usage is usage. Language **79**(4), 682–707 (2003)
27. Sun, Y.-C.: Learner perceptions of a concordancing tool for academic writing. Comput. Assist. Lang. Learn. **20**(4), 323–343 (2007)
28. Timmis, I.: Corpus Linguistics for ELT. Research and Practice. Routledge, London (2015)
29. Wichmann, A., Fligelstone, S., Knowles, G., McEnery, T.: Teaching and Language Corpora. Longman, London (1997)
30. Whistle, J.: Concordancing with students using an 'off-the-web' corpus. ReCALL **11**(2), 74–80 (1999)
31. White, D., Manton, M.: Open Educational Resources: The Value of Reuse in Higher Education. JISC-Funded OER Impact Study. University of Oxford, Oxford (2011). http://www.jisc.ac.uk/media/documents/programmes/elearning/oer/OERTheValueOfReuseInHigherEducation.pdf, 27 February 2014
32. Wiley, D.: The Current State of Open Educational Resources (2006). http://opencontent.org/blog/archives/247, 27 February 2014
33. Xu, J., Morgan, M., McKenny, J.: Chinese learners' use of formulaic sequences in spoken interaction. In: Boulton, A., Thomas, J. (eds.) Input, Process and Product: Developments in Teaching and Language Corpora, pp. 244–257. Masaryk University Press, Brno (2012)

Electronic Chinese Learning Materials for Ethnic Minority Students

Madeleine Tsoi, Kat Leung(✉), and Man-Koon Ho

Caritas Institute of Higher Education, Hong Kong SAR, China
{mtsoi,kleung}@cihe.edu.hk

Abstract. The Chinese proficiency level of over 60 % of Ethnic Minority (EM) students in Hong Kong aged between 12 and 23 is not on a par with their local counterparts. Between March and July 2014, City University and Hong Kong Christian Service surveyed 378 EM students and asked them to rate their own Chinese competence, their experience and evaluation of how Chinese language education would impact on their career and education opportunities. Most respondents felt that although the Education Bureau had introduced some measures to help them in recent years, these measures failed to significantly boost their written and spoken competencies. The survey also interviewed 107 EM job seekers, 60 per cent of whom were unable to read or write Chinese. Not only did they fail to respond and send timely applications because they could not understand Chinese recruitment advertisements, but also there was a shortage of positions for them as they were severely impeded by their poor language skills in Chinese. A thematic report on the education of EM students in 2011 indicated that the number of EM secondary school graduates who were able to proceed to tertiary education showed a low figure of 0.6 % as compared with their Chinese counterparts of 18 % [2]. This paradoxical situation is caused by the fact that universities prescribe at least a Level 3 pass for the Chinese Language subject in the Hong Kong Diploma of Secondary Education (HKDSE) as an entrance requirement which consequently hampers these students from moving upwards in education, and to a larger extent, in the social hierarchy. After conducting a series of pilot studies, our research team has established that the set of electronic teaching and learning materials we have designed are suitable and effective for Chinese as Second Language (CSL) learners to improve their writing and speaking skills.

Keywords: Ethnic minority · Chinese · Education · Social hierarchy

1 Introduction

In the context of education, Hong Kong has a relatively big South Asian student population which includes three main ethnic groups: Pakistani, Nepalese and Indian, many of these students are second- or even third-generation Hongkongers. However, they still face the problem of being unable to learn Chinese due to a lack of suitable Chinese as a Second Language (CSL) curriculum. Some may know how to speak it, but can neither read nor write it. The Chief Executive's policy address in 2014 included a provision for

J. Lam et al. (Eds.): ICTE 2015, CCIS 559, pp. 32–41, 2015.
DOI: 10.1007/978-3-662-48978-9_4

the development of a CSL curriculum. Advocates have long been calling for this – many of them have argued that without an adequate curriculum for studying the Chinese language, the low Chinese level of students from EM backgrounds is likely to persist and this will prevent them from moving upwards in education, and to a larger extent, in the social hierarchy. The present study attempts to design electronic teaching and learning materials suitable for CSL learners.

2 Literature Review

To many EM students, Chinese remains an "alien" language which they can neither read nor write, let alone using Cantonese to express their meaning. In the realm of "Systematic Assessment" [16], these student groups fail to meet the minimum requirement. Training should be provided in the following areas:

2.1 Assisting Ethnic Minority Students to Strengthen Their Fundamental Knowledge of the Chinese Language

Helping ethnic students to strengthen their basic ability is synonymous with strengthening their ability in word recognition. 謝錫金, 羅嘉怡 [16] point out that many CSL students visualize Chinese characters as picture images. Devoid of concepts about the positions of strokes and dashes of Chinese characters, these students have to memorize and imprint these picture images into their heads in order to learn them. In writing, it is easy for these students to combine a few strokes and dashes into one [17], e.g. 「幻想」 could be turned into 「幼想」, or could miss the top right part of the character 「梁」. They tend to make mistakes with characters containing fused brushstrokes as they have scant knowledge of compound brushstrokes [18].

Writing competency in Chinese is often judged on stroke order, stroke accuracy and elimination of wrongly written characters [19]. The occurrence of wrong characters is often associated with stroke order and character structure, attributing to the two extremes of "underwriting" for complicated characters and "overwriting" for simple characters [20]. 戴汝潛, 郝嘉傑 [21] define one aspect of Chinese writing skill as the ability to master the order of brushstrokes. Wrong stroke order may adversely impact on the shape, balance and structure of a character; conversely, familiarity with the stroke order increases character quality and writing efficiency.

Understanding both the meaning and function of words and terms are essential for reading and writing. CSL students often have a poor memory for Chinese vocabulary [16]. Gershkoff-Stowe & Hahn [6] discover that word frequency and neighborhood density affect the connection between words and the concepts they depict. Repeat practice of a particular word in reading or writing would increase the action level of that word [6]. Besides, it is important to have some knowledge of the components of lexical structure which will improve ability in both reading and writing [9]. Results from the research study of 蕭炳基, 范國等人 [22] reflect that secondary school students who have a repertoire of 2,000 to 6,000 frequent words possess better power of expression.

2.2 Assisting Ethnic Minority Students to Strengthen Their Reading and Writing Abilities

Reading ability is fundamental to most students as it affects their understanding of words and the content of an article. Compared with other language abilities, reading ability is frequently included as one of the assessment items in language tests [11] as it directly impacts on academic performance. Reading is in fact a thinking act, a cognitive process of getting meaning from language written in books [23–25]. According to Daneman [3], reading ranges from lower-level processes of word recognition and decoding, through to high-level processes of combining words and terms to form propositions, and propositions to form a series of concepts [26].

To raise their reading ability, students must read more. In the long run, 謝錫金, 羅嘉怡 [16] suggest that Chinese language learning should focus on training ethnic minority students to employ different strategies to advance their reading ability; helping them to develop their writing ability and high-level thinking through reading; and guiding them to discuss the content of their reading in order to reinforce their listening and speaking skills. Therefore, it is paramount to raise students' motivation in reading.

Planning, organizing, translating and reviewing constitute the four stages in the writing process. Writing involves a thinking process [4, 8]. To write better is to think better [7, 13–15]. In the pre-writing process, the writer must make an effort to think, analyze, integrate and select to ascertain the central idea of the article. In other words, the central idea is derived from reading materials after careful thinking, not an idea by chance without thinking. During the process of writing [5, 10], inapt students may not be capable of using multiple skills simultaneously, but instead get bogged down by trivialities (word writing and usage, etc.) and fail to use high-level writing skills, such as determining the theme and forming linkages between thoughts. Research verifies that students with inferior writing ability are also disorganized in thoughts and they lack confidence. Paying too much attention to word choice and language accuracy during writing would lead to the problem of cognitive overload [1, 27, 28]. Therefore, we must take their focus away from trivialities, such as writing wrong words, and help them to concentrate on high-level writing problems.

Besides, teachers should guide students towards solving low-level problems themselves during the writing process, such as word formation and vocabulary usage. Some students could not control their thinking; have scanty knowledge of grammatical structures; make sentences at random; or forget the theme of the article in the process of writing [29, 30]. 謝錫金, 羅嘉怡 [16] discover that the writing ability of CSL students is generally inferior to that of local students, and therefore the articles they write are usually short and content deficient. Even if some of these students are capable of writing longer articles, they fall short of providing interesting content, only to repeat old ideas. Besides, the articles they have written often contain wrong or mispronounced words, and awkward structures so they tend to score low on the assessment scale [29, 30].

3 Electronic Training Materials for Learning Chinese

3.1 Training on Basic Knowledge

This module focuses on basic knowledge of Chinese with the main aim of arousing learners' interest and motivation in learning. Topics include character structuring, character framing, parts and components, and correct writing of characters. For example, students will be taught to recognize the shape, sound and meaning of Chinese characters to refrain from writing wrong words. Understanding sentence structure and developing ability in sentence composition and restructuring also constitute the essence of this module.

Character Structuring. In order to guide students towards the understanding and mastering of the correct stroke order in Chinese characters, as shown in Fig. 1, the computer will:

- demonstrate correct stroke order on the monitor;
- analyze students' stroke order and display on the monitor; and
- record students' stroke order and store in the computer for future retrieval.

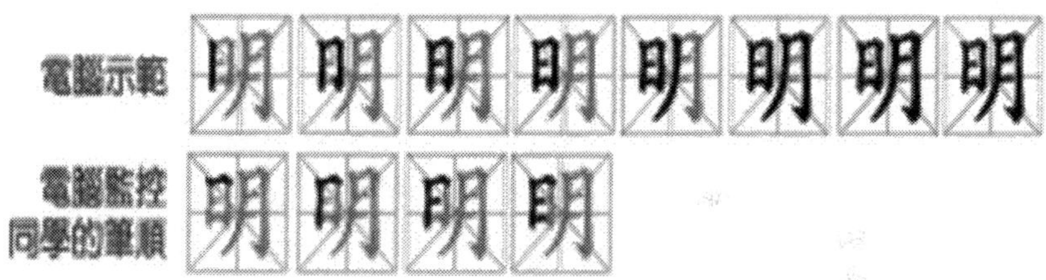

Fig. 1. Computer display (top) and computer monitoring a student's stroke order (bottom).

Students can choose squares of different sizes to write the characters. Repeat practice is pertinent in order to strength the coordination between hand and eyes.

Character Framing. The objective of this part is to guide students towards character recognition and framing, enabling them to master ways of structuring and framing characters. As shown in Fig. 2, the computer will:

- show character structure through diagrams;
- strengthen a student's ability to recognize character frame and structure by repeat demonstrations; and
- reinforce a student's memory and observation of character structure through sharp, recurrent images.

Students can choose squares of different sizes to write the characters. Repeat practice is pertinent in order to strength the coordination between hand and eyes.

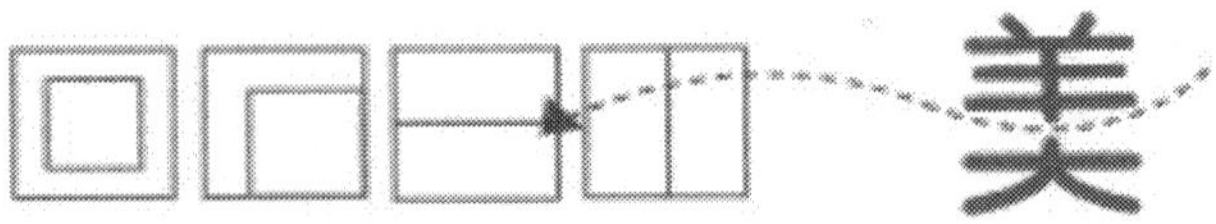

Fig. 2. Computer displays progressive character structure through a series of diagrams.

Parts and Components. This part enables students to understand the fact that each Chinese character contains different parts and components as shown in Fig. 3. Different colors are used for students to identify and distinguish between the various parts and components of each Chinese character on the screen. Students will also discover that parts and components impact on character structure, sound and meaning.

忄 + 青 → 情 the radical "忄" + young = love
日 + 青 → 晴 the radical "日" + young = fine (weather)
目 + 青 → 睛 the radical "目" + young = eye
氵 + 青 → 清 the radical "氵" + young = clear

Fig. 3. Computer progressively configures by displaying parts and components of each character.

3.2 Training on Writing

Word Combination. This part trains students' ability in combining words. Modern Chinese contains many two-word expressions, for instance, the Chinese term for "music" constitutes the words "sound" and "happiness", and the words in this two-word expression can be configured in different ways to form different expressions.

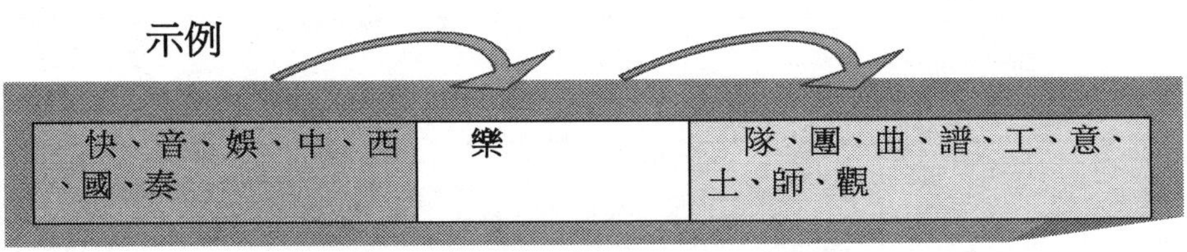

Fig. 4. Word combination example.

As illustrated in the example shown in Fig. 4, "sound" can be combined with suffixes, such as "sign", "symbol", "volume", "gamut", "color", "acoustics" and "quality" to form a diverse range of two-word expressions. "Happiness" can be combined with suffixes such as "notes", "band", "song", "theory" to form a multitude of two-word expressions. Prefixes such as "western", "sad", "fast", "enjoy" can also be used to form other two-word expressions. The practice exercise displayed on the screen requires students to use the prefixes in the first column and the suffixes in the second column to form as many two-word expressions as they can.

Word Matching. The objective of this part is to assist students in mastering ways of matching words as expressions are units used to form sentences. Well-matched words lead to well-matched expressions which become sentences to narrate things, express feelings and emotions. Whether one expression matches well with another expression depends on different characteristics. In Chinese, nouns cannot overlap each other and cannot be modified by auxiliaries. However, they match perfectly well with measure words, e.g. "three school units". In writing compositions, we have to be aware of the characteristics of each word and phrase so we can mix and match them to make perfect sense.

Table 1. Sample exercise displayed on screen.

Word combination	English translation	Expression formed by combining the two words
解決--- ---問題	solve-----problem	"solve a problem"
提高--- ---警惕	raise-----alertness	"raise alertness"
改善--- ---生活	improve-----life	"improve life"
接受--- ---考驗	take-----test	"take the test"
支持--- ---改革	support-----reform	"support the reform"

Table 2. Interactive exercise.

Word combination interactive exercise	English translation
如何解決兄弟之間的 (問題), 確實令他很頭痛。	How to solve the (problem) between the two brothers really gives him a headache.
這裏龍蛇混雜, 我們必須提高 (警惕)。	As this place is full of lowlifes, we must (raise our alertness).
他希望憑著一雙手去改善 (生活), 而不想靠領取「綜援」津貼維生。	He hopes to work to (improve life) and not to rely on the "CSSA".
小明願意接受 (考驗), 挑戰自我。	Young Ming wants to (take the test) to challenge himself.
香港醫生和病人都支持 (改革), 希望醫療服務出現新的局面。	Both doctors and patients in Hong Kong (support the reform), longing for a new phase in medical services.

The sample word combination exercise displayed on screen is shown in Table 1 whereas the interactive exercise is shown in Table 2. Exercise should be submitted electronically for immediate feedback.

Sentence Structuring and Restructuring. The objective of this part is to train students' ability in structuring and restructuring sentences. An e-tutorial segment guiding students to recognize the basic structure of a sentence, i.e. subject, predicate and object, will be incorporated in the training materials. Samples displayed on the monitor depict the logical reasoning and construction of each sentence as shown in Fig. 5.

Today is Sunday and we stay home to watch TV together.

Fig. 5. Sample sentence configuration.

3.3 Training on Reading Comprehension

This module aims to help students understand words and text content. Students will also be trained to employ reading strategies to grasp contextual clues, to shadow and to apply what has been read. In fact, time clues, space clues, signpost language, cause and effect illustrations, etc. all contribute to the understanding of the content of a passage. In reading, students should be taught to make use of content to understand the structure, clues and expressions of a passage.

Sample Exercise. It is common to use the comparison method in passages for readers to have proper understanding and conceptualization of abstract ideas and phenomena. The emphasis is on creating a repertoire of articles with different themes and topics. There will be a collection of articles pitched at different levels of difficulty and lexical density grouped under each theme. The concept can best be illustrated by the first paragraph of the following articles, all bearing the same theme and name "Their Lunch".

他們的午餐(29 字)
中午時分, 澳門的一些建築工人一字排開, 坐在人行道邊上吃飯。

At noon, some construction workers in Macau sit in single file on the sidewalk eating their lunch (29 words in Chinese).

他們的午餐(58 字)
中午時分, 澳門的一些建築工人一字排開, 坐在落閘的店鋪門前吃飯。能夠像這樣好好地飽餐一頓, 對他們來說, 似乎已經足夠了。

At noon, some construction workers in Macau sit in single file in front of a closed shop to have their lunch. As long as they can eat heartily like this, it seems good enough for them (58 words in Chinese).

他們的午餐(85 字)
中午時分, 澳門的一些建築工人坐在落閘的店鋪門前吃飯。儘管這樣, 但能夠好好地飽餐一頓, 對他們來**說**, 似乎已經足**夠**了。他們對澳門的發展貢獻不小, 卻要求不多, 這種精神, **值**得尊敬。

At noon, some construction workers in Macau sit in front of a closed shop to have their lunch. Despite their predicament, they still eat heartily because this is good enough for them. Although they make considerable contribution to Macau's development, they do not ask for much. Their spirit should be respected (85 words in Chinese).

他們的午餐(114 字)

中午時分, 澳門的一些建築工人一字排開, 坐在落閘的店鋪門前吃飯。他們吃的當然不是什麼山珍海味, 只是很普通的盒飯。儘管這樣, 但能**夠**好好地飽餐一頓, 對他們來**說**, 似乎已經足**夠**了。他們對澳門的發展貢獻不小, 卻要求不多, 這種精神, **值**得尊敬。

At noon, some construction workers in Macau sit in single file in front of a closed shop to have their lunch. Their lunch boxes only contain plain food, not some luxury and exotic delicacies. Despite their predicament, they enjoy their food heartily. To them, this is good enough. Although they contribute significantly to Macau's development, they do not ask for much. Their spirit should be respected (114 words in Chinese).

4 Conclusion

According to the Census and Statistics Department, the term Ethnic Minority applies to people of non-Chinese race, comprising Asians other than Chinese (81.0 % in 2011), Whites (12.2 % in 2011), Mixed (6.4 % in 2011) and Others (0.3 % in 2011). From education perspectives, the dominant student groups are from South Asian countries comprising Pakistani, Indian and Nepalese [2]. Most South Asian EM residents are local citizens who hold Hong Kong SAR identity cards and/or passports and the main languages they speak are Urdu, Hindi, Punjabi and Nepali. Many activists insist that education should be an "equalizing, balancing" factor which offers young people the hope of a better life irrespective of their gender or race. Unfortunately, students from EM backgrounds are confronted with great obstacles as it is virtually impossible for them to meet requirements for a university place without strong Chinese-language skills. If such conditions persist, abilities of minority students may often go unrecognized, and we may even deprive them of ways of getting better jobs and breaking cycles of poverty. In this respect, language has wrongly been used as a way to allow racial/ethnic hierarchies, leading to more racial segregation and dissension. As Hong Kong has been globally known as a world city where East meets West, such discriminatory policies should not be made to continue!

The present study, although limited in scope, will shed some light on the education needs of this group of students and on how best we can address their wishes of attaining an acceptable standard in the Chinese language in order to pursue further studies, and to advance in careers or professions of their choosing.

References

1. Brossell, G.: Rhetorical Specifications in essay examination topics. Coll. Engl. **45**, 165–173 (1983)
2. Census and Statistics Department: 2011 population census: Summary results. (2012). Accessed http://www.census2011.gov.hk/pdf/summaryresults.pdf
3. Daneman, M.: Individual differences in reading skills. In: Barr, R., Kamil, M.L., Mosenthal, P., Pearson, P.D. (eds.) Handbook of Reading Research, vol. 2, pp. 512–538. Longman, White Plains (1991)
4. Flower, L.A., Hayes, J.R.: The Dynamics of Composing: Making Plans and Juggling Constraints. In: Gregg, L.W., Steinberg, E.R. (eds.) Cognitive Processes in Writing, pp. 31–50. Lawrence Earlbaum Associates, Hillsdale (1980)
5. Flower, L., Hayes, J.R.: A cognitive process theory of writing. Coll. Compos. Commun. **32**(4), 365–387 (1981)
6. Gershkoff-Stowe, L., Hahn, E.: Fast mapping skills in the developing lexicon. J. Speech Lang. Hear. Res. **50**(3), 682–697 (2007)
7. Hall, D., Emblen, D.L.: A writer's reader. Little Brown, Boston (1976)
8. Hayes, J.R.: A new model of cognition and affect in writing. In: Levy, M., Ransdell, S. (eds.) The Science of Writing. Erlbaum, Hillsdale (1996)
9. Leung, P.W.L., Hung, S.F., Ho, T.P., Lee, C.C., Liu, W.S., et al.: Prevalence of DSM-IV disorders in Chinese adolescents and the effects of an impairment criterion: a pilot community study in Hong Kong. Eur. Child Adolesc. Psychiatry **17**, 452–461 (2008)
10. Matsuhashi, A.: Pausing and planning: The tempo of written discourse production. Res. Teach. Engl. **15**(2), 113–134 (1981)
11. Rivera, C., Vincent, C., Hafner, A., LaCelle-Peterson, M.: Statewide Assessment Programs: Policies and Practices for the Inclusion of Limited English Proficient Students. ERIC Digest. Washington D.C.: ERIC Clearinghouse on Language and Linguistics. ED 362 073 (1997)
12. South China Morning Post: Newspaper articles in July issues (2014)
13. Sulzby, E.: Children's Emergent Reading of Favorite Storybooks: A Developmental Study. Read. Res. Q. **20**(4), 464 (1985). Copyright 1985 by the International Reading Association
14. Widdowson, H.G.: Explorations in Applied Linguistics. Oxford University Press, Oxford (1979)
15. Johnson, A.B., Tsang, C.D.: Chapter name in an edited book. In: Lee, K.L. (ed.) Understanding Student Engagement, pp. 234–256. Longman, Hong Kong (2010)
16. 謝錫金, 張慧儀, 羅嘉怡 (2008)。《中國語文課程, 教材及教法:面向有特殊學習需要的學童》香港大學出版社。
17. 李錚 (1964)。<六岁左右儿童的**汉**字字形知**觉**形位的初探>。《心理学**报**》1964 年 02 期。
18. 何萬貫, 葉穎暉 (1998)。 <小學高年級學生對漢字筆畫的認識>。《初等教育學報》。頁 15–42 。
19. 謝錫金, 祝新華 (2001) <識字教與學心理>, 見謝錫金主編 (**2001**) 《高效漢字教與學》。香港:青田教育中心。頁 44–79 。
20. 祝新華 (1993)。語文能力發展心理學。杭州:杭州大學出版社。
21. 戴汝潛, 郝嘉傑 (1999) <中國**內**地兒童識字教育>, 見戴汝潛主編 (**1999**)《漢字教與學》。山東:山東教育出版社。頁 110–232。
22. 蕭炳基, 范國等人 (1986) 製訂的《常用詞語表》。
23. 歐佩娟 (1982)。《三種**閱**讀方法與中文**閱**讀理解能力的關係之研究》, 碩士論文。
24. 蕭炳基 (1993)。《篇章文理線索對**閱**讀過程之效應》第 8 卷, pp. 12–18。
25. 何萬貫 (2002)。 <教學的反思—中文科課程改革的幾個問題>。周漢光編 (2002) 《創意中文教學》。香港:香港中文大學教育學院課程與教學學系。頁 3–10。

26. 蘇月華等 (1995)。《中文閱讀理解能力訓練》(中一教師本)。香港:香港中文大學。
27. 何萬貫 (2003)。<高中作文技巧>(多媒體教學系列)。香港:中文大學出版社。
28. 何萬貫 (2007)。<香港中學生中國語文科作文卷語誤分析>。《中國語文通訊》。頁 8–18。
29. 何萬貫 (1997)。<有效的作文批改—錄音批改作文>。《語文教學與研究》(華中師大)。第 7 期。頁 12–13。
30. 何萬貫, 歐佩娟 (1998)。<中學, 預科與大學學生運用題性寫作聯繫策略的能力>。

Blended Learning: A Case Study of Korean Language Course

Edwin Chan Chiu Wai(✉), Norris Lau Ka Yin,
Jimmy Yau Kwok Chau, and Shirley Huang Mei Yee

Centre for Cyber Learning, HKU SPACE,
University of Hong Kong, Hong Kong SAR, China
{edwin.chan,norris.lau,jimmy.yau,
my.huang}@hkuspace.hku.hk

Abstract. Advances in technology foster a proactive approach to provision of support and solutions to learners. One common approach is blended learning in which online learning plays a complementary role in traditional face-to-face classroom learning. With the popularity of mobile devices, more studies on the use of mobile devices in learning or training process have been conducted. In this paper, we describe the features and functionalities of a Korean e-learning website which supports both learning with desktop computers and mobile devices. Instructional design strategies are discussed. Surveys were conducted to investigate the learners' perceptions of the e-learning materials in three consecutive intakes and the results of these intakes were compared. Finally, we pinpoint the areas of improvement in developing language materials for blended learning courses which can serve as a reference for future development.

Keywords: Online resources · Language courses · Blended learning · Instructional design · Online learning · e-learning · m-learning

1 Introduction

Technologies have changed our lives in numerous aspects compared with those in the past few decades. One of them which is considerable is education. Introduction of online learning components including interactive elements like animation, audio and video to traditional face-to-face classroom learning, which is called blended learning, has received positive attention [8]. This provision of support not only leverages effective and relevant learning resources, and also arouses interest of learners, and most importantly, brings the utmost learning experience for learner-centric pedagogy [24, 28]. Keeping pace with evolving technology in education is challenging as technology offers lots of opportunities and possibilities [20] in enhancing teaching and learning, especially with the growing trend of learning through mobile devices [38].

Undoubtedly, a move from electronic learning (e-learning) to mobile learning (m-learning) is noticeable, owing to the continuation of Moore's Law [34], the ubiquity of mobile devices and the widespread coverage of wireless network. According to a prediction made by International Data Crop (IDC) in 2013, the average cost of smartphone is expected to drop more than 20 % in 2017 [16]. Meanwhile, the processing

J. Lam et al. (Eds.): ICTE 2015, CCIS 559, pp. 42–60, 2015.
DOI: 10.1007/978-3-662-48978-9_5

power of mobile devices is rapidly improving and becomes comparable to that of desktop [4]. In addition, statistics from Hong Kong Office of the Telecommunications Authority (OFCA) showed high mobile subscriber penetration rate reaching 239 % in 2014 [30]. Besides, popularisation in mobile devices also drives new learning habits. According to a research report on Search behaviours of Internet users in China, "to get information related to work and study" ranked the second, following "to get information I am interested in" [7]. It is obvious that the importance of m-learning is paramount and the shift of learning behaviour from PC-end to mobile-end is significant [40]. Educators and content developers should be aware of this trend and consider how to facilitate m-learning in the planning of online learning materials so as to deliver better learning experience.

Previous studies on online material development were centred on instructional design for desktop computer learners [6, 17, 35]. With the emergence of m-learning, more studies focus on issues and design principles of pure m-learning [1, 9, 13]. Ally [1] discussed the learning theories and instructional design principles for the design of learning materials for mobile devices. Elias [9] analysed the application of universal instructional design principles in distance education to the design of mobile learning. However, studies on a mixed mode, that is, instructional design that supports both learning with desktop computers and mobile devices are thin on the ground, bearing device variability as the patent challenge. With the increasing prevalence of smartphone with large screen size in the market [37] and better coverage of wireless network, can the accessible design of the learning materials with solid pedagogical approaches can remove the barriers to education diversity in desktop computer learning and mobile learning?

This paper aims to evaluate the effectiveness of the use of supplementary e-learning materials that support learning with desktop computer and mobile devices in a language course. Features and functionalities of these e-learning materials were described in the perspective of instructional design strategies. Surveys were conducted at the end of three consecutive intakes for this course. By comparing the survey results, differences in learners' perceptions of the e-learning materials and the level of their engagement in the blended mode of learning were discussed. Moreover, the results also shed some light on the areas of improvement in developing language resources for blended learning courses.

2 Recent Development of Language Resources

Successful cases in foreign language learning with incorporation of information and communication technology (ICT) were reported. These learning resources facilitated learner-centred learning environment, enhanced learner motivation, and helped achieve ubiquitous learning. Hirata [14] showed that the key point of high student acceptance of foreign language learning was to address the learner's needs and preferences in different modes of instructions. Japanese e-learning system developed by the HKU SPACE was proved helpful to learners' studies, complementing traditional face-to-face teaching [21]. Other examples like, "Let's go Korea!" was a public Korean e-learning website developed by the collaboration of RTHK, City University of Hong Kong and Consulate General Republic of Korea [32] in 2005.

Owing to rapid evolution of mobile devices in recent years, more and more language mobile apps are available at different application distribution platforms. In Korean language, there are “Learn Korean” from Bravolol containing numerous Korean phrases and vocabularies with authentic pronunciation [5]. “Learn Korean 6,000 Words” from Fun Easy Learn is another example, which provides different topics related to Korean culture such as food and music. For Japanese, an Android mobile application for beginners to learn Japanese in a self-pace mode was developed [29].

Recent researches had been conducted to study the language learning with m-learning [19, 23]. Tsang [39] evaluated the effectiveness of instructional design principles in multimedia learning for mobile learning. The study showed that learners’ language proficiency for English and Chinese was enhanced by the mobile learning modules and positive student feedback towards the learning materials was reflected. It also listed out a number of recommended guidelines on instructional design for mobile learning and pointed out that catching up with the frequent update of mobile operation system would be a challenge to them to maintain the compatibility of the learning modules. All of these researches pinpointed that effective instructional design strategies played an indispensable role in online language study, both in e-learning and m-learning.

3 Instructional Design of Korean e-learning Website

Instructional design is to analyse the learning needs and manipulate the knowledge with systematic approach so as to develop effective learning materials which can improve the delivery of instruction. Learning materials are designed from learner’s perceptive that can help learners build up knowledge. Different instructional design strategies and learning theories are adopted to enhance and provide valuable learning experience to learners.

In this study, the course “Introductory Korean” under the HKU SPACE is being investigated. This course is offered to part-time leaners of different disciplines and is a beginner course among a Korean language programme. Learners are provided with online learning materials via a Korean e-learning website to supplement their weekly 3-h face-to-face classroom learning. Learners can access the Korean e-learning Website via the HKU SPACE e-Learning Management System, SOUL 2.0.

The Korean e-learning Website consisted of 3 major sections. First, Pronunciation section provides the information of Korean characters (Hangeul) including vowels, consonants and Batchim. The audio file and the corresponding stroke-order animation of each vowel and character are provided. In addition, a Hangeul generator (by selecting vowel and consonant) is included for learners to create Korean characters on the fly, followed with the corresponding pronunciation and stroke-order animation. Second, Chapter section offers different resources like Vocabulary, Grammar and Practice Exercises. In Vocabulary, Chinese translation and foreign source of vocabularies are listed out, together with the native-speaker audio file. Grammar consists of explanation of rules in the Korean language, supplemented with example sentences (with audio files) and instant quizzes for quick revision. Practice Exercises section comprises questions on vocabulary, grammar, listening and comprehension for learners to review the levels of knowledge in each chapter. Third, Tools section consists of learning functions like Vocabulary Search, Vocabulary Flash Card and Typing Game of Korean Characters.

By applying the instructional design principles in multimedia learning (Mayer, 2008) and universal instructional design principles for mobile learning [9], the Korean e-learning website were incorporated with instructional design principles in the following six major areas.

3.1 Simple and Intuitive - User Interface and Navigation

User interface design is one of the critical factors to provide effective learning experience [36]. Good user interface can provide a comfort digital learning environment to learners and make learning more engaging. The Korean e-learning website was designed to open in a pop-up window. Being noticeable, it helped learners focus on the current learning site. With a dimension of 1000 pixels x 700 pixels, the Website can fit most of the screen sizes and match with the common screen scale, both for desktop and mobile devices. With cautious consideration of reading comfortableness and efficiency, font size and the page layout were persistently adjusted to minimise the user scrolling effort, either by mouse or fingers. Moreover, learning content was clearly organised into a self-explanatory and intuitive way. For instance, the basic explanations about Hangeul and tools such as Flash Card were separated from Chapter section whereas Chapter-related content like Vocabulary, Grammar and Practice Exercises was consistently put under Chapter section. Simple user interface with textual navigation facilitated learners to quickly familarise with the Website navigation, and thus to concentrate on the learning materials.

3.2 Use of Multimedia

To align with the multimedia strategies used in mobile learning, various types of multimedia were widely used in the Korean e-learning website [1]. In Pronunciation section, stroke-order animations worked with the corresponding audio files of Korean characters (Temporal contiguity). In addition, learners could have a hands-on experience of character creation with vowel and consonant, which was supported with instant pronunciation. Moreover, over 600 common vocabularies were presented with translations and native-speaker audio. In order to reduce the cognitive load of learners [1, 25], visual-auditory instructional technique was adopted. Relevant graphics as well as clear and simple instructions/text (Spatial contiguity) were placed next to the questions in Practice Exercises. Audio flashcards on Hangeul and vocabularies were introduced for learners to revise Korean characters/vocabularies and practise pronunciation from time to time.

3.3 Flexible of Use - Chunk of Information

In order to utilise the limited capacity of learner's memory, learning content was divided into manageable learning parts whenever possible [3]. For example, Hangeul was classified into vowels, consonants, double vowels and Batchim, rather than presenting all the content on a single page. Grammar content in each Chapter was displayed in small meaningful chunks [33] in tabs, allowing learners to view sub-topic one after the other. All these design strategies benefited learners in memorization and the process of information absorption [27].

3.4 Low Physical and Technical Effort - Interactive Activities

Interactive design helps enrich the learning experience and encourage participatory learning [2]. Interactive design in learning activities can make learning more engaging by arousing learner's interest, and can extend their retention time in the learning materials. Thus, different types of interactive activity such as drag-and-drop question, matching exercise were developed in the Korean e-learning website. On the other hand, with the support of touch response in mobile devices, these interactive activities also addressed the tedious issue of inputting text data into mobile devices.

3.5 Individualised Activities

In Flash Card of Pronunciation and Vocabularies, learners were allowed to set the speed (from fast to slow) and option (characters/vocabularies are grouped by categories/levels) of the displayed characters/vocabularies, based on their language/vocabulary acquisition. With these individualised activities, learners could gain greater control of their learning experience [12]; besides, it could cater different learning needs and backgrounds of individual learners.

3.6 Gamification

Typing game in the theme of fishing game was developed for engagement, challenge creation and achievement of learning objectives [31]. In the Korean e-learning Website, a typing game with Korean vocabularies was designed and developed. Korean vocabularies were drawn randomly from the database and displayed on some moving fish. Learners were instructed to hook as many fish as possible within a minute by typing the Korean characters timely and accurately. Learners could compete with each other as their scores would be shown on the scoreboard. This game was designed to motivate learners to practise Korean typing skill and to revise the Korean vocabularies at the same time. This game was designed to associate the learning objectives with an incentive of gaining high score and to harness competitive urges [15] (Fig. 1).

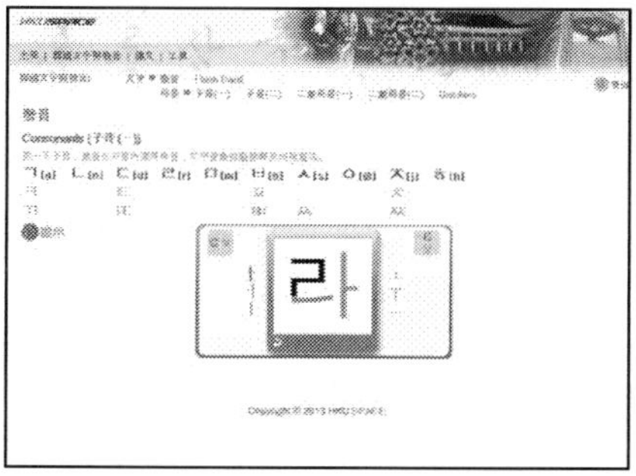

Pronunciation (Stroke order animation and audio)

Practice Exercises

Practice Exercises (audio and visual)

Practice Exercises (Drag and Drop)

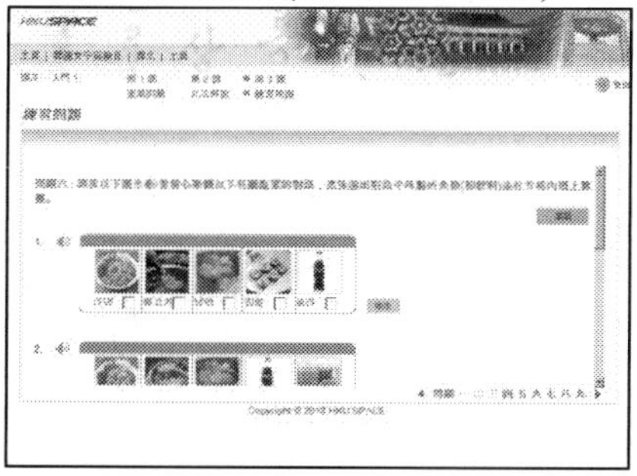

Interactive activites (Listening quiz)

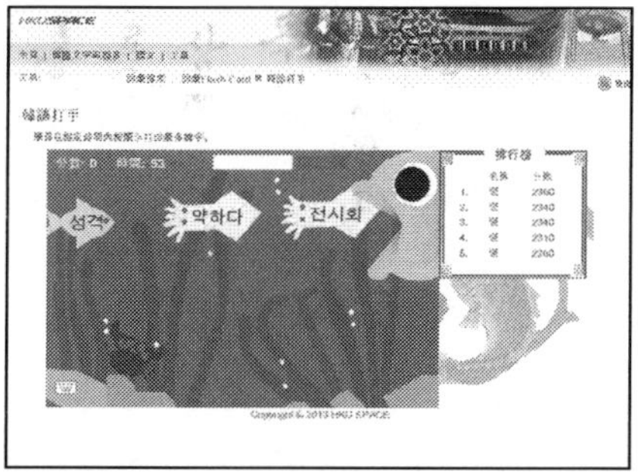

Typing Game

Fig. 1. Screen captures of the Korean e-learning Website

4 Evaluation Study

4.1 Methodology

Adopting a blended learning approach, the language course "Introductory Korean" was conducted in a traditional face-to-face learning mode supplemented with a Korean e-learning website. It was a three-month course, comprising three-hour weekly classes of lecturing. At the end of each course intake, learners were invited to a survey. Learners' feedback on taking this language course and their perceptions of the online learning materials were collected. Three consecutive surveys were conducted started from the first intake (February 2013) (Table 1).

From the three surveys, a total of 1,770 responses were received, constituting an overall response rate of 71.1 %. Details of each survey are listed below.

Table 1. No. of respondents in each survey

Intake	No. of respondents	No. of learners	Response rate
February 2013	536	764	70.2 %
September 2013	620	835	74.3 %
February 2014	614	892	68.8 %

4.2 Summary of Survey Results

Each survey comprised three parts of questions covering Part I - Online Course Design, Part II - Online Course Materials and Part III – Overall Comments. In Part I, learners' general perceptions of the online learning website were evaluated. In Part II, more detailed questions about the usefulness of online learning materials such as Pronunciation, Vocabulary, Grammar, Practice and Tools were asked and learners could reflect their opinions and perceptions of each learning material in open-ended questions. In Part III, learners were asked to comment on their overall learning experience of the e-learning website. In particular, learners were asked whether they had encountered any technical problems in using the website and whether they had used any mobile devices to access the website.

The Korean e-learning website was first launched in February 2013 and new features likes Vocabulary Flash Cards, Vocabulary Search and Typing Game (under Tools section) were launched in February 2014. Additional questions about Tools were included in the questionnaire of the third intake. As such, results of the Tools section would be analysed independently. In the following section, major survey results were highlighted and discussed.

4.2.1 Part I – Online Course Design

A screening question was asked to check whether the respondents had accessed the online learning materials in the Korean e-learning website. Figure 2 showed that the

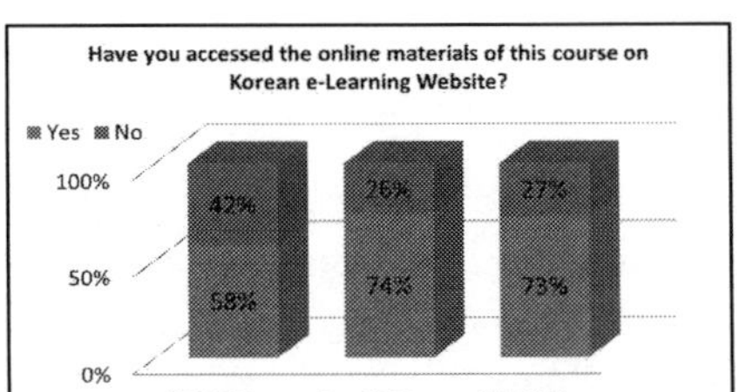

Fig. 2. Comparison of percentages of learners who have accessed the Korean e-learning website in the three intakes.

percentage of learners who had accessed the online learning materials in the three intakes. The percentage rose significantly from 58 % to 74 % in the first two intakes and levelled off at 73 % in the third intake. The rapid increase of access rate in the second intake could be explained by the fact that learners might not recognise the presence of the e-learning resource in its initial launch. More promotion of the e-learning website by the teaching staff was done in the subsequent two intakes.

Over the three intakes, an average of 75 % of respondents agreed that the instructions on the e-learning website and activities were very clear and clear (Fig. 3). Besides, over 66 % of respondents agreed that it was very easy or easy to navigate the learning materials in the e-learning website (Fig. 4). This percentage climbed gradually to 72 % in the third intake. These two findings give a positive indication that the instructional design employed in the e-learning website did not bring big barrier to accessible materials for the learners. More discussion about this finding can be found in the Discussion section.

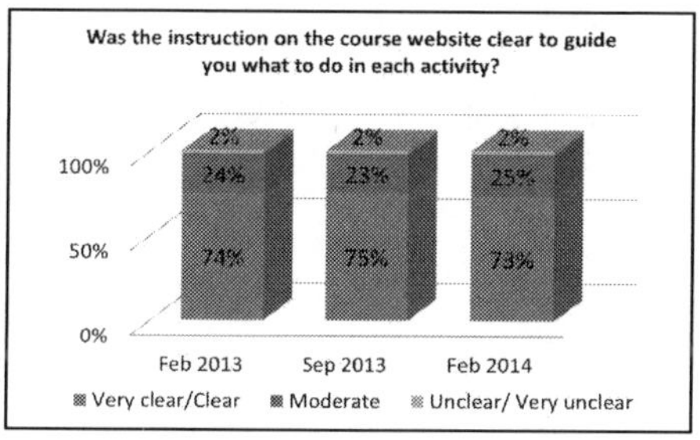

Fig. 3. Comparison of learners' feedback on whether the instruction on the Korean e-learning website was clear in the three intakes.

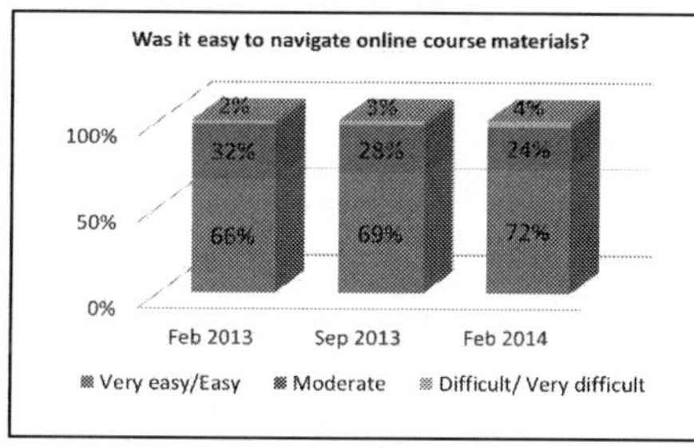

Fig. 4. Comparison of learners' feedback on whether the navigation of online course materials was easy in the three intakes.

4.2.2 Part II - Online Course Materials

In this section, more detailed learners' perceptions of various learning materials available in the e-learning Website were evaluated. The questions were grouped into 6 areas, namely Pronunciation, Chapter, Vocabulary, Grammar, Practice Exercises and Tools.

Pronunciation. In the first intake, 79 % of respondents strongly agreed or agreed that Pronunciation section helped them to start with Korean language (Fig. 5). This percentage gradually increased to 84 % and 85 % in second and third intakes respectively. For the sub-questions under Pronunciation, around 80 % of respondents consistently strongly agreed or agreed that the audio and content of Pronunciation was clear and easy to follow/read in the three intakes (Figs. 6 and 7).

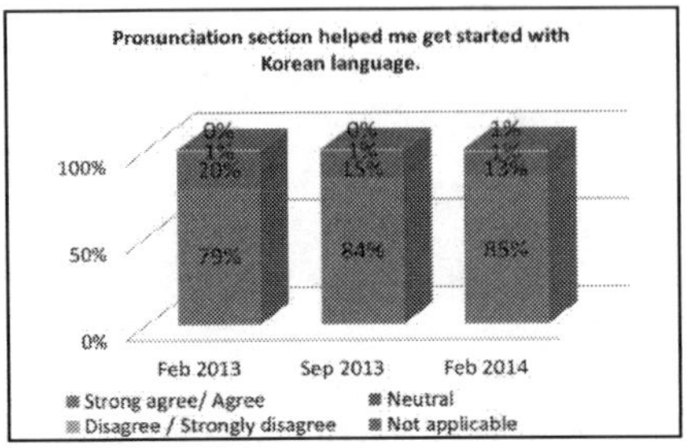

Fig. 5. Pronunciation section helped me get started with Korean language.

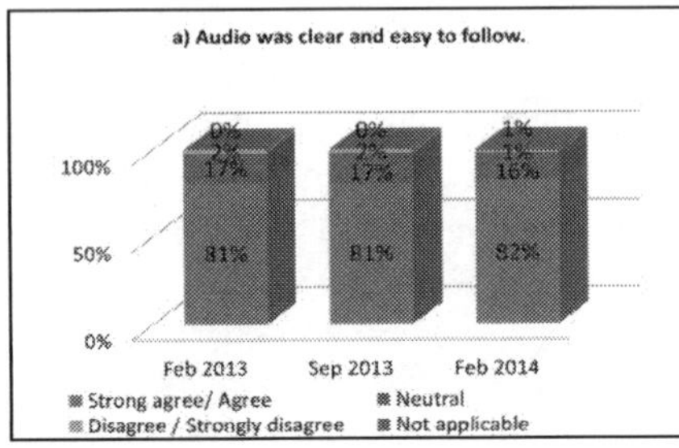

Fig. 6. Audio was clear and easy to follow.

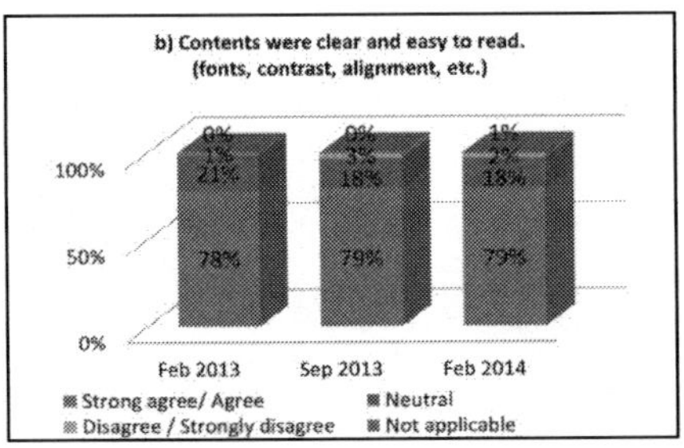

Fig. 7. Contents were clear and easy to read. (fonts, contrast, alignment, etc.)

Chapter. Around 70 % respondents strongly agreed or agreed that Chapter section helped them consolidate and deepen their knowledge (Fig. 8). This percentage rose to 76 % and 77 % respectively in second and third intakes respectively.

Vocabulary. Regarding learners' perception of Vocabulary section, 74 % of respondents in the first intake strongly agreed or agreed that this section was useful and

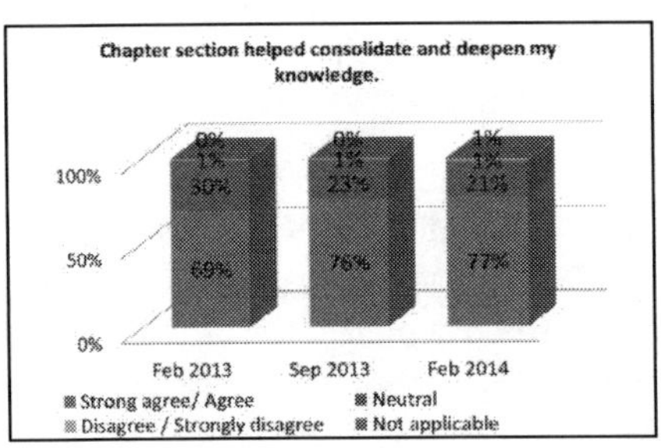

Fig. 8. Chapter section helped consolidate and deepen my knowledge.

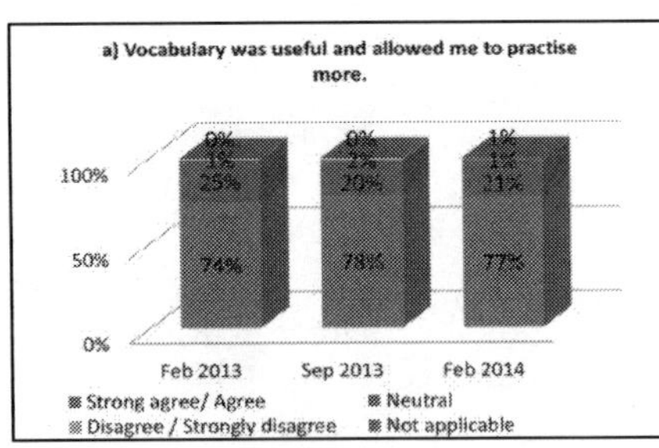

Fig. 9. Vocabulary was useful and allowed me to practise more.

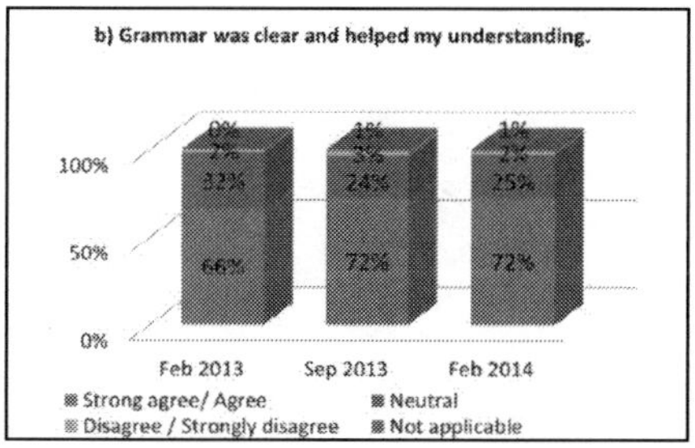

Fig. 10. Grammar was clear and helped my understanding.

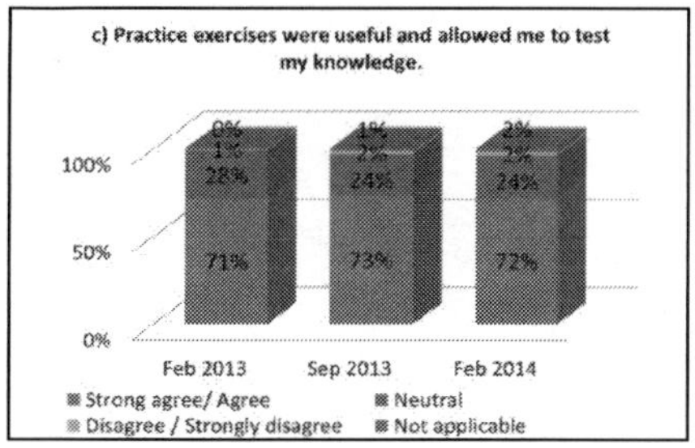

Fig. 11. Practice Exercises were useful and allowed me to test my knowledge.

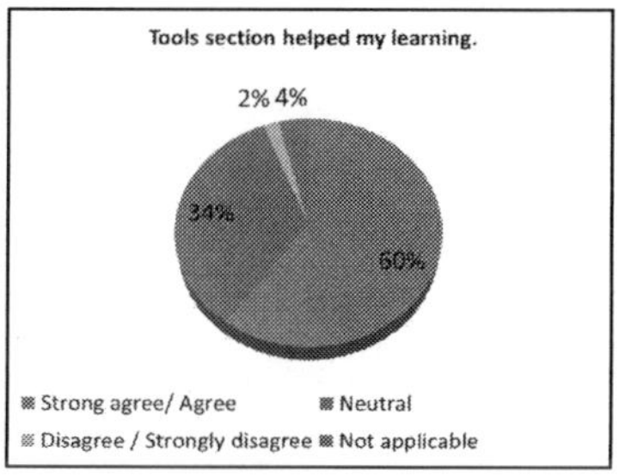

Fig. 12. Tools section helped my learning.

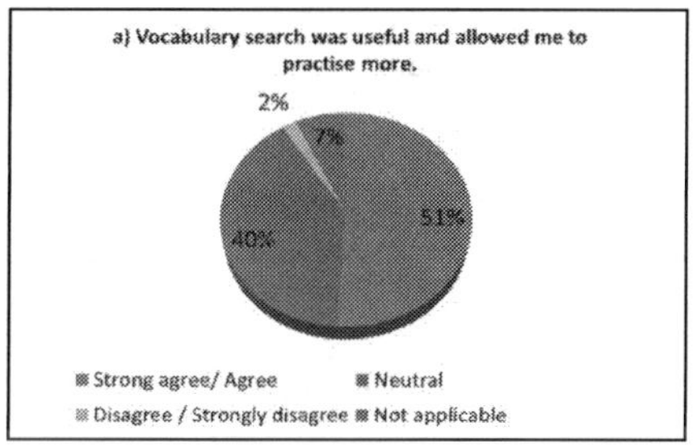

Fig. 13. Vocabulary search was useful and allowed me to practise more.

allowed them to practise more (Fig. 9). This percentage climbed to 78 % in the second intake and levelled off in the third intake.

Grammar. In the first intake, around 66 % of respondents strongly agreed or agreed that Grammar was clear and helped their understanding (Fig. 10). Similar to the trend of Vocabulary, the positive feedback of Grammar section grew in the second intake and became stable at 72 % in the third intake.

Practice Exercises. Among the three intakes, around 71–73 % of respondents strongly agreed or agreed that Practice Exercises were useful and allowed them to test their knowledge (Fig. 11).

Tools. This Tools section was launched before the third intake. The results of this section were analysed independently. Learners gave a moderate feedback towards two learning functions - Vocabulary Search and Vocabulary Flash Card. 51 % of respondents strongly agreed or agreed that Vocabulary search was useful and allowed them to practise more (Fig. 13). 54 % of respondents strongly agreed or agreed that Vocabulary Flash Card was practical and helped strengthen their vocabulary (Fig. 14). Around 42 % of respondents gave neutral feedback on the Korean typing game and only 38 % of respondents strongly agreed or agreed that the Korean typing game was interesting

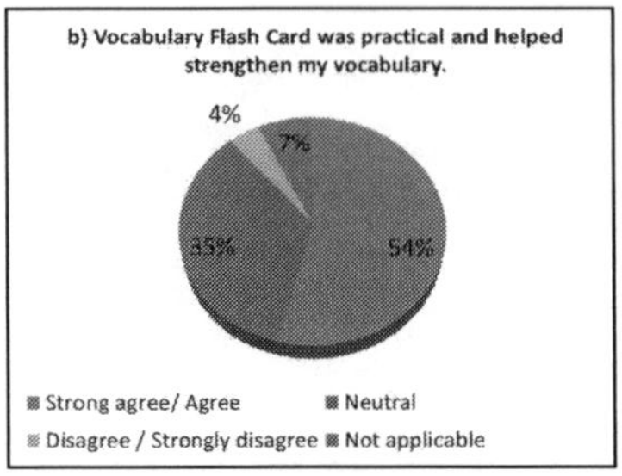

Fig. 14. Vocabulary Flash Card was practical and helped strengthen my vocabulary.

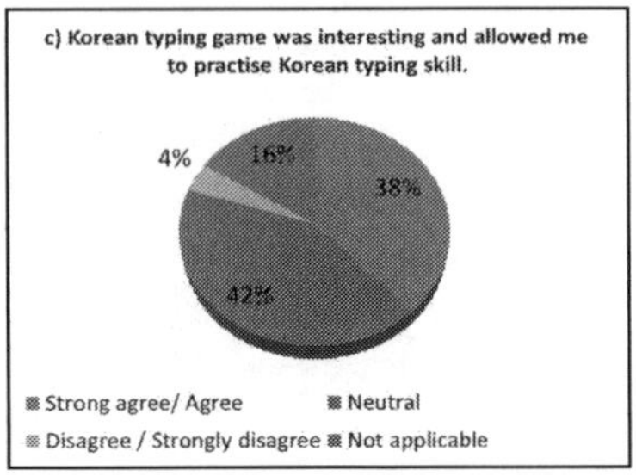

Fig. 15. Korean typing game was interesting and allowed me to practise Korean typing skill.

and allowed them to practise Korean typing skill (Fig. 15). Regarding the whole Tools section, 60 % of respondents agreed that this section helped their learning (Fig. 12).

4.2.3 Part III - Online Course Materials

Table 2 showed a quick summary of the learners' online learning experience. Over 70 % of respondents strongly agreed or agreed that the online course materials made their learning more flexible and accessible, and enriched their learning experience over the three intakes. Most important, on average, 74 % of respondents strongly agreed or agreed that the online course materials enhanced their understanding of the topics covered, while less than 3 % of respondents gave negative feedback on this view. In addition, an average of 74 % of respondents satisfied with the quality of the online course materials.

Learners were also asked to choose the most useful materials for their learning on the course website. They were allowed to choose more than one among four sections, Pronunciation, Vocabulary, Grammar and Practice Exercise. Among the three intakes, the most useful learning materials selected are listed in descending order as below (Fig. 16):

Pronunciation > Practice Exercise > Grammar > Vocabulary

Regarding learners' view on continuity of learning support, around 98 % of respondents would like to have online course materials available in other modules. It went up to 99 % for the second and third intakes (Fig. 17).

In Fig. 18, it showed that around one-third of respondents had used mobile devices to access the online course materials. This figure gradually grew from 32 % in the first intake, to 37 % in the second and third intakes. Among them, they were asked about the frequency of accessing online course materials with mobile devices. A large proportion (over 65 %) of this group of respondents used mobile devices more than 2 times in every 10 times (Fig. 19).

Table 2. Summary of overall feedback

Questions	Intake	Strongly agree/Agree	Neutral	Disagree/Strongly disagree	Not applicable
The online course materials made my learning more flexible and accessible	Feb 2013	71 %	26 %	3 %	0 %
	Sep 2013	75 %	22 %	3 %	0 %
	Feb 2014	76 %	21 %	2 %	1 %
The online course materials made my learning more interesting and engaging	Feb 2013	62 %	33 %	5 %	0 %
	Sep 2013	58 %	35 %	7 %	0 %
	Feb 2014	64 %	32 %	3 %	1 %
The online course materials enhanced my understanding of the topics covered	Feb 2013	74 %	24 %	2 %	0 %
	Sep 2013	74 %	23 %	3 %	0 %
	Feb 2014	74 %	24 %	1 %	1 %
The online course materials enriched my learning experience	Feb 2013	71 %	25 %	4 %	0 %
	Sep 2013	73 %	24 %	3 %	0 %
	Feb 2014	72 %	25 %	2 %	1 %
Overall, I was satisfied with the quality of the online course materials	Feb 2013	70 %	26 %	4 %	0 %
	Sep 2013	77 %	20 %	3 %	0 %
	Feb 2014	74 %	22 %	3 %	1 %
Overall, the facilitation by the instructor for online learning was helpful in achieving my learning goals	Feb 2013	68 %	28 %	4 %	0 %
	Sep 2013	75 %	23 %	2 %	0 %
	Feb 2014	76 %	21 %	2 %	1 %

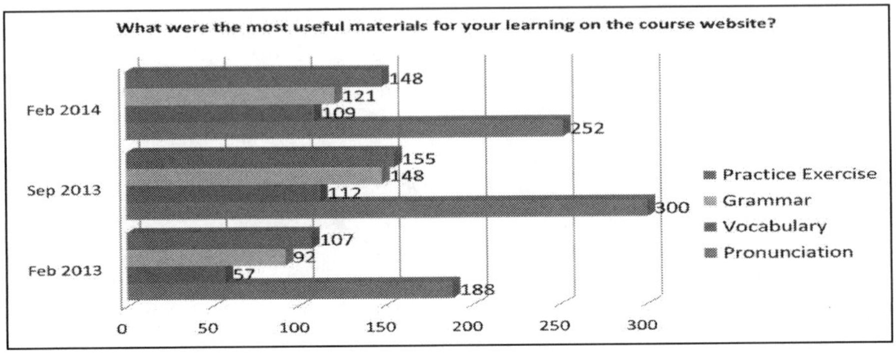

Fig. 16. The most useful materials for learning on the e-learning Website

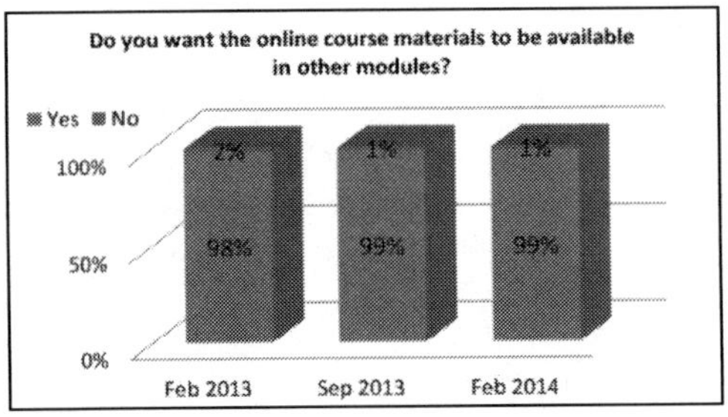

Fig. 17. Do you want the online course materials to be available in other modules?

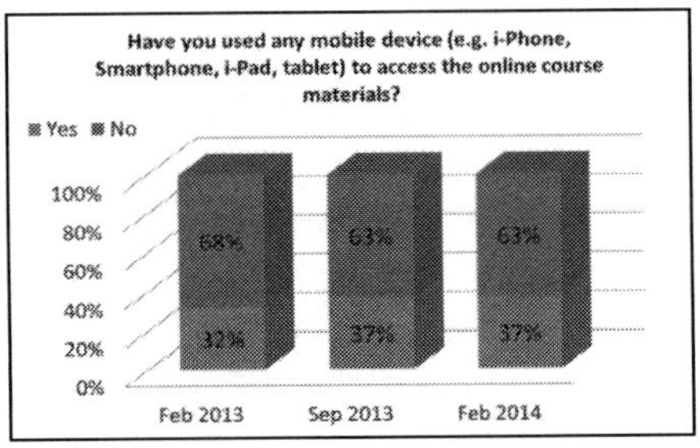

Fig. 18. Have you used any mobile device to access the online course materials?

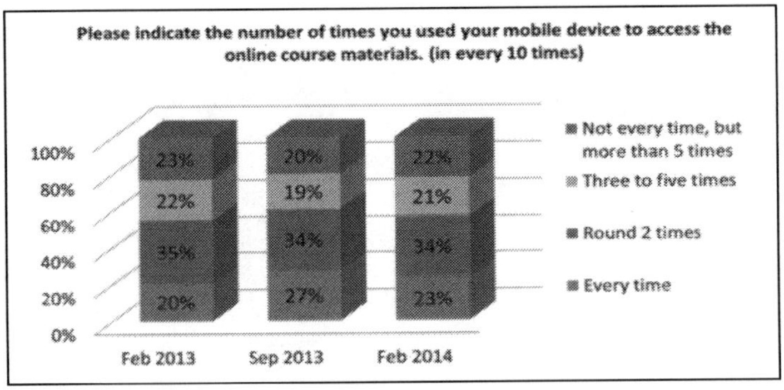

Fig. 19. Frequency of using mobile device to access the online course materials. (in every 10 times)

5 Discussion

5.1 Instructional Design in Online Course Materials

5.1.1 Simple and Intuitive – Use Interface and Navigation

According to the survey results in Sect. 4.2.1, positive results were given to the online course materials. Up to 72 % of respondents claimed the e-learning Website was clear and easy to use. Simple user interface with textual navigation facilitated minimised file sizes and increased download speed [9]. Thus, better overall user experience could be accomplished.

5.1.2 Use of Multimedia

With proper use of multimedia in online learning Website, learning experience can be enhanced and learning objectives can be achieved [21, 22]. Learners could make use of the Pronunciation section to practice speaking skills for language acquisition. A learner stated in the questionnaire, "Pronunciation can be played repeatedly and thus enhance my listening & pronunciation." Some learners also reflected that pronouncing a word correctly was the most difficult part when learning a foreign language. Therefore, the Pronunciation section is the most useful learning materials. Moreover, they also pointed out that there were not many online website providing Korean pronunciation, and the Korean e-learning website provided was a reliable support for them. Another learner stated that "I can revise other parts of learning materials from the book or from my notes, but it is not possible for pronunciation." Multimedia such as graphics, stroke animation, and audios were employed for effective presentation in Pronunciation. It not only helped arouse learners' interest, and also facilitated learners' interaction with learning content [42].

5.1.3 Flexible of Use – Chunk of Information

Taught topics in Grammar were separated into chunk of manageable learning parts in each Chapter. Learners could learn progressively from online materials in an organised way. Some feedbacks expressed that the e-learning website helped learners prepare before quizzes and examinations, thus learners found that it was easier to revise online and they could focus on the main points. Besides, some learners stated in the survey that they could understand better the taught topics with online materials than textbook, and could revise the Korean language at anytime, anywhere without textbook.

5.1.4 Low Physical and Technical Effort – Interactive Activities

Practice Exercises section consisting of interactive activities was chosen as the second most useful learning material in the Korean e-learning website. This could be attributed to the goal of low physical and technical effort in instructional design of the activities, in which MC questions, drag-and-drop and matching game were employed instead of activities requiring intensive text input. A learner stated in the questionnaire about Practice Exercise "From simple to complex, questions are designed with different levels and different types. It is very practical but not boring."

5.1.5 Individualised Activities

Pronunciation was ranked as the most useful learning material among the features in the Korean learning website. It was believed that the Flash Card of Pronunciation and the Hangeul generator ascribed mostly to this result. According to the learners' feedback, the Flash Card allowed them to practice the pronunciation of the Korean Characters and it met their needs with ease of use. In addition, Hangeul generator allowed learners to revise Korean characters according to level of language acquisition.

5.1.6 Gamification

Korean typing game was designed to build an entertaining learning experience, i.e. learners could revise the taught vocabularies, while at the same time, they could learn and practise their Korean characters typing skills through a game. It was expected this game could create excitement and engagement. However, the survey result indicated that only 38 % of respondents were interested in it while 42 % of them gave neutral feedback. Some learners reflected that the typing game was too difficult for beginner learners. Modification of instructional design of this activity was required.

5.2 PC-mobile End and PC-end Learners

To further evaluate the effective of the online learning materials in the Korean e-learning website, perceptions of the PC-mobile end learners (who accessed the website via PC and/or mobile devices, constituting over 32 % of the respondents in each survey) were compared with those of PC-end learners (who accessed the website via desktop computers or notebook) in each intake. By using the screening question in each survey, data of each question are grouped under PC-end and PC-mobile end. Scores were assigned to different levels of perception, namely 'Strongly agreed' as 5, 'Agreed' as 4, 'Neutral' as 3, 'Disagreed' as 2, 'Strongly disagreed' as 1 and 'Not applicable' as 0.

Table 3 showed that PC-mobile end learners gave a higher mean than PC-end learners in all aspects of study: flexibility and accessibility, extent of interest and

Table 3. Comparison of PC-mobile and PC-end learners 3 intakes

Perception	Feb 2013			Sep 2013			Feb 2014		
	Mean		Variance	Mean		Variance	Mean		Variance
	PC-mobile (a_1)	PC (b_1)	(a_1-b_1)	PC-mobile (a_2)	PC (b_2)	(a_2-b_2)	PC-mobile (a_3)	PC (b_3)	(a_3-b_3)
I	3.99	3.78	+0.21	4.00	3.81	+0.19	3.91	3.77	+0.14
II	3.88	3.78	+0.10	3.94	3.74	+0.20	3.93	3.82	+0.11
III	3.78	3.59	+0.19	3.76	3.47	+0.29	3.77	3.60	+0.18
IV	3.95	3.81	+0.14	3.94	3.79	+0.15	3.90	3.83	+0.08
V	3.93	3.70	+0.23	3.91	3.76	+0.14	3.84	3.77	+0.07
VI	3.87	3.68	+0.19	3.98	3.76	+0.22	3.91	3.76	+0.16

Perception I - The overall online course materials helped me review the course contents after class.
Perception II - The online course materials made my learning more flexible and accessible.
Perception III - The online course materials made my learning more interesting and engaging.
Perception IV - The online course materials enhanced my understanding of the topics covered.
Perception V - The online course materials enriched my learning experience.
Perception VI - Overall, I was satisfied with the quality of the online course materials.

engagement, understanding to the content, learning experience and satisfaction of learning materials. It strongly indicated that the instructional design employed in the Korean e-learning website, was optimised for both learning with desktop computers and mobile devices.

5.3 Improvement

The survey results in Sect. 4.2.3 illustrated that number of learners using mobile devices to access online learning materials increased gradually. This ascertains the growing trend of m-learning. To provide effective learning experience, designing and developing online materials that fit mobile devices becomes critical and essential. In the design phase of the Korean e-learning website, we had taken m-learning into our consideration. Pronunciation (including stroke animation and audio for Korean characters) and Flash Card were developed to fit both desktop computers and different types of mobile devices. To achieve the best learning experience, the Korean website was built on HTML5 and Flash for browsers running on desktop computer, iOS devices and Android devices. Keeping effective development and maintenance in perspective, we had adopted a generic solution with a unique content repository and unified strategy in the Korean e-learning website which was optimised for learners' access by both desktop and mobile devices.

To review the instructional design of the Korean e-learning Website, here are some areas that need to be reconsidered. First, owing to the device variability of the mobile devices, the issue that small fonts and layouts in small screen size with poor resolution [11] was still encountered, which was reflected by a few learners from the surveys. Even with the prevalence of smartphone with large screen size, care for learners using small screen size is still required. Second, significant amount of resources would be required to maintain and test the learning materials on various platforms like different desktop browsers, iOS and Android devices, especially the audio playback issue.

Here are some suggestions to tackle the above issues. First, to further optimise the learning experience in mobile devices, responsive Web design (RWD) would be one of the alternatives in this case [41]. Responsive Websites are made of fluid grids to control the design and the content can be scaled up or down depending on browser or device screen size. Page layouts, images, text and even video will be more flexible and can be re-adjusted automatically to fit for the device. Learner learning experience will be improved since they can get the best presentation of the online content via mobile devices. From the perspective of course developer, working on both mobile site and desktop site is no longer necessary. Cost effectiveness is enhanced so as the efficiency of website management. Responsive mobile web design would be a feasible way to provide a spectrum of possible solutions for both desktop and mobile learning. This approach has been applied in the development of one of our language courses and promising results are observed.

Second, regarding the audio issue for mobile devices, the audio support of mobile browsers has been improving with higher compatibility among different devices as observed in these 2 years. We believe that this issue will be solved in the coming future.

Third, the Typing game of Korean characters could be improved through re-application of instructional design; the typing speed in this game could be refined and classified into multiple levels [18]. The speed of the disappearing of the vocabularies for beginners could be slower than that for intermediate learners, so as to create an adaptive and individualised game for learners with suitable challenges.

6 Conclusion

With the advances in technologies, it is believed that mobile device will be a game changer in e-learning because of its breakthrough in geographic and time limitation in learning as well as its opportunity in enhancing learning experience. Instructional design strategies play an important role in the development of online learning materials for blended learning courses as the gap between the desktop learning and mobile learning has become less substantial from learners' point of view. The Korean e-learning Website was incorporated with various instructional design strategies and the factor of m-learning with a view to achieving the best learning experience. Positive learners' perception of learning materials were collected from learner surveys conducted in three consecutive intakes. Learning materials need to be: (1) simple and intuitive, (2) information-rich (multimedia), (3) flexible of use (chuck of information), (4) interactive (low physical and technical effort from learners) (5) individualised (design for learners with differences). This study reinforces the importance of instructional design in developing language materials for blending learning courses which can serve as reference for future development.

References

1. Ally, M.: Using learning theories to design instruction for mobile learning devices. Learning and Skills Development Agency, Mobile learning anytime everywhere. A book of papers from MLEARN 2004, 2 (2005) Accessed from http://stu.westga.edu/~bthibau1/MEDT%208484%20Baylen/mLearn04_papers.pdf#page=14
2. Barkley, E.F., Cross, K.P., Major, C.H.: Collaborative Learning Techniques: A Handbook for College Faculty, p. 300. Jossey-Bass, San Francisco (2005)
3. Bradley, C., Haynes, R., Cook, J., Boyle, T., Smith, C.: Design and development of multimedia learning objects for mobile phones. In: Ally, M. (ed.) Mobile Learning: Transforming the Delivery of Education and Training, pp. 157–182. Athabasca University Press, Edmonton (2009)
4. Bonnington, C.: In Less Than Two Years, a Smartphone Could Be Your Only Computer. Wired, 10 February 2015. http://www.wired.com/2015/02/smartphone-only-computer/
5. Bravolol, Learn Foreign Languages, Mobile Apps: Learn Korean – KR Translator (iTunes: 3 April 2015; Google Play: 24 February 2015). http://bravolol.com/products/learn-korean
6. Cheung, K.S., Lam, J., Lau, N., Shim, C.: Instructional design practices for blended learning. In: International Conference on Computational Intelligence and Software Engineering (CiSE) (2010)

7. China Internet Network Information Center: Statistical Report on Internet Development in China, January 2014. http://www1.cnnic.cn/IDR/ReportDownloads/201404/U020140417607531610855.pdf
8. Delialioglu, O., Yildirim, Z.: Students' perceptions on effective dimensions of interactive learning in a blended learning environment. J. Educ. Technol. Soc. **10**(2), 133–146 (2007)
9. Elias, T.: Universal instructional design principles for mobile learning. Int. Rev. Res. Open Distrib. Learn. [S.l.] **12**(2), 143–156 (2011). ISSN 1492-3831
10. Fun Easy Learn, Mobile Apps: Learn Korean 6,000 Words (Google Play: 27 November 2014). http://www.funeasylearn.com/app/learn-korean/
11. Gipple, J., Lord, E.: Understanding Mobile Learning and Best Practices. Retrieved from ICS Learning Group, 18 May 2015. http://www.icslearninggroup.com/whitepapers/understanding-mobile-learning-and-best-practices/
12. Guy, R. (ed.): Mobile Learning: Pilot Projects and Initiatives. Informing Science, Santa Rosa (2010)
13. Herrington, A., Herrington, J., Mantei, J.: Design principles for mobile learning. In: New Technologies, New Pedagogies: Mobile Learning in Higher Education, pp. 129–138. University of Wollongong, Wollongong (2009)
14. Hirata, Y., Hirata, Y.: Japanese students' attitudes towards hybrid learning. In: Fong, J., Kwan, R., Wang, F.L. (eds.) ICHL 2008. LNCS, vol. 5169, pp. 439–449. Springer, Heidelberg (2008)
15. Horton, W.: E-Learning by Design, pp. 141–144. Pfeiffer, San Francisco (2006)
16. IDC, IDC Finds Worldwide Smartphone Shipments on Pace to Grow Nearly 40 % in 2013 While Average Selling Prices Decline More Than 12 %, 26 November, 2013. http://www.idc.com/getdoc.jsp?containerId=prUS24461213
17. Jones, K.T., Chen, C.: Blended learning in a graduate accounting course: student satisfaction and course issues. J. Acc. Educ. **18**, 15–28 (2008)
18. Kapp, K.M.: The Gamification of Learning and Instruction: Game-based Methods and Strategies for Training and Education. Wiley, Hoboken (2012)
19. Kukulska-Hulme, A.: Will mobile learning change language learning? ReCALL **21**(2), 157–165 (2009)
20. Lam, J., Chan, R., Yan, K.: A report on the online learning experience of students in accounting course. Engaging Learners Through Emerg. Technol. Commun. Comput. Inform. Sci. **302**(2012), 31–44 (2012)
21. Lam, J., Cheung, K.S., Ng, J., Yau, J., Seto, W., Im, T.: Students' needs of e-courses as complement to traditional learning: A Japanese studies e-course case. In: IEEE International Symposium on IT in Medicine and Education, ITME 2008, pp. 876, 880 (2008)
22. Lee, K.K., Chong, M.P.: Blended learning: a case study for Japanese language studies. In: Fong, J., Kwan, R., Wang, F.L. (eds.) ICHL 2008. LNCS, vol. 5169, pp. 450–462. Springer, Heidelberg (2008)
23. Liu, M., Navarrete, C.C., Maradiegue, E., Wivagg, J.: mobile learning and english language learners: a case study of using iPod touch as a teaching and learning tool. J. Interact. Learn. Res. 25(3) (2014)
24. Macdonald, J.: Blended Learning and Online Tutoring: A Good Practice Guide, 2nd edn. Gower, Hampshire (2006)
25. Mayer, R.E., Moreno, R.: Nine ways to reduce cognitive load in multimedia learning. Educ. Psychol. **38**(1), 43–52 (2003)
26. Mayer, R.E.: Applying the science of learning: Evidence-based principles for the design of multimedia instruction. Am. Psychol. **63**(8), 760–769 (2008)
27. Miller, G.A.: The magical number seven, plus or minus two: some limits on our capacity for processing information. Psychol. Rev. **63**(2), 81 (1956)

28. Naidu, S.: Learning and teaching with technology: principles and practices. Kogan Page, London (2003)
29. Ng, S.C., Lui, A., Wong, Y.K.: An adaptive mobile learning application for beginners to learn fundamental japanese language. In: Li, K.C., Wong, T.-L., Cheung, S.K., Lam, J., Ng, K.K. (eds.) ICTE 2014. CCIS, vol. 494, pp. 20–32. Springer, Heidelberg (2015)
30. OFCA - Hong Kong Office of the Telecommunications Authority, Key Communication Statistics, Telecommunications Services, December 2014. http://ofca.gov.hk/en/media_focus/data_statistics/key_stat/index.html
31. Prensky, M.: Digital game-based learning. Comput. Entertainment (CIE) **1**(1), 21 (2003)
32. Radio Television Hong Kong, Consulate General Republic of Korea and City University of Hong Kong: Let's go Korea! (2005). http://rthk.hk/elearning/gogokorea/chapter.htm
33. Schmidt-Weigand, F., Kohnert, A., Glowalla, U.: A closer look at split visual attention in system-and self-paced instruction in multimedia learning. Learn. Instr. **20**(2), 100–110 (2010)
34. Shankland, S.: Moore's Law: The rule that really matters in tech. CNET Sci-Tech: 15 October 2012. http://www.cnet.com/news/moores-law-the-rule-that-really-matters-in-tech/
35. Shim, C., Lam, J., Lau, N., Hung, A., Yuen, K., Tsang, D.: The role of instructional design in blended accounting courses. In: Blended Learning: Maximization of Teaching and Learning Effectiveness, pp. 65–74. City University of Hong Kong, Hong Kong (2011)
36. Singh, H.: Building effective blended learning programs. Educ. Technol.-Saddle Brook Englewood Cliffs NJ- **43**(6), 51–54 (2003)
37. Statista.com. Feature phone and smartphone shipments in Asia from 2008 to 2020 (in 1,000 units) http://www.statista.com/statistics/225406/feature-phone-and-smartphone-shipment-forecast-in-asia/
38. Traxler, J.: Defining, Discussing and Evaluating Mobile Learning: The moving finger writes and having writ….. The Int. Rev. Res. Open Distrib. Learn. 8(2), June 2007. ISSN 1492-3831
39. Tsang, E., Yuen, K.S., Cheung, B.: Effective instructional design for mobile learning. In: Emerging Modes and Approaches in Open and Flexible Education, pp. 59–80. Open University of Hong Kong Press (2014)
40. Wellman, S.: Google lays out its mobile user experience strategy, 11 April 2007. http://www.informationweek.com/blog/main/archives/2007/04/google_lays_out.html
41. Yan, H., Poon, L.: Thinking of everyone: responsive web design for a math OER project. In: Chen, G., et al. (eds.) Emerging Issues in Smart Learning, pp. 329–336. Springer, Heidelberg
42. Zhang, W.Y.: Entering the 3rd generation of e-Learning: characteristics and strategies. In: Blended Learning: Maximization of Teaching and Learning Effectiveness, pp. 1–9 . City University of Hong Kong, Hong Kong (2011)

Mobile Learning and Ubiquitous Learning

Students' Typical Usage of Mobile Devices in Learning Activities

Simon K.S. Cheung(✉)

The Open University of Hong Kong,
Good Shepherd Street, Ho Man Tin, Kowloon, Hong Kong, China
kscheung@ouhk.edu.hk

Abstract. Mobile devices have been widely used by higher education students for learning purposes. This paper explores the students' typical usage of mobile phones, tablet devices and notebook computers in different learning activities, based on the online surveys conducted to the full-time undergraduate students in the Open University of Hong Kong over the past three years. It is revealed that, besides e-mail access and internet browsing, mobile phones are often used for social networking. They were not usually used for reading e-books and doing assignments. Tablet devices are often used for reading e-books, connecting to learning portal and internet browsing, but not for doing assignments. Notebook computers are frequently used in almost all learning activities, especially for doing assignments. The results affirm that the usage depends on the nature of the learning activities and the technical features and limitations of the devices.

Keywords: Mobile learning · Mobile device · Learning support

1 Introduction

Generally referring to smart phones, tablet devices and notebook computers, mobile devices have been widely used by higher education students for both learning and non-learning purposes. This concurs with the increasing penetration rate of mobile devices over the past few years. According to Pew Research Centre, as of 2014, 90 % and 64 % of American adults own a cell phone and a smart phone, respectively [1]. The percentage of ownership of a smart phone is almost double in three years. The growth is even more prominent for tablet devices, where the percentage of ownership increased from 8 % to 10 % in 2011 to 42 % in 2014.

With the advent of modern mobile devices equipped with processors, wireless and broadband network adaptor, mobile learning has evolved as another new mode or style of learning. Mobile learning is conventionally regarded as an extension or a variety of e-learning or online learning that further expand and make learning available anywhere and anytime through mobile devices [2]. It is also defined as the learning across multiple and different contexts using mobile devices, through social and content interactions [3]. From the techno-centric perspective, mobile learning is characterized by the use of mobile devices, which are small in size, portable, and interactive, for learning anywhere and anytime [4].

J. Lam et al. (Eds.): ICTE 2015, CCIS 559, pp. 63–72, 2015.
DOI: 10.1007/978-3-662-48978-9_6

According to Cheung, the successful adoption of mobile learning depends on the technological feasibility of mobile learning, learners' needs of flexible learning, and pedagogical benefits [5]. Unquestionably, mobile learning offers the flexibility and convenience of learning anywhere and anytime. Apart from these, it is recognized and reported in the literature that mobile learning provides many unique pedagogical benefits [6–9]. In brief, mobile learning transforms the learning process and changes the ways of learning, creates new opportunities beyond the traditional face-to-face learning, offers more flexibility and mobility in learning, expands learning experience in terms of time and place, and facilitates communications and interactions among teachers, students and course administrators as well as encourages the mode of peer learning or collaborative learning.

In recent years, a number of studies have been conducted to explore the students' usage of mobile devices. In 2014, ECAR conducted a study to explore the students' technology experience and expectation through a survey on University undergraduate students in the United States and 15 other countries [10]. According to the survey, in 2014, 86 % of the students owned a mobile phone, 47 % owned a tablet device, and 90 % owned a notebook computer. Mobile devices are typically used in learning activities, such as communicating with the peers, accessing learning portal, receiving messages on events and activities, reading e-books or e-resources, accessing library resources such as e-books and e-databases, and recording the lectures and other in-class activities. Another study conducted by the University of Central Florida in 2013 showed that the ownership of mobile devices was high among students, and that tablet devices were the most popular mobile devices for academic purposes [11]. It also revealed that mobile learning typically occurred outside the classroom, with limited guidance from the instructors.

This paper investigates higher education students' typical usage of mobile devices in learning activities. Surveys have been conducted at the Open University of Hong Kong [12]. Starting from 2013, at the beginning of each year (usually in January or February), the University conducted a survey to study how mobile devices (including mobile phones, tablet devices and notebook computers) are used by the students for learning purposes. These surveys were conducted using online questionnaires to full-time undergraduate students. The students were asked on whether mobile phones, tablet devices and notebook computers were usually used in different learning activities, including checking e-mails, accessing learning portals, reading e-books or e-resources, communicating via social networking tools and online chats, doing assignments, and browsing the internet.

Based on the surveys in 2013, 2014 and 2015, this paper reports some findings on the students' typical usage and preference of mobile devices in different learning activities. The patterns of using mobile devices in the learning activities are derived. The rest of this paper is structured as follows. Following this introduction, Sect. 2 gives an overview of mobile devices in terms of technical features and limitations. Section 3 shows the above-mentioned surveys conducted by the Open University of Hong Kong over the past three years. Section 4 briefly concludes this paper with a discussion on the key findings.

2 Overview of Mobile Devices

Mobile devices generally refer to small, hand-held or portable computer devices with a display screen, touchpad, and physical or virtual keyboard. Having a weight of less than 2 kg, these devices broadly cover mobile phones or smart phones, tablet devices and notebook computer. They can readily access the internet through wireless network, 3G or 4G broadband networks. Internet browser, e-mail, e-book reader, social networking tools, online chat and message communication facilities are typical functional features of these devices.

This paper investigates the students' usage of mobile devices in different learning activities, where mobile devices cover mobile phones, tablet devices and notebook computers. They are briefly defined as follows.

Mobile Phones. Mobile phones broadly refer to mobile phones and smart phones which provide computing functions and internet accesses in addition to the usual phone communication. Also characterized by a flat touch-screen display with a few physical buttons, mobile phones use solid state storage, built-in or through a SIM card. Virtual keyboard, writing pad or voice recognition are provided to serve as the input devices. With specific processors and chip sets, mobile phones run on specific operating systems such as Android, iOS and Windows mobile. A typical mobile phone has a small screen display of less than 7 inch width. Like tablet devices, mobile phones adopt touch-screen based navigation. Its weight is less than 1 kg. If fully charged, a mobile phone can be continuously used for up to 9 or 10 h. All mobile phones support wireless network, 3G or 4G broadband network. Table 1 summarizes the technical features of mobile phones. Two representative examples are Apple iPhone [13] and Samsung Galaxy Note [14].

Table 1. Technical features of mobile phones.

Key items	Technical features
Screen size	Less than 7 inch
Disk storage	Solid state drive
Input device	Virtual keyboard
Pointing device	Touch screen navigation
Weight	Less than 1 kg
Battery life	up to 9 or 10 h
Network adaptor	Wireless network and 3G or 4G broadband network
Operating system	Mobile operating systems, such as Android and IOS
Application software	Mobile applications

Tablet Devices. Tablet devices broadly cover tablet computers and slate computers. They are characterized by a flat touch-screen display without any physical keyboard and pointing device. Solid state storage is used. Although a pop-up virtual keyboard is provided to serve as the main input device, a few physical buttons are provided for convenient controls. The processors and chip sets are different from that of notebook computers. Also, tablet devices run on specific operating systems such as Android, iOS and Windows mobile. A typical tablet device has a screen display of 7 to 11 inch width, supporting touch-screen based navigation. Its weight is around 1 kg. If fully charged, a tablet device can be continuously used for up to 7 or 8 h. For network connectivity, all tablet devices are equipped with wireless network adaptor. Many of them also support 3G or 4G broadband network. Table 2 summarizes the technical features of tablet devices. Two representative examples are Apple i-Pad [15] and Microsoft Surface [16].

Table 2. Technical features of tablet devices.

Key items	Technical features
Screen size	7 inch to 11 inch
Disk storage	Solid state drive
Input device	Virtual keyboard
Pointing device	Touch screen navigation
Weight	around 1 kg
Battery life	up to 7 or 8 h
Network adaptor	Wireless network and 3G or 4G broadband network
Operating system	Mobile operating systems, such as Android and IOS
Application software	Mobile applications, such as browser and e-book reader

Notebook Computers. Notebook computers broadly refer to the conventional laptop computers which are functionally identical to desktop personal computers (PC). As notebook computers use the conventional PC processors and chipsets, PC operating systems and application software can run on notebook computers. A typical notebook computer has a screen display of 10 to 15 inch width, a physical keyboard with touch pad or track stick as the pointing device. Its weight ranges from 1 to 2 kg. In recent years, notebook computers tend to use solid state drives which consume lesser power than the traditional hard disk drives, thus having longer battery life. If fully charged, a notebook computer may be continuously used for up to 5 or 6 h. For network connectivity, all notebook computers are equipped with wireless network adaptor, and many of them also provide wired network adaptor. It is not common for notebook computers to support 3G or 4G broadband network. Table 3 summarizes the technical features of notebook computers. Two representative examples are Lenovo Thinkpad [17] and Apple MacBook [18].

In brief, notebook computers are the portable or mobile version of PCs that run on the conventional PC operating systems and application software. With the use of solid state drives instead of hard disk drives, notebook computers consume less power, and therefore, have longer battery life. Tablet devices and mobile phones are purpose-built for mobile usage, for example, touch-screen based navigation, virtual keyboard, small in size, longer battery life and built-in features for connecting wireless network and 3G or 4G broadband network. They are equipped with mobile applications, such as Internet browser, e-book reader, social networking tools, etc. Tablet devices can be

Table 3. Technical features of notebook computers.

Key items	Technical features
Screen size	9 inch to 15 inch
Disk storage	Magnetic-based hard disk drive or solid state drive
Input device	Physical keyboard
Pointing device	Touch pad or track stick
Weight	1 to 2 kg
Battery life	up to 5 or 8 h
Network adaptor	Wireless network (some supporting wired network)
Operating system	Conventional PC operating system
Application software	Conventional PC application software

regarded as mobile phones with a larger screen and more storage capacity but without phone communication functions.

3 Use of Mobile Devices in Learning Activities

In order to study the students' typical usage and preference of mobile devices in different learning activities, online surveys were conducted to full-time undergraduate students in the Open University of Hong Kong. At the beginning of each academic year starting from 2012/13, the students were asked on whether mobile phones, tablet devices and notebook computers were usually used in different learning activities. These learning activities include accessing e-mails (on the e-mail account provided by the University), connecting to the learning portal, reading e-books or e-resources, communicating via social networking tools and online chats, doing assignments, and browsing the internet.

In the following, we report and analyze the result of the online surveys in 2012/13, 2013/14 and 2014/15.

Possession of Mobile Devices for Learning Purposes. Table 4 reports the percentage of student possessing mobile devices for learning purposes. Almost all the students used at least one type of mobile devices for learning purposes. It is also found that the percentage of students possessing tablet devices is steadily increasing over the past three years.

Table 4. Possession of mobile devices for learning purposes.

Mobile devices	% of students possessing the devices for learning purposes		
	2013 (n = 385)	2014 (n = 368)	2015 (n = 359)
Mobile phones	95 % (367)	93 % (342)	94 % (337)
Tablet devices	29 % (111)	37 % (137)	43 % (153)
Notebook computers	53 % (204)	53 % (194)	64 % (228)
Nil	0 % (0)	1 % (2)	0 % (0)

Usage of Mobile Phones in Different Learning Activities. In the surveys, students were asked if mobile phones were usually used in different learning activities. Table 5 reports the results in term of the percentage of students using mobile phone for each learning activity. It is shown that, among other learning activities, accessing e-mails, connecting to learning portal, communicating using social networking tools or online chats, and browsing the internet are frequently used by students (where over 70 % of students indicated that they usually used mobile phones in these learning activities). It is also shown that less than half (44 % to 47 %) of the students usually use mobile phones in reading e-books or e-resources. It is very clear that the highest usage (over 94 %) of mobile phone is on social networking and online chats whilst the lowest usage (less than 30 %) is on doing assignment. Over the past three years, there were no significant variations (1 % to 7 %) on the percentage of students using mobile phones in the individual learning activities.

Table 5. Usage of mobile phones in different learning activities.

Learning activities	% of students using mobile phones in learning activities		
	2013 (n = 367)	2014 (n = 342)	2015 (n = 337)
Accessing e-mails	76 % (279)	75 % (257)	75 % (252)
Connecting to learning portal	74 % (271)	77 % (265)	79 % (267)
Reading e-books or e-resource	44 % (163)	44 % (150)	47 % (157)
Social network or online chat	93 % (342)	94 % (323)	94 % (316)
Doing assignments	29 % (106)	30 % (101)	23 % (78)
Browsing the internet	73 % (268)	76 % (261)	74 % (251)

Mobile phones have the definite advantages of the mobility and portability of the devices. They are small in size, light in weight and easy to carry. Moreover, mobile applications on communications are well available for mobile phones. These explain why students usually used mobile phones for communication, including e-mail access, social networking and online chats. However, mobile phones have the disadvantages on screen size and input devices. The screen of mobile phones is too small (usually less than 7 inch) for students to read e-books or e-resources. There is also a lack of convenience input devices, such as physical keyboard and pointing device. These are the reasons of low usage of mobile phones for doing assignments.

Usage of Tablet Devices in Different Learning Activities. In the surveys, students were asked if tablet devices were usually used in different learning activities. Table 6 reports the results in term of the percentage of students using mobile devices for each learning activity. It is shown that, except for doing assignment, tablet devices are usually used by the students in all learning activities (where over 60 % of students indicated that they usually used tablet devices in these learning activities). However, there is no particular learning activity with very high usage (for example, over 90 %) of tablet devices. The highest usage of tablet devices is on connecting the learning portal and browsing the internet. Over the past three years, there were no significant variations (2 % to 11 %) on the percentage of students using tablet devices in the individual learning activities.

Table 6. Usage of tablet devices in different learning activities.

Learning activities	% of students using tablet devices in learning activities		
	2013 (n = 111)	2014 (n = 137)	2015 (n = 153)
Accessing e-mails	66 % (73)	64 % (88)	61 % (94)
Connecting to learning portal	74 % (82)	73 % (100)	75 % (115)
Reading e-books or e-resource	64 % (71)	68 % (93)	67 % (102)
Social network or online chat	71 % (79)	63 % (86)	65 % (99)
Doing assignments	50 % (56)	39 % (53)	48 % (73)
Browsing the internet	73 % (81)	69 % (94)	71 % (109)

Tablet devices have a clear advantage over mobile phones on the screen display. A wider screen (7 inch to 11 inch) is usually provided by table devices. Although tablet devices are bigger in size and heavier in weight as compared to mobile phones, they have advantages on the mobility and portability, and are still easy to carry. Moreover, mobile applications on communications and e-book readers are well available for mobile phones. These explain why students usually used tablet devices not only for communication but also for reading e-books, e-resources and browsing the internet. Since mobile devices lack convenience input devices, such as physical keyboard and pointing device, they are not usually used in doing assignments.

Usage of Notebook Computers in Different Learning Activities. In the surveys, students were asked if notebook computers were usually used in different learning activities. Table 7 reports the results in term of the percentage of students using mobile devices for each learning activity. It is shown that, except for social networking and online chats, notebook computers are usually used by the students in all learning activities (where over 60 % of students indicated that they usually used tablet devices in

Table 7. Usage of notebook computers in different learning activities.

Learning activities	% of students using notebook computers in learning activities		
	2013 (n = 204)	2014 (n = 194)	2015 (n = 228)
Accessing e-mails	64 % (130)	62 % (120)	68 % (155)
Connecting to learning portal	79 % (161)	74 % (143)	77 % (176)
Reading e-books or e-resource	70 % (142)	67 % (130)	70 % (160)
Social network or online chat	67 % (136)	54 % (105)	59 % (135)
Doing assignments	99 % (201)	93 % (181)	98 % (224)
Browsing the internet	70 % (142)	65 % (127)	72 % (164)

these learning activities). It is very clear that the highest usage of notebook computers is on doing assignments (over 90 %) whilst the lowest usage is on social networking and online chats (less than 60 %). Over the past three years, there were no significant variations (3 % to 13 %) on the percentage of students using notebook computers in the individual learning activities.

Notebook computers have a number of advantages over mobile phones and table devices. Besides providing a larger screen display (9 inch to 15 inch) and convenient input devices, such as a physical keyboard together with touch-pad or track stick, they can run on the conventional PC operating system, and hence, PC application software. These explain why notebook computers were usually used in almost all learning activities, especially doing assignments. However, notebook computers are rather less portable, as compared to mobile phones and tablet devices. They are also heavier in weight. For this reason, notebook computers are not usually used for interactive communication, such as social networking and online chats.

Usage Patterns of Mobile Devices in Different Learning Activities. Summarizing the above findings, some usage patterns of mobile devices can be derived. Table 8 states these usage patterns in different learning activities. For accessing e-mails and learning portal and browsing the internet, all three categories of devices (mobile phones, tablet devices and notebook computers) are usually used. For reading e-book or e-resources, tablet devices and notebook computers are usually used whilst mobile phones are less frequently used. For social networking and online chats, the usage of mobile phones is the highest. For doing assignments, notebook computers are almost always used whilst mobile phones and tablet devices are rarely used.

Table 8. Usage pattern of mobile devices in different learning activities.

Learning activities	% of students using tablet devices in learning activities (in 3 years)		
	Mobile phones	Tablet devices	Notebook computers
Accessing e-mails	frequent (75 % to 76 %)	frequent (61 % to 64 %)	frequent (62 % to 68 %)
Connecting to learning portal	frequent (74 % to 79 %)	frequent (73 % to 75 %)	frequent (74 % to 79 %)
Reading e-books or e-resource	not frequent (44 % to 47 %)	frequent (64 % to 68 %)	frequent (67 % to 70 %)
Social network or online chat	very frequent (93 % to 94 %)	frequent (63 % to 71 %)	less frequent (54 % to 67 %)
Doing assignments	not frequent (23 % to 30 %)	not frequent (39 % to 50 %)	very frequent (93 % to 99 %)
Browsing the internet	frequent (73 % to 74 %)	frequent (69 % to 73 %)	frequent (65 % to 72 %)

4 Discussion and Conclusion

Todays, almost every student owns at least one mobile device for learning purposes. In this paper, we investigate the students' typical usage of mobile devices in different learning activities, where mobile devices are generally categorized as mobile phones, tablet devices and notebook computers. Following a brief review of mobile devices, this paper reports the results of the surveys on the usage of mobile devices, which were conducted to the full-time undergraduate students in the Open University of Hong Kong over the past three years.

In summary, it is found that the majority of students usually used mobile phones on e-mail access, connecting to learning portal, social networking and online chat, and browsing the internet. This is because of the definite advantages of mobile phones on mobility, portability and network connectivity. It is not often to use mobile phones for reading e-books or e-resources, and doing assignment due to the limitation of the screen size and lack of convenient input devices. With a balance between portability and usability, tablet devices provide a larger screen display than mobile phones. They were usually used in different learning activities except doing assignments. However, tablet devices were not usually used in doing assignment because of lacking some convenient input devices. Notebook computers offer very comprehensive functional features and are compatible with the conventional PC application software. Therefore, they were usually used in almost all the learning activities. Owing to the deficiency on portability and mobility, it is not common for using notebook computers in interactive communication such as social networking and online chats.

Besides, over the past three years, there are slight variations on the usage patterns of mobile phones, tablet devices and notebook computers. According to the survey, there were no significant variations on the percentage of students using mobile phones in individual learning activities, and so for tablet devices and notebook computers. This essentially reflects that the patterns of how mobile phones, tablet devices and notebook computers are generally used in different learning activities have been established and become stabilized. The findings further affirm that the usages depend on the nature of the learning activities and the technical features as well as limitations of the mobile devices. This indeed aligned to some previous studies on the topic, including the author's earlier studies [19, 20]. It is hoped that the findings and sharing can provide some insights on the students' typical usage of mobile devices in learning activities for higher education institutions.

References

1. Pew Research Center: *Device Ownership Over Time*, Internet, Science and Technology Report, Pew Research Center (2015)
2. Ellis, K.: Moving into m-Learning. Training J. **40**(10), 56 (2003)
3. Crompton, H.: A Historical Overview of mobile learning: Toward learner-centered education. In: Berge, Z.L., Muilenburg, L.Y. (eds.) Handbook of Mobile Learning, pp. 3–14. Routledge, Florence (2013)

4. Winters, N.: What is mobile learning? In: Sharples, M. (ed.) Big Issues in Mobile Learning: Report of a Workshop by the Kaleidoscope Network of Excellence Mobile Learning Initiative, pp. 7–11. University of Nottingham, Nottingham (2007)
5. Cheung, K.S., Yuen, K.S., Tsang, E.: A study on the readiness of mobile learning in open education. In: Proceedings of the IEEE International Symposium on IT in Medicine and Education, pp. 133–136, IEEE Press (2011)
6. Kim, S.H., Mims, C., Holmes, K.P.: An introduction to current trends and benefits of mobile wireless technology use in higher education. AACE Journal **14**(1), 77–100 (2006). Association for the Advancement of Computing in Education
7. Lam, J., Yau, J., Cheung, S.K.: A review of mobile learning in the mobile age. In: Tsang, P., Cheung, S.K., Lee, V.S., Huang, R. (eds.) ICHL 2010. LNCS, vol. 6248, pp. 306–315. Springer, Heidelberg (2010)
8. Gikas, J., Grant, M.M.: Mobile computing devices in higher education: student perspectives on learning with cellphones, smartphones and social media. Int. High. Educ. **19**, 18–26 (2013)
9. Cheung, S.K.: A case study on the students' attitude and acceptance of mobile learning. In: Li, K.C., Wong, T.-L., Cheung, S.K., Lam, J., Ng, K.K. (eds.) ICTE 2014. CCIS, vol. 494, pp. 45–54. Springer, Heidelberg (2015)
10. ECAR: ECAR Study of Undergraduate Students and Information Technology 2014, Educause Center for Analysis and Research, Educause (2014)
11. Chen, B., Denoyelles, A.: Exploring Students' Mobile Learning Practices in Higher Education Educause Review, 7 October 2013, Educause (2013)
12. OUHK: Website of the Open University of Hong Kong, the Open University of Hong Kong (2015). http://www.ouhk.ed.hk
13. iPhone: Website of iPhone, Apple (2015). https://www.apple.com/iphone
14. Galaxy: Website of Galaxy Note, Samsung (2015). http://www.samsung.com/hk_en/consumer/mobile/galaxy-note
15. iPad: Website of iPad, Apple (2015). https://www.apple.com/ipad
16. Surface: Website of Surface, Microsoft (2015). https://www.microsoft.com/surface
17. Thinkpad: Website of Thinkpad X Series, Lenovo (2015). http://shop.lenovo.com/us/en/laptops/thinkpad/x-series/x1-carbon
18. Macbook: Website of Macbook, Apple (2015). https://www.apple.com/macbook
19. Cheung, S.K.: A study on the use of mobile devices for distance learning. In: Cheung, S.K., Fong, J., Kwok, L.-F., Li, K., Kwan, R. (eds.) ICHL 2012. LNCS, vol. 7411, pp. 89–98. Springer, Heidelberg (2012)
20. Cheung, K.S.: A survey on the use of mobile devices for learning purposes. Int. J. Innov. Learn. **16**(2), 192–202 (2014)

Wearables in Education: Expectations and Disappointments

Daniyar Sapargaliyev(✉)

Almaty Management University, Almaty, Kazakhstan
dsapargalieff@gmail.com

Abstract. This paper describes the current state in the use of wearable technology in learning and teaching. It is becoming increasingly difficult to ignore the wide dissemination of wearable technology in everyday life. Today various types of wearables (such as watches, fitness trackers, clothing and glasses) are used in libraries, medical schools and universities. We have analysed more than 30 academic sources and found out that the emergence of new technologies in the classroom is almost always associated with high expectations of its effective implementation. The main aim of our theoretical research is to identify the examples of successful pilots in wearable learning and perhaps we tried to predict the possible barriers and problems in using new wearables (such as Google Glass) in the classroom. The results of our research will be used in further large scale projects and can be helpful for understanding the new trends in using emerging technologies in education.

Keywords: Wearable technology · Wearables · Google glass · Hands-free learning

1 Introduction

There is a growing body of literature that recognises the importance of the use of wearable computers in education. According to the 'Encyclopedia of human-computer interaction', wearable computing is 'the study or practice of inventing, designing, building, or using miniature body-borne computational and sensory devices' [15].

One of the first wearable versions of the computer was created in the early 1960s [30]. In 1999, Steve Mann presented the 'EyeTap Digital Eye Glass' that was the one of the first attempts to create new type of peripheral head-mounted display computer [14]. Today, wearable technology is 'poised to see significant growth in the coming years, spurring experimentation in higher education because the demand for wearables is seen to be coming in large part from college-aged students' [11].

In recent years, Google Glass is one of the best known wearables. This head-mounted wearable computer allows communicating with the Internet via natural language voice commands. In 2013, Google started selling a prototype of Google Glass to qualified 'Glass Explorers' mostly in the USA [10].

The aim of this paper is to review recent research works in the use of wearables for teaching and learning.

J. Lam et al. (Eds.): ICTE 2015, CCIS 559, pp. 73–78, 2015.
DOI: 10.1007/978-3-662-48978-9_7

2 Literature Review

Last years, a few authors have begun to study the problems of using wearable technology (such as Google Glass) in education [22, 37]. Buchem & Pérez-Sanagustín [6] have considered the possible scenarios of learning with Google Glass. Petrovic [24] argues that wearable computing is still poorly used in education.

Probably, in the nearest future, Google Glass will assist learners to access and share information with human-like interface [18]. Students will improve their learning capacities and will strengthen their motivation for learning by using wearables [26].

Alternatively, a teacher can follow student's actions and movements through Google Glass in the classroom [2].

Together these studies provide important insights into the using wearable technologies in medical education, library practice and learning process.

2.1 Google Glass in Medical Education

Recently, researchers have shown an increased interest in using wearable technology for medical education [28, 32].

Nosta [19] suggests that wearable technology changes medical education and shortens distance between the patient and caregiver. For example, Google Glass can help to predict glucose levels in the food diabetics eat [16]. Also, Google Glass can be used to video record students during standardized patient encounters and provides a novel perspective for the analysis and evaluation of their interpersonal communication skills and nonverbal behaviors [31]. Russell *et al.* [25] present the feasibility of telementored instruction in bedside ultrasonography using Google Glass. Students were able to obtain adequate imaging to determine a healthy patient's ejection fraction through telementored education.

There has been an increasing amount of literature on using wearable technology in surgical education [13]. A number of authors have considered the concept of teaching surgical skills and anatomy through live stream [35] and have used Google Glass to solve surgical education challenges in the operating room [17]. Brent *et al.* (2014) suggested that the combination of real-time augmented reality and wearable computing devices such as Google Glass holds much promise in the field of surgery. At the same time Waxman [33] has attempted to criticize the possible ways of using wearables in surgical training.

There is a volume of published studies describing the using wearables in learning of anatomy. Benninger [4] investigates the method that melds traditional medical palpation with wearable technology. Google Glass has provided a platform to position a live ultrasound image to view while examining the patient. Also, wearables have demonstrated clinical and educational value within anatomic pathology. The Glass allows taking quality photographic and video records of the intact and fresh specimens at the time of initial dissection. It is important for diagnoses, reporting and potential error reduction [7].

Despite the successful implementation of wearable technology on medical, surgical education and anatomy, there are some limitations and barriers of using wearables for educational purposes:

-The hospitals are still slow to digitalise.

-The battery life of Glass allows for only about 45 min of recording.

-The doctors can not upload patient data onto Glass because that information is streamed through Google's server. The hospital legislations do not allow a third party to access patient information [9].

2.2 Wearables at Libraries

Numerous studies have attempted to explain how wearables are used at public and universities' libraries. For example, students explored the potential of Google Glass in enhancing classroom instruction and the research experience at the Yale University Library. They developed the scan and deliver application which would allow library staff to fulfill patron scanning requests directly from the library stacks, as well as using Google Glass to assist library patrons with disabilities [21].

The readers and students of Honnold Library at Claremont University use Google Glass as a tool for enhancing their studying and providing of access to information. For example, they plan 'to record debates from the first-person perspective to examine speech techniques and track eye patterns in public speaking' [29].

The Claremont Colleges Library has potential to be constantly reset and linked to new users' accounts, and innovative design affordances that seem to capture the popular imagination. Claremont's early experience with Glass indicates that providing access to the interesting and inaccessible can be quite successful, and that endorsement effects can be moderated by encouraging broad (rather than elite) experimentation and dialogue about the complex and inherent ramifications technology itself [5].

The Ames Library of the Illinois Wesleyan University was accepted into Google's Glass Explorer program in 2014. The library staff is searching for opportunities to use this cutting edge technology in higher education. They think the Glass is a valuable tool for faculty who are investigating a design initiative [8].

Public libraries also use the Glasses to attract new readers. The library of Arapahoe District (Colorado) bought Google Glass as technology is just out of reach to the common person and new or risky for most people to purchase [1].

The studies presented thus far provide evidence that a library plays an important role in the process of interaction between old forms of accessing information and new possibilities of the wearables.

2.3 Wearable Technologies in Learning

A considerable amount of literature has been published on studying potential of wearable technology for different types of learning. These studies focus on using wearables in STEM (science, technology, engineering and mathematics) education, collaborative fieldwork, classroom management and learning at museums. Barker *et al.* [3] presented a pilot study that utilised a wearable technologies intervention as a way to increase attitudes towards STEM content areas for students. The findings indicated that wearable technologies may indeed increase STEM attitudes and could particularly be a viable way to increase participation in STEM for females.

Some research works demonstrate the effective use of wearables for studying STEM subjects such as biology [20], physics [34] and geography [23]. For example, Weppner *et al.* [34] have created a fully functional gPhysics App based on the Google Glass platform which is designed to perform an educational physical experiment in the area of acoustics. Paterson & Glass [23] have demonstrated another successful example of evaluating Google Glass as a research tool and using videography during field research.

Whitmeyer [36] described the example of using wearable technologies for collaborative fieldwork. In this experimental work, one of learners played the role of an agile instructor wearing Google Glass and the other played the role of sessile student in a synchronous field class, viewing the instructor's Glass video in real time. Silva *et al.* [27] considered the potential of Glassist App, aiming at helping teachers' management tasks. This application allows teachers to create individual portfolios for students, manage their information and share it with peers.

One of the directions in using wearable technology in education is study aims to assess how Google Glass enhances visitors' learning outcomes within museum and art gallery environment [12].

3 Discussion

Prior studies have noted the importance of assisting learners to access and share information with human-like interface. Very little was found in the literature on the question of the use of wearables for large-scale projects.

For the last three years, there were many attempts to understand the importance of the use wearable technologies in education. But probably we should find the explanations how to transfer the previous experience in the use of mobiles and other devices in education for the new direction in the implementation of wearables in teaching and learning.

We think that wearable technology is allowing the opportunities that should help to improve the relationship between students and teachers. In the case of wearable technology, the expectations of teachers and students will be matched. We found that wearable devices provide unrestricted access to information together with the hands-free use voice control. This freedom allows professors and students to interact in a more seamless mode and at the same time creates the illusion of easy access to the knowledge and practical skills. The permanent interaction and teaching support can significantly improve the academic achievements, but at the same time can reduce the ability for the independent learning. Here is the problem of the correct use of wearable technology that should justify many positive expectations of professors and students. Further studies, which take these results into account, will need to be undertaken.

References

1. Asgarian, R.: Arapahoe library invests in Google Glass. Libr. J. **139**(1), 16–18 (2014)
2. Bailey, J.: Google Glass: an evolution in education or the next segway? AGU Fall Meet. Abs. **1**, 728 (2013)

3. Barker, B., Melander, J., Grandgenett, N., Nugent, G.: Utilizing wearable technologies as a pathway to STEM. In: Slykhuis, D., Marks, G. (eds.) Proceedings of Society for Information Technology & Teacher Education International Conference 2015, pp. 1770–1776. Association for the Advancement of Computing in Education (AACE), Chesapeake (2015)
4. Benninger, B.: Google Glass, ultrasound and palpation: the anatomy teacher of the future? Clin. Anat. **28**(2), 152–155 (2015)
5. Booth, C., Brecher, D.: Ok, library: implications and opportunities for Google Glass. Coll. Res. Libr. News **75**(5), 234–239 (2014)
6. Buchem, I., Pérez-Sanagustín, M.: Personal learning environments in smart cities: current approaches and future scenarios. Learn. Divers. Cities Future **15**, 136 (2014)
7. Ciomek, N., Zhu, H., Cordon-Cardo, C.: Diagnostic and educational uses of Google Glass in anatomic pathology. Lab. Invest. **95**(1), 395A (2015)
8. Dhue, H.: University Part of Google's Glass Explorer Program (2014). https://www.iwu.edu/news/2014/03-google-glass.html
9. Glauser, W.: Doctors among early adopters of Google Glass. Can. Med. Assoc. J. **185**(16), 1385 (2013)
10. Google. Google Glass (2013). http://www.google.com/glass/start/
11. Johnson, L., Adams, B.S., Estrada, V., Freeman, A.: NMC Horizon Report: 2015 Higher Education. The New Media Consortium, Austin (2015)
12. Leue, M.C., Jung, T., Tom Dieck, D.: Google Glass Augmented Reality: Generic Learning Outcomes for Art Galleries. In: Tussyadiah, I., Inversini, A. (eds.) Information and Communication Technologies in Tourism 2015, pp. 463–476. Springer, Switzerland (2015)
13. Lindeque, B.G., Ponce, B.A., Menendez, M.E., Oladeji, L.O., Fryberger, C.T., Dantuluri, P.K.: Emerging technology in surgical education: combining real-time augmented reality and wearable computing devices. Orthopedics **37**(11), 751–757 (2014)
14. Mann, S.: Through the glass, lightly. IEEE Technol. Soc. Mag. **31**(3), 10–14 (2012)
15. Mann, S.: Wearable computing. In: Soegaard, M., Dam, R.F. (eds.) The Encyclopedia of Human-Computer Interaction, 2nd edn. The Interaction Design Foundation, Aarhus (2014)
16. Marks, P.: A healthy dose of Google Glass. New Sci. **219**(2936), 22–23 (2013)
17. Moshtaghi, O., Kelley, K.S., Armstrong, W.B., Ghavami, Y., Gu, J., Djalilian, H.R.: Using Google Glass to solve communication and surgical education challenges in the operating room. Laryngoscope **125**(10), 2295–2297 (2015)
18. Nooriafshar, M.: Google Glass and its potential uses in digital education. Research Colloquia and Showcase (2013)
19. Nosta, J.: How Google Glass is changing medical education . Forbes (2013). http://goo.gl/3t593R
20. Parslow, G.: Commentary: Google Glass: a head-up display to facilitate teaching and learning. Biochem. Mol. Biol. Edu. **42**(1), 91–92 (2014)
21. Patrick, A.: Google Glass Available for Faculty and Student Groups during Spring Semester. Yale University Library News (2014). http://www.library.yale.edu/librarynews/2014/01/google_glass_available_for_fac.html
22. Penny, C., Schugar, J.: Ok Class…Google Glass in Education. In: Proceedings of Society for Information Technology & Teacher Education International Conference, pp. 2059–2060 (2014)
23. Paterson, M., Glass, M.: The world through Glass: developing novel methods with wearable computing for urban videographic research. J. Geogr. High. Educ. **39**, 1–13 (2015)
24. Petrovic, B.: Wearable Computing in Education. ICT Manag., 849, 934 (2014)

25. Russell, P.M., Mallin, M., Youngquist, S.T., Cotton, J., Aboul-Hosn, N., Dawson, M.: First "Glass" education: telementored cardiac ultrasonography using Google Glass-a pilot study. Acad. Emerg. Med. **21**(11), 1297–1299 (2014)
26. Salamin, A.: Using Google Glass to enrich printed textbooks in a blended learning environment to meet digital natives' expectations. In: World Conference on E-Learning in Corporate, Government, Healthcare, and Higher Education, vol. 1, pp. 1741–1748 (2014)
27. Silva, M., Freitas, D., Neto, E., Lins, C., Teichrieb, V., Teixeira, J.M.: Glassist: using augmented reality on Google Glass as an aid to classroom management. In: Virtual and Augmented Reality (SVR), XVI Symposium, pp. 37–44 (2014)
28. Sultan, N.: Reflective thoughts on the potential and challenges of wearable technology for healthcare provision and medical education. Int. J. Inf. Manag. **35**(5), 521–526 (2015)
29. Thomas, J.: Library to lend Google Glass. The Student Life (2014). http://tsl.pomona.edu/articles/2014/2/14/news/4709-library-to-lend-google-glass
30. Thorp, E.O.: The invention of the first wearable computer. In: Second International Symposium on Wearable Computers. Digest of Papers, pp. 4–8. IEEE (1998)
31. Tully, J., Dameff, C., Kaib, S., Moffitt, M.: Recording medical students' encounters with standardized patients using Google Glass: providing end-of-life clinical Education. J. Assoc. Am. Med. Coll. **90**(3), 314–316 (2015)
32. Vallurupalli, S., Paydak, H., Agarwal, S.K., Agrawal, M., Assad-Kottner, C.: Wearable technology to improve education and patient outcomes in a cardiology fellowship program-a feasibility study. Health Technol. **3**(4), 267–270 (2013)
33. Waxman, B.: Medicine in small doses. Google Glass: a new dimension in surgical education or just another gimmick? ANZ J. Surg. **84**(11), 810 (2014)
34. Weppner, J., Lukowicz, P., Hirth, M., Kuhn, J.: Physics education with Google Glass gPhysics experiment app. In: Proceedings of the 2014 ACM International Joint Conference on Pervasive and Ubiquitous Computing: Adjunct Publication, pp. 279–282 (2014)
35. Whitaker, M., Kuku, E.: Google Glass: the future for surgical training? Bull. R. Coll. Surg. Engl. **96**(7), 223 (2014)
36. Whitmeyer, S.: Using Wearable Technologies for Collaborative Fieldwork. GSA Annual Meeting in Vancouver, British Columbia (2014)
37. Woodside, J.M.: Wearable technology acceptance model: Google Glass. In: Slykhuis, D., Marks, G. (eds.) Proceedings of Society for Information Technology & Teacher Education International Conference 2015, pp. 1800–1802. Association for the Advancement of Computing in Education (AACE), Chesapeake (2015)

A Novel Mobile Application for Training Oral Presentation Delivery Skills

Andrew Kwok-Fai Lui(✉), Sin-Chun Ng, and Wing-Wah Wong

School of Science and Technology, The Open University of Hong Kong, Ho Man Tin, Kowloon, Hong Kong SAR, China
{alui,scng,s1095992}@ouhk.edu.hk

Abstract. Oral presentation is one of the most desirable soft-skills of university graduates. One proven way to train oral presentation is to put students through authentic presentation sessions and facilitate them to improve through feedbacks from their peers, teachers, and self-observation. However, such authentic situations with real audience and genuine high-stakes objectives are not frequent due to the difficulty to holding one. This paper presents a self-regulated mobile learning approach of training oral presentation. A mobile application with feedback functions will allow presenters to practice certain elements of effective presentation that do not require authentic training. A mobile application called PresentMate was developed for the evaluation of this approach. The mobile application can provide instant or delayed feedback on timing, body motion, and voice level to the user. The user can practice at any place and at any time to improve presentation skills based on consideration of the feedback. A preliminary survey indicated that this approach is viable and a number of suggestions on enhancing the design are given in the paper.

Keywords: Oral presentation · Mobile application · Accelerometers · Self-regulated learning · Authentic learning · Mobile learning

1 Introduction

The importance of oral presentation skills could not be stressed anymore. You could well be the latest victim of yet another uninspiring paper presentation given by the authors of this paper. We have wasted enough of our time, our attention, and our youth in conference rooms and lecture halls across the world. This rather bold statement could become amusing if we considered the fact that for decades universities have vowed to emphasize communication skills in their curriculums. Beder [1] quoted a number of renowned Australian engineering scholars calling for curriculum reform because engineering graduates were lacking communication skills. As early as the 1970s, Kelsall (as cited in [7] pointed out communication skills and interpersonal skills should feature alongside technical knowledge of the graduate specifications. The situation seemed to have worsened recently, especially in the computing and information technology sector. Vicinanza [16] spoke for employers in the sector and suggested changes in the curriculum to develop so-called soft skills, of which communication is rank number one.

J. Lam et al. (Eds.): ICTE 2015, CCIS 559, pp. 79–89, 2015.
DOI: 10.1007/978-3-662-48978-9_8

A major challenge to become a capable oral presenter is usually attributed to the demand and anxiety of speaking publicly. A suitable dose level of pressure should help promote the focus and energy of the presenter. For some people, however, the anxiety can adversely affect the delivery. According to a well-known survey, over 75 % of the population considered public speaking as their number one fear [6]. That many students found to be poor in presentation should not come as a surprise. Smith & Sodano [13] pointed out that the uncertainty of the actual delivery could be a key reason, as students would normally not have the opportunity to observe their own presentation. Audience response or the lack of it would be open to interpretation of the speaker and causing uncertainties.

1.1 Effective Training of Oral Presentation Skills

Studies on improving student oral presentation skills have largely covered educationally proven approaches such as self-regulated learning [18], authentic learning [9], and feedback [10]. The idea of practice makes perfect remains the underlying principle, but delivering presentations and receiving feedback repeatedly may not be enough. Smith & Sodano [13] stressed the role of making observations and using self-assessment to reflect and take actions to improve. De Grez et al. [4] also included self-assessment as part of the feedback to inform students of how they performed against a standard, and stated, "… ultimate goal is that the learner becomes self-monitoring". The study discovered that student performance improved each time in a series of three presentation practice sessions. The essential requirement for such practices is authenticity. There are contextual-sensitive aspects of oral presentation such as stress-handling, time management and audience control that could not be assessed without real experience of speaking in front of a crowd. In addition, students see greater meaning in authentic tasks and the learning is more motivated [8].

Setting up an authentic environment for oral presentation practices is demanding. The ideal conditions include audience of the right type and size, a venue with proper presentation aide, and a genuine high-stakes objective of doing the presentation. Even if educational cost were not a concern, it would be highly innovative if the stress and weight of a multi-million sales presentation could be simulated in a classroom. For students, giving several talks in a course teaching effective presentation is no match for explaining their final year projects to their professors and peers before graduation. Practices in simulated situations are still important for preparation and development of skills, but the experience gained in authentic contexts is not replaceable. In the midst of global cost-cutting trend in higher education, we should turn to innovation and technology for new approaches of learning oral presentation effectively.

1.2 New Approach

This paper advocates an effective approach of improving oral presentation delivery based on a mobile application supplementing standardized instruction. This approach still considers authentic presentation practices as an essential part of the instruction. However, the training of some factors of effective presentation does not really need the unique situation of a genuine presentation, and could be offloaded to supplementary learning opportunities purposely created. For example, a full house of audience would not necessarily help improve pronunciation, and it is more sensible to practice pronunciation in other less involving situations. The mobile application is designed to facilitate self-regulated learning through multi-facet monitoring and instant feedback. Students can engage with the mobile application alone to make improvements in certain skills suitable for training in less authentic situations. They can then make better use of the authentic opportunity to focus on other aspects.

The mobile application, called *PresentMate*, runs on smart phones with a reasonably large screen. The current version of *PresentMate* has implemented three training aspects, including time management, voice management, and body movement. The practice begins with the speaker holding the smart phones with one or two hands. *PresentMate* serves as an electronic cue card, and it supports the pre-loading of slides and notes. As the presentation practice going one, the application receives signals from the phone sensors and makes inference of the presenter's performance. Instant alerts such as voice too low or hand trembling are available. After the practice, a report will be generated for the presenter, together with voice recordings of the presentation, allowing the presenter to review and reflect.

The mobile application approach should reduce the trouble of organizing genuine presentation tasks for training. It does not replace the authentic learning opportunities, and it recognizes delivering a genuine presentation is still important in training certain skills such as audience control and stress control. However, the mobile application allows repeated practices at any place convenient to the presenter. Including the mobile application in the instruction should make learning effective without additional cost.

2 Related Work

Research work on using technology to help developing oral presentation skills is rather fragmented. Most approaches acknowledged the value of situated learning and genuine presentation opportunities, but there are at least two directions for improving the effectiveness of the instruction.

The first direction is to extract maximum benefits from genuine presentation opportunities. In addition to the authentic experience gained, students can receive teachers' and peers' feedback as elements for further reflections. Another commonly used instruction is self-review, which is based on video recordings of one's performance. The use of videotaping has been part of the oral presentation education for computing final year project students for many years. The latest video-taking technology, such as lecture video capture, has simplified the arrangement. Smith & Sodano [13] studied the effect of integrating lecture video capture and self-assessment for improving presentation skills. Students had access to recordings of their presentations giving them opportunities to carefully observe and to reflect on their performance. A comprehensive self-assessment was designed to guide their reflections, and findings showed that there was increased awareness of factors contributing to effective presentations. De Grez et al. [4] found that self-assessment had the same impact as teacher-assessment and peer-assessment.

The second direction is to supplement the genuine presentation opportunities with alternative learning activities. Chun [3] demonstrated the use of speech analysis software to provide visual feedback for correcting intonation problems. Visual feedback based on spectrograms was also found to improve significantly the learning of segmental pronunciation for second language learners [11]. Intonation and pronunciation training does not require specific situations or contexts, for example, the home can be a good place for this. Advance in natural user interface has made assessment of body posture, body language, and even eye contact possible. Echeverría et al. [5] developed a presentation skills assessor based on video and Microsoft Kinect. The system was found to be in general agreement with human assessor on predicting the performance level. Perhaps the most interesting recent development is virtual reality training for oral presentation [15, 17]. Making use of virtual audience to give timely, rational, and emotional responses could create an authentic experience for presenters. At the time of writing, this is still very much an emerging research area, and no detailed study on a complete system could be found from the body of literature.

3 System Design and Implementation

The main objective of *PresentMate* is to facilitate self-regulated learning through sensor-based monitoring, instant alert, and performance feedback. From the user perspective, *PresentMate* offers the following features.

- Presentation aide with functions such as electronic cue cards, slide viewer, notepad, and timer.
- Instant alert to notify variations in voice level and body movement.
- End of presentation report with performance indicators and audio playback for self-assessment and self-reflection.

PresentMate includes three modes of operation:

1. *Preparation mode*. Before starting a presentation practice, there are functions for uploading of slides and cue cards and note, re-arranging slides, and editing of notes.
2. *Presentation mode*. During a presentation practice, a cue card viewer, a slide viewer, timer, and instant performance indicators and alerts are available.
3. *Self-assessment mode*. After the end of a presentation practice, there are functions for viewing performance report, reviewing audio recordings, and browsing old reports.

3.1 Components of the System

Figure 1 shows the component view of *PresentMate*. The system is designed to operate in a standalone way on smart phones or other mobile devices with three-axis accelerometers and a microphone.

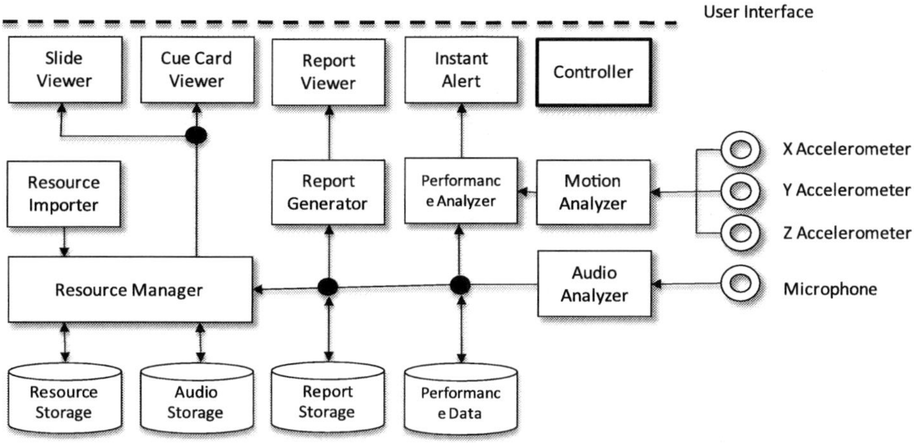

Fig. 1. Component view of *PresentMate*

The components relevant for the *preparation mode* are described in the following.

- *Resource importer*. Resource files from local storage or remote storage can be added to *PresentMate* through this component. The resource file types include slide images and text files.
- *Resource manager and resource storage*. The resource manager supports operations including resource removal, text editing, and slide rearrangement. It also manages the files kept in the resource storage.

Most system functions are active in the presentation mode. A lot of system components are involved, including the resource manager that provides slides and notes for the electronic cue cards. Other components are described below:

- *Slide viewer* and *cue card viewer*. These components serve as electronic cue cards to provide manuscripts to follow or the main points to make. Presenters can flip the slides or the cards through direct manipulation on the screen.
- *Motion analyzer and audio analyzer*. The motion analyzer receives signal from a three-axis accelerometer and applies algorithms to infer the presenter's state of motion, whether the presenter is standing, walking, and shuddering. The audio analyzer receives audio signal from a microphone and monitors the voice level of the presenter. Results of analysis are passed to the performance analyzer for further processing.
- *Performance analyzer*. It collects the output from the motion and audio analyzers, and makes a judgment on the performance. The performance data is stored away for report generation later. It also notifies the instant alert component of any identified performance-related events.
- *Instant alert*. It keeps the presenters informed of critical performance issues such as voice level too low or trembling hands.

The components for the self-assessment mode include the following:

- *Report generator*. It is responsible for generating a performance report of a presentation practice based on the stored performance data.
- *Report viewer*. It supports viewing of a performance report and browsing of stored reports in the report storage.

3.2 Motion Analyzer

The prototype motion analyzer is able to distinguish four states of body motion: standing, walking, hand trembling and other. Figure 2 shows the structure of the motion analyzer.

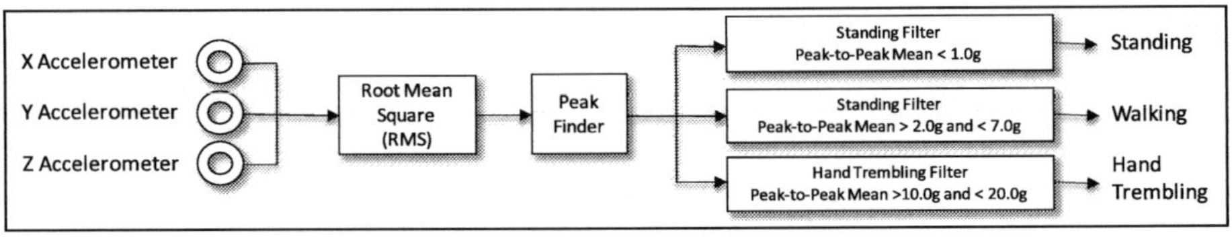

Fig. 2. Structure of the body motion analyzer

The three-axis accelerometer provides three continuous streams of accelerometer data. To eliminate the variations caused by holding the mobile device in different orientations, the three streams are combined into one using a root-mean-square (RMS) filter. The root-mean-squared data stream is then passed to a peak finder. The peak finder considers peaks with sufficiently large magnitude as true peaks, and uses one standard deviation from the mean as the threshold. In addition, if two or more consecutive true peaks are found to be above the mean or below the mean, only one true peak will be kept. With these techniques, small fluctuations, which could be caused by minor hand or body motion, can be filtered out. Figure 3 shows how peaks are identified with this method.

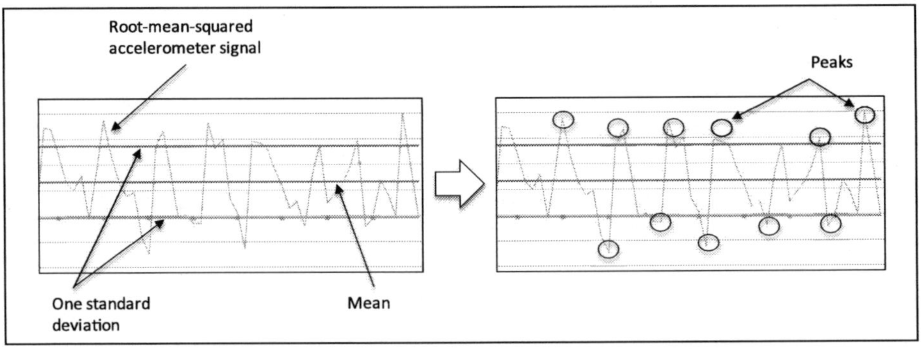

Fig. 3. Illustration of how true peaks are identified in motion analyzer

The list of true peaks is then passed to three body motion recognizers for standing, walking, and hand trembling. The mean peak-to-peak is calculated in a 10-second window, and this is used as the feature for the recognition. We carried out an empirical study that involved carrying a smart phone with one or two hands and performed the three motion states. A collection of over 30 samples of the motions states enabled us to find out the threshold values that distinguish the states. Examples of root-mean-squared data streams of the three motions states are shown in Fig. 4.

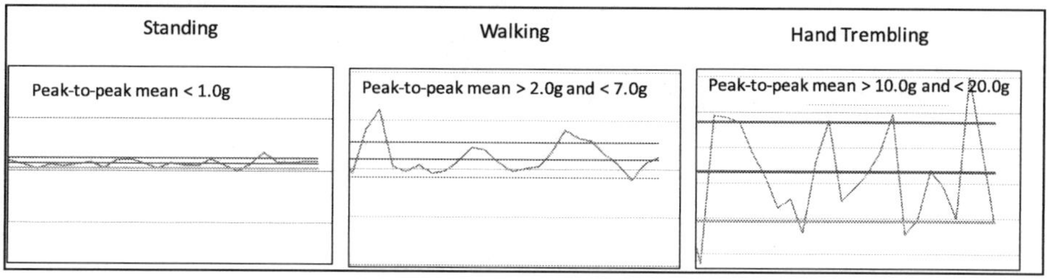

Fig. 4. The different magnitude of peak-to-peak means for the three motion states

3.3 Audio Analyzer

The audio analyzer is used to detect if the voice level is adequate or is fluctuating. Finding the absolute voice level requires careful calibration based on a particular microphone and audio system. In addition, the voice level is affected by the relative position of the smart phone and the indoor sound system. Despite all these insurmountable problems, as a proof of concept, we demonstrated that voice level fluctuations could be detected with some assumptions:

- The venue has a broadcast sound system.
- There is an arm's length between the mouth and the smart phone.

3.4 System Implementation

A prototype of *PresentMate* was implementation as a proof of concept. The prototype was developed based on the Android platform.

Figure 5 shows screenshots of the preparation mode for import of presentation resources. The user can select files from local or remote storage.

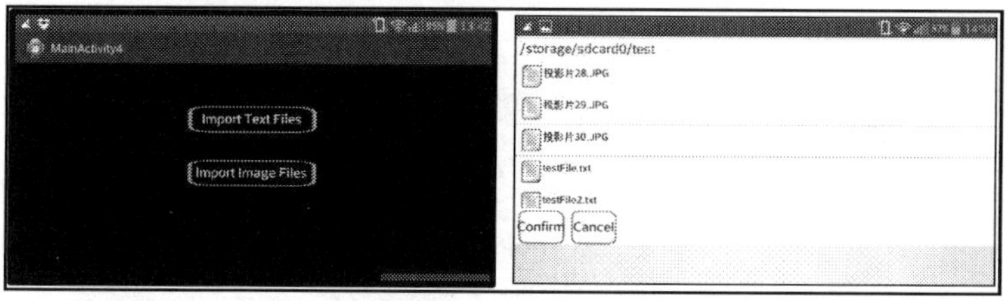

Fig. 5. Screenshots of loading resource page in the preparation mode

A browser is available for checking and re-arranging the slides. Figure 6 below shows the screens after loading text files and loading slide images. There are two buttons on the right edge for starting and stopping the presentation mode.

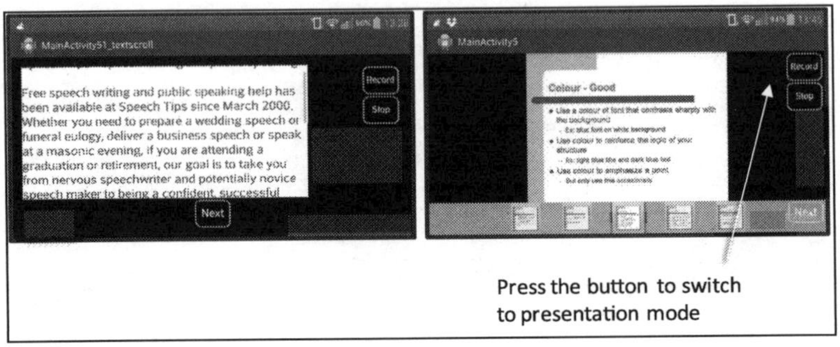

Fig. 6. Screenshots of the resource browsing page.

In the presentation mode, the sensors and analyzers become active and monitor the presenter's performance. The presenter is expected to hand-hold the mobile device and glance at the screen occasionally. Figure 7 shows examples of on-screen alert messages that are designed to remind the presenter.

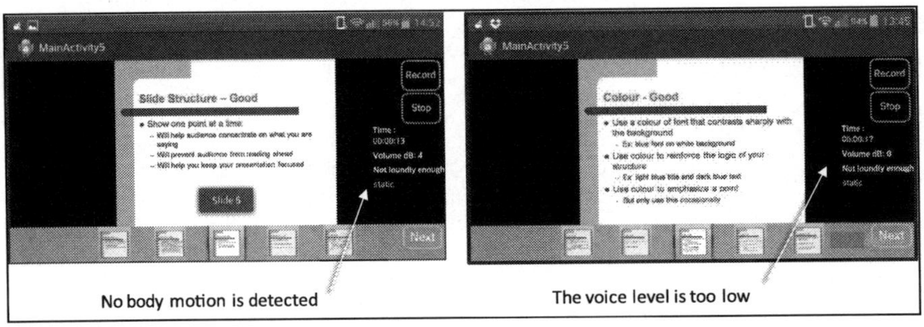

Fig. 7. Screenshots showing the on-screen alerts.

The presentation mode ends when the stop button is pressed. The user can then obtain a report of the presentation, of which a screenshot is shown in Fig. 8.

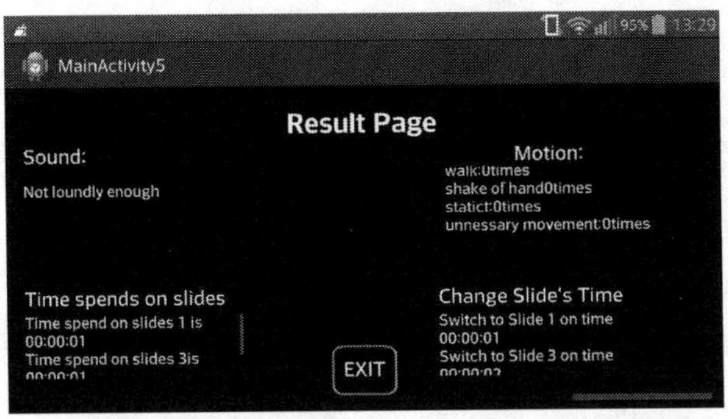

Fig. 8. Performance report page.

4 Evaluation

The objective of building the prototype is to demonstrate the idea of smart-phone based oral presentation training. Based on various smart-phone sensors, certain elements of oral presentation performance could be inferred and feedback to the user. A descriptive study was carried out to evaluate the feasibility of our approach.

A total of 20 testers took part in the study. The 20 testers were acquaintances of one of the authors. The age range was between 12 and 20. None of them reported any experience of using a product help develop their oral presentation skills. The testers were asked to simulate using the mobile application to perform a presentation. The usage time was limited to 10 min. At the end, the testers were asked to fill in a survey.

Figure 9 shows that 60 % of them felt fear when doing an oral presentation but 20 % did not. The other 20 % did not have such an experience.

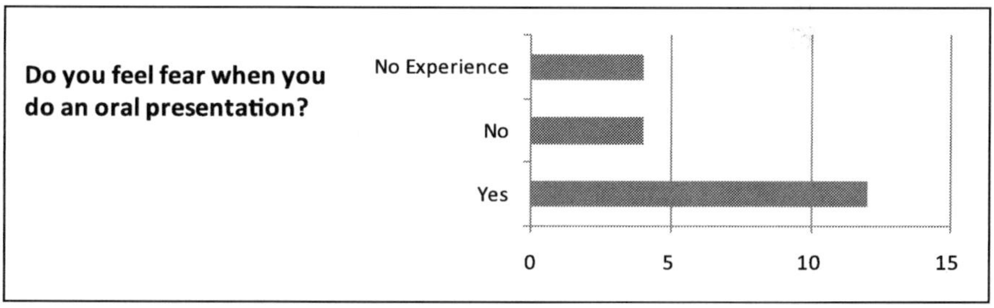

Fig. 9. Statistics of the testers feeling fear in an oral presentation.

Figure 10 shows whether the testers agreed with using a smart-phone and the mobile application. Among the testers, 70 % of them used a smart-phone to help do an oral presentation. They were mostly positive about the training aspect of the mobile application.

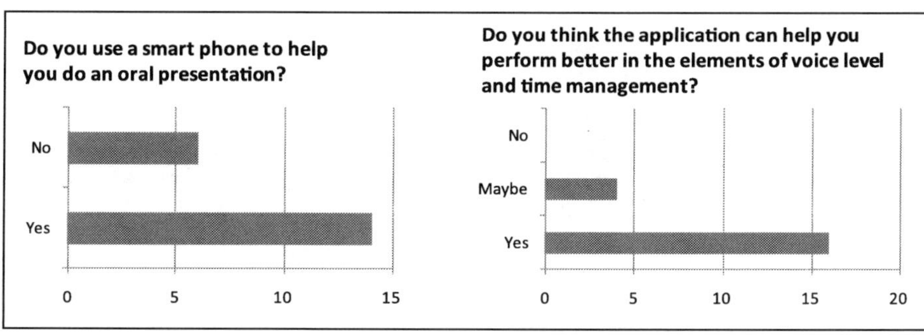

Fig. 10. Results concerning the testers' perception of the mobile application

The survey also included open-ended questions. When asked if the motion analyzer helpful for presentation, the students responded:

- *"It tells me how static I am in the presentation."*
- *"It let me aware of some bad habits such as trembling."*
- *"It tells me if I had changed positions when I gave the presentation, and moving around is a kind of interaction with the audience."*

When asked which page was the most useful, 15 of them reported the performance report page, mostly because the page gives useful details and information.

In general, there are preliminary indications that:

- The mobile application can help train oral presentation.
- The application can help manage the voice level and time management.
- The performance report page is most useful that it can be a good reference.

5 Conclusion

This paper illustrated with a solid example how mobile application could be effective in oral presentation training. Based on a review of the literature, the cost of holding an authentic oral presentation training session would be more worthwhile if suitable pre and post learning activities could bring out more value from the training. This paper suggested a self-regulated mobile learning approach could improve certain elements of effective oral presentation. The mobile application developed, called *PresentMate*, allowed the training to happen anywhere and anytime. The application provides instant and delayed feedback to enable self-reflection, which is regarded as the key to learning oral presentation (Smith & Sodano, 2011). *PresentMate* does not require special devices other than a smart-phone.

A prototype implementation of *PresentMate* was used for preliminary evaluation of the approach. With the standard sensors, the mobile application demonstrated that providing feedback related to elements of presentation performance is feasible. The results of a survey indicated that the testers found the feedback functions useful and relevant to learning presentation. While the novelty effect could be a significant factor, there are at least some merits evolved from this approach. The evidenced feasibility of this approach is the main contribution of this work.

The current design of *PresentMate* is still very limited. Only body motion, timing of presentation, and voice level are included in the elements of feedback. The accuracy of the motion and audio analyzers is yet to be evaluated. It was also reported that accurate detection of voice level is subject to many environmental factors. The accelerometers however have potential to reveal more bodily motion patterns that could be related to presentation performance. In addition, future smart phones are expected to carry more kinds of sensors. For example, one fitted with ultrasound, electromyography sensors could give feedback on the stress level.

Another limitation of *PresentMate* is the performance report. The current design presents only low-level information such the time spent walking around. It is up to the presenters to interpret and integrate into their self-reflection. Further computational analysis might be able to infer higher-level information such as the level of audience interaction. This new type analysis might involve taking into consideration of data from multiple sensors, and possibly using machine learning for classification.

References

1. Beder, S.: Towards a more representative engineering education. Int. J. Appl. Eng. Educ. **5**(2), 173–182 (1989)
2. Busà, M.G.: Sounding natural: Improving oral presentation skills. Lang. Value **2**, 51–67 (2010)
3. Chun, D.M.: Signal analysis software for teaching discourse intonation. Lang. Learn. Technol. **2**(1), 61–77 (1998)
4. De Grez, L., Valcke, M., Roozen, I.: How effective are self-and peer assessment of oral presentation skills compared with teachers' assessments? Act. Learn. High Educ. **13**(2), 129–142 (2012)
5. Echeverría, V., Avendaño, A., Chiluiza, K., Vásquez, A., Ochoa, X.: Presentation skills estimation based on video and kinect data analysis. In: Proceedings of the 2014 ACM Workshop on Multimodal Learning Analytics Workshop and Grand Challenge, pp. 53–60. ACM (2014)
6. Furmark, T., Tillfors, M., Everz, P.O., Marteinsdottir, I., Gefvert, O., Fredrikson, M.: Social phobia in the general population: prevalence and sociodemographic profile. Soc. Psychiatry Psychiatr. Epidemiol. **34**(8), 416–424 (1999)
7. Harvey, L.: New realities: the relationship between higher education and employment. Tert. Educ. Manag. **6**(1), 3–17 (2000)
8. Kearney, M., Schuck, S.: Spotlight on authentic learning: student developed digital video projects. Australas. J. Educ. Tech. **22**(2), 189–208 (2006)
9. Lombardi, M. M.: Approaches that work: how authentic learning is transforming higher education. EDUCAUSE Learning Initiative (ELI) Paper, 5 (2007)
10. Nicol, D., Milligan, C.: Rethinking technology-supported assessment practices in relation to the seven principles of good feedback practice. Innovative Assessment in Higher Education, 64–77 (2006)
11. Olson, D.J.: Benefits of visual feedback on segmental production in the L2 classroom. Lang. Learn. Technol. **18**(3), 173–192 (2014)
12. Reeves, T., Herrington, J., Oliver, R.: Authentic activities and online learning. In: Goody, A., Herrington, J., Northcote, M. (eds.) Quality Conversations: Research and Development in Higher Education, vol. 25, pp. 562–567. Jamison, ACT: HERDSA (2002). Accessed http://www.ecu.edu.au/conferences/herdsa/main/papers/ref/pdf/Reeves.pdf
13. Smith, C.M., Sodano, T.M.: Integrating lecture capture as a teaching strategy to improve student presentation skills through self-assessment. Act. Learn. High Educ. **12**(3), 151–162 (2011)
14. Sueyoshi, A., Hardison, D.M.: The role of gestures and facial cues in second language listening comprehension. Lang. Learn. **55**(4), 661–699 (2005)
15. Tudor, A.D., Mustatea, I., Poeschl, S., Doering, N.: Responsive audiences—Nonverbal cues as reactions to a speaker's behavior. In: Virtual Reality (VR), pp. 119–120. IEEE (2014)
16. Vicinanza, S.: Information technology as a discipline: what employers want in an IT graduate. ACM Inroads **4**(4), 59–63 (2013)
17. Wiederhold, B.K., Riva, G.: Designing virtual audiences for fear of public speaking training–an observation study on realistic nonverbal behavior. Annu. Rev. Cybertherapy Telemedicine. Adv. Technol. Behav. Soc. Neurosci. **181**, 218 (2012)
18. Zimmerman, B.J.: Self-regulated learning and academic achievement: an overview. Educ. Psychol. **25**(1), 3–17 (1990)

FluteKit - A Mobile Learning Application for Beginners to Train Rhythmic Skills and Learn Flute Fundamentals

Sin-Chun Ng(✉), Andrew Kwok-Fai Lui, and Cheuk Hei Cheng

The Open University of Hong Kong, 30 Good Shepherd Street, Ho Man Tin, Kowloon, Hong Kong SAR, China
{scng,alui,s1098053}@ouhk.edu.hk

Abstract. Flute beginners often suffer from rhythmic errors as they may play a note longer or shorter than its correct duration. Sometimes, the rhythms written in the music sheets are too complicated for them to comprehend. Flute beginners may lose their interests when they keep performing unsatisfactorily. This paper describes the development a mobile e-learning application for flute learners to train their rhythmic skills and help them learn flute fundamentals so that they can play a new song in a better way with fewer mistakes. This application focuses on helping users to learn rhythmic skills and sight reading. The rhythms that the learners have played will be recorded, recognized and analyzed. Comments and improvement tips will be provided to the learners according to the weaknesses found. Relevant results of sight reading exercises will be used to find out the errors that the individual learner have made so as to improve his/her performance.

Keywords: Mobile learning application · Android apps · Rhythmic skill · Learn to play flutes

1 Introduction

Learning musical instrument becomes a trend in Hong Kong in which learning flute is a popular choice. Beginners usually will have problems in reading notes from a music sheet, following the rhythm of a song, or playing notes with correct pitch and correct fingering. This paper introduces a mobile application as an assistive tool for flute learners to practice their own skills. The application includes a digital score renderer/player, a voice recording and playback system, voice-to-note converter, note track analyzer, a sight-reading assessment system, a flute tuner, a metronome and a flute fingering chart. It aims to help users identify their problems in playing flutes, give comments to users and assist them to play a song correctly. It also helps users develop skills in sight reading by giving them sight reading exercises.

Sight-reading is a vital skill for mastering the learning of a music instrument. Assume that the learners already have some fundamental music theory concepts, there are mainly two problems that learners may encounter: (1) not able to count rhythms accurately; (2) having difficulties in identifying notes on the staff. Most learners can read music notes faster by reading more scores but they still find it hard to learn rhythm counting.

J. Lam et al. (Eds.): ICTE 2015, CCIS 559, pp. 90–102, 2015.
DOI: 10.1007/978-3-662-48978-9_9

To teach learners rhythmic skill, how to present the rhythm is important. Most flute teachers use auditory means, demonstrating the rhythm by flute or singing it out. Shehan [1] found that learners need fewer trials to repeat the rhythm accurately if the rhythm is presented through multiple media, combinations of visual and auditory means. However, Persellin's findings showed that presenting rhythms through multiple media, combinations of visual, auditory, and kinesthetic means, does not lead to learners' better rhythm accuracy [4]. One explanation is that Shehan counted the number of trials the learners repeated until the rhythm is accurately played while Persellin used one-time assessment to validate if the learners repeated the rhythm accurately. Therefore, the rhythms presented through multiple media can reduce the times learners take to play a rhythm accurately. Also, Persellin found that Grade 1 students were weak when reading notes. Presenting the rhythm in multimedia can solve the problems that some individuals have difficulties learning rhythms due to particular sensory weakness.

Moreover, rhythm learning procedure is essential. Most flute teachers use clap-count method, which is defined as counting aloud while coordinating clapping at the start of notes, to tell learners how to count rhythms which learners, in contrast, may be unable to follow. Pierce [3] carried out an experiment on using different learning procedures and found that clap-count method is not effective as it is too difficult. Some flute teachers ask learners to follow the melody they are playing. It may be an effective way for learners to learn a rhythm by memorizing it, but most importantly, learners have to repeat it so that teachers can validate whether they understand the rhythm well. The loopholes of this approach are as follows:

1. Learners may not know how to count the rhythm thoroughly as they can only memorize it temporarily. They may fail to count a similar rhythm next time.
2. Learners may find it complicated to play the notes and rhythms at the same time as they cannot focus on only one part. Learning effectiveness will then be lowered.
3. Learners cannot practice on their own using this procedure as no one can demonstrate the melody nor validate the accuracy of the rhythm repeated.

To address the problem that learners may find it hard to play the notes and rhythms simultaneously, both single-pitch rhythms and melodies should be used. Boisen [2] found that for both single-pitch and matching melodies are presented, the accuracy of rhythms repeated by learners is almost the same. Therefore, single-pitch rhythms can be given to learners, followed by the melodies. Learners can focus on the rhythm part only when repeating single-pitch rhythms. They can then learn the melody more easily. Also, this lengthens the attention span of learners on the rhythm. Learners can have a greater understanding of the rhythm, memorize it better and may respond better when they encounter similar rhythms.

Recently, mobile learning provides a platform for learners to gain access to learning resources at anytime and anywhere by just bringing along with their mobile devices. Mobile learning can be argumentative, acting as a helper or substitution of the current tools with some improvements [5, 6]. Mobile learning applications can help users collect data such as photos, recordings, text inputs and help users learn and improve themselves by giving solutions or advices.

2 Current Applications for Learning Music

There is no flute learning application that can integrate both the sight reading skill and flute learning skill into one application in the market. Mobile applications of the two categories, flute fundamentals and sight-reading, are reviewed. "*Sight Reading Machine*" [9] is an app which can generate a melody unit on the staff and play it through speakers. "*Music Tutor (Sight Reading)*" [8] can generate a note on staff and ask learners to select the corresponding pitch in keyboard. "*Flute Notes Flash Cards*" [7] can generate a note on staff with the key. Learners can flip the flash card to see the corresponding flute fingering. "*How To Play Flute*" [10] provides a keyboard and a flute model. Learners can press on a key and the corresponding fingering positions are shown on the flute in the app. "*Learn To Play The Flute*" [11] provides videos on flute fundamentals. The comparison of these apps is listed in Table 1.

Table 1. Comparison of the existing mobile flute fundamentals and sight-reading learning applications

Application name	Pros	Cons
Sight Reading Machine	Different music instruments can be chosen when playing the melody.	The melody is randomly generated which may have a strange music style.
	The set of notes and rests can be defined.	The melody can only be played once and then it will generate a new one. Learners cannot practice again and again.
	The range of pitch can be defined.	The application does not record learners' performance and give them feedbacks.
Music Tutor (Sight Reading)	With large pitch range of notes is available.	The application is not designed for flute which does not help learners in flute fingering.
Flute Notes Flash Cards	The application generates a note on staff with the key. Learners can flip the flash card to see the corresponding flute fingering.	The application cannot help learner in reading the key of the note.
How To Play Flute	The application can help learners to look up and memorize flute fingering.	Learners may not know the keys on the piano.
		The application cannot help learner in reading the key of the note.
Learn To Play The Flute	Learners can learn from videos instead of text.	The app does not record learners' performance and give them feedbacks

3 Implementation of the Application

The mobile application for flute beginners is called *FluteKit*. It is composed of six major components as shown in Fig. 1: Score Reader with Practicing Helper, Sight Reading Training System, Flute Fundamentals e-learning System, Metronome, Tuner, and Flute Fingering Chart.

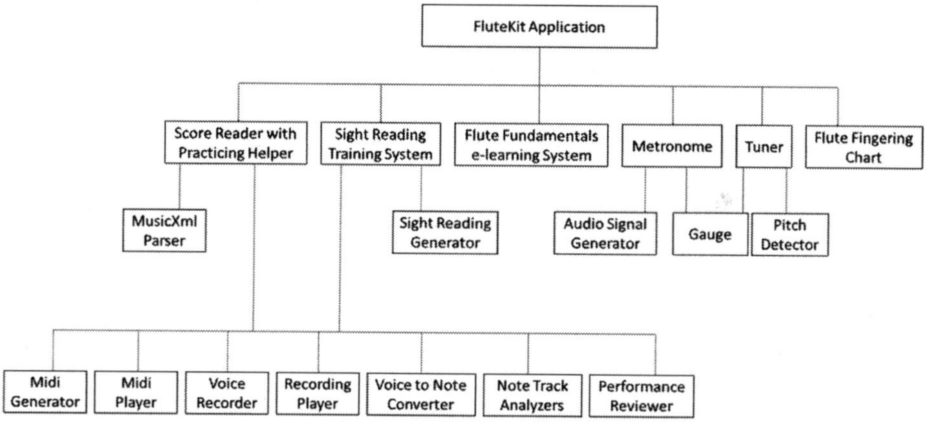

Fig. 1. The system architecture of *FluteKit*

The application is developed for Android devices with touch screen, microphone and speaker. The technologies used in the platform include Android (Java), HTML, CSS, JavaScript, SQLite. Score Reader with Practicing Helper, Sight Reading Training System, Metronome, Tuner, and Flute Fingering Chart are developed by using Java, which provides faster computation to process Audio data. Flute Fundamentals e-learning System is developed by HTML, CSS and JavaScript which is easier to update content and can present multimedia of e-learning materials in a better way. Flute Fundamentals e-learning System is integrated to the application by Android WebView.

3.1 Score Reader with Practicing Helper

Score Reader with Practicing Helper allows users to practise playing a music sheet by providing the corresponding MusicXML file. It aims to help users familiarize with the music and figure out any errors made when playing the song. Users should provide MusicXML to the system in order to render the music scores (Fig. 2), generate score playback (Fig. 3), and analyze the recording for users' performance (Fig. 4).

Fig. 2. Screenshot of score renderer

Fig. 3. Screenshot of the comparator. (upper row: the original score, lower row: the notes detected)

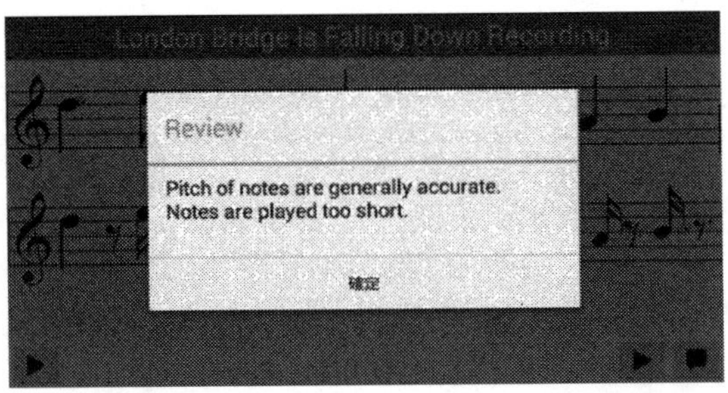

Fig. 4. Screenshot of the comment dialog.

MusicXML format is chosen because it is fully and openly documented, and can be freely used under a Public License. It is an XML-based file format for representing Western musical notation. Many music score writing programs (e.g. MuseScore, Finale, Sibelius) supports importing and exporting MusicXML file so MusicXML file of a music sheet can be easily obtained from the internet or created by using these software.

The practicing helper validates the correctness of the song played by users through recording. The performance of learners is recorded by *Audio Recorder* and analyzed by *Voice to Note Converter*. Information is then processed by *Note Track Analyzer* and *Performance Reviewer*.

The results are then presented to the users in a music sheet which have the original notes shown on the upper row while the notes recognized are shown on the lower row (Fig. 3). It enables users to compare notes that they played easily so that rhythmic errors and pitch errors can be identified.

Score Reader with Practicing Helper consists of the following subsystems:

(1) MusicXML parser. MusicXML parser reads MusicXML files for rendering the music score. It enables users to practice any songs they want as long as they have the file, which can be downloaded online or created with score writing programs.
(2) Midi Generator and Midi Player. The system can generate the audio of the music sheet. It is done with Midi Generator and Midi Player sub-systems. Midi Generator writes the midi file to the internal storage in android device which is private to the application. Midi Player reads the midi file written and allow users to play or pause it.
(3) Audio Recorder and Audio Player. The system enables users to record their play and playback the recording. Audio Recorder records audio signals and store as PCM values and Audio Player allows the playback of the recording. The PCM raw data can be written to internal storage in android device which is private to the application.
(4) Voice to Note Converter. It is challenging to distinguish notes from recordings. In the system, it is assumed that users do not perform slur notes. To recognize notes, samples of a note should firstly be separated from each other. Then, the frequency of each note can be found by frequency-domain approaches with the Fast Fourier transform (FFT) algorithm.
(5) Note track analyzer and performance reviewer. The note track analyzer identifies problems from the notes identified. Here are some examples on how problems are identified: pitch accuracy can be found by comparing the frequency of the original note with that of the user input, and rhythmic errors can be identified if the duration of the note is inconsistent with the original note. Performance reviewer gives comments to users based on the findings of note track analyzers. It gives different comments and advices on different cases.

3.2 Sight Reading Training System

Sight Reading exercises are provided to the learners. It aims to allow users exposed to different rhythms to develop sight reading skills. The working principle is similar to Score Reader with Practicing Helper but Sight Training System generates notes instead of using MusicXML picked by users.

The training system checks the users' understanding of the section of notes through recording their performance. The performance of learners is recorded by Audio Recorder and analyzed by Voice to Note Converter. Information is then processed by Note Track Analyzer and Performance Reviewer.

The results are presented to users in a music sheet which have the original notes shown on the upper row while the notes recognized are shown on the lower row. It enables users to compare notes easily so that rhythmic errors and pitch errors can be identified. Results and advices are provided to users based on the performance of melodies they played. Overall pitch accuracy, length, stability, etc. are evaluated.

3.3 Flute Fundamentals E-Learning System

Learners can build a solid flute foundation through reading articles and following instructions of video tutorials are provided. E-learning materials will cover the followings:

- Mouthpiece Lip Placement Tutorial
- Posture and Hand Position Tutorial
- Tone Practice
- Octave Slur Practice
- Harmonic Series Practice.

The Flute Fundamentals e-Learning System (Fig. 5) is built with web pages. HTML, CSS, JS are good to present articles and multimedia. It is also easy to update contents of HTML so web based presentation is adopted.

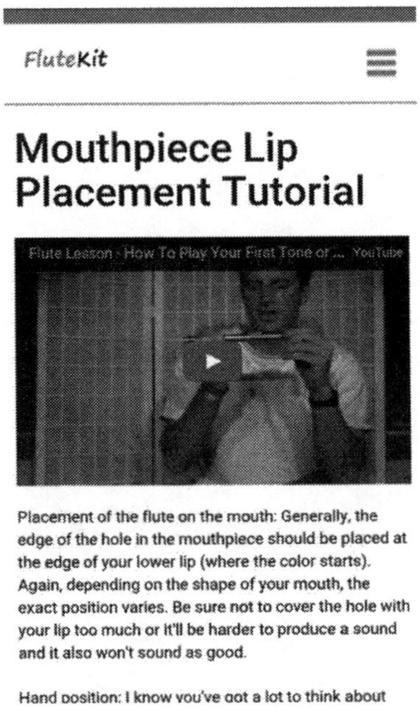

Fig. 5. Screenshot of the flute fundamentals e-learning system

3.4 Tuner

A tuner is important for flute learners. Flute player should tune their flutes before playing. A screenshot of the flute tuner is shown in Fig. 6. The Tuner provides two modes of tuning:

1. Auto mode. When flute learners activate the auto tuning mode, the application will record the voice and analyze the frequency of the voice. The recognized frequency and its corresponding pitch are shown on the screen. There is also a gauge to show the accuracy of the pitch. The needle of the gauge deflecting left indicates the pitch played is flat and vice versa. If the pitch played is accurate, the needle should remain in the center of the gauge.
2. Manual mode. The tuner will produce the sound of the selected pitch. Tuning is done aurally by playing the pitch on flute and adjusting the float so that it matches the one produced by the tuner.

   The theory of this mode of tuning uses interference beats to measure the accuracy of tuning. If the two pitches are closer to the harmonic, beating will occur at lower frequency. Therefore, flute player should adjust the flute until the beating is not audible.

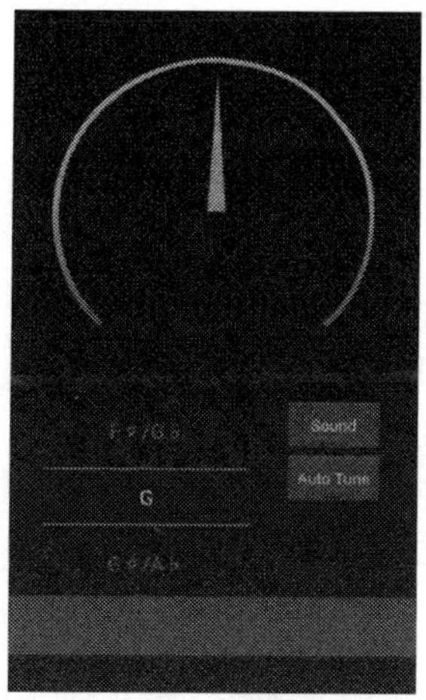

Fig. 6. The screenshot of tuner in *FluteKit*

The tuner consists of the following subsystems:

(1) Pitch Generator. Pitch Generator is a sub-system which can generate sinusoidal wave signal of specified frequency and output it to the speaker. It is used to generate sound of selected pitch when manual tune is chosen.
(2) Pitch Detector. Pitch Detector samples regularly from the microphone. It finds the frequency with the highest volume from the recorded signals by using frequency-domain approaches with the Fast Fourier transform (FFT) algorithm. The scientific pitch notation (e.g. Middle C is C4) of the note frequency can be found by comparing with sorted note pitch maps and get the notation with the nearest frequency. The note pitch maps can be generated by Piecewise linear approximation:

$$\text{Frequency of } n \text{ th successive semitone of current note} = \textit{current frequency} \times 2^{\frac{n}{12}}$$

The accuracy is calculated by comparing with the frequency of the corresponding scientific pitch notation.

(3) Tuner Gauge. Tuner Gauge shows the accuracy of the pitch detected visually by the needle. It supports deflection animation of the needle.

3.5 Metronome

The metronome is useful for flute learners to practice. The beat of flute beginners is often inaccurate. With the metronome, they can follow the beats and play the rhythm accurately.

The metronome in *FluteKit* gives users the beats by both visual and audio means. Flute learners can see the needle oscillating on a regular interval at a constant speed while listening the beating of the metronome (Fig. 7).

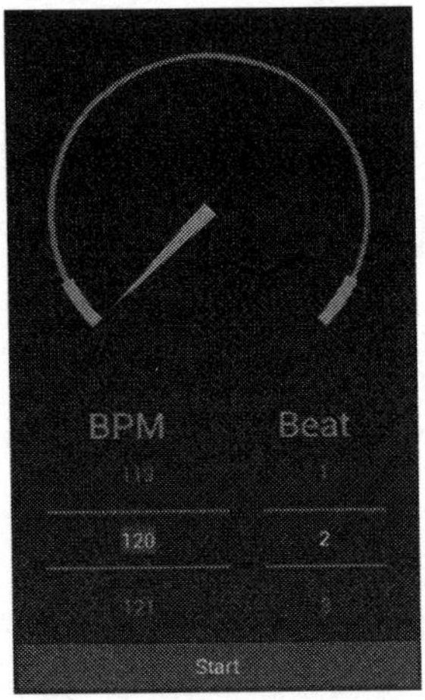

Fig. 7. The screenshot of metronome in *FluteKit*

3.6 Flute Fingering Chart

Flute learners often forget the fingering of some keys of flute, especially for those high pitch notes. Flute Fingering Chart enables user to look up the fingering as shown in Fig. 8. Flute Fingering Chart shows the fingering with the corresponding note in staff. Users swipe up and down to change the note and obtain the corresponding fingering.

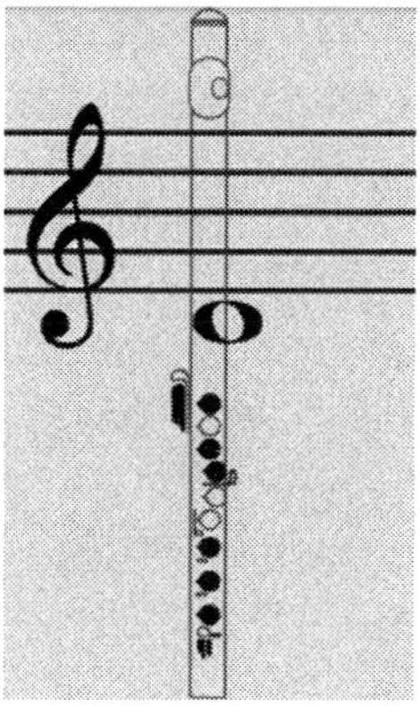

Fig. 8. The screenshot of flute fingering chart

The implementation of Flute Fingering Chart is relatively simple. GestureDetector is developed to monitor swiping gestures. On swiping up or down, the note on the staff is updated and the keys of the flute (changing the image/background image of the flute key) are updated according to the states of key of the corresponding pitch.

4 Evaluation

Questionnaires were given to users who have tried the application to evaluate the effectiveness of the application. The evaluation is based on the following areas:

1. Effectiveness of learning a piece of score with the application. This evaluates if the Score Reader with Practicing Helper can select the difficult part out and help the user to cope with the problem. Also, the accuracy of comments and advice given to users should also be evaluated.
2. Improvement in sight reading after using the application. This evaluates if the Sight Reading Helper can help train the sight reading skill of the user.
3. Effectiveness of the flute fundamentals materials. This evaluates the completeness and effectiveness of the training materials provided.
4. User acceptance of the user interface. This evaluates the ease of use of the application.

Twelve questionnaires were collected and ten of them were flute learners. Their ages were in the range of 18–25.

4.1 Effectiveness of Learning a Piece of Score with the Application

From the above Table 2, users agreed the score reader with practicing helper could help them learn songs. Score playback helps them learn songs effectively.

Table 2. Result – Effectiveness of learning a piece of score with the application

	Definitely Agree	Agree	Disagree	Definitely Disagree
Score Reader helps me to learn a song	100 %(5)	0 %(0)	0 %(0)	0 %(0)
Score Reader can show music scores clearly	0 %(0)	100 %(12)	0 %(0)	0 %(0)
Score Playback helps me to learn a song	83 %(10)	17 %(2)	0 %(0)	0 %(0)
Recording playback helps me to identify errors	50 %(6)	50 %(6)	0 %(0)	0 %(0)
FluteKit detects note pitch accurately from recordings	75 %(9)	25 %(3)	0 %(0)	0 %(0)
FluteKit detects note length accurately from recordings	67 %(8)	25 %(3)	8 %(1)	0 %(0)
Detected notes from recordings helps me to identify errors	8 %(1)	92 %(11)	0 %(0)	0 %(0)

In general, they agreed that the notes identified are accurate and the function can help them figure out the errors.

4.2 Improvement in Sight Reading After Using the Application

From the above Table 3, all users agreed that the sight reading training system could help them improve sight reading skill. Some users thought that the melodies were quite strange and it was unlikely to be met in real life.

Table 3. Result – Improvement in sight reading after using the application

	Definitely agree	Agree	Disagree	Definitely disagree
Sight Reading Training helps me to improve sight reading skills	0 %(0)	100 %(5)	0 %(0)	0 %(0)

4.3 Effectiveness of the Flute Fundamentals Materials

From the above Table 4, all users agreed that the articles and video tutorials could help users build fundamental skills but they thought the resources were not enough. It should link to score reader and provide some exercises to practice in each chapter.

Table 4. Results – Effectiveness of the flute fundamentals materials

	Definitely agree	Agree	Disagree	Definitely disagree
Flute fundamentals e-learning system is clear and easy to use	0 %(0)	100 %(5)	0 %(0)	0 %(0)
Videos and articles on flute fundamentals help me to improve my skills	0 %(0)	100 %(5)	0 %(0)	0 %(0)

4.4 User Acceptance of the User Interface

From the above Table 5, all users agreed that the user interface design was simple, clear and easy to use in general. However, users indicated some parts should be improved.

Table 5. Results – User acceptance to the user interface

	Definitely agree	Agree	Disagree	Definitely disagree
FluteKit is easy to use	0 %(0)	100 %(12)	0 %(0)	0 %(0)
Metronome is easy to use	83 %(10)	17 %(2)	0 %(0)	0 %(0)
Tuner is easy to use	17 %(2)	83 %(10)	0 %(0)	0 %(0)

- A tutorial should be given to tell users how to use score reader for the first time as users may not know the usage of each button.
- Tuner should provide an indicator (e.g. a signal light, green for accurate, yellow for acceptable, red for inaccurate pitch) for auto tune mode to tell users if the pitch is accurate.
- A tutorial should be given to tell users how to use flute fingering chart for the first time.

5 Conclusion

The purpose of developing a new mobile application called *FluteKit* is to help flute learners learn flute efficiently. Through practicing and learning from e-learning materials, they can have a solid foundation which helps them read music scores and build up self-learning ability.

FluteKit provides an all-in-one platform which provides practicing tools, self-learning materials and assistive tools which are suitable to be used in different situations. As *FluteKit* is an Android application, users can install it to their smartphones and access them anytime and anywhere. It is a more comprehensive mobile music e-learning application when compared to the existing applications on Google Play.

Score Reader with Practicing Helper assists users practice a song. It can help users figure out and correct the errors made when playing a song. The performance of the user is presented by rendering it on a music sheet with comments. *Sight reading training system* train users' sight reading skills by practicing and help them figure out and correct the errors made when playing the song. *Flute fundamental e-learning system* help users build up fundamental skills. It provides articles and video tutorials. *Assistive tools* including tuner and metronome help users play the songs accurately with correct rhythm and pitch.

References

1. Shehan, P.K.: Effects of rote versus note presentations on rhythm learning and retention. J. Res. Music Educ. **35**(2), 117–126 (1987)
2. Boisen, R.: The effect of melodic context on students' aural perception of rhythm. J. Res. Music Educ. **29**(3), 165–172 (1981)
3. Pierce, M.A.: The effects of learning procedure, tempo, and performance condition on transfer of rhythm skills in instrumental music. J. Res. Music Educ. **40**(4), 295–305 (1992)
4. Persellin, D.C.: Responses to rhythm patterns when presented to children through auditory, visual, and kinesthetic modalities. J. Res. Music Educ. **40**(4), 306–315 (1992)
5. Hockly, N.: Mobile learning. ELT J. **67**(1), 80–84 (2013)
6. Zimmermann, M.: Adaption of multimedia E-Learning services to mobile environments. In: IEEE Global Engineering Education Conference (EDUCON 2011), 4–6 April 2011, pp. 671–678 (2011)
7. Apt App: Flute Notes Flash Cards - Google Play Store (2014). https://play.google.com/store/apps/details?id=air.fluteNotesFlashCards&hl=zh_TW
8. JSplash Mobile: Music Tutor (Sight Reading) - Google Play Store (2011). https://play.google.com/store/apps/details?id=com.jsplash.apps.sightreadingimprover&hl=zh_TW
9. Vivace Studio: Sight Reading Machine - Google Play Store (2015). https://play.google.com/store/apps/details?id=com.thefoakhouse.sightreadingmachine&hl=zh_TW
10. Josef Pavlik: How To Play Flute - Google Play Store (2014). https://play.google.com/store/apps/details?id=com.spintec.android.HowToPlay.Flute&hl=zh_TW
11. CakeHendrik: Learn To Play The Flute - Google Play Store (2014). https://play.google.com/store/apps/details?id=com.hendrikflute&hl=zh_TW

Easy-to-Learn Piano: A Mobile Application for Learning Basic Music Theory and Piano Skill

S.C. Ng(✉), Andrew K.F. Lui, and Alvin C.H. Kwok

The Open University of Hong Kong, 30 Good Shepherd Street, Ho Man Tin, Kowloon, Hong Kong SAR, China
{scng, alui, s1109202}@ouhk.edu.hk

Abstract. This paper presents a mobile learning application for piano beginners to learn fundamental knowledge of music theory in a funny and interesting way. This mobile application provides different materials and exercises, which help users learn basic music theory, practice keyboard playing, listen and distinguish different keys and chords, and compose music. Since most of the piano beginners are weak at sight-reading, this application provides a sight-reading practice to improve their sight-reading skill. This practice provides a music sheet, allows users to follow it and play on the keyboard. The application will show the correct records and mistakes of the users. There are also games and listening exercises for learners to practice with fun so as to arouse their interests in music. After using this mobile application, learners are supposed to be able to read music sheet, play simple songs on the keyboard, compose songs, and discern different tones through training their ears.

Keywords: Applications of mobile devices · Music theory · Playing piano

1 Introduction

In modern days, many parents want their kids to learn at least one music instrument, piano is a popular choice. Music can improve the quality of personal accomplishment and culture. Music plays an important role in the development of a child's brain. Piano can promote the use of right and left half-brains in coordinating both hands. Parents normally send their kids to music schools or invite piano teachers to have piano lessons. Most of the people will have lessons in a music school, because not all families have their own pianos at home. However, learners must practise playing the piano in order to make progress, so they need a way to do practice at home. It is difficult for beginners to have self-learning without the teachers' guidance, they are hard to know what they are playing are correct or not. Most importantly, musical beginners don't have any basic knowledge of music theory, it is difficult for them to learn how to play piano by themselves.

Music can enhance the development in emotion, intelligence, memory and creativity [4]. There are many methods of learning piano, but the important thing is how to arouse the children's interest in learning. 'Interest is the best teacher [1].' If the children

J. Lam et al. (Eds.): ICTE 2015, CCIS 559, pp. 103–112, 2015.
DOI: 10.1007/978-3-662-48978-9_10

are interested in playing the piano, they will have initiative to practice and think about how to play the songs in a better way.

Although the skill of playing the piano is important, music theory is indispensable in learning music. Learners can practice music theory by listening, singing and reading.

Music sheets are used to record the notes of music. If the learners know how to read music sheets, they will know the rhythms and thus can play the songs correctly. The speed of reading music sheets is the key of playing the song successfully, which can reduce the chance of mistakes and play the music more smoothly. Most of the teachers said when the learner plays the first line of music, he or she should read next line synchronously [6]. If the players cannot read fast, only rely on the eyes to read the notes and press the keys accordingly, it will be easy to miss out some keys when playing the piano. Therefore, sight reading is an important part in learning piano.

Listening and singing can help learners to feel the music and the rhythms of the songs. When the learners sing and play together, they will not just sing the pitch, they can feel the music simultaneously. Learners may listen when they are playing the piano, they can find out where they need to improve. Auditory frequency discrimination of children is better than adults, so it is better to train the rhythm when they are young [2].

Nowadays, e-learning and mobile learning (m-learning) are getting popular, students can learn without textbooks, they can study using e-learning platforms [7]. Teaching materials can be updated easily as the publisher can release an updated package or update the website [3]. The use of multimedia instructional materials such as games and animation can make the learning fun and interesting. When the learners get interested in it, they will spend more time to study [5]. An e-learning or m-learning program may provide numerous features conducive to learning. Those features should achieve the learning objectives, allow the learners find the best way to learn [8].

This paper introduces a mobile learning application called "Easy-to-Learn Piano" that allows users learn fundamental knowledge of music theory and basic piano skill. Users can learn music in a funny and interesting way with games and exercises. This application provides functions for users to learn basic music theory, practice keyboard playing, listen and distinguish keys and chords, and compose a song. Since most piano beginners are weak at sight-reading, this application provides a sight-reading practice for the users. The application will show the correct records and mistakes of the users. Learners can also import their own music sheets by the composer tools for practice. After using this mobile application, learners are supposed to be able to read music sheet, play simple songs on the keyboard, compose songs, and discern different tones through training their ears.

2 Current Applications for Learning Music

There are a lot of piano learning mobile apps in the app store, most of them provide functions like reading a music sheet and practicing through the piano keyboard, but there isn't any practice of singing or listening in those mobile apps. Also, there are some apps for listening practice and composing music, they don't have the piano keyboard practicing. Table 1 lists out the functions of different mobile applications including *Pianist* [9], *Perfect Ear 2* [10] and *Ensemble Composer* [11] for comparison.

Table 1. Comparison of current piano learning applications

		Pianist	Perfect Ear 2	Ensemble composer	Easy-to-Learn Piano
Keyboard practicing	Music sheet	Y	N	N	Y
	Piano game	Y	N	N	Y
Composer	By keyboard	N	N	N	Y
	By music sheet	N	N	Y	Y
Listening exercise	Listen and press	Y	Y	N	Y
Piano learning materials	Notes	N	Y	N	Y
	Keyboard	N	N	N	Y

Y = Yes; N = No

3 Implementation of the Application

For learning a language, the learner needs to practice on reading, writing, listening and speaking. Learning music is similar to learning a language, the learners need to develop skill in reading scores, listening and distinguish different notes, writing and composing pieces of music, and playing the piano. The mobile application "Easy-to-Learn Piano" is developed for IOS touch screen tablet PC (iPad), it provides functions including the learning materials, keyboard practicing tool, composer tool and listening exercises for the users to learn music in a funny and interactive way.

The system components, start page and main menu are shown (Figs. 1, 2 and 3).

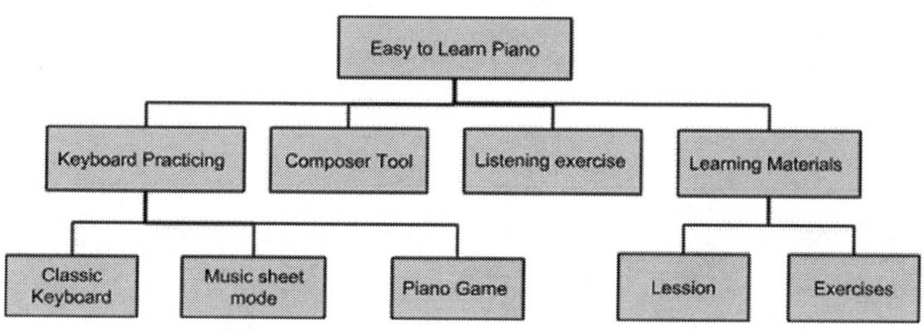

Fig. 1 The system components of Easy-to-Learn Piano

3.1 Learning Materials

This feature assumes the users do not have any knowledge in music. It includes learning materials for introducing basic music theory, such as duration of different notes, note names and the corresponding sounds on the staff, different clefs (treble clef and bass clef) shown in Figs. 4 and 5. Those topics are of great importance to

Fig. 2 The startup page of the application

Fig. 3 The main menu

beginners. There are two parts of learning materials: music lessons and music exercises. "Music lesson" provides an e-book for users to learn the music theory. "Music exercises" includes multiple-choice exercises and fill-in exercises to test whether the users understand the materials given in the music lessons (as shown in Figs. 6 and 7).

Fig. 4 Screen shot of music lesson

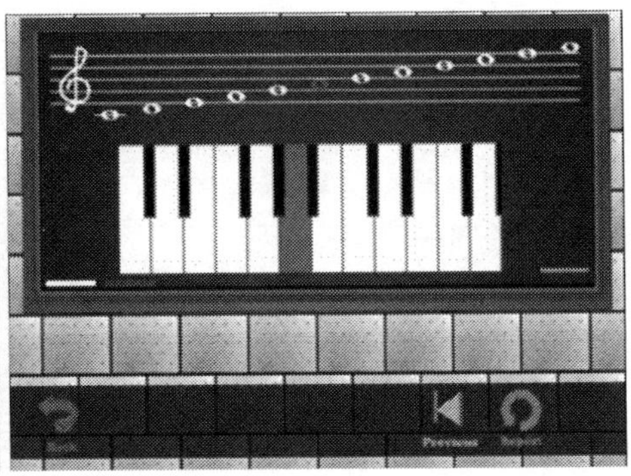

Fig. 5 Screen shot of music lesson

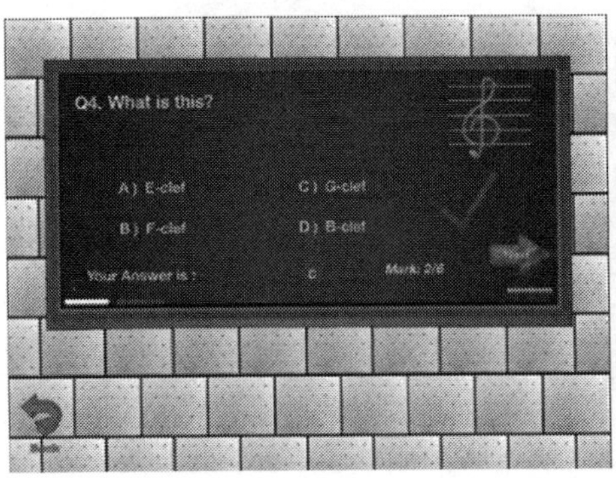

Fig. 6 Multiple-choice exercise

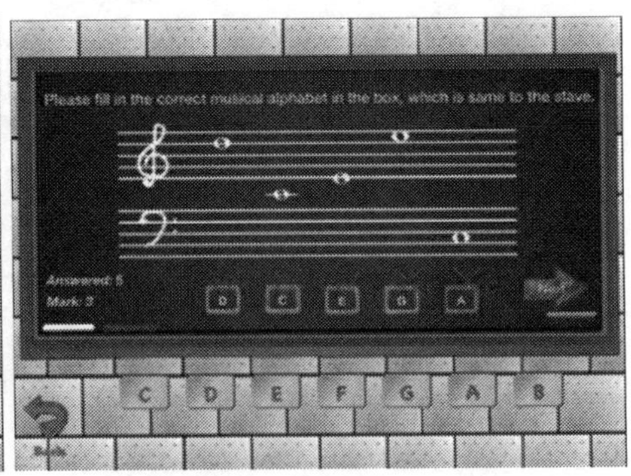

Fig. 7 Fill-in the letter name of the notes

3.2 Keyboard Practicing

3.2.1 Classic Mode Keyboard

It includes a piano keyboard that allows users to key in and play songs. When the user presses any key on the keyboard, the corresponding note will be shown in the stave (Fig. 8). The user can also switch to another mode to check for the corresponding letter name for the key being pressed (Fig. 9).

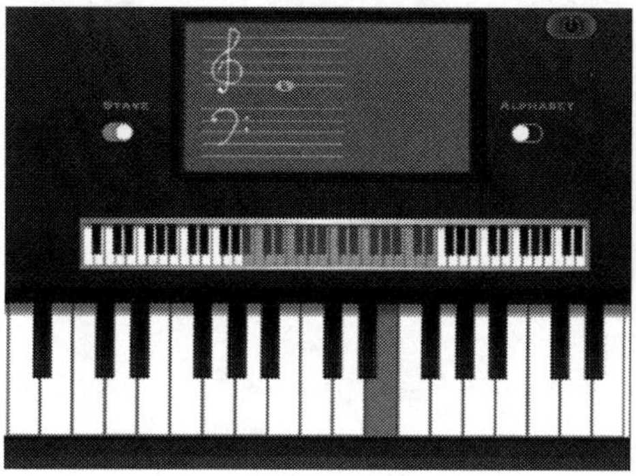

Fig. 8 Keyboard with stave

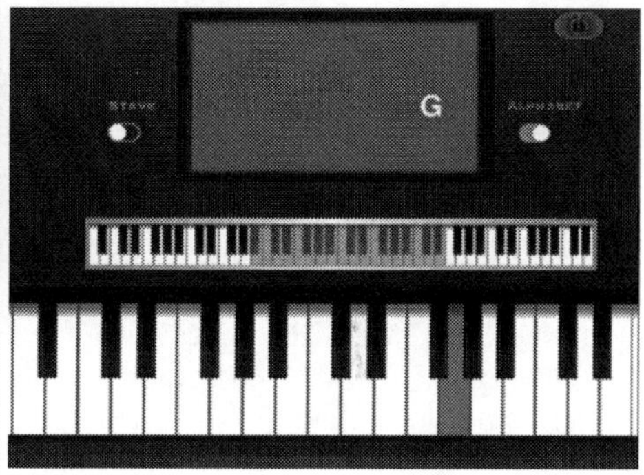

Fig. 9 Keyboard with letter name

3.2.2 Shooting Game

There is a piano game in the section. The boxes are generated from the top of the screen and they will fall slowly onto the keyboard. After the game is started, the user needs to press the key to remove the boxes. If the box is blue, it will drop to one of the white keys. If the box is red, it will drop to one of the black keys. The user should press the correct key as long as the box drops to the blue line (Fig. 10). If the user hit the corresponding key when the box falls on the blue line, it will generate a 'perfect' or 'good' score. When the game is finished, a score view will be shown (Fig. 11). Different states of results including 'perfect', 'good', 'miss', 'wrong' and 'combo' are defined by the using the following rules.

- Perfect
  - ➢ Correct key is pressed
  - ➢ The box is on the blue line when key pressed

Perfect status

- Good
  - ➢ Correct key is pressed
  - ➢ The box is near to the blue line

Good status

Good status

- Miss
  - ➢ The box hits the keyboard without any key pressed
  - ➢ Or the box is too far away from the blue line when key is pressed

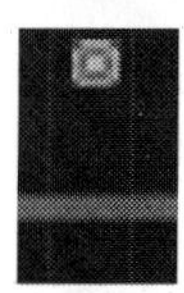

Miss status

- Wrong
  - ■ Incorrect key is pressed
- Combo
  - ■ Continuously get perfect or good status

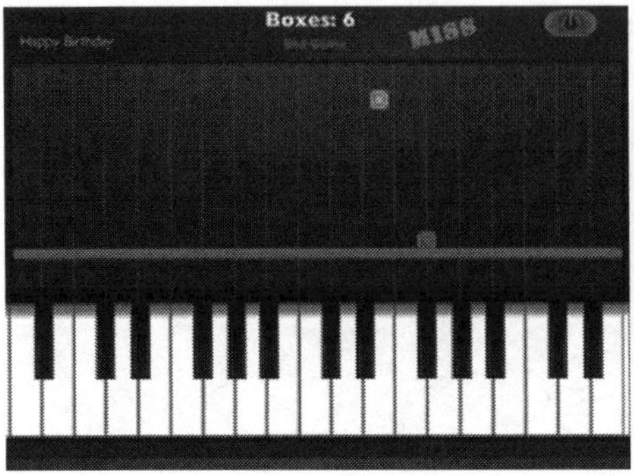

Fig. 10 Keyboard shooting game

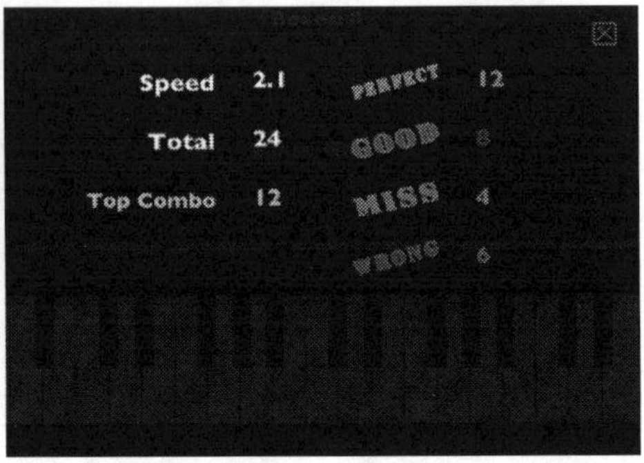

Fig. 11 Results of shooting game

3.2.3 Music Sheet Practice

This feature provides a music sheet to show the notes, the user should follow the notes to play the song written on the music sheet. It allows the user to practise sight reading skill. Users should read and follow the beats and pitches of the notes. When the user starts this feature, the screen will show 8 notes at a time on each line. The user needs to follow the beat and the pitch of the written note to press the corresponding key on the keyboard. There is a red rectangle showing which note the user needs to press (see Fig. 12). When the practice ends, it will show the summary of the correct records and mistakes of the users (as shown in Fig. 13).

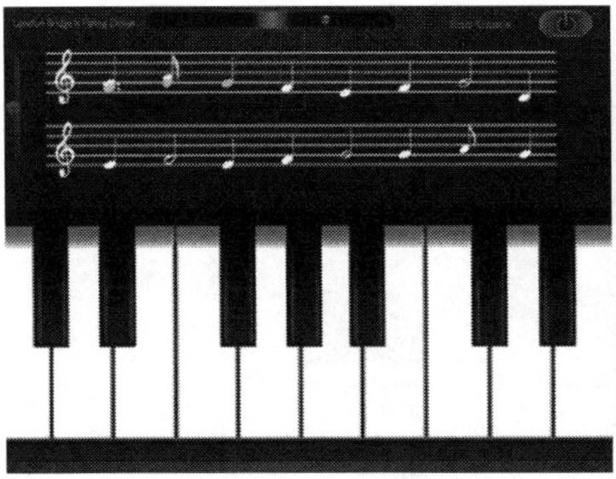

Fig. 12 Music sheet practice

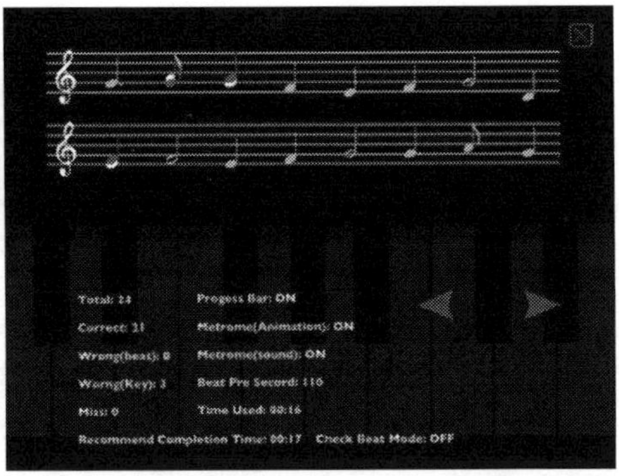

Fig. 13 Score view of music sheet

This feature contains three parts: *music sheet generator*, *user input recognizer*, and *the checking system*. Music sheet generator can either generate a song randomly or read a song from an existing music sheet. After reading a song from a file, the music sheet generator will put all the pitches and beats of the song into an array, it will then calculate the positions of the notes and display them in the stave. The user input recognizer will get the user's input from the keyboard. It will calculate the time between the key pressed and the key released as the beat of the note, then put all the pitches and beats in an array and display them in the stave. The checking system will compare the two arrays from the music sheet generator and the user input recognizer. If the checker finds a note from the user is incorrect, the note will be shown in red colour, else the note will be shown in cyan colour (in Fig. 13). The user can also choose to have metronome available when he or she is playing the music. If the metronome is enabled, it will play "tick" sounds for every one beat. The user can follow the beat to play the music.

3.3 Composer Tool

This feature allows users to compose music onto the music sheet. Users can create a new music sheet or load the existing music sheet to modify. After the user has created a music sheet, he/she can add, edit, insert or delete notes using the buttons shown in Fig. 14. Users can select different types of notes for composing music. Examples of different notes are given in Fig. 15.

Fig. 14 Buttons of the composer

Fig. 15 Example of different notes

The interface for the composer is shown in Fig. 16. User can assign the title of the song and save the file accordingly. The file can be retrieved in Composer tool and also the Music sheet under the "Keyboard practicing". A sample song in the preview mode is shown in Fig. 17.

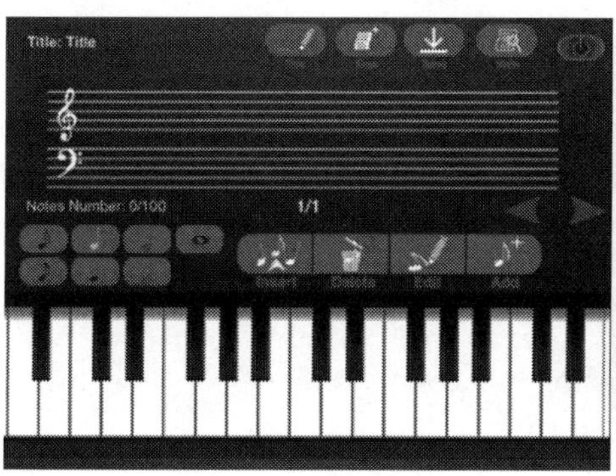

Fig. 16 Interface of the composer

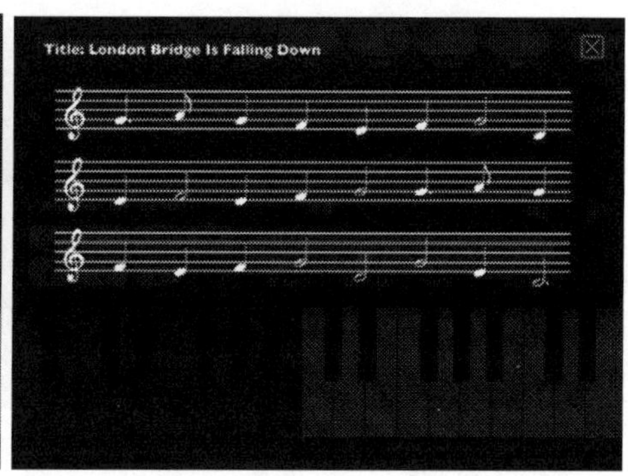

Fig. 17 Music sheet preview in composer

3.4 Listening Exercises

Listening exercises are used to train the aural ability of the users. It is a practice for users to train the ability to discern different tones and chords. There are two levels in the exercises: normal level and hard level.

- Normal level: The system will play a sound randomly selected from any key on the keyboard. The user should listen and then guess the key.
- Hard level: The system will play a chord (three notes that played together simultaneously, when C, E, G played together, it is the C major chord), the user has to distinguish which three notes are being played, and press the corresponding keys.

After the user has listened to notes, he or she needs to guess and enter the key. If the user's answer is correct, a "tick" image will be given. Otherwise, a "cross" image will be given, it will also show the correct keys (Figs. 18 and 19).

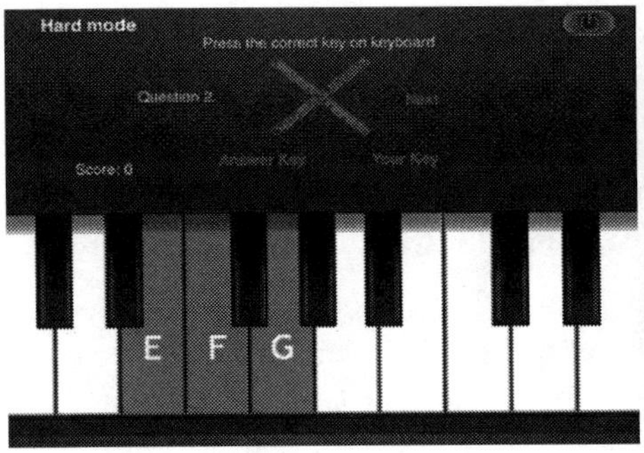

Fig. 18 Wrong user input

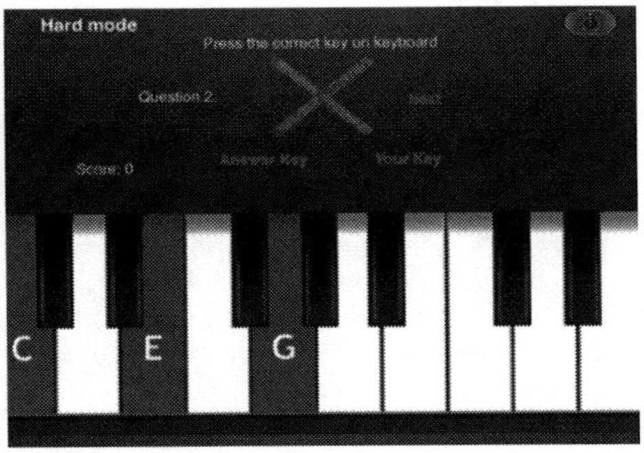

Fig. 19 Correct answer is shown

4 Evaluation

To test the effectiveness of the application, an evaluation was carried out for 20 different users. Their ages are ranged from 18 to 25. Most of the users did not learn piano before. Users were invited to learn music through the application in 1 week time. They are then asked to fill in a questionnaire with eight questions and give feedbacks about the application. Users can choose from the five-level likert scale: 5 (Strongly agree) to 1 (Strongly disagree). Users can give comments and feedbacks on the application in the questionnaire. The questions and the average scores for corresponding questions in the questionnaire are listed in Table 2.

From Table 2, most respondents agreed the music lesson can help them learn basic music theory. However, there are some respondents pointed out that some terminologies are too hard for them. It is better to change them into simple words. Respondents generally agreed that the exercises are useful for the review. The exercises summarized the basic knowledge that the users should grasp, but the exercises did not help them to memorize the concept. The exercises may be modified to focus on how to let the users memorize the basic concept. Respondents agreed that "Music Sheet" can

Table 2. List of questions in the questionnaire

Question	Average score
1. "Music Lesson" in "Learning Materials" can help you learn basic music theory	3.60
2. The exercise in "Learning Material" is useful for review	3.55
3. "Shooting Game" in "Keyboard Practicing" can foster your learning interest in piano	3.60
4. "Music Sheet" in "Keyboard Practicing" can improve your skill of reading music sheet	4.25
5. "Music Sheet" in "Keyboard Practicing" is friendly for beginners	3.05
6. "Composer tool" is user-friendly	3.40
7. You will use "Composer tool" to create music sheet again	4.45
8. "Learning exercise" can improve your abilities of discriminating sound	4.05

improve the skill of sight reading, but there are quite a number of respondents choosing "Neither". To improve the sight reading skill, it takes a long time. It is better to add some simple music sheets and let users start with the easy level. A majority of respondents agreed that the music sheet is friendly for beginners. This tool can help the beginners to play music without any piano skill. It can let beginners get interested in playing piano. Let the user practise and follow the song step by step. Some respondents pointed out that the "composer tool" isn't user-friendly for the first time. Once when the user knows how to use for the first time, he/she thinks that the tools can help users to create a music sheet easily.

Nearly all respondents agreed the "Listening Game" can improve their skill of discriminating sounds. This game is easy to play. Also, most respondents will play it again and again for many times. According to the results, an easy game can attract people to play it. If the user can play it repeatedly, it will improve their skill of discriminating different keys and chords.

Most respondents agreed the "Shooting" game can foster the learning interest of the users in piano. We can't only do practice for learning. Those games are provided for students to arouse their interests in playing piano. The "Shooting" game is a funny keyboard game which can help users to practice and relax at the same time.

5 Conclusion

In this paper, a mobile application to assist the learning of piano is introduced. There are four main parts in the application. "Learning Materials" includes an e-book of the basic music theory and exercises. "Keyboard Practicing" provides a piano keyboard game and piano keyboard practicing. "Composer" provides a tool for users to create a music sheet. "Listening Exercise" provides a listening game for users to discern different tones.

"Learning Materials" can help the users learn the basic music theory, such as knowledge of notes, beat and so on. "Keyboard Practicing" can improve the skills of reading music sheet and playing on the keyboard. "Composer" can let users practice in the use of note and train their creativity. "Listening Game" can help learners to feel the sound and rhythm. It can also train learners to discern different tones.

There is still much room for future development that can enhance the system. The following items are some suggestions:

- Learning materials: Some words in "Music Lesson" are too hard in the current system. The original intention of this function is helping learners in learning. If the words are too hard, it can't help the learners. It will be better to change those words to simple words in the future.
- Keyboard practicing: According to the evaluation, the learners are hard to find a way to do practicing. Some simple music sheets for beginners level can be added, which has only 1 or 2 different pitches in the music sheet only. Also, it will be better to provide a learning guide in the future, let them have a way to follow how to learn piano.
- Composer tool: Currently, the composer tool is not user-friendly for the first time users to use. Most of the users need so much time to find out how to use the functions in the composer. It will be better to add some hint or user guide for the users in the future.

References

1. Wei, Y.: On piano-teaching for children. J. Jiangxi Inst. Educ. **33**(02), 161–163 (2012)
2. Ng, S.C., Lui, A.K., Lo, W.S.: An interactive mobile application for learning music effectively. In: Lam, J., Li, K.C., Cheung, S.K., Wang, F.L. (eds.) ICT 2013. CCIS, vol. 407, pp. 148–157. Springer, Heidelberg (2013)
3. Seddon, F., Biasutti, M.: Evaluating a music e-learning resource: the participants, perspective. Comput. Educ. **53**(3), 541–549 (2009)
4. Jin, X.: On the values and characteristics and education of childrens piano learning. Stud. Preschool Educ. (5), 37–39 (2007)
5. Bragg, J.: Piano for all launches e-learning guide to aid beginners in learning the piano. Marketers Media (2013). Accessed from http://marketersmedia.com/piano-for-all-launches-e-learning-guide-to-aid-beginners-in-learning-the-piano/7624
6. Lewis, M.B.: Teaching sight-reading (2002). Accessed http://www.marthabeth.com/teaching_sight_reading.html
7. Kukulska-Hulme, A.: Will mobile learning change language learning? ReCALL **21**(2), 157–165 (2009)
8. Badrul, H.K.: Components and Features of E-learning, Design, Delivery, Implementation, and Evaluation Managing E-learning, pp. 6–12. Information Science Pub., Hershey (2005)
9. Rubycell: Pianist [Mobile application software] (2015). Accessed https://play.google.com/store/apps/details?id=com.rubycell.pianisthd
10. EDuckAppsSV: Perfect Ear 2 [Mobile application software] (2015). Accessed https://play.google.com/store/apps/details?id=com.evilduck.musiciankit&hl=zh_TW
11. Lotuz Studio: Ensemble composer [Mobile application software] (2014). Accessed https://play.google.com/store/apps/details?id=com.lotuz.musiccomposer

A Bandwidth Saving Mobile Application for e-Learning

Jeff K.T. Tang[1(✉)], Chor-Yi Leung[2], Yuen-Kwan Chan[2], and Chun-Kit Lam[2]

[1] Caritas Institute of Higher Education, 18 Chui Ling Road, Tseung Kwan O, New Territories, Hong Kong, China
jtang@cihe.edu.hk

[2] The Open University of Hong Kong, 30 Good Shepherd Street, Ho Man Tin, Kowloon, Hong Kong, China

Abstract. In this paper, we proposed a bandwidth saving e-learning system for mobile learners who wish to save their bandwidth. In the meantime we provided a more user-friendly and comprehensive administration tool for teachers to prepare and deliver course materials (in form of presentation slides) more efficiently and easily. The teachers can create their presentation slides through the back-end user interface by a few clicks, or upload existing MS Power Point slides onto the system. The slides can be converted into smaller sized files (e.g. compressed image files) that saves the bandwidth of the mobile device of the user. In addition, teachers may record their audio narration in order to give a clearer explanation to the contents. Furthermore, the teacher can monitor the students' learning progress and their performances through the system generated analysis reports. User studies have been conducted to verify whether the app interface is user-friendly for the learners. We have collaborated with Hong Yip (a property management company) and deliver online courses to the front-line workers on trial basis.

Keywords: e-learning · Ubiquitous learning · Teaching materials storage

1 Introduction

A successful mobile learning app should be eye-catching and effective in order to make the learners willing to spend time and pay great attention learning through the app. Most of the time the users are unwilling to read instructions, so an effectively and efficiently app is required such that they can self-learn the content easily without supervision of instructors.

In this paper, we are going to develop a mobile learning app for the front-line property management workers in collaboration with Hong Yip Service Co. Ltd.[1], a local property management company. From time to time, they need to attend training courses about safety and professional development. To be more cost efficient, it is desirable to put the course (as well as the assessment) online. However, the majority of the workers are aged people and most of them are not familiarize with smartphone user interface. Moreover,

---

[1] www.hongyip.com.hk.

J. Lam et al. (Eds.): ICTE 2015, CCIS 559, pp. 113–123, 2015.
DOI: 10.1007/978-3-662-48978-9_11

they mostly use cheap mobile data plan and they are reluctant to download online material for work. These issues became the challenges of our system design.

On the other hand, we need to provide the instructor or course coordinators capabilities to upload and update the course material conveniently and easily. Sometimes, to make the delivery of online course more clearly and less boring, the instructors like to record videos like Coursera[2]. However, movies are always demanding a high bandwidth usage. In our design, we traded off the quality, usability and cost. In addition, it is desirable to record the learners' learning result and allow them to check their progress at any time. In our design, the learners will be asked to take a post-course online test via the app, which will automatically check their performance determine whether they need to retake the course once again.

The paper is organized as follows. We will describe the existing learning systems and related researches in Sect. 2. In Sect. 3, we will introduce our proposed mobile learning app and back-end support system, in the usability point-of-view. The system will be evaluated with a user study described in Sect. 4, followed by a concluding note at Sect. 5.

2 Relevant Studies

2.1 Existing Online Learning Systems

Nowadays, learning online using web-based system or mobile app is very popular. Web-based online learning makes learning way become very different, for example, Metafora [2] is a platform that support "learning to learn together" in science and mathematics education. They support a featured discussion tool that allows general communication and collaboration for teams, their discussion spaces is ability to include snapshots and links to artifacts from the different tools, it enables students learning together and easy to share their comments of the materials and make a record of the comments. This feature makes online learning be more efficiency, but it leads to copyright problems because students download/copy and save the materials to the mobile device but the teachers who own the right cannot control the leakage of their material to outside world.

Another one which also make online learning have discussion is called Teachable Agent [1]. Student can share concept maps in real time by drawing conclusions based on what they have been taught visually through this application. Besides it provides interactive feedback through a chat room, so it can improve their agents' knowledge in real time as well. It is difficult of intelligent tutoring systems to deploy in currently educational platforms without additional work. This limitation is caused by the tutoring system that requires considerable time and resources for their implementation. A new approach to implement open-source and interoperable intelligent tutors is through standardization, which lets tutors be shared, and used by many stakeholders, and easily loaded onto different platforms without using any standardized peripheral systems or databases. It remains a challenge for instructors and teachers to designing, monitoring, and managing their lesson in higher education. Florian-Gaviria et al. [3] used a software

---

[2] https://zh-tw.coursera.org/.

suite that extends course design based on well-defined learning outcomes, monitoring performance and competence acquisition.

The mobile app Lecturio e-Learning [7] can show the details of the lessons so the learners can jump to read/revise particular lessons on demand. However, it mainly uses video for delivering the materials so the users should have good Internet connection. Moreover, there is learning app focusing on one type of course such as IPA e-Learning Platform[3], which is easy and convenient for users to give feedback and send message to teacher for asking question.

Overviewing those existing systems above, we found that all of them have well organized types of lessons by some difference icons, and then user can choose which course they want by icons easily and clearly. But all of them use video to present the lesson mainly so it will require large bandwidth of user's mobile device. We need to solve this problem to match our requirement.

2.2 Related Research

In this sub-section, we will describe the existing work regarding the material content and the methods that save data usage.

Material Content. Regarding to "Progress in International Reading Literacy Study" [11], we found that an item called "Student like reading" which mentions only 21 % of students are interested in reading. As for "Student put in reading" item, 24 % of students put in the lesson only. We found that many people do not like reading.

According to low reading ability, we found that the majority of students are not interested in reading physical materials such as books, newspaper, and printed notes. One of the reasons is that they like the rich contents with multimedia like animations, graphic, or photo more than texts. A lightweight e-learning system should enhance the attractiveness for the students. In addition, most of students do not get enough time for the rest after work. They may fall asleep while viewing the materials with less interesting factors but our resources and materials can improve and enhance the learning and reading interests. Hence, teachers can add multimedia content such as images, audio and interactive functions to the teaching materials.

Bandwidth and Data Usage. Nowadays, it is so popular to use mobile device to access to the Internet and get the information the users need. We have found 2 surveys about bandwidth and data usage of the Internet users which are Mobile Data Usage Survey 2014 and Data plans are the biggest obstacle to mobile video's future.

According to the result of Mobile Data Usage Survey [8], about half of the interviewees own a smartphone. 41 % of the smartphone owners will mostly access mobile apps about social media. However there are only 7 % of the smartphone owners getting content from accessed APPs. Making an app with media for e-learning is a trend so that it can improve the interests of getting online courses for the students. However, the other survey mentions that consumers are increasingly turning to their phones to stream video,

[3] https://play.google.com/store/apps/details?id=com.ipa.elearning.

but there's one major obstacle that still holds many back from watching video on mobile devices while outside of their own home: data plans. Almost half of consumers (46 percent) believe the data cost for accessing video on mobile devices is too high. At the same time, the Mobile Data Usage Survey [8] also mentioned that there are only 20 % of the smartphone owners always or sometimes accessing the Internet on their mobile phone when abroad via a mobile whereas over half of (57 %) them accessing via Wi-Fi. It says that we must solve the problems about media and bandwidth.

Referring the relevant studies, we have concluded some points in our proposed system: Firstly, in order to avoid the copyright problems, we will forbid the student download the learning materials. Moreover, we will not allow the student to capture the screen for stay the materials in the mobile device. Secondly, although discussion tools are good for learning among the students, we will not provide this function for avoid cheating problems. Thirdly we will use multimedia in our app for the sake of attract the students to learn and have an interesting learning experience as they are not interested in plain text or more text than graphics. Finally we have to reduce the data usage of the mobile plan of the users so that they are more willing to use our app. Also, we will avoid using video for teaching materials, so we will use images and audio instead.

3 Proposed System

The front end will show the slides for attend the online course. The App provides a platform for students to learn from the materials created by the teachers. To enter the app, the student should login first. If he/she does not have the account, registration is needed. When the admin accepts the user to take course and the class of the course is started, student can start for the lecture (Fig. 1).

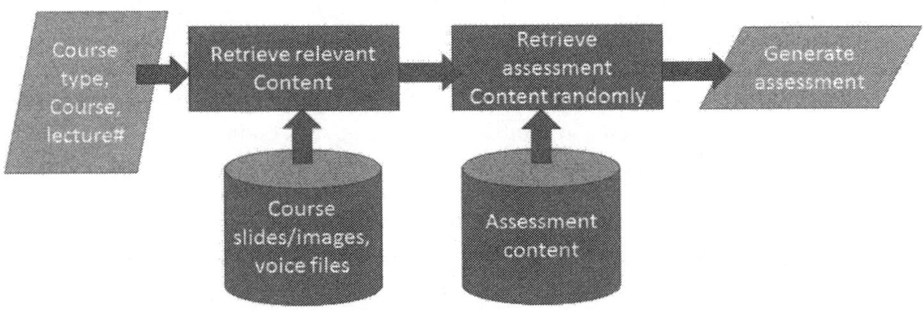

Fig. 1. The workflow of the frontend mobile application.

Student can view the course material, do an assessment to test user's ability and do an evaluation. If the student cannot pass at the first time, he/she can do it once more. Also, he/she can enrol courses before the date starts. Student can view all courses every time they want. Moreover, each student has a profile that shows the user information and detailed assessment result. The student can also set the e-mail notification for being notified about the latest information.

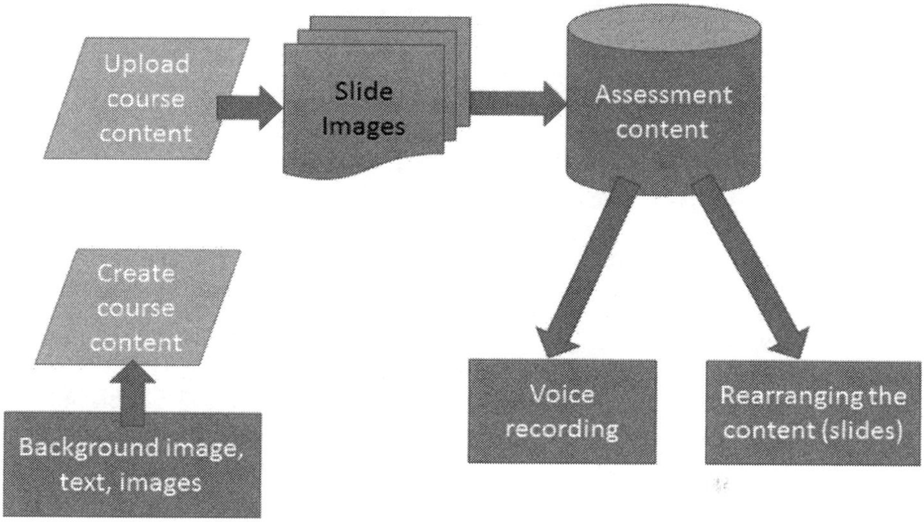

Fig. 2. The workflow of the backend system of material and student management.

The backend system allows teachers to create material and manage students, courses, and classes. Teacher adds a course type of the course and adds a new course. Then, add a course material which a course should have more than one material and create slide or upload material. We also provide material recording online and re-ordering. Teacher can preview all slides. Teacher needs to set questions for assessment and evaluation before students start to take the course and finally to create classes with different date periods for students to enrol the course. Teacher can accept or decline the enrolment in the system. In addition, teacher can view the report for checking the assessment results, user log and evaluation results. Besides, each teacher will have their permission which is handled by the system administrator (Fig. 2).

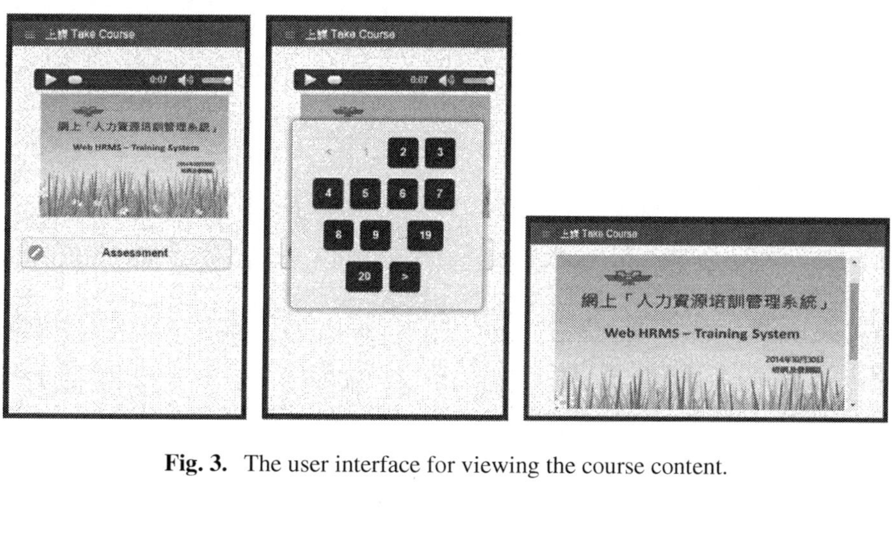

Fig. 3. The user interface for viewing the course content.

3.1 Student Attend the Online Course

The student will get into the slide for the course. There is an audio bar on the top, and the assessment button on the bottom. Figure 3 shows the user interface. Each slide gets one audio recording of the content. While the student have done enough reading, he/she can take the assessment anytime afterwards. When the student clicks on the image, the page numbers will pop up whereas they will hide when the student reads the material. The student can rotate the monitor 90 degrees in order to read a larger slide (full screen mode), which is clearer and more comfortable for aged readers.

3.2 Teacher's Material Handling

The major functions of backend system are creating, uploading, recording and managing the course contents. Our system allows the users to upload Microsoft PowerPoint file, and it will convert its slides into separated compressed image files. Besides, our system provides web tools for the teachers to create content (slides) on demand. They can insert

Fig. 4. The user interface for uploading the course content.

Fig. 5. The user interface for creating course content.

text, images and background to a pre-defined template, and then saved into an image file. The system also allow the teachers to record their voices that would play along showing a slide. The teachers can view and rearrange the slide sequence by simply drag-and-drop the slide and move them to the desired positions (Figs. 4, 5, 6, and 7).

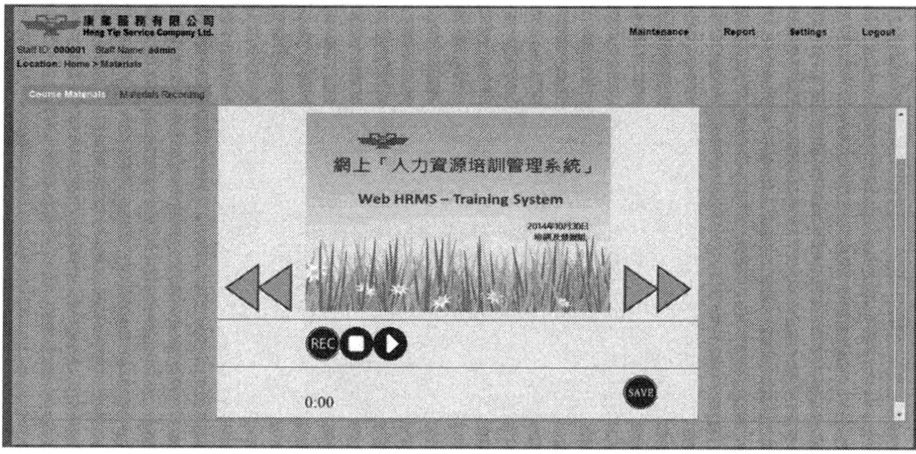

Fig. 6. The user interface for recording the teacher's voice.

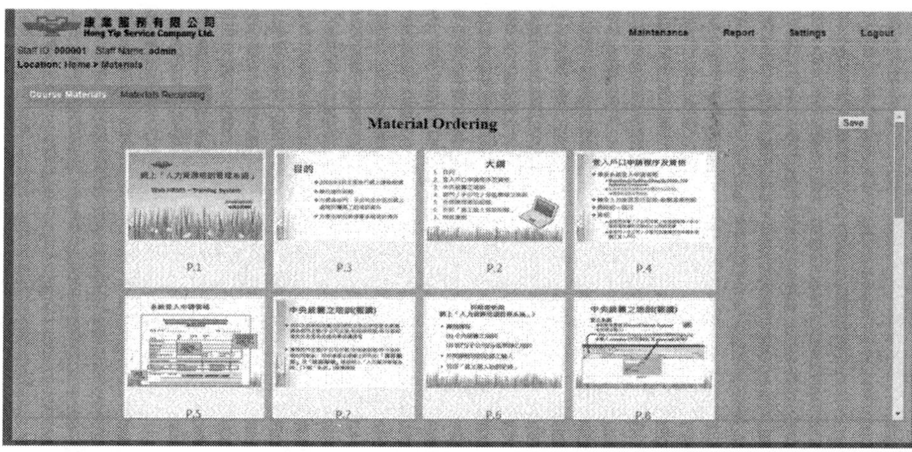

Fig. 7. The interface for rearranging the sequence of content/slides.

4 System Evaluation

We have conducted two sets of experiments in order to evaluate the system in both subjective and objective ways. Firstly, we conducted a user study with a post-test questionnaire; followed by a performance evaluation that verifies whether the course material (converted from PPT) are actually smaller in storage size.

The user study aims at capturing the users' feeling and opinions through answering a questionnaire after using our proposed system. So, we called it the post-testing questionnaire. Table 1 shows the 10 statements used in the questionnaire. The users are told to rate in a 7 point scale: the larger the score, the more they agree with the statement.

Table 1. The questions in the questionnaire.

No	Statement
1	It helps me be more effective
2	It does everything I would expect it to do
3	It makes the things I want to accomplish easier to get done
4	I can use it without written instructions
5	I can recover from mistakes quickly and easily
6	It is user friendly
7	I easily remember how to use it
8	I am satisfied with it
9	It works the way I want it to work
10	I feel I need to have it

4.1 The Result of the Post-test Questionnaire

The overall user study result is shown in Fig. 8. We have evaluate the feedback by 20 users, who are told to rate the questionnaire statements after using the front-end mobile app that designed for the front-line property management workers. The bold dotted horizontal line represents a threshold $T = 4$, where score $> T$ means the user had a good feeling otherwise the user felt bad. For each item, a score above/below this line means the users felt positive/negative about our app. Overall, the users are positive about our app, as the average score is 5.905 for all questions, which is above the goodness threshold T. Hence, in overall the users are feeling positive to our mobile learning app.

Let us see their feedback in detail. Question 7 received the highest average score. This means the users considered our app is easy to remember how to use. It proved that the design of our app is concise, in which the users do not click many times with complicated steps to go to the pages that the users want. In Question 1, 65 % users gave 7 marks that means they agree the app help them be more effective in learning. It proved that our app filled up the expectations of the front-line workers. In Question 5, many users gave 4 to 6 marks mainly. We considered that some users might not know well about the app in the first time. There is still a room to improve as particular user feedback that some steps were not so easy to remember for them.

Next, we are going to discuss the evaluation result of the backend system for administrator users. Similarly, we invited 20 users to try out the backend. For each item, a

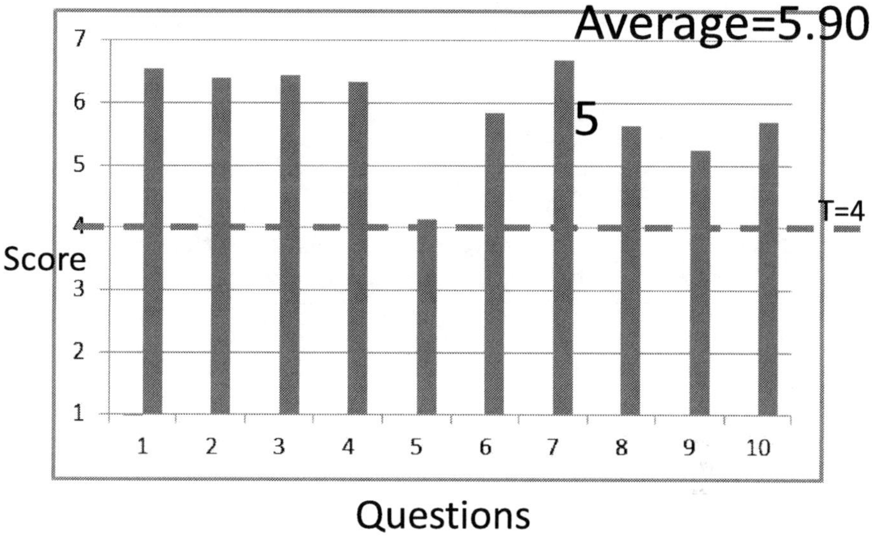

Fig. 8. The result of the feeling about front-end.

score above/below this line means the users felt positive/negative about our system. In overall, the users are positive about our system, as the average score is 5.28 for all questions, which is also high above the goodness threshold T (Fig. 9).

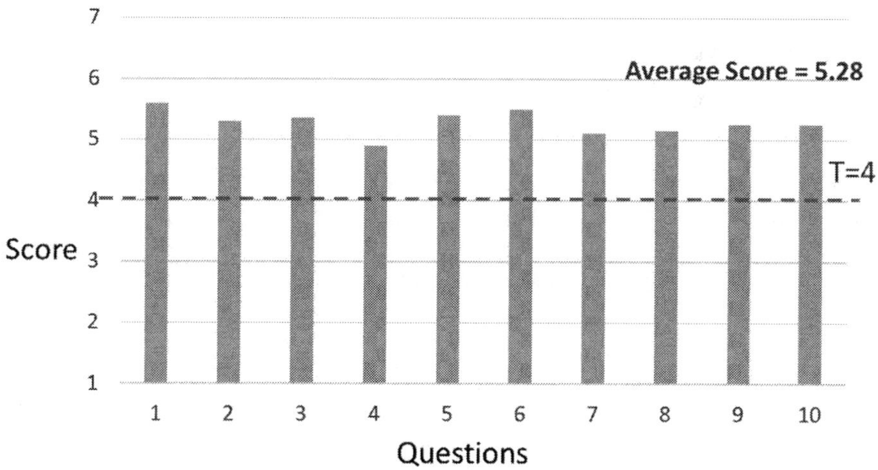

Fig. 9. The result of the feeling about back-end.

In Question 1, many users gave 6 marks that means they agreed the system could help them to create/manage course content more effectively. In Question 6, users considered our system is user friendly, which 55 % users give 6–7 marks. It proved that the design of our backend utility is concise enough. Users do not click many times with complicated steps to go to the page that the users want. However, Question 4 received an average score of 4.9 only. It seems it is needed to show more instruction and guides in the administrator's page because many functions are provided and they may easily get lost in the first time they used the system.

4.2 Performance Evaluation

Finally, we conducted a performance evaluation to verify the performance of reducing storage size of course materials. Table 2 shows the evaluation result.

Table 2. The performance of reducing the sizes of the course materials.

Power point type	Number of samples	Average size
Mainly text	10	Before upload: 785 KB
		After upload: 509 KB
		Size reduced: 35 %
Text and picture	10	Before upload: 1.15 MB
		After upload: 458.5 KB
		Size reduced: 61 %
Mainly picture	10	Before upload: 6.39 MB
		After upload: 360.9 KB
		Size reduced: 94 %

Our system could convert MS PowerPoint files into compressed images. We try to upload 10 PowerPoint files for each type of testing PowerPoint samples, which are Mainly Text, Text and Picture, and Mainly Picture, so there are total 30 PowerPoint file. As you see the results of all the type of PowerPoint files have good performance to reduce average size after uploading, and we know that mainly image files have the best performance on reducing size that it can reduce 94 % average size.

5 Conclusion

In this paper, we proposed a mobile learning app that aims at saving the amount of data to be downloaded by the front-line property management workers. Besides, an easy to use and effective backend user interface is implemented for teachers/instructors to create, upload, edit course material and record audio content. According to the results of the user studies, the users are feeling positive to our proposed system (both frontend and backend). Especially, they felt easy to use and their needs (such as saving mobile data) are satisfied. However, more instructions are demanded by both the backend and frontend users, which can be part of our future enhancement of the system. Finally, the performance evaluation showed the size of course materials are reduced efficiently (up to 94 %).

In the future, we will deploy the system to Hong Yip in their coming training courses. So, in the next step we will study how to enhance the security when this system goes live on Internet. In a long run, this system will stored a vast amount of learners' data. We will apply Big-data method to analyse the behaviours of the workers, such as the learning attitude and how serious when they were taking online course.

References

1. Chin, D.B., Dohmen, I.M., Schwartz, D.L.: Young children can learn scientific reasoning with teachable agents. IEEE Trans. Learn. Technol. **6**(3), 248–257 (2013)
2. Dragon, T., Mavrikis, M., McLaren, B.M., Harrer, A., Kynigos, C., Wegerif, R., Yang, Y.: Metafora: a web-based platform for learning to learn together in science and mathematics. IEEE Trans. Learn. Technol. **6(3)**, 197–207 (2013)
3. Florian-Gaviria, B., Glahn, C., Gesa, R.F.: A software suite for efficient use of the European qualifications framework in online and blended courses. IEEE Trans. Learn. Technol. **6**(3), 283–296 (2013)
4. Santos, G.S., Jorge, J.: Interoperable intelligent tutoring systems as open education resources. IEEE Trans. Learn. Technol. **6**(3), 271–282 (2013). Guidance on Preparing Personal Information Collection Statement and Privacy Policy Statement. https://www.pcpd.org.hk/english/publications/files/GN_picspps_e.pdf
5. Johnson, J.: Designing with the Mind in Mind: Simple Guide to Understanding User Interface Design Rules. © 2010 Elsevier Inc., Burlington (2010). (P. 37, Fig 3.5)
6. Krug, S.: Don't Make Me Think, Revisited: A Common Sense Approach to Web Usability. Pearson Education, US (2013)
7. Lecturio e-Learning (2015). https://play.google.com/store/apps/details?id=de.lecturio.android
8. Mobile Data Usage Survey 2014 – Results. https://www.mca.org.mt/sites/default/files/attachments/surveys/2014/mobile-data-usage-survey-2014.pdf
9. Parker, S.: The Web Designer's 101 Most Important Decisions: Professional Secrets for Winning Website, 2HOW Books (2012)
10. Plumley, G.: Website Design and Development: 100 Questions to Ask Before Building a Website. John Wiley & Sons, Hoboken (2010). (Character 5)
11. Post-testing questionnaire's question setting, Daniel K. Schneider. http://edutechwiki.unige.ch/en/Usability_and_user_experience_surveys
12. Seckler, M., Heinz, S., Bargas-Avila, J.A., Opwis, K., Tuch, AN.: Designing usable web forms: empirical evaluation of web form improvement guidelines. In: CHI 2014, One of a CHInd, Toronto (2014)
13. The Progress in International Reading Literacy Study (PIRLS). Institute of Education Science (2011). https://nces.ed.gov/surveys/pirls/. Accessed, dated 31 July 2015

Open Learning and Online Learning

A Big Data Framework for Early Identification of Dropout Students in MOOC

Jeff K.T. Tang[1], Haoren Xie[2], and Tak-Lam Wong[3(✉)]

[1] School of Computing and Information Sciences, Caritas Institute of Higher Education, Hong Kong, China
jtang@cihe.edu.hk

[2] Centre for Excellence, Caritas Institute of Higher Education, Hong Kong, China
hrxie2@gmail.com

[3] Department of Mathematics and Information Technology, The Hong Kong Institute of Education, Hong Kong, China
tlwong@ied.edu.hk

Abstract. Massive Open Online Courses (MOOC) became popular and they posted great impact to education. Students could enroll and attend any MOOC anytime and anywhere according to their interest, schedule and learning pace. However, the dropout rate of MOOC was known to be very high in practice. It is desirable to discover students who have high chance to dropout in MOOC in early stage, and the course leader could impose intervention immediately in order to reduce the dropout rate. In this paper, we proposed a framework that applies big data methods to identify the students who are likely to dropout in MOOC. Real-world data were collected for the evaluation of our proposed framework. The results demonstrated that our framework is effective and helpful.

Keywords: MOOC · Big data · Dropout rate · Decision tree

1 Introduction

Massive Open Online Courses (MOOC) caught much attention from the education society in recent years [1, 9]. Coursera[1], edX[2], and Khan Academy[3] are three examples of well-known MOOC online platforms. Students are able to enroll and attend any online courses at anytime and anywhere through the MOOC mobile app. An MOOC contains a series of lessons that scheduled in a number of weeks that is similar to traditional face-to-face lectures. The course materials are normally delivered in the form of online videos. Hence, the students can attend the lessons by watching the videos according to their own learning progress.

[1] www.coursera.org.
[2] www.edx.org.
[3] www.khanacademy.org.

J. Lam et al. (Eds.): ICTE 2015, CCIS 559, pp. 127–132, 2015.
DOI: 10.1007/978-3-662-48978-9_12

According to the figures released by Coursera, they have got over 22 million[4] users around the world. It shows that MOOC have already achieves an extremely high penetration and attracts a huge number of learners. However, the dropout rate of in MOOC is also known to be very high. The completion rate for most courses is lower than 13 % even though several thousands of participants enrolled on these courses [11]. Such a high dropout rate becomes a barrier for the success of MOOC because too many students failed to complete their study through it. As a result, this raises the need to identify the factors leading to the dropouts from MOOC. Early identification of those students who are likely to dropout allows lecturers to provide assistance or remedial measures to them.

In this paper, we aim at applying big data technique to predict the students who have high chance to dropout or discontinue of learning in MOOC. In essence, decision tree model, which is an automatic classification method, is applied to identify the potential dropout students. Early intervention such as email reminder, additional remedial measures, can then be provided in order to keep the students to continue their learning.

2 Related Work

Big data methods are techniques for automatically or semi-automatically analyzing data-rich environment such as huge marketing databases as well as fast-changing and dynamic financial data [6]. In human factor point-of-view, the features of community activity as well as individual activity can be identified by big data method [15]. Big data method helps to analyze the data collected by various sources, and then predict the potential challenges, which is useful for higher education institutions to make decisions [4].

Recently, educational big data analysis is able to discover useful knowledge or interesting patterns from the unique type of data coming from educational settings, became an emerging research area [2, 12, 13]. For example, different methods have been utilized to analyze the online course management system data to discover student usage patterns [14]. Another example is to discover genres of online discussion threads [8]. Besides, the students' behavior can be identified by analyzing their history click-stream data with SVD [7].

A recent research predicts the instructor's intervention in the discussion forums on MOOC, and it shows machine learning methods such as Linear Chain Markov Model, Global Chain Model, Logistic regression, and Decision Tree are usable in such kind of prediction task [3].

3 Proposed Method

In order to identify potential dropout students in MOOC, we have developed an automatic framework[5]. Figure 1 shows the overview of the proposed framework. Essentially, our framework considers the historical data of MOOC.

---

[4] https://www.coursera.org/about/community, retrieved on 1 September 2015.

[5] We employed Weka, which is an open-source data mining tools to implement our framework. (URL: http://www.cs.waikato.ac.nz/ml/weka/).

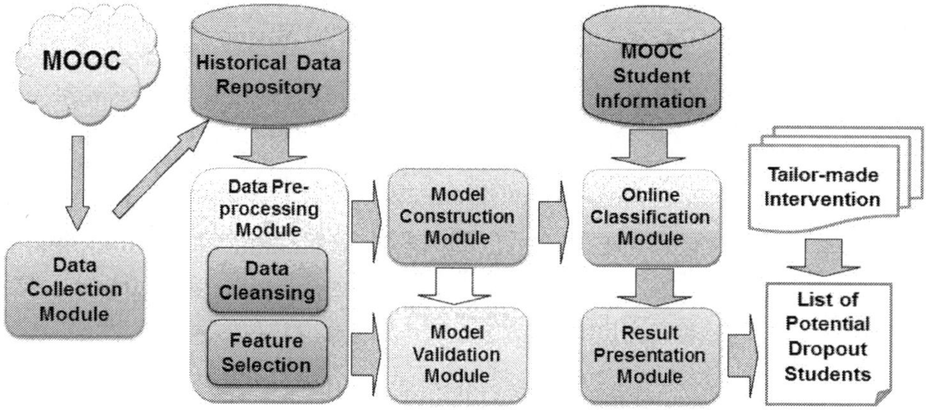

Fig. 1. Overview of our framework.

Each entry of the data refers to an enrollment of a student to a course and other relevant information. These historical data will be used to automatically construct a classification model to identify the potential dropout students. After obtaining a trained classification model, this model can then be applied in an ongoing MOOC to predict the students who have high chance to dropout from the course. Appropriate intervention can then be made by the lecturer to retain students' learning. In particular, our framework consists of the following modules:

Data Collection Module: Each MOOC consists of information including the course details and the students' enrollment information. This module serves as the interface between MOOC platforms for collecting all information available in the MOOC. The collected data will be stored in a historical data repository. Each entry of the data contains a list of features corresponding to the demographical information, enrollment information, activity information of the student in a MOOC, etc.

Data Pre-processing Module: The data collected from MOOC may contain incomplete or inconsistent information due to input errors by human or missing values. These noise and incomplete information may lead to inaccurate predication in later processing. This module aims at creating a set of informative and meaningful data for the construction of the classification model. It is composed of two sub-modules, namely Data Cleansing Sub-Module and Feature Selection Sub-Module.

Data Cleansing Sub-Module: Since the collected raw data by the data collection module may consist of noisy and incomplete data. For example, some MOOC students may not fill in their gender, age, etc. when creating accounts. This results in missing values in some features, and affect to classification performance. Such adverse effect can be reduced by, for example, filling the most frequent value or average value for the missing feature. On the other hand, discretization, which divides a feature of continuous values into a number of discrete groups, may need to be conducted on some of the features such as age, so that the collected data can be feed to the classification model construction module.

Feature Selection Sub-Module: After data cleansing, feature selection needs to be conducted to remove some uninformative features. For example, some features such as the time average time interval between watching videos may be useful and indicative for predicting the dropout of a student, while some other features such as the gender may not be indicative. Using non-indicative features in prediction may reduce the efficiency of the model training process, or even degrade the performance. Feature selection can be carried out by using typical feature selection methods like Chi-Square method or information gain method.

Model Construction Module: One essential step in our framework is to train an effective prediction model to predict dropout of some new students in a MOOC. The trained model can then be applied to predict how likely a student will dropout in a MOOC. The Model Construction Module aims at applying data mining techniques to construct a classification model by making use of the training examples, which are pre-processed data from the historical data repository. As described above, the model will consider those features which are expected to be useful and indicative after the invoking the Data Pre-processing Module. In particular, we employed a decision tree method, namely, ADTree [5], to accomplish the classification task.

Model Validation Module: To ensure that the predicted model trained in the Model Construction Module is effective, this module will test the accuracy of the constructed classification model by making use of the validation data. The validation data are historical data, but not used in the construction of the classification model. In practice, we will divide the set of historical data into training data, which is used in Model Construction Module, and validation data, which is used in this Model Validation Module. Only the validated prediction model achieving certain classification accuracy will be adopted in actual application.

Online Classification Module: Once a prediction model has been trained and validated, it can be applied to predict the potential dropout students. The ongoing information of students of MOOC will be the input to this module. The validated prediction model will be applied to predict the potential dropout students. The results consist of a list of students who have high chance to dropout.

Result Presentation Module: A graphical user interface is used to present the resulting list of potential dropout students. This interface allows the lecturer to browse the information of the potential dropout students who are automatically predicted by the system. The lecturer can then decide appropriate actions to retain the students' learning.

4 Experiment

To demonstrate the effectiveness of our framework, we implemented a prototype and conducted experiments to evaluate our framework. We collected real-world MOOC dataset for the experiments to evaluate our framework [10]. This release of dataset is comprised of de-identified data from MITx and HarvardX courses on the edX platform. The dataset consists of over 600,000 entries, each of which refers to a student-course enrollment information. The dropout information of each entry is also included for evaluation purpose in the experiment.

The objective is to evaluate the performance in predicting the dropout students in the dataset by our framework. In this experiment, the entire set of data was randomly divided into two portions. Two-third of data was treated as training examples in the model construction module and the model validation module for constructing the classification model. The remaining one-third of data was treated as testing data. In the testing data, the dropout information of the data is excluded to simulate the real MOOC setting. The dropout information of the testing data is only used in the evaluation of the performance of our framework. Next, the constructed prediction model was then used to classify the potential dropout students in the testing data. This procedure was conducted repeated for 10 times, aiming at obtaining a more objective performance results.

We measured the performance of our framework by adopting the evaluation metric accuracy, which is equal to the actual number of dropout students who are correctly predicted by the system in the testing data divided by the predicted number of dropout students in the testing data. Our framework achieves an average accuracy of 94.9 % in the dataset.

5 Conclusion

We developed a framework which applied a big data technique, namely decision tree, to automatically identify the potential dropout students in MOOC. We evaluated the performance of our framework using real-world dataset. The results demonstrated that our framework is effective and helpful. Lecturers can decide necessary actions based on the prediction to retain the students in MOOC.

The proposed framework can be applied to predict other student behaviors. Similarly, the learning paths, participation etc. of individual student can be predicted. In this sense, students who have high potential failing the course could be spotted out in early stage and hence the lecturers can take care of these students more.

As future work, it would be interesting to incorporate some visualization technologies to demonstrate the results. Besides, our framework will be evaluated with different data mining and machine learning methods and the best model for predicting the student dropout could be determined. Moreover, the individual learning needs and paces of students could be catered as their individual learning paths are identified with data mining techniques.

Acknowledgement. This work is partially supported by the Small Research Grant (MIT/SRG10/14-15) and the Internal Research Grant (IRG 30/2014-2015) of the Hong Kong Institute of Education.

References

1. Alraimi, K.M., Zo, H., Ciganek, A.P.: Understanding the MOOCs continuance: the role of openness and reputation. Comput. Educ. **80**, 28–38 (2015)
2. Baker, R.S., Yacef, K.: The state of educational data mining in 2009: a review and future visions. J. Educ. Data Min. **1**(1), 3–17 (2009)
3. Chaturvedi, S., Goldwasser, D., Daume III, H.: Predicting instructor's intervention in mooc forums. In: Proceedings of the 52nd Annual Meeting of the Association for Computational Linguistics, pp. 1501–1511. ACL (2014)
4. Daniel, B., Butson, R.: Foundations of big data and analytics in higher education. In: International Conference on Analytics Driven Solutions: ICAS 2014, p. 39. Academic Conferences Limited (2014)
5. Freund, Y., Mason, L.: The alternating decision tree learning algorithm. In: Proceeding of the Sixteenth International Conference on Machine Learning, pp. 124–133 (1999)
6. Han, J., Kamber, M., Pei, J.: Data Mining: Concepts and Techniques. Morgan Kaufmann, San Francisco (2005)
7. Kloft, M., Stiehler, F., Zheng, Z., Pinkwart, N.: Predicting MOOC dropout over weeks using machine learning methods. In: Proceedings of the EMNLP Workshop on Modeling Large Scale Social Interaction in Massively Open Online Courses, pp. 60–65 (2014)
8. Lin, F.-R., Hsieh, L.-S., Chuang, F.-T.: Discovering genres of online discussion threads via text mining. Comput. Educ. **52**(2), 481–495 (2009)
9. Margaryan, A., Bianco, M., Littlejohn, A.: Instructional quality of massive open online courses (MOOCs). Comput. Educ. **80**, 77–83 (2015)
10. MITx and HarvardX. HarvardX-MITx Person-Course Academic Year 2013 De-Identified dataset, version 2.0 (2014). http://dx.doi.org/10.7910/DVN/26147
11. Onah, D.F.O., Sinclair, J., Boyatt, R.: Dropout rates of massive open online courses: behavioural patterns. In: Proceedings of the Sixth International Conference on Education and New Learning Technologies, pp. 5825–5834 (2014)
12. Rabbany, R., Takaffoli, M., Zaiane, O.: Analyzing participation of students in online courses using social network analysis techniques. In: Proceedings of Educational Data Mining, pp. 21–30 (2011)
13. Romero, C.: Educational data mining: a review of the state of the art. IEEE Trans. Syst. Man Cybern. Part C Appl. Rev. **60**(6), 601–618 (2010)
14. Romero, C., Ventura, S., Garcia, E.: Data mining in course management systems: moodle case study and tutorial. Comput. Educ. **51**(1), 368–384 (2008)
15. Zhang, Y., Chen, M., Mao, S., Hu, L., Leung, V.: CAP: crowd activity prediction based on big data analysis. IEEE Netw. **28**(4), 52–57 (2014)

Do Massive Open Online Courses Offer a Viable Solution for Essential Problems in Higher Education?

Ali Simsek(✉)

Institute of Communication Sciences, Anadolu University,
Yunus Emre Campus, Eskisehir, Turkey
asimsek@anadolu.edu.tr

Abstract. Higher education institutions have been suffering from serious problems for decades. Many reform programs have been implemented to overcome these problems. Some of the solutions have worked well but others have failed. As a promising initiative, the movement of massive open online courses (MOOCs) has generated enormous excitement among educators. Many prestigious universities have created educational partnerships and offered MOOCs worldwide. The market has been expanded with the joining of commercial establishments, and millions of students around the world have registered to such courses. However, the average completion rate is extremely low and a great majority the students attend these courses for enjoyment than for credentials. Similarly, almost none of the universities, which include the leading providers, do not recognize the credits earned through these courses for their diploma programs. There is also a serious concern that MOOCs may cause hegemony of the Ivy League institutions on other universities.

Keywords: Distance education · Massive open online courses · Higher education · Online learning · Open educational resources · Educational technology

1 Introduction

The field of education has gone through serious transformations in the last several decades. Almost all elements and aspects of education have changed dramatically. Along with many other factors, emerging technologies have played a vital role in this process. With the help of omnipotent and omniscient technologies, educational services have been provided with greater audiences regardless of their personal and social conditions. Students have also received better education which is sensitive to their individual differences and circumstances. In other words, both the reach and the quality of education have been improved at a global scale.

On the other hand, it is still a heart-breaking reality that hundreds of millions of school-age children do not have access to elementary education. More than half of the students completing the elementary school cannot proceed to the secondary school for a variety of reasons. The access rate in higher education is disappointingly low. Particularly developing countries lack sufficient physical and financial resources to provide proper education to their citizens. However, they have been seeking solutions for these problems and many of them are keen to take advantage of new educational technologies.

J. Lam et al. (Eds.): ICTE 2015, CCIS 559, pp. 133–142, 2015.
DOI: 10.1007/978-3-662-48978-9_13

Higher education has a highly strategic role in the knowledge society. Particularly universities conduct research to produce scientific information, teach the most valid knowledge to their students, and disseminate up-to-date information to all segments of the society by various means. Although these are the fundamental functions of universities worldwide, they have not been very successful in performing relevant tasks. Therefore, universities have been working on developing alternative approaches and means to serve the world better.

Massive open online courses (MOOCs) have received considerable interest among educators as a promising alternative to provide more and better learning opportunities to global audiences. Many universities have established partnerships with both public and private institutions to offer MOOCs. Millions of students around the world have registered to thousands of such courses. New York Times called 2012 "The Year of the MOOC" [4]. Advocates of MOOCs often claim that this virtually unprecedented movement will change higher education completely by supporting small universities and allowing their students to take courses from more prestigious universities [9]. On the other hand, critics of MOOCs emphasize that this movement may cause the hegemony of well-financed and globally-recognized Ivy League institutions on insufficiently-supported and less-reputable universities around the world without solving the essential problems [7].

This paper analyzes the promises and realities of the MOOCs movement for higher education. First, it discusses essential problems of higher education. Secondly, it describes potentials of MOOCs for solutions of these problems. Third, it presents the evidence whether MOOCs really provide effective solutions. Finally, it draws some conclusions and makes recommendations for possible courses of actions in order to improve MOOCs in higher education.

2 Essential Problems in Higher Education

Higher education has long been experiencing serious problems. Although the areas and arrays of the problems have stayed relatively same, the intensity and priority of the problems have changed from time to time. Consequently, institutional efforts and actions toward possible solutions for essential problems have focused on the nature and impact of the current problems. When one looks at the field of higher education from outside, today's challenges appear not to be different from yesterday's struggles. However, an insider may convincingly argue how and why yesterday's solutions may not be valid for today's problems.

There are a number of problems regarding higher education at the global scale today. All problems have negative effects on functioning of universities one way or another. Some do not directly affect educational services but the others are at the core of educational applications. The following appear to be the most essential challenges that higher education faces today.

Increasing student enrollments: The number of students has constantly increased and physical resources have not been sufficient to provide quality education for them. As a result, class sizes are getting bigger and bigger. Then the simple rule works: the larger the class size, the lesser the interaction. Considering that today's students demand more flexibility and higher interactivity, their motivation and satisfaction will be low in large classes. In addition to burgeoning number of student enrollments, student demographics have also changed. However, universities do not appear to recognize dramatic shift in student demographics. The fact is clear: Today's typical student is no longer an 18 to 24 year old studying full-time on a campus. In fact, there is strong evidence that fewer than 20 % of the existing student population fit the traditional description of a college student [1]. The majority of students are young adults, working part-time, and expecting to receive their education through Internet-based technologies [7]. Yet, higher education institutions still provide services based on the assumed needs of a shrinking minority.

Financial crisis: Universities have been in the midst of a financial crisis for some time and they do not know how to find additional resources or generate new revenues to balance their budgets. The highest cost increases have been at public colleges and universities where more than three quarters of students are enrolled. State funding for higher education is generally shrinking. Because the governments are not capable of providing further funding due to their other obligations, universities should either reduce their expenses or use available resources more efficiently, which is not an easy task. Efforts to balance the budgets have eventually resulted in more cuts in services and less spending. Many universities are seeking alternative ways of reducing costs by developing technology-based courses.

Difficulty in hiring talented faculty: It is not easy to hire and keep talented faculty members with limited financial resources and traditional employment policies. Many small or mid-size universities cannot compete with nationally and internationally renowned universities in getting distinguished faculty members. It is simply because their offers do not match personal expectations of established professors. Then, what happens? Big universities select the prominent scholars, and small universities get the rest. This certainly affects the reputation and quality. It is not a coincidence that most of the technology-based instructional innovations have emerged in top universities that employed the gifted scholars.

Lack of focus on education: It appears that education is not the focus of many universities. Faculty members concentrate more on research and publications than teaching and supervision due to requirements of the tenure policies. Performance indicators encourage the faculty assign higher value to producing more publications than teaching better courses. Of course, students suffer from this preference because having a strong publication record does not necessarily translate to being a talented instructor due to the absence of serious pedagogy. Thus, it is often emphasized that professors should value good teaching as well as good research. In order for this to happen, pedagogical support for professors should be increased toward creating a paradigm shift in their mental sets as well as academic priorities.

Circumventing instructional design: A typical university course is offered just because the faculty member is an expert in the relevant area. There is no such thing as "instructional design" when offering a new course in the departmental curriculum. Actually, some institutions use the concept of 'course development' but it generally refers to planning a course, getting the approval from relevant bodies, and listing that course in the curriculum without giving serious attention to instructional elements. What happens after several years? They cannot find time to improve their courses for the workload of professors is heavy.

Inadequate use of technology: University learning is usually linear, one fits all. An instructor delivers the lecture to all students in a big auditorium and expects that all students benefit from it regardless of their differences. This is not acceptable to the generation of digital natives who would like to get their education anywhere, anytime, and anyway based on their own needs and circumstances. For example, why does typical university education last for four years? It is too long for many students who have lots of life experiences and learning credentials. Self-directed learning and virtual curriculum may be effective solutions in this regard. Ample evidence of research suggests that self-determination is a primary motive for humans. Why not give higher education students more power to explore their passions and determine their own learning? Well, this may be appealing to say but research also suggest that students should be educated about learning strategies and best educational practices before given complete control over their learning. One should not forget that there are also problems with instructors' technology skills. Low digital fluency among faculty, lack of rewards for teaching through technology, and competition from new models of teaching (online versus offline) may be discouraging.

Restrictive assessment of learning outcomes: Most university courses aim at increasing general awareness of students without considering specific competencies or learning outcomes. Universities educate/train their students for skills needed for employment in the work life. However, employers often do not often find needed skills in graduates and feel that they have to retrain them. This is called "workforce development" for closing the skills gap. It is frequently suggested that educators and employers should focus on what the university is producing and how it measures up. There is much to be done here. There is a wide variety of highly reliable, valid, and commonly accepted assessment tools and methods that can be employed to evaluate knowledge and skill acquisition.

Rudimentary accreditation and quality assurance: Accreditation is generally concerned with granting equivalency to similar learning within an academic institution. Accreditation reform appears to be one of the few issues that universities agree on to assure quality both within and among programs. There is also growing consensus that a need exists for acceptable standards and greater transparency in the process for determining the credit worthiness of learning attained outside the academy. This means that all courses and programs should be accredited in order to be accounted for credits at the level of higher education.

International partnerships with commercial interests: On the one hand, more institutions in North America and Western Europe find themselves looking at enrollment shortfalls due to declining number of high school graduates. On the other hand, a limited number of universities in developing countries cannot meet the growing demand for higher education. This double-edge situation forces higher education institutions around the world to form partnerships for providing education particularly to those under the age of 25 as regular college students. Worldwide, the majority of universities give a high importance to internationalization, with Europe topping the list, followed by North America. The Middle East and Latin America are at the bottom [3]. When asked about the most important benefits of internationalization, the top three reasons at the global level listed in order of relevance were: increasing international awareness of students, strengthening research and knowledge production and fostering international cooperation and solidarity.

Insensitivity to copyright and intellectual property: The world of higher education is in the midst of change, often driven by technologies that are profoundly affecting the work of faculty members. They are reshaping the processes of teaching and learning, redefining the roles of faculty members in organizing and overseeing the curriculum, and altering the bases for evaluating student achievement as well as faculty performance. When the professors produce knowledge and share it with students in the form course materials, their copyright or intellectual property rights are often violated by both employers and students. The problem is more common in online courses. Some university administrators think that they have already paid for property rights because the authors are their employees. Similarly, many students think that sharing the course materials in the Internet or even in social media do not violate property rights just because the material becomes public once it is delivered to them. There are serious ethical violations in this regard.

Problems in higher education are not limited to the ones mentioned above. There are many other problems concerning the governance of higher education systems, research and publication issues, human resources management, promotion and tenure policies, infrastructure, physical facilities, technological investments, employment and following up of graduates etc. Here we focus more on educational challenges for which MOOCs may offer some solutions. Thus, promises and deliveries of MOOCs are discussed below.

3 Expectations and Realities

It is frequently mentioned that MOOCs may provide solutions for many problems in higher education worldwide. Considering that these courses are developed basically for varying audiences of higher education, this assertion sounds reasonable. However, MOOCs are also criticized by many for not being able to deliver what they promise. Therefore, we have to look at the expectations and realities regarding the effects of MOOCs on higher education systems.

An international group of experts from MOOCs-providing universities such as Harvard, Stanford, Cornell, Georgetown, Texas, Athabasca, Carlos III de Madrid, Hong Kong etc. jointly indicated that MOOCs had some visible effects on higher education. These are: (a) increased institutional consciousness around the future of digital education (i.e. future models of higher education); (b) elevated appreciation for the profession on teaching (focusing attention on teaching and learning process); (c) team-based course design; (d) privileging institutional capacity building over outsourcing (to shape rather than be shaped by the digital era); and (e) creation of new space for experimentation (i.e. learning analytics). All of these effects are related to educational function of universities with a heightened focus on teaching and learning [6].

On the other hand, Simsek [7] pointed out that the MOOCs movement has failed based on basic educational indicators: (a) The average completion rate is lower than 10 percent; (b) Two-thirds of students quit the course before the midterm exam, most of them do not even complete an assignment; (c) 74 percent of undergraduate students and 80 percent of graduate students study the material only by sampling instead of reading, listening, or watching the full content; (d) 82 percent of students consider enjoyment important or very important, while 23 percent of students say that learning the content is important or very important for them; (e) Four out of five students registered to MOOCs are above the age of 25, which means that a great majority of students are not regular college students but young working adults.

Proponents of MOOCs suggest that this movement has impacted higher education systems in many ways and the influences will continue in the future because MOOCs are proliferating very fast. In fact, as of February 2014, there were 1533 registered MOOCs worldwide and approximately 2500 are scheduled to be effective by July 2015. Considering that the first commonly known MOOC started in 2011 with Professor Sebastian Thrun's Artificial Intelligence course at Stanford, growing rate is speedy [10].

Moreover, most of the MOOCs are offered by globally recognized providers such as edX, Coursera, Udacity, Udemy, ALISON, Canvas Network, Khan Academy, iversity, FutureLearn, Open2Study, P2PU etc. They provide three kinds of MOOCs as far as their instructional approaches are concerned. These are: cMOOCs (designed as independent courses based on the connectivist theory), xMOOCs (university courses are extended for other audiences), and vMOOCs (designed for teaching vocational skills or practical training). Most of the courses offered are cMOOCs and more than 20 million students have registered to MOOCs worldwide [10].

It is obvious that the MOOCs movement has created so much excitement among educators, particularly in higher education. Hundreds of institutions have involved, thousands of educators have taken part, and millions of students have attended. For example, Professor Thrun, a pioneer in MOOCs and co-founder of Udacity, predicted that in the next 50 years, 10 institutions would be responsible for delivering higher education [5]. A lot of promises were made and there is now ample evidence for judging the worthiness and influences of these courses. Here are some questions and possible answers for them. We hope that the explanations below will also help deciding whether MOOCs provide a viable solution to essential problems in higher education.

Are MOOCs more motivating than traditional courses? Considering that most MOOCs have video-based lectures, individual assignments, frequent quizzes, online discussions, collaborative projects, and rubrics-based peer evaluation, they are envisaged to satisfy student expectations more than traditional courses. However, students generally stop watching videos after the first 5 min. Completion rates are typically in single digits (lower than 10 %), with a sharp participation drop starting in the first week. Even a simple reasoning suggests that students do not leave a course too early if they are really motivated. It seems that MOOCs do not generate sufficient motivation so that students quit the courses at early stages. Thus, it is difficult to say that MOOCs are more motivating than regular courses.

Are MOOCs equivalent to face-to-face courses? The claim is that MOOCs are designed by teams of experts with the most current content and effective instructional strategies so that they will produce at least the same quality of instruction, if not superior. Nevertheless, most faculty members do not see MOOCs equivalent to their face-to-face courses. They tend to assume that MOOCs may best be considered supplementary material in diploma programs or they may be good for those who would like to empower themselves for career development purposes. In fact, a great majority of learners taking MOOCs are working adults who indicate that they register to these courses for advancing their skills or closing the skills gap between university education and work life. The top two reasons for enrolling MOOCs are career skills and personal enjoyment. It appears that both instructors and students do not assign the same value to MOOCs [7].

Are MOOCs accredited and transferable? Theoretically speaking, most MOOCs are developed and delivered by prestigious universities and their approved partners based on certain standards. Hence, one expects that these courses meet the criteria applicable to a typical university course. In fact, many of the MOOCs have the same content with traditional courses or taught by the same instructors so that they should be considered equivalent and transferable. Unfortunately, the reality is different. With the exception of few courses, none of the MOOCs are accredited by the relevant authorities of higher education. This makes the transfer of earned credits impossible for diploma or degree programs, although certificates are awarded to students who complete a MOOC successfully. For example, Harvard and MIT provide MOOCs through edX consortium for worldwide audiences but they disregard the academic credits when their own students complete the same MOOCs.

Are MOOCs time-efficient? Developing MOOCs requires extended amount of time and many professors do not have enough time for taking part in the design team. For example, when median values are taken into account, a professor spends 100 h for developing a MOOC and he/she spends 8 h per week for a MOOC while it is in session [2]. This means about 200 h for a quarter-based course. Considering these figures, it becomes difficult to embed the expertise and experience of gifted (for the very same reason busy) professors in MOOCs. In addition, there are no meaningful rewards or fiscal incentives for a faculty offering quality a MOOC. Tenure systems in many established universities do not give credits for developing and delivering MOOCs. Taken all together, it does not make much sense to offer MOOCs for a professor who is concerned about tenure policies and research-based publications.

Are MOOCs inexpensive? Development of MOOCs may be a costly process for universities that already have fiscal challenges. Depending on the complexity of the design, the cost for the development of a MOOC ranges from $30,000 to $300,000. When one looks at the cost of the least expensive and the most expensive cost of MOOCs, the latter requires a ten times bigger budget than the former. On the other hand, the registration fee for a sensible MOOC ranges from $30 to $90 (Wikipedia, 2015). Depending upon the number of students registering to MOOCs, universities may not afford the total cost if they outsource them. Furthermore, when smaller or regional universities collaborate with big universities or consortia and encourage their students to take as many MOOCs as possible, their system will be dependent upon the MOOC providers in the long run.

This represents a potential threat for their system because they may be subjected to the hegemony of the big universities.

Are MOOCs based on the best instructional strategies? Advocates of the MOOCs movement indicate that these courses are designed in teams of subject matter experts, instructional designers, graphics experts, web specialists etc. In fact, most of these teams are more of task forces than instructional design teams. Also, the percentage of such courses is very low and often a professor provides the content and a computer specialist uploads it to the system. Vardi [9] criticizes the format of "short, unsophisticated video chunks, interleaved with online quizzes, and accompanied by social networking." Yes, there are templates or rubrics of some providers based on assumed best practices but their strategies are not necessarily the most effective [11]. For example, some MOOCs are online-only while others integrate blended learning. Similarly some universities prefer flipped classrooms where students watch lectures online at home and work on collaborative projects and interact with the faculty while in class. Such an approach may increase pass rates significantly. However, when asked about the major reasons for taking MOOCs, 51 % of students mentioned 'convenience' and 17 % mentioned 'knowledge gain' [8].

Are MOOCs free of cultural barriers? Many proponents of the MOOCs movement indicate that higher education is going global on digital platforms so that students from all countries can attend. Because these courses are offered for worldwide audiences, instructors demonstrate sensitivity to cultural differences. They also embed international perspectives in their content so that students develop a comprehensive view on the world issues. Does the reality support these assertions? Not much. Most MOOCs are developed in universities in the United States and the contents of the courses are usually based on popular textbooks. MOOC providers do not pay much attention to different views on international matters unless they develop their MOOCs specifically for Asian or African audiences. For example, the majority of students registering to MOOCs offered by ALISON, an Ireland-based provider, are from India so that content developers as well as instructors may show some sensitivity to cultural differences outside the western world. It is accurate to say that the MOOCs movement contributes to internationalization of higher education but it does not mean that all courses promote intercultural perspectives.

Are MOOCs changing the focus of higher education? The answer is a partial yes. As previously mentioned, the MOOCs movement increased the level of attention given to education within the university systems. Teaching and learning processes have been the main focus of MOOCs because these are just courses aiming at facilitating learning. However, commercialization of educational services by for-profit enterprises presents a serious risk for future since most commercial providers run their systems based on profit-driven business models. This may expand the digital market of MOOCs but may run contrary to the true nature of education. Therefore, particularly universities taking part in for-profit partnerships should be definitely concerned about educational outcomes. Otherwise, pedagogical bases of the MOOCs will be delicate and students will get easily lost in them.

Are MOOCs technology-enhanced? Pioneers of the MOOCs movement indicated that this new but powerful approach was a response to the needs of the knowledge society. This is true because the current information technologies have certain characteristics such as multimedia, interactivity, navigation, direct access, and user control. Today's students do not want linear and boring lectures, nonfunctional assignments, compulsory attendance, and in-class tests. Instead, they want to take courses at home, on the road, in the workplace etc. with the help of contemporary technologies. Virtual, mobile, and social media have been an inseparable part of their lives. Many MOOCs are provided through virtual platforms so that students can take these courses anytime and anywhere. However, the most important problem is that many MOOCs are developed by taking advantage of state-of-the-art capabilities of new technology but the real learning occurs only based on appropriate pedagogical approaches not on the use of the most current technology.

4 Conclusion

Based on the sound theoretical discussions and findings of empirical research, we can conclude that MOOCs have the potential to help educators overcome some of the problems in higher education. Of course, MOOCs can help universities only in their educational function and cannot solve other problems. However, universities should change their conventional policies and practices to benefit from this movement. As practiced so far, MOOCs do not offer a viable solution to essential problems in higher education. For example, MOOCs may present certain solutions for extending learning opportunities to increasing number of students but students will not take MOOCs seriously as long as universities disregard and do not transfer academic credits gained through these courses. Similarly, many MOOCs use technology more than traditional courses but pedagogical foundations are not strong enough so that students get disappointed and quit the courses after selectively watching a few short segments of video lectures. Institutions should undoubtedly recognize that it is not the technology but the pedagogy that will bring about learning.

Moreover, the MOOCs movement itself creates new concerns and challenges among educators. Discussions about the hegemony of the Ivy League institutions on other universities, violating intellectual property rights of professors even by their own institutions, losing the humanly nature of education, and diminishing socializing effects of campus life are just among them. Thus, one can say that MOOCs cannot replace existing higher education systems, although such contentions are often made in the literature. Institutions should carefully think about benefits and pitfalls of MOOCs before making radical decisions regarding the diffusion of these courses or increasing their weights in academic programs. This is particularly important when MOOCs are offered by external providers which serve a wide array of audiences worldwide. If universities do not keep control or participate actively in the design process of MOOCs offered to their students, they will soon become dependent on other universities, if not on commercial providers. Then, their mission will be recruiting students as customers for the Ivy League institutions. This will also create an awkward environment in which their professors serve either as teaching assistants for remedial instruction or proctors in exams.

Higher education is certainly going digital. This is a response to the architecture of knowledge and expectations of learners in the information society of the digital age. The MOOCs movement appears to be a catalyst for the development of technology-based approaches and innovative programs that reply to demands of the changing world. Universities cannot close their eyes or turn their backs to progressive dynamics of distance education that ease the pressure on higher education systems by serving massive audiences through technology-abled learning environments. In today's world, students can connect with professors in the digital marketplace of education which is not costly because it does not require expensive physical infrastructures. Therefore, universities should balance traditional courses and MOOCs in meaningful ways for their students. Higher education institutions do not need to choose between online learning and offline learning. The truth is neither delivery model is intrinsically better than the other. Hence, educators need to strategically balance both models and think about how to support the never-ending nature of today's learning that extends beyond the classroom or the campus.

References

1. Clark, D.: Report on 6 MOOCs turns up surprises (2013). http://donaldclarkplanb.blogspot.de/2013/05/report-on-6-moocs-turns-up-10-surprises.html. Accessed 9 April 2015
2. Kolowich, S.: The professors who make the MOOCs (2013). http://chronicle.com/article/The-Professors-Behind-the-MOOC/137905/#id=overview. Accessed May 12, 2015
3. Marmolejo, F.: Internationalization of higher education: The good, the bad, the unexpected (2010). http://chronicle.com/blogs/worldwise/internationalization-of-higher-education-the-good-the-bad-and-the-unexpected/27512. Accessed 12 February 2015
4. Pappano, L.: The year of the MOOC (2012). http://www.nytimes.com/2012/11/04/education/edlife/massive-open-online-courses-are-multiplying-at-a-rapid-pace.html/pagewanted=all&_r=0. Accessed 10 February 2015
5. Pope, J.: What are MOOCs good for? (2014). http://www.technologyreview.com/review/533406/what-are-moocs-good-for. Accessed 10 February 2015
6. Salisbury, A.D.: Impacts of MOOCs on higher education (2014). https://www.insidehighered.com/blogs/higher-ed-beta/impacts-moocs-higher-education. Accessed on 15 April 2015
7. Simsek, A.: The great failure of the MOOCs movement. In: Keynote address at the International Conference on Contemporary Issues in Education. Dubai, United Arab Emirates (2015)
8. Stiles, K.: Massive open online courses (MOOCs) - Are they challenging or not? (2015). http://www.surveycrest.com/blog/massive-open-online-courses-challenge/. Accessed 12 May 2015
9. Vardi, M.Y.: Will MOOCs destroy academia? Commun. ACM **55**(11), 5 (2012). doi: 10.1145/2366317
10. Wikipedia. Massive open online course (2015). http://en.wikipedia.or/wiki/Massive_open_online_course. Accessed 10 February 2015
11. Yuan, L., Powell, S.: MOOCs and open education: Implications for higher education. University of Bolton: CETIS (2013). http://publications.cetis.ac.uk/2013/667. Accessed 23 February 2015

An Attempt to a Reconstruction of HSK Chinese-English Dictionary: A Search for Self-study of Mandarin Chinese

Jette C.H. Tsoi(✉), John C.T. Chow, and David W.K. Chu

School of Humanities and Languages, Caritas Institute of Higher Education, 18 Chui Ling Road, Tseung Kwan O (Tiu Keng Leng MTR Station), New Territories, Hong Kong SAR, China
{jtsoi, jchow, dchu}@cihe.edu.hk

Abstract. Hanyu Shuiping Kaoshi (thereafter HSK) Chinese-English Dictionary is an online search system for testing the proficiency of HSK examinees, in accordance with the Searching Handbook Stroke Sequence, integrating and newly editing with reference to Cantonese Pronunciation Database, CEDICT Cantonese-English Dictionary and JFJ (Simplified-Traditional Chinese Converting). The paper focuses on: (1) enhancement of flexibility and effectiveness on self-learning of Mandarin Chinese, targeting at those students whose mother tongues are not Chinese; (2) further development of student's reading and writing proficiency in the perspective of nurturing their language feelings from speaking and listening in the context of teaching strategy; (3) building up of basic Chinese characters database in order to enhance the speed and number of Chinese words acquired by the students and (4) attempts to overcome the difficulties of students in their learning process, with the addition of grammatical elements.

Keywords: Online learning · Quality assurance · Student engagement · Student satisfaction

1 Introduction

Chinese as a foreign language has become more and more popular in different parts of the world. Hong Kong as an international city is not only not an exception, but also a metropolitan where foreign people learn Chinese for business or other purposes. Yet to acquire a language successfully requires access and exposure to various kinds of materials which are engaging, authentic and comprehensible but very demanding. They are also often limited whether in classrooms or self-study settings. In response to this need, language educators have long been searching the feasibility of information and communication technologies in its solution [13].

In the field of information and communication technologies, more digital multimedia technologies than printed media or audio recorders have always been adopted in learning materials because its (visual, audio, and text) presentations can strengthen memory connections than a single medium alone and digital technology facilitates instant and accurate playbacks. As a result, learners can be provided with specific

J. Lam et al. (Eds.): ICTE 2015, CCIS 559, pp. 143–151, 2015.
DOI: 10.1007/978-3-662-48978-9_14

segments much more easily without wasting efforts to locate them. This is called a tedious and time consuming process [13]. Notwithstanding it, the importance of technology application in language learning for students as well as in learning Chinese as a foreign language is still in its infant stage whereas in pursuance of this theme, it should explore the construction and further development of language materials addressing the difficulties encountered by non-Chinese learners in Hong Kong.

This paper aims at introducing the proposed HSK online dictionary with its features which try to address the difficulties met by foreign learners of Chinese and assessing the comprehensive design in terms of its feasibility.

2 Literature Review

Previous studies have so far tended to focus on the roles played by online electronic dictionaries in foreign language learning with English as examples. On one hand, they put emphasis on their demerits of synthetic and unclear features of pronunciation, their incomplete lexical content [6] and distortion of word-to-word mapping with the target language [3]. On the other hand, they also have not overlooked their merits on the speed of reference [12] and the liberation from 'the stress and anxieties in the process of language learning' [5].

Only a few of scholars have conducted studies on Chinese-English dictionaries which have concentrated on their (1) design in immersion model, aiming at nurturing learners in the foreign language environment; (2) categorization of words in different levels; (3) their objectives in speed of reference, easiness to learn, easiness to understand, multi-search function, clear explanation with ample examples and demonstration of grammar function and (4) its integration with computer technology but limited to methods of search and application of multi-media. Firstly, Lu [7] summaries the process leading to the publication of a Chinese Dictionary published by the Commercial Press exploring the aim, objectives, principles and methods in editing the captioned dictionary. He furthers that the dictionary addresses the difficulties encountered by foreign learners and users in difficulty of reference, of understanding, of learning. The work lastly explains the principle of meaning explanation, of word entries, of giving examples and of footnotes; therefore a user-friendly dictionary can be written through the improvement of search functions. Wang [10] lists some important rules governing the construction of a dictionary encompassing the necessity of offering parts of speech in a systematic way, suitability of describing grammar function and the meaning as well as the collocation of words. Thirdly, the fundamental concepts of introduced by Guo [4] demonstrates the explanation of Chinese words in terms of Chinese with data-base source as well as the understanding of Chinese words with authentic examples. They are reflected in the following three aspects: (1) the arrangement of words in terms of the priority of sequence of learning and the frequency of its use, with reference to the frequency of its use based on the numerical figures of character frequency and word frequency; (2) the provision of multi-search function of order, with the reflective characteristics of computers and (3) the availability of Multi-function.

However, the previous studies have not fully been conducted in the following areas: (1) they did not address the difficulties encountered by Chinese learners in a systematic manner; (2) lack of integration with the computer technology and (3) nonexistence of interaction between the learners and the on-line dictionary.

3 The Challenges to Learning Chinese as a Foreign Language

The difficulties met by foreign learners of Chinese can be categorized in different aspects. Wang, Kong and Farren [1] summarize their analysis in the following three ways, namely (1) the way as how to write the Chinese characters, (2) the accurate pronunciation of these words and (3) memorizing the meaning of these words. Their analyses of group interview data (11.7 %) further showed that students expressed frustration with learning the Chinese language in various ways. First, students identified that learning how to write Chinese characters is a difficult process. Second, students also identified pronunciation and memorization of specific Chinese words to be difficult.

The documents of the Hong Kong Education Bureau also provide us with other difficulties among foreign language of Chinese. According to the supplementary instructions on Chinese Language Programme (Non-Chinese learners), they are the shape of Chinese characters, the tonic accents, vocabulary, partitive and word order.

As for the interactions with the computer, Zhao (2003) provides detailed comments on communicative interactions which can take place in either written or spoken language or a combination of both. At the simplest level, a computer program can generate utterances either in oral form or in written form that ask the learners to respond through an answer with a mouse click or providing simple writing responses. With the advancement of speech synthesis and recognition technologies, the learner can also conduct near-natural conversations with a computer programme around 'pre-selected and programmed topics' [13].

Lastly, Swan [9] states that researchers have identified three kinds of interactivity in computer-based education. They are: interaction with content, interaction with instructors, and interaction among peers and they can be adapted to the construction of electronic HSK Chinese-English Dictionary, especially when the interactivity would facilitate enhancing the learning effectiveness.

4 The Responses to the Difficulties of Foreign Learners of Chinese: Proposed HSK Chinese-English Dictionary

4.1 The Responses to the Difficulties of Chinese Learning

The proposed dictionary will address the shortcomings mentioned above in the manifestation of the following characteristic features: (1) the introduction of voice recognition and pronunciation function; (2) priority given to listening and reading – language input; (3) demonstration of applications in everyday life and grammar functions; (4) stroke order and frequency order and (5) an attempt to include the interactions in the learning process.

4.2 Software Features

The proposed Dictionary helps foreign learners of Chinese to prepare well the HSK Proficiency Test. It takes into account the needs of different regions: (1) Mainland Chinese character input software mainly for simplified service; (2) Mandarin, Chinese character input software Taiwan mainly for traditional and Mandarin service and (3) Hong Kong Chinese character input software taking care of traditional Chinese characters, simplified and Mandarin, as well as Cantonese (Zhangxiao Heng & Qun display, 2002). Therefore, it is designed in the form of a table, which covers several areas, namely traditional Chinese, simplified Chinese, Mandarin pinyin, Cantonese Pinyin, HSK grade, frequency order, stroke order, meaning and examples.

Each of the entries is annotated with Pinyin numbers indicating the tone it is used. That is, the Mandarin pinyin tone with 1,2,3,4,5 is marked at the end of a syllable (four tones plus soft); and 1,2,3,4,5,6 is marked in Cantonese pinyin six syllables. Moreover, the letter ü is represented by v, ê is represented by e. As this dictionary is integrated with the internet, internal code dictionary will make use of Unicode.

The proposed Dictionary integrates some dictionaries such as "The YES-CEDICT Chinese Dictionary (to be published)", "CEDICT English Dictionary", "Simplified-Traditional Chinese Converting and Proofreading", "Chinese Character Database: With Word-formations Phonologically Disambiguated, According to the Cantonese Dialect" and "Frequency Order Number in the List of Frequently-used Words of Modern Chinese". The production of the online dictionary is conducted with the use of Adobe Dreamweaver and JavaScript. Adobe Dreamweaver is used for Html and CSS while JavaScript is the main software used for word search and online interactive version of Adobe Dreamweaver will be produced.

4.3 Use of the Software

The dictionary has two different menus: (1) Main Menu (See Fig. 1) and (2) Advanced Menu (See Fig. 2) in which there is a total of six input modes, namely (1) simplified input, (2) traditional input, (3) tonal Mandarin pinyin input, (4) Cantonese Pinyin input, (5) wildcard search, and (6) atonal Mandarin pinyin input. Learners are free to choose either keyboard or voice version (See Fig. 3). In such areas as Hong Kong or Taiwan where traditional Chinese characters and Cantonese are used, Cantonese Pinyin input mode with tone would be found easier to use whereas atonal way Pinyin input system is useful to those Chinese learners who find difficult to accurately grasp the tones of Chinese language, particularly fail to correctly distinguish between the third and the soft tones. Moreover, there is also a wildcard search function where the dictionary will display all words at HSK level 1 if 'HSK1' is entered while it also supports arbitrary searches in which all words containing 'wo' as an example will be displayed when 'wo' is inputted. Lastly, voice recognition function is also introduced.

The dictionary provides a variety of learning material to learners, with information on HSK 5000 word entries. Firstly, each entry in the dictionary covers multi-content, namely simplified characters, traditional characters, pinyin Mandarin, Cantonese spelling, word meaning and other associated words. For example, from the entry on "you", it is understood whether traditional or simplified characters or both exist. The entry with

Fig. 1. Main menu

Fig. 2. Advanced search

Fig. 3. Voice input function

only one type of character means that it does not have the difference between Simplified Chinese and Traditional Chinese characters (Refer to Fig. 4). On the contrary, an entry with two types of characters means that it has both the Simplified and Traditional Chinese characters (See Fig. 5). Secondly, the meaning for each entry based on CEDICT English Dictionary contains more than one sense with the inclusion of colloquial sense as well. For example, the entry "convenience" word would refer not only to do things conveniently, but also to indicate, in colloquial meaning, 'going to the toilet' in its pragmatic use. Thus, the dictionary covers the basic meaning of a word's meaning and oral communication, providing support for Chinese learners' daily communication. Third, this dictionary provides a multi-word associated word function. Words associated with the entry in the proposed Dictionary will also be displayed when any one word is searched (See Fig. 5). Learners clicking any word can be linked to the interpretation of the word, so that learners can remember similar words in order to improve the efficiency of learning. Finally, the example sentences in either simplified or traditional character version are available in the dictionary with learners' search function.

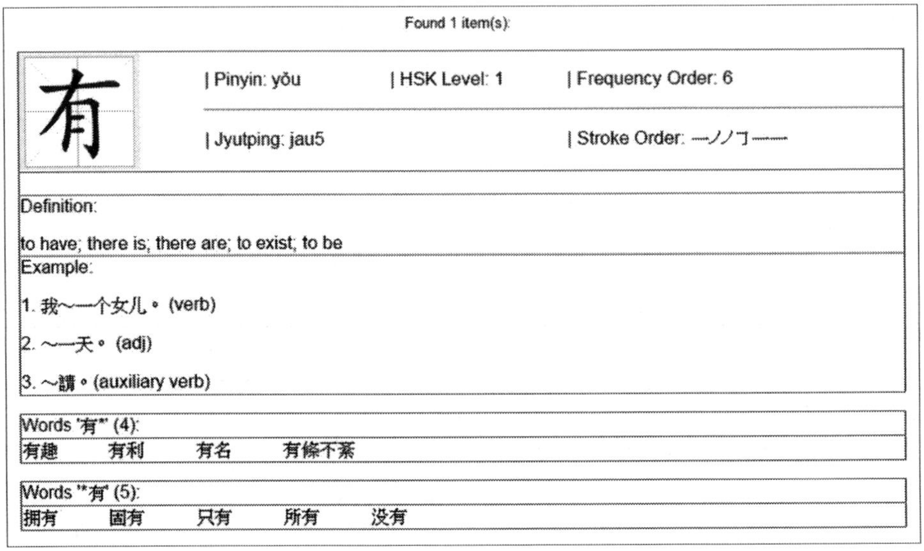

Fig. 4. Search result 1

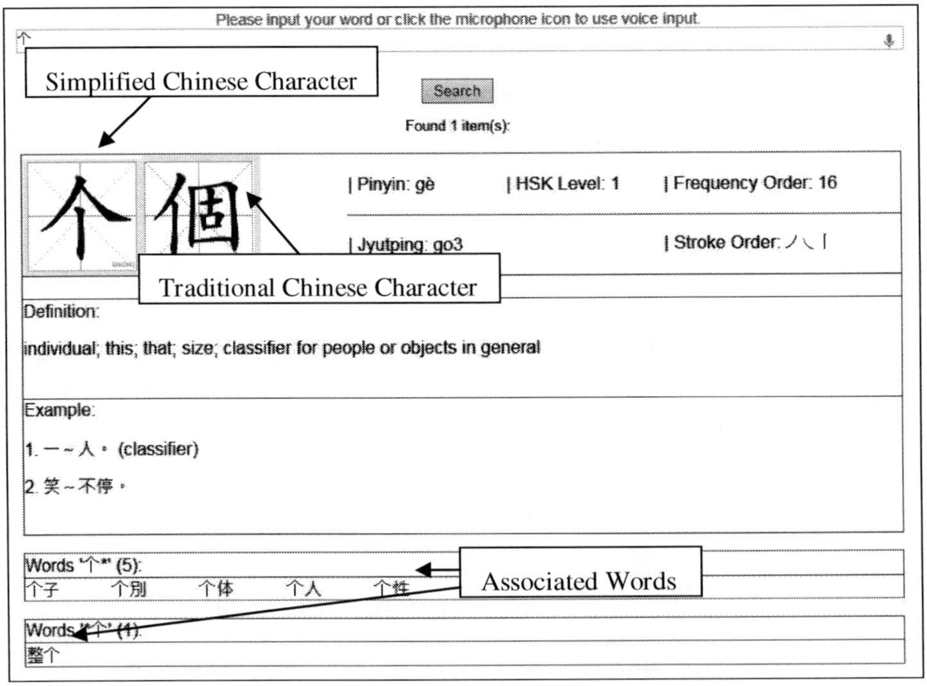

Fig. 5. Search result 2

5 The Anticipated Problems Encountered in the Proposed HSK Chinese-English Dictionary

The proposed HSK Chinese-English Dictionary is only at the design stage and it should have its problems. Firstly, users may find the choice of options in the Main Menu is not sufficient to meet their demands. Secondly, because of the technology limitation, the voice recognition input can only be operated with the provision of CHROME browser of GOOGLE. Lastly, the database used to support the system is of a limited range; therefore users are not satisfied with the limited availability of the words and examples provided in the entries. We have to address that usages on Chinese words vary from one region/country to another, for example, Mainland, Hong Kong, Taiwan, Singapore, etc. This leads to misunderstanding on the meaning of some frequently-used Chinese words in different backgrounds. The inclusion of overseas Chinese Language education, the native Chinese Language teaching as well as teaching Chinese as a foreign language, could perhaps provide a fuller picture for the learning of commonly used words at the same time without sacrificing the local characteristic features in different regions/countries [11]. The limit on provision of multimedia function and the voice function demonstrate its characteristic features of Chinese used in different regions/countries although this point was not mentioned in the difficulties encountered by various foreign learners of Chinese in this paper. The examples given in the proposed dictionary are offered with simplicity as the principle, targeting at the majority of learners without strong linguistic background of Chinese Language since the issues of syntax and semantics in Chinese Language entails complex application.

6 The Anticipated Problems Encountered in the Proposed HSK Chinese-English Dictionary

In short, the significance of the proposed HSK Chinese-English Dictionary lies in its inclusion of not only Mandarin Pinyin but also Cantonese Spelling search modes. The additional arrangement of entries with consideration of the frequency in terms of their use in everyday life language communication is another special feature of the dictionary which meets the demands from the HSK examinees. Moreover, stroke order is also available for each entry with attention to those beginner learners of Chinese as a foreign language. Lastly, the dictionary highlights the differentiation of Chinese word list at different levels to help students on their Chinese learning. This strives to ensure the user-friendly feature, trying to solve the difficulties of learning Chinese as a foreign language.

Obviously the paper has merely provided a preliminary set of ideas on how to reconstruct a proposed HSK Chinese-English dictionary, but an empirical study is the next step in order to further fine-tune the design of the proposed dictionary through a questionnaire survey targeting at major minorities in Hong Kong such as Pakistan people or Filipino. Secondly, relying solely on on-line electronic dictionary cannot be the full picture of learning a foreign language; therefore an assessment of the degree to which on-line electronic dictionary helps learners in the process of foreign language acquisition should be conducted. In other words, an empirical research is needed to ascertain which areas it assists the learners and in which areas it does not. Lastly, the dictionary has too focused on how to help learners acquire mastering Chinese characters, reading Chinese passages, listening to Chinese presentation, speaking with native Chinese speaker, without attention paid to assist learners in writing Chinese. In this connection, account should later be taken into the incorporation of the handwriting technology in helping them to write Chinese characters. All in all, the project has brought light the ideas on the construction of an elementary electronic HSK Chinese-English dictionary but it also hopes to be leading to more profound researches based on scientific and empirical information and strategies.

References

1. Aubrey, H., Wang, A.K., Tom, F.S.: What learning environment factors motivate non-heritage language learners in middle grades to learn chinese? Electron. J. Foreign Lang. Teach. **11**, 312–326 (2014)
2. Prikola, Ari, Hedlund, Turid, Keskustalo, Heikki, Jarvelin, Kalervo: Dictionary-based cross-language information retrieval: Problems, Methods and Research Findings. Inf. Rev. **4** (3/4), 209–230 (2001)
3. Carter, R., McCarthy, M.: Developments in the teaching of vocabulary. In: Carter, R., MaCarthy, M. (eds.) Vocabulary and Language Teaching, pp. 39–59. Longman, New York (1988)
4. Guo, Shu Guan (郭曙綸): Ji Yu Yu Liao Ku De HSK Duo Gong Neng Li Jie Ci Dian (基於語料庫的HSK多功能例解字典): She Xiang Yu Yang Li 《(設想與樣例). In Zhang Shao Lin (張紹麒) (2005):Ci Shu Yu Shu Wei Hua Yan Jiu (辭書與數位化研究). Shanghai: Shanghai Ci Shu Chu Ban She (上海辭書出版社), 1-4 (2005)
5. Lai, C.: The advantages and disadvantages of computer technology. Reading Foreign Lang. **17**(2), 125–143 (2006)
6. Liu, S.S.C.: Electronic dictionaries and ESL students. In: Proceedings of International Conference on English Education. Shih Chih University, Taipei (2007)
7. Lu, Jian Ji (魯健驥) and Lue, Wen Hua (呂文華). Bian Xie Dui Wai Han Yu Dan Yu Xue Xi Ci Dian De Chang Shi Yu Si Kao (編寫對外漢語單語學習詞典的嘗試與思考)——Shang Wu Guan Xue Han Yu Ci Dian Bian Hou (商務館學漢語詞典編後). In Shi Jie Han Yu Jiao Xue (世界漢語教學), Issue No.1, 59–69 (2006)
8. Shires, G., Wennbord, H.: Web Speech API Specification (2012). Retrieved from https://dvcs.w3.org/hg/speech-api/raw-file/tip/speechapi.html. Last access: June 6 2015
9. Swan, K.: Learning effectiveness: what the research tells Us. In: Bourne, J., Moore, J.C. (eds.) Elements of Quality Online Education, Practice and Direction, pp. 13–45. Sloan Center for Online Education, Needham (2003)
10. Wang, Hui (王惠):Yu Wen Ci Dian Zhong De Yu Fa Gong Neng Miao Xie (語文詞典中的語法功能描寫) – Jian Ping Xian Dai Han Yu Gui Fan Yong Fa Da Ci Dian (兼評《現代漢語規範用法大詞典》). In Ci Shu Yan Jiu (辭書研究), 2000(3), 84–93 (2000)
11. Wang, Hui (王惠): Oversea Chinese Language Education from the Perspective of Vocabulary (從詞彙差異看海外華語教育). In Journal of Chinese Language Studies (漢語教學學刊), Vol.3, 228–242 (2007)

12. Yonally, D., Gilfert, S.: Electronic dictionaries in the classroom!? Bah, humbug! In The Internet TESL Journal 1 (1995). http//iteslj.org/Articles/Weschler-ElectroDict.html. Last accessed 3 August 2009
13. Zhao, Yong: Recent developments in technology and language learning: a literature review and meta-analysis. CALICO J. **21**, 7–27 (2003)
14. Zheng, Ding Ou (鄭定歐): Dui Wai Han Yu Xue Xi Ci Dian Xue Chu Yi (對外漢語學習詞典學芻議). In Shi Jie Han Yu Jiao Xue (世界漢語教學), Issue No. 4, 85–94 (2004)

A Study on Use and Acceptance of Book Apps among College Students in a University

Yang Li, Shan Wang, and Wenge Guo(✉)

Department of Educational Technology, GSE, Peking University, Beijing 100871, China
st13431m@gse.pku.edu.cn, 15210922066@163.com, wgguo@pku.edu.cn

Abstract. With the development of wireless Internet, mobile reading, especially book app reading, has been important parts of everyday reading. This study designs an online questionnaire and inquires how college students read e-books with apps and what they think of book apps. The results show that college students read books with apps wide-rangedly, frequently but fragmentally, skimmingly and leisurely. Many factors lead college students to choose and use an app, mainly including recommendation from friends, free and a wide variety of books in the book apps. However, even though apps have many advantages over printed books, paper reading is their favorite.

Keywords: Book apps · Mobile reading · College students

1 Introduction

With the development of Internet and wireless Internet, people have spent more and more time reading with mobile devices, such as smart phones, tablet PCs and so on. Mobile reading is becoming important parts of everyday reading. Some phenomena happened in our daily life could also support this results. In the past, people passed the time by reading newspaper or books in the subway, which doesn't occur any longer. Nowadays people replace the newspaper with mobile phones. For most people, mobile reading is a way of killing time by reading news and network literature. Many people think mobile reading is a convenient way to access to information and have fun. They read with mobile devices mainly for relaxation [1–3].

As an important tool for mobile reading, book app contributes to mobile reading. 148apps.biz, a website that tracks app download on the Apple App Store, announced that there were over 6,000 book apps on the App Store which occupied 11 % of the all Apps [4]. Book Apps combining pleasing interface, convenient operation and abundant reading resources have been more and more popular and become an important platform for mobile reading.

The young people, especially college students accept new things easily and they are good at learning new technologies, which makes them the majority of the book apps users. How the college students use book apps? What happened when they read books with apps? Which do they prefer, paper books or e-books in the apps? This study will

J. Lam et al. (Eds.): ICTE 2015, CCIS 559, pp. 152–160, 2015.
DOI: 10.1007/978-3-662-48978-9_15

try to find the answers to these questions by investigating the reading habits of college students who use book apps.

2 The Method to Inquire Current Situation of Use and Acceptance of Book Apps

To explore the transformation of reading of students in universities, we design an online questionnaire to investigate what college students think of book apps and how they use them. After data collection, descriptive statistical method is used to analyze the data.

2.1 Online Questionnaire

The questionnaire is made up of two parts including individual information and current situation of use and acceptance of book apps. Part 1 individual information is at the beginning of the questionnaire. The gender and educational background information are collected. Part 2 includes fifteen questions. These questions are about reading contents, reading strategies, reading time and so on. In addition, the advantages and disadvantages of book apps are also investigated to compare the book app reading with paper reading.

2.2 Data Collection and Analysis

The questionnaire is distributed randomly on the Internet among the college students in a university sponsored by 985 project. Finally, 426 questionnaires are retained and 418 of those which accounted for 98.12 % of the total, were effective.

Excel 2007 is used to analyze the data. Bar and pie charts are generated to show the frequency and percentage to make it clear that current situation of use and acceptance of book apps among college students.

3 Information of Respondents to Questionnaire

3.1 Gender Ratio

As Fig. 1 shows, there are 245 males which make up 58.61 % of all of respondents. The remaining 41.39 % are females. Males are a little more than females, but the gender ratio is approximately 1:1.

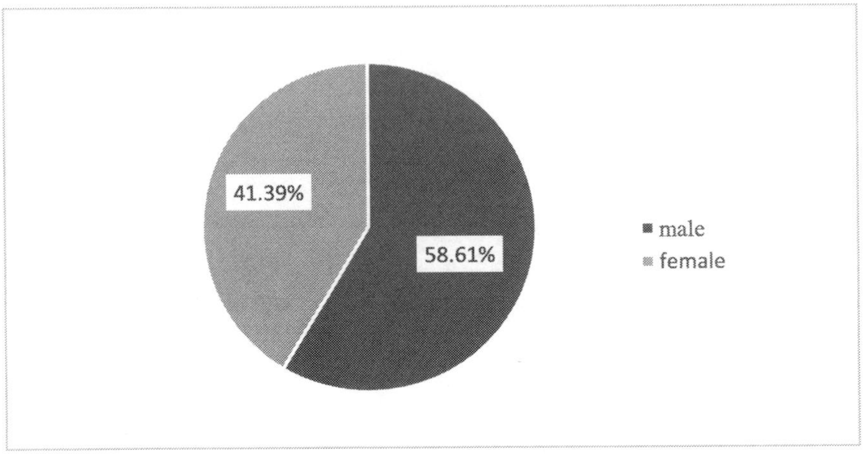

Fig. 1. Gender ratio

3.2 Educational Background

This study is conducted in a university, so educational background of respondents is various, including undergraduate students, masters and doctors. 38.52 % respondents are at the underground level, 39.71 % at the master level and 21.77 % at the doctor level. The number of doctors is a bit less, which is normal because in each university doctor students are the least (Fig. 2).

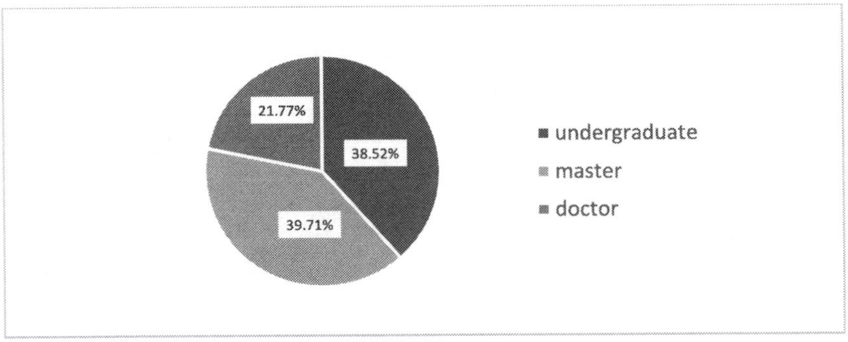

Fig. 2. Educational background of respondents

4 Current Status of Using Book Apps Among College Students

We inquire the current status of using book apps from many aspects, mainly including reading contents, reading time, reading duration, reading strategies and so on. The results are as follows.

4.1 College Students Read Books with Apps Wide-Rangedly and Frequently, but Fragmentally, Skimmingly and Leisurely

College Students Read Books with Apps Wide-Rangedly. When college students are asked what they read with book apps, the answers are very various. The data in the Fig. 3 shows that the contents college students read with book apps relate to literary, language, humanities, management, economics, life & fashion, biography and so on. It can be seen that reading with book apps is of very wide range.

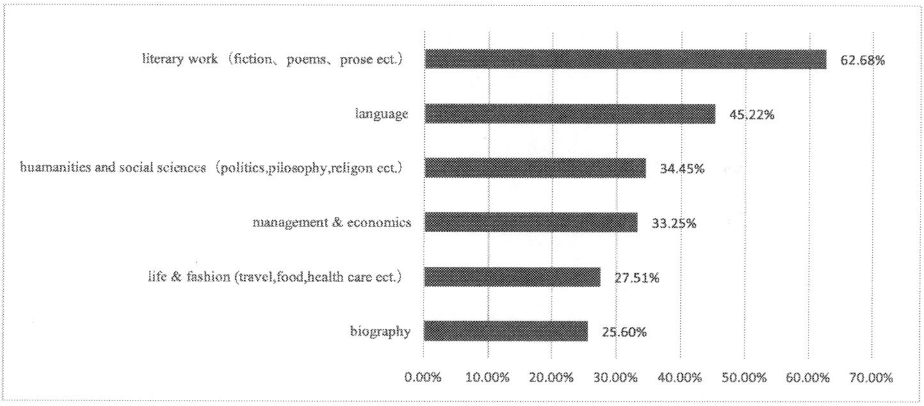

Fig. 3. Reading contents

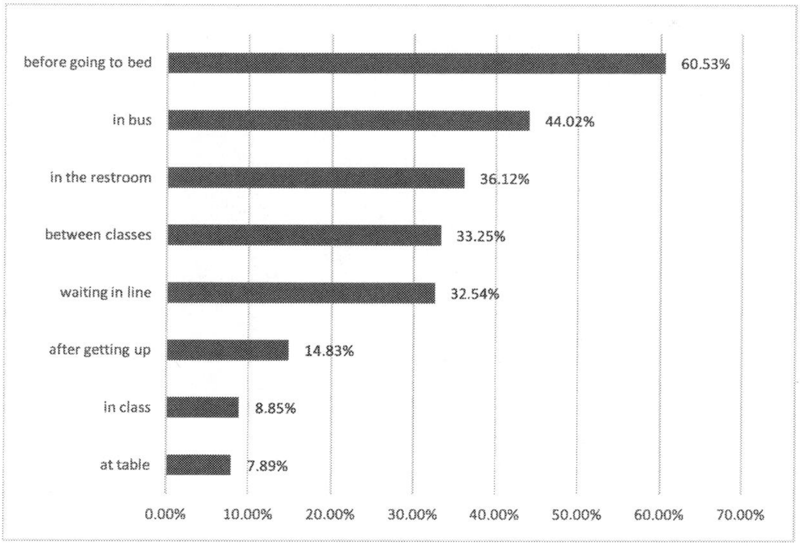

Fig. 4. Time to read books with apps

College Students Use Book Apps Fragmentally, Mostly for Leisure. Figure 4 shows that the most frequent time when college students use book apps is before going to bed, followed by while being in bus and in the restroom. In addition, some students read books with apps when waiting in line and being between classes.

Two conclusions could be drawn from the data in Fig. 4. Firstly, college students read books with apps fragmentally because these time, such as before going to bed, being in bus and in the restroom etc. is very fragmented. The reading duration in the Fig. 5 has also proved this conclusion. Figure 5 shows that only 15.55 % students use book apps for more than 2 h every day and most students spend less 2 h, even less 30 min on book apps. The time students spend on book apps is short.

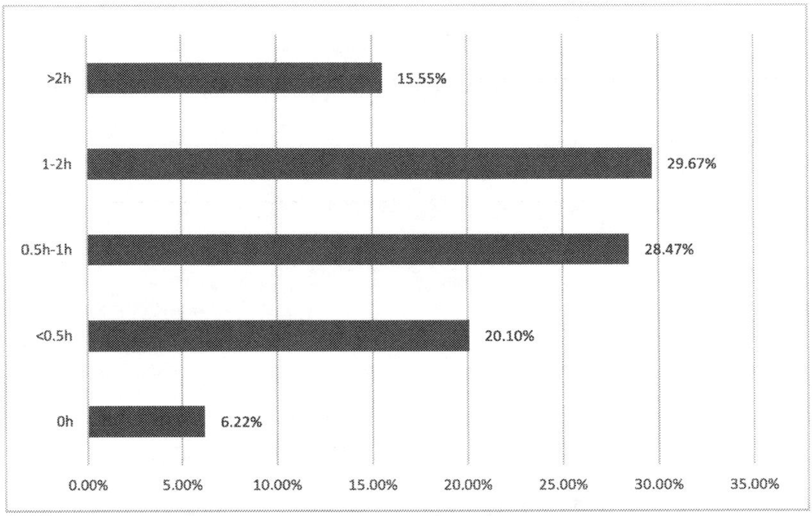

Fig. 5. Duration time of reading books with apps every day

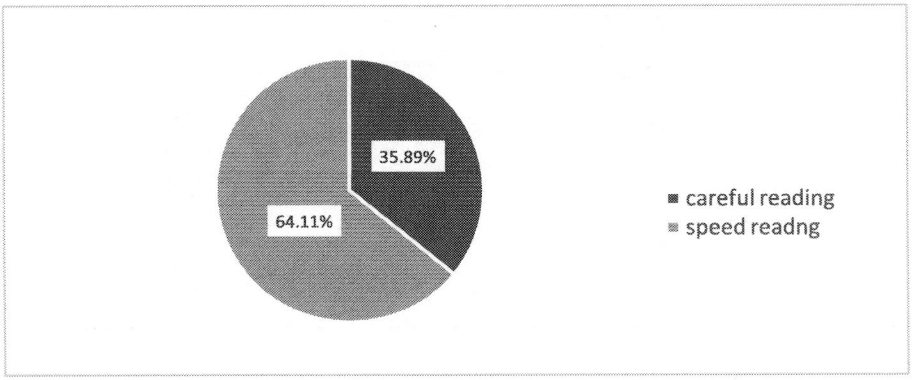

Fig. 6. Way of reading e-books with apps

Secondly, these time, for example before going to bed, between classes and at table, is for rest and relaxation so we could infer that among college students, books apps are used for leisure, which is actually a way of informal learning. In a word, college students read books with apps fragmentally and leisurely.

Speed Reading is Used Frequently When Reading Books with Apps. Paper and app are two different ways of presenting knowledge, which results in different reading ways. The data in Fig. 6 shows that nearly 2/3 of respondents read books in skimming way and 1/3 read carefully when using book apps. The time to use book apps may account for this results. As shown in the Figs. 4 and 5 above, college students use book apps when they are in bus, in the restroom, at table and they spend less 2 h on book apps every day. Careful reading needs more time and attention than speed reading. In such short and fragmentary time, it's difficult to read carefully. Even for college students themselves, books app itself is just a tool for relaxation.

4.2 Factors Leading College Students to Choose and Use an App

Students know a book app from various channels, but mainly from friends' recommendation. The data in the Fig. 7 shows that nearly half of the respondents know about an app by recommendation from friends and 39.95 % by application rankings in app store. Some else students know an app by news and ads built in system. So for app promotion, it's very important to have good reputation and top ranking on the app store. In addition, working with phone makers is also a good way to introduce a new app. However, built-in ads is not a good way for app introduction.

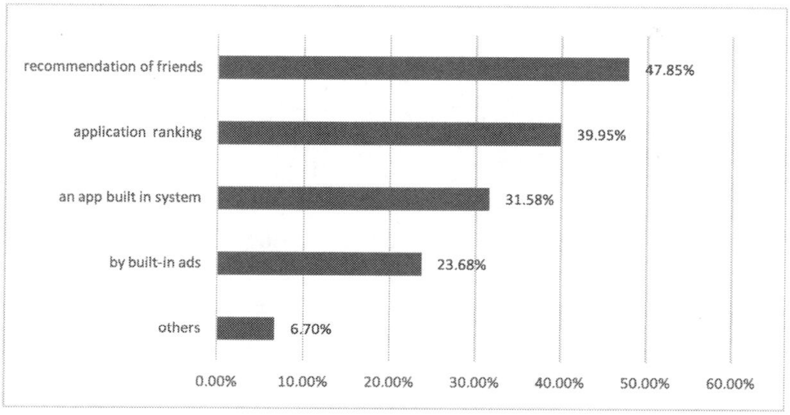

Fig. 7. Ways to know about an App

The most important factors, free and a wide variety of books, affect students to choose a book app. Figure 8 shows that for college students who have no income, free is the most important factors affecting them to choose a book app, followed by having a wide variety of books, well-organized interface and convenient operation. However, whether the app offer push-based personalized information delivery and social sharing service is not very significant to college students. Actually, free, having wide variety of books, well-organized interface and convenient operation are the most basic services of a book app while the push-based personalized information delivery and social sharing are auxiliary. So it' clear that college students have relatively low demand for advanced service offered by book apps.

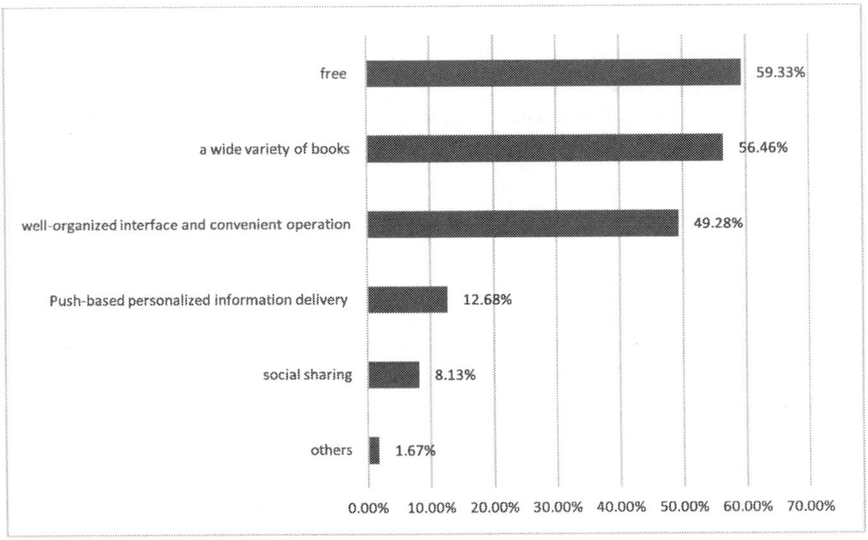

Fig. 8. Factors leading to college students' choice of book apps

4.3 Even Though Apps Have Many Advantages Over Printed Books, Paper Reading is Their Favorite

College students have been in the transformation from paper reading to digital reading. Book app reading is one important way of digital reading. Facing book app reading and paper reading, college students think the former have some advantages over the latter. For example, book apps are cheaper, even cost nothing. Book apps make books more accessible and they don't need to spend time getting to library for books. Moreover, by book app, they could read books anytime and anywhere. In addition, more portable is also one of advantages book apps have (Fig. 9).

Except the advantages, book apps have many disadvantages compared to paper book. More than 80 % of all respondents point that reading books with apps causes eye fatigue easier than reading printed books does. Some college students think they cannot make notes when reading books with apps and after reading they remember fewer contents than they do with paper books. A small number of students state they are less patient when using book apps (Fig. 10).

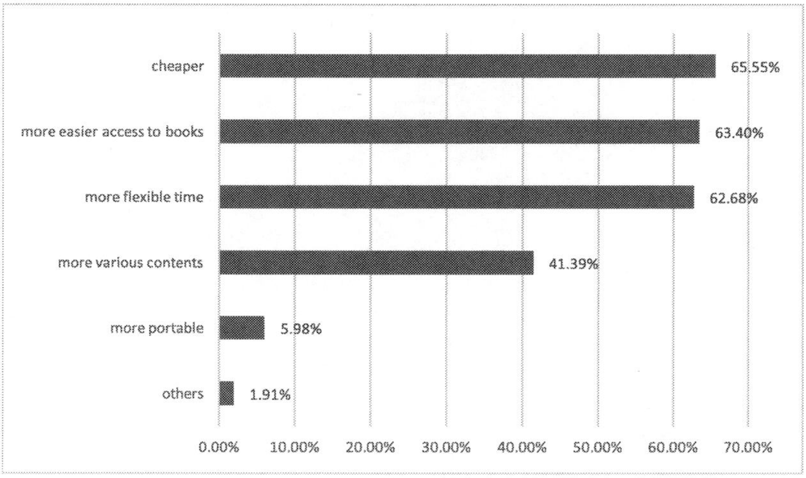

Fig. 9. Advantages of book apps over paper books

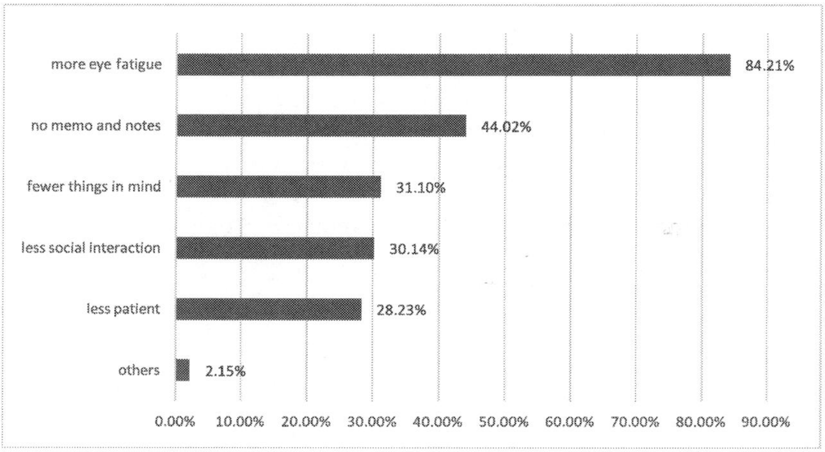

Fig. 10. Disadvantages of book apps

Now that book apps have some strength and weakness, which do college students prefer facing book apps and paper book? Fig. 11 shows that 63.63 % college students will choose to read printed books if both are accessible while only about 1/3 of respondents prefer book apps. Besides of the disadvantages book apps have, this reason may be that paper reading is the first way when they began to learn to read from childhood and it's hard to change a long-term reading habit.

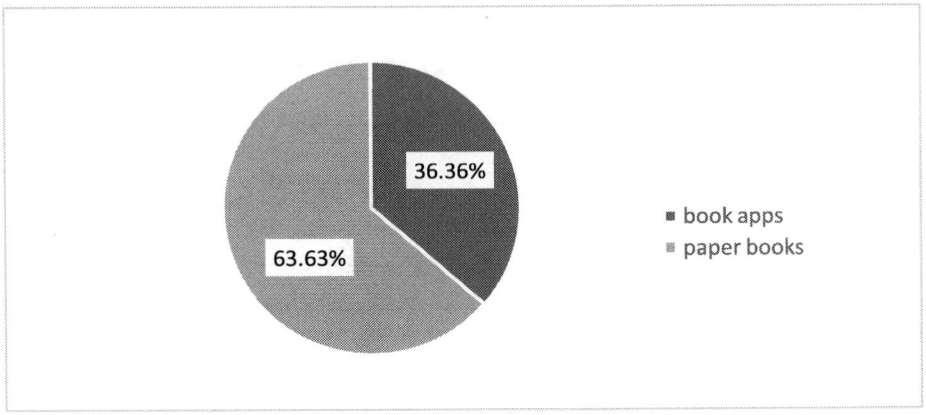

Fig. 11. Choice between book apps and paper books

5 Conclusion

In this study, college students in a university are investigated to inquire their book app reading habits including reading contents, reading time, reading strategies and so on. The data shows that college students read books with apps widely, fragmentally and leisurely, and facing with paper books and e-books on apps, most students prefer the traditional printed books. However, what factors lead college students to prefer paper book reading? Why do college students choose to speed reading when using book apps? The future research continues to explore the reasons of this current status of reading habits of college students.

References

1. Mao, Y.: Comments on reading with smartphone. J. Acad. Libr. **6**, 5–11 (2010)
2. Sun, J., Jing, N.: An study on service for mobile reading of libraries in universities by investigating readers. Res. Libr. Sci. **8**, 57–62 (2011)
3. Ye, T.: Analysis of mobile reading preference of college students based on grounded theory method. Res. Libr. Sci. **7**, 78–81 (2011)
4. Wen, Y.: App and Journal App in mobile and wireless Internet. J. Publishing Res. **9**, 82–85 (2012)

The Analysis of the Application of Cloud Computing in the Field of Basic Education

Xiaoling Wang(✉) and Qiong Cai

School of Educational Information Technology, South China Normal University, Guangzhou 510631, China
qfnuwangxiaoling@sina.com, qiongtsai@163.com

Abstract. In recent years, Cloud Computing raised rapidly and has been applied in all aspects of life. In 2008, Cloud Computing was introduced to China, and then favored by educators. The paper starts from the current situation in the application of cloud computing in the field of basic education, analyzes the presence of problems in the process and proposes appropriate measures with a view to the development of cloud computing and basic education services.

Keywords: Cloud computing · Basic education · Application

1 Introduction

"Cloud Computing" was first put forward by Google in the Search Engine Conference in August, 2006. In the recent 10 years, the technology of Cloud Computing is developing rapidly, and permeating to all aspects of life. As a new field of research, cloud computing has attracted the attention of researchers in the field of Education, since it's introduction to China in 2008. Currently, the application of Cloud Computing in Education is still in the primary stage, and the development status is influenced by the regional economic and education level. And the institutions that focused on Cloud Computing is mainly colleges and universities. They focused their eyes mainly on the application and development of Cloud Computing technology, as to the application mode of Cloud Computing in education, is mainly reflected in higher education and general education.

When they use Cloud Computing in higher education, they generally classified it into four stages: the infrastructure construction of Cloud Computing, the construction of high performance platform of Cloud Computing, the construction of application of Cloud Computing and the construction of the sharing resources of Cloud Computing. Cloud Computing is mainly applied in the management of colleges and universities, the computer rooms and libraries. However, the application of Cloud Computing in the field of basic education is less than that in higher education, and there is less analysis of the application of Cloud Computing in the field of basic education either.

The paper starts from the current status of the application of Cloud Computing in basic education, summarizes the current application status of Cloud Computing in basic education, and hopes to put forward the corresponding countermeasures. The paper also

J. Lam et al. (Eds.): ICTE 2015, CCIS 559, pp. 161–169, 2015.
DOI: 10.1007/978-3-662-48978-9_16

wants to forecast the trend of the application of Cloud Computing in the field of basic education, with a view to the development of Cloud Computing and the basic education services.

2 The Current Situation of Cloud Computing in Basic Education

The technology of Cloud Computing is mostly used in the field of higher education, but they have not found some efficient mode of cloud computing to be used in basic education. While in the field of basic education, because of the lack of the basic hardware, technical personnel, theoretical basis, there is few application of cloud computing in basic education.

2.1 The Current Situation of Cloud Computing in Basic Education in China

2.1.1 The Current Situation of the Construction of Educational Resource Platform in Basic Education Based on Cloud Computing

In the field of education, educational resource always takes a very important role. In the current stage, researchers mainly focus their eyes exploring the construction of the cloud educational resource platform when they looked at the application of cloud computing technology in basic education. Researchers analyze the current construction mode of educational resource platform, combined with the characteristic of cloud computing and the requirement of the consumers, they proposed the idea that they can construct a big educational resource platform based on the thinking of cloud service. Due to the hardware facilities and the theoretical basis, there is few educational resource platform based on cloud computing in the field of basic education. And the existing platforms are still in the exploring stage. In conclusion, there is no perfect educational resource platform based on cloud computing so far.

2.1.2 The Current Situation of the Construction of Education Mode in Basic Education Based on Cloud Computing

When there is new technologies used in the field of education, there is change. And the application of cloud computing technology used in the field of basic education brings the change in education mode. Cloud computing makes distance education more convenient. The shared resources make some new education mode, such as mobile learning and fragmentation learning more accepted by human beings. And also, it is more convenient for educators too. It makes the student can do whatever they want, and it is easy to cultivate students' individualized learning. Students can be their own center, and they can increase their own characteristics, broaden the space for their own, and etc. But it also makes great challenge for teachers and educators: How to do to make the technology of cloud computing play the biggest role in the field of basic education? What kind of education mode is the most suitable for the technology of cloud computing applied in the field of basic education? What kind of evaluation should be used to adapt to the application of cloud computing technology in the field of basic education?

2.1.3 The Current Situation of the Construction of Education Informationization in Basic Education Based on Cloud Computing

The construction of education informatization mainly includes following contents in China: First is the construction of campus information network; Second is the construction of education informatization resource; Third is the opening of the information technology curriculum; Forth is the integration of information technology and other subject curriculum; Fifth is the comprehensive application of education information network.

If cloud computing is used in the educational informatization construction in primary and secondary schools, the level of sharing education information resource in primary and secondary schools will be improved efficiently. In this way, we can avoid the duplication investment during the construction of educational informatization, and we can save the money, also, we can provide more abundant services and applications for primary and secondary schools. There is no doubt that cloud computing pointed out a very clear direction for the educational informatization construction in primary and secondary schools, and it may be a big improvement. However, there are lots of problems in the process of the construction of educational informatization so far, for example, how to make it more reasonable in the process of educational informatization construction based on cloud computing in primary and secondary schools [1].

2.2 The Current Situation of Cloud Computing in Basic Education in Foreign Countries

In foreign countries, cloud computing has begun to be used in basic education, but most of them are focused on the application of educational resources, education platform and etc. In America, Graham primary school in North Carolina has begun a program of cloud computing, as a part of the SIMtone Education Thunder Program. The terminal that SIMtone Education Thunder Program provided for the teachers and students meets their growing digital learning needs, and it can provide a virtual desktop for teachers and students through the instant connection with the Simon's general cloud computing services in order to provide the courses, assignments, and other learning materials for students. So that no matter students is in the classroom, in the library or at home, they can access to the same desktop, and no additional computer is needed. Also in the North Carolina in America, the state university has a cloud computing platform called "Virtual Computing Lab" with collaboration with IBM, to provide services for colleges, universities, primary schools and secondary schools, and etc. The services that they provided include the use of online educational resources, application software, computing and storage [2].

3 The Advantage that Cloud Computing Used in the Field of Basic Education

3.1 Data Storage More Secure

The security of information is particularly prominent in primary and secondary schools because of the lack of professional personnel. Cloud computing can provide more reliable and secure data storage center for schools. If school use the cloud computing technology service, they can store their data in the cloud. There will be professional staff to store data, and there will be professional technical management team to manage the submitted data and procedures, and the data will be shared by a certain limit. So that school will not worry about the loss of data caused by the virus and hacker intrusion or hardware damage any more. If we do so, educators will not have to spend their time and effort to store and manage the data of education, they can devote more time and energy to the optimization of the curriculum. So they have more chance to dig into the education theory and practice, students may have a different experience of study.

3.2 Cloud Services Is More Convenient

With the development of the Internet, it is a trend that we can search on the Internet at anytime, anywhere, so that they can enjoy the cloud computing service whenever and wherever they want. And for primary and secondary schools, teachers can work at anywhere and they can share data in all kinds of devices, and also, they can share the education resource with others and work with other teachers even though they are at two different point on the earth. In China, if we use cloud computing, we can provide a new way to narrow the gap between east and west. Teachers in the east and west of China can share education resource by the technology of cloud computing, and at last realize the goal of education informatization.

3.3 Unlimited Possibilities

Cloud computing has a strong power of calculating, and the power provide a unlimited space for storing and managing the power. And it also provide unlimited possibilities for the education on the Internet, and basic education. Suppose that you can manage and monitoring the distribution server of primary and secondary schools in the city or even in the country just in a room, it may be amazing. It makes the maintenance of the server and the sharing more simple, and it can also realize the IT operations with lower cost and higher efficiency.

3.4 Economic Benefit Optimization

There is a lower requirement for the user's terminal equipment with cloud computing, and so there is no need for primary and secondary schools to replace the expensive servers, computers and network equipment frequently. All we need, is just a connection with the Internet, or the installation of a browser. You can leave the rest to the cloud, thus you can greatly save the hardware equipment purchase and maintenance cost, so that we can achieve economic benefit optimization.

3.5 Virtualization

Virtualization is the main feature of cloud computing. As for users, they usually download resources they need on the cloud, as for the storage and management on the cloud, they feel like that it dosen't matter. And they think the cloud is a virtual existing. In the cloud, when the server in use is overloading, it can change to another server automatically. It is amazing when it refers to education informatization in basic education. If it comes to use, we can effectively solve the part of server overload, but some of the server is idle, and we can make best use of the efficiency of the education resources.

3.6 Solving the Problem of High Repetition of Educational Resources and Lack of Quality Resources

When primary and secondary schools establish education resources, because of technology, communication, coordination and etc., the quality of education resource is not the same, and there is also some education resource that we establish more than once, and the utilization of the resource is not so high as we thought. And we can solve all the problems with cloud computing. Based on the construction of education informatization in cloud computing, it can effectively solve the problem of the island of education information, solving the problem of high repetition of educational resources and lack of quality resources.

4 The Problems that Cloud Computing Used in the Field of Basic Education

Cloud computing is used in basic education just in education resource platform or education platform, it is a limit. And as for the practice in daily life, there may be some problems.

4.1 Lack of Thinking

Cloud computing is raising the researchers' focus in the education technology field as a new start thing, especially in higher education. But there is less application in basic education. And the fundamental reason is that teachers, researchers, and other educators are not aware of the huge advantages of cloud computing when it is applied in the field of basic education. And because the teachers are not aware of the huge advantages of cloud computing, they don't have the consciousness to use cloud computing in their teaching life. They are the direct implementation of the basic education, and they have important effects on the understanding, mastering and using of cloud computing technology. But in China, primary and secondary teachers have little access to new technology. They just teach based on the textbook and the teaching program. Even for information technology teachers, they only have heard about cloud computing, and they have no more knowledge of it, and not to mention applied cloud computing in their daily teaching.

4.2 Lack of Hardware Device

Material base determines the superstructure. Cloud computing is the integration of traditional computer and network technology, such as distributed computing, parallel computing, utility computing, network storage, virtualization, load balancing, and so on. One of the reasons that why cloud computing is applying less in education, including higher education and basic education, is that the technology is not mature. Without enough support of technology, it is difficult for cloud computing to be applied in basic education. In our country, the difference between the East and West is quite obvious, and the difference between the coastal areas and the inland areas is also very obvious. And the difference reflected in the basic education is the specific performances in teaching hardware devices. For example, to apply cloud computing in basic education, the basis is computer, but in most areas in the west of our country, many schools have no this kind of hardware devices.

4.3 Theoretical Overview and Technical Support for Development is Less

The majority of scholars in China in education technology field is still limited their eyes to the theory of cloud computing. The practical technology of cloud computing education application is relatively lack of research. And researchers had pay more attention to the cloud computing resources upload, acquire and how to create a simple and high-efficient resource acquisition rote. But the research of the creative application of cloud computing technology is relatively a shortage, which is unfavourable for the application of cloud computing in education. A new technology applied in the field of education, theoretical research, of course, is indispensable, because this is the key to guide the application of technology in practice. However, the reason why technology can be applied in basic education is due to the characteristics of basic education and educational needs, so that the technology will be better to serve the education [3].

4.4 The Small Number and Uneven Quality of Education Resource with Cloud Computing

In China, the basic education resources platform based in cloud computing is being established, but so far, the number is not too much, and the quality, you know, is hard to say. This is because that the researchers that devoted themselves to cloud computing in cloud computing are not so many. And most of the education resource database platform is built mainly by two ways: self-development or commercial purchase.

If the school establish the resource database by themself, they can built it from their own needs, in order to meet the needs of the school. However, they are limited by the ability of development and the economic investment restrictions, so that they can't meet their teaching needs, no matter in quality or in quantity. There is another limitation too. If the schools do that by themselves, the platform they built might be isolated, and the database technology and data dictionary will be different. If there is no unified data conversion interface, it will be difficult for them to exchange resources. And if so, the information isolated island phenomenon will be intensified [4]. Purchase of commercial resource platform is based on the information market management, and if you want to use their platform, you should pay for it. But these platforms are mostly universal, and they can't provide personalized service according to the characteristics of different schools. And also, they packaged the code of the business platform, which makes the user unable to develop further any more, and so, it is difficult to expand outreach.

4.5 Lack of Unified Management Mechanism

In the present situation, there is no complete management mechanism about the application of cloud computing in the field of basic education. If the school develop the platform by themself, there will be difference in hardware, software and programming language. So that it will be difficult to share education resource between two schools, and the phenomenon of isolated information island will be more common. This shows that we are lack of unified construction standards for the construction infrastructure, resource and platform for cloud computing. And when cloud computing applied in basic education, how to operate, how to maintain, and other problems will appear.

5 The Improving Measures that Cloud Computing Used in the Field of Basic Education

5.1 Combination of Theory and Practice

Theory can guide practice, while practice provide feedback for theory. The research about the theory of cloud computing is indispensable, and so as to the practice. The reason why researchers pay so much attention to the theory of cloud computing is to known how to applied cloud computing in education. It is very important for researchers to pay more attention in practice as well as the theory, so cloud computing will serve well in the basic education. Actually, when researchers start to researching how to apply cloud computing in basic education, they will find more problems, which will enrich the theory. And it is a challenge for teachers and educators who work in the field of basic education, they must keep advancing with the times, learning the theory about cloud computing, and design their teaching process according to students' needs. And in this way, they can make the students know that they are in charge of the class and they are the most important in the class. What the teacher need to do is to encourage students to study by their own step, encourage students to learn personalized and stimulate students' personality.

5.2 Focus on the Development of Resource Platform and Promote Technological Progress

Education resources occupy a very important position in education. Cloud computing can take great advantage for basic education, and it may take a very important role in education resources. 《The development planning in education informatization for the later ten years (2010–2020)》 pointed out that: To construct education resources platform, and gather hundreds of enterprises and institutions, develop the excellent resources with thousands of teachers and students. Our country will help all the teachers and students to get access to brilliant education resources with the construction of the platform which is built by the country digital education resource service, so that we can achieve the goal of high-quality resources sharing and sustainable development.

The document published by the government can bring cloud computing a broad prospect, and the government can strength in construction of cloud computing platform, promote effective sharing of education resource, which might be a new trend of research in China. In addition, we should also pay more attention to the functionality of the service platform. We should not focus on the speed of visit, the simplification of information searching, the articulation of the guide, system stability and security, and so on. What we should do is to achieve the function of innovation, and design a multivariate service platform. Of course, we need some support of the technology, and the promotion of the cloud computing by the researcher, in order to serve the education [3].

5.3 Support for the Government to Increase the Use of Cloud Computing Application in Basic Education

The government should give some support for applying the cloud computing in basic education. Without the support of the government, there is a long way to go to apply cloud computing in basic education. For example, the government should increase the investment to remote areas and poverty-stricken areas of education, so that the secondary and primary schools in these areas can have certain hardware to implement cloud education. And we should give the teachers there a chance to be trained, so they can apply cloud computing in their class.

Furthermore, the government should publish a unified cloud computing resources standard as soon as possible. To say it simply is to set a set of standards at first, then implement the constructions. It is equal to say that we design and develop the education resource on the basis of the standard we set already, in order to facilitate the follow-up and share. As to the development of the cloud computing technology, the government needs investment also, to encourage researchers to do something creative, and apply in education finally. And also, we can see that cloud computing has a lot of things to do in education informatization, so government should encourage researchers try in the field, and finally narrow the gap in China.

6 The Development Trend that Cloud Computing Used in the Field of Basic Education

In summary, if cloud computing is applied in basic education, these will happen:

Cloud computing technology and its application will gain popularity and promotion in the field of basic education, state and society will also pay more attention to cloud computing education application, and they will increase input of human, material and financial resources.

Cloud computing and teaching methods will be better integration. The theory of education might be the basis of cloud computing in education, and when cloud computing is applied in education, we will be more careful about the feedback, and if we do so, cloud computing will better serve in basic education.

More research about the mode and method about how cloud computing could apply in basic education would occur, and it may give great advice, so that cloud resource and cloud education platform could be better applied in basic education.

Cloud computing will do something to speed up the process of education informatization in China.

7 Conclusion

Cloud computing is still in the primary stage in basic education, and it may bring many unexpected benefits of the education and teaching. But at present, there are still lost of problems when cloud computing is applied in basic application, and there will be more problems in the future. What the researchers can do is to find the problem, and solve the problem. With the growing popularity of big data, cloud computing must solve some problems in the current situation of basic education in our country.

References

1. Hongjian, Liao: Research on the construction of primary and secondary education information based on Cloud Computing. Sci. Technol. Inf. **4**, 293 (2012)
2. Suqing, Y., Li, P.: Cloud computing and its inspiration to China's basic education. Technol. Appl. **6**, 77–78 (2010)
3. Huainan, Zhang, Cheng, Yang: A survey of the application of cloud computing in China. Distance Educ. China **1**, 20–26 (2013)
4. Qiao, C., Xinping, H.: Construction of teaching resources platform based on cloud service. Mod. Educ. Technol. **12**, 112–115 (2011)
5. The development planning in education informationization for the later ten years (2010–2020)[EB/OL].[03-13-2012]. http://www.moe.edu.cn/Publicfiles/business/htmlfiles/moe/s3342/201203/xxgk_133322.html

Institutional Strategies, Policies and Practices

A Review of Learning Analytics in Educational Research

Kam Cheong Li(✉), Hoi Kuan Lam, and Sylvia Siu-Yin Lam

The Open University of Hong Kong, Hong Kong SAR, China
{kcli,hlam,ssylam}@ouhk.edu.hk

Abstract. An increasing amount of research work is now focused on the topic of learning analytics. Gathering the facts from the literature is important for identifying issues and features in 'the state of the art' and the way forward. This paper aims to examine the research literature published in the last five years and construct a systematic review of learning analytics. A document analysis method is used to classify the research work in 51 articles, selected from the Web of Science, which report educational research studies using a learning analytics approach. The details of the studies are categorised according to their research questions or objectives, the methodology (such as input data, techniques used or software tools for data collection and analysis) and the findings. This paper offers an overview of the emerging field of learning analytics, provides a foundation for exploring this promising area of educational research, and identifies a series of future challenges.

Keywords: Learning analytics · Education research · Systematic review

1 Introduction

Learning analytics (LA) is an emerging field in the education sector. It focuses specifically on the learning process [1] and involves the use of big data techniques to capture, model and predict the behaviours of diverse target groups from a massive volume of unstructured data. At academic institutions, LA is used to examine the relevant data on students and instructors at a micro-level which target individual learners and the courses taken in order to understand student performance and promote student success [2]. With the sophisticated analytic tools and techniques of LA, student performance and learning outcomes can be improved by enhanced targeting of support and intervention, thus promoting learning and education [3]. The study and advancement of LA involves the development, usage and integration of new processes and tools in order to improve the practice of learning and teaching for individual students and instructors.

2 Background

In communities of educators, LA and educational data mining (EDM) form two research areas oriented towards the inclusion and exploration of big data capabilities in education for gaining insights into the learning activities of learners [4]. EDM is an area for "developing, researching, and applying computerized methods to detect patterns in large collections of educational data that would otherwise be hard or impossible to analyse

J. Lam et al. (Eds.): ICTE 2015, CCIS 559, pp. 173–184, 2015.
DOI: 10.1007/978-3-662-48978-9_17

due to the enormous volume of data within which they exist" [5]. LA is defined as "the measurement, collection, analysis and reporting of data about learners and their contexts, for the purposes of understanding and optimizing learning and the environments in which it occurs" [6]. There are other definitions of the term LA which are different in some details, but the definitions share an emphasis on converting educational data into useful actions to foster learning [7].

Although EDM and LA share the common goal of gaining insights into learners' activities, they are different in their origins, techniques, fields of emphasis and types of discovery [5, 7, 8]. Nonetheless, the two research areas are complementary [4]. The research results on EDM do not focus on empirical evidence but on the objectives, methods, processes and tools for knowledge discovering. LA, on the other hand, adopts a holistic approach when seeking insights into the learning processes. An overview of LA argues that teachers should engage with LA for richer conceptions of learning and improvements in teaching [9]. Another study supplements the insights for students, stating that "receiving information about their performance in relation to their peers or about their progress in relation to their personal goals can be motivating and encouraging" [1].

The concepts and methods of LA are drawn from a variety of related fields [7]. It is "an area of research related to business intelligence, web analytics, academic analytics, action analytics and predictive analytics" [4]. LA is also a field in which several related areas of research in technology-enhanced learning converge, including academic analytics, action research, EDM, recommender systems and personalized adaptive learning [7]. The more concrete examples of LA practice comprise predictive modelling, social network analysis (SNA), usage tracking, content analysis and semantic analysis, and recommendation engines [9].

Given the common emphasis on converting educational data to support the learning process and foster learning, as well as the different practices of LA, there is however no concrete theoretical model or framework of LA in the literature. As Clow states, "Learning analytics is not so much a solid academic discipline with established methodological approaches as it is a 'jackdaw' field of enquiry, picking up 'shiny' techniques, tools and methodologies …. This eclectic approach is both a strength and a weakness: it facilitates rapid development and the ability to build on established practice and findings, but it — to date — lacks a coherent, articulated epistemology of its own" (pp. 685–686) [9]. In Papamitsiou and Economides's literature review of empirical evidence of LA and EDM, they assert that "The motivation for this review derived from the fact that empirical evidence is required for theoretical frameworks to gain acceptance in the scientific community…. Consequently, there was a need to supply the audience with an accredited overview" (p. 50) [4]. Based on the LA reference model, Chatti and others reviewed relevant studies in LA applications and mapped the studies onto the four dimensions of the model, namely data and environments, stakeholders, objectives and methods [7]. The review, however, was confined to two years, 2010 and 2011. A search in the relevant literature did not find any review of empirical evidence of LA for a longer period, which motivated us to produce a critical review of empirical studies of LA over a five-year period to indicate the extent of maturity and deployment of LA applications for useful actions to foster learning.

3 Methodology

3.1 Aim and Objectives

Though LA has demonstrated its potential as a promising research area in educational technology, only limited systematic literature reviews have been carried out on the topic. This paper, which aims to collect and summarize information derived from the literature about the applications of LA in educational research, addresses the following research questions:

1. What kinds of educational research have been conducted using an LA approach?
2. What kinds of data have been used for educational research using an LA approach?
3. What kinds of techniques/software tools are available for educational research using an LA approach?
4. What kinds of key findings are observed from educational research using an LA approach?

3.2 Data Collection and Analysis Methods

This paper aims to examine the research literature about LAs published in scholarly journals. Studies from this research have been chosen by accessing electronic sources. The literature is limited to studies published in the last five years, between 2011 and 2015, in the Web of Science from international databases. The data sources for this study are summarized in Table 1(A). The Web of Science includes such journals as the *Journal of the Learning Sciences*, *Computers & Education*, *The Internet and Higher Education*, the *International Journal of Computer-Supported Collaborative Learning*, *Learning Media and Technology*, the *British Journal of Educational Technology*, *Sport Education and Society*, *IEEE Transactions on Learning Technologies*, the *Australasian Journal of Educational Technology*, the *Journal of Geography in Higher Education*, *Educational Technology and Society*, *Distance Education*, *Teaching in Higher Education*, the *International Review of Research in Open and Distance Learning*, and *Culture, Education and Communication*. While searching, the word 'LA' has been used as the search topic and the search category has been limited to 'education educational research'. The resulting search gained access to a total of 51 studies, in which 47 were articles, two were reviews and two were editorials. In this study, document analysis has been used to examine each article and the content was identified through objective, systematic and quantitative categorization [10]. Through document analysis, the information extracted from the selected literature has been examined and revised using a particular encoding system and has been used as collected data [11]. Subsequently, the data gathered by document analysis have been made into content analysis, according to the mathematical representation of the data based on the characteristics observed [12]. The literature has been examined carefully and categorized into three main criteria. These criteria within the framework of the research approach were (1) the research question or objective of the studies; (2) the methodology used in the studies; and (3) the key findings of the studies. The second criterion — the methodology used — was further divided into five sub-criteria. They were (2.1) the data source, i.e. the kind of system in which the data were gathered, managed and used for the analysis; (2.2) stakeholders, i.e. the participant(s) targeted by the analysis; (2.3) study group, i.e. the characteristics of the participants; (2.4) instrument(s), i.e. the technique(s) used to perform the analysis of the collected data; and (2.5) course or field of the study, i.e. the area that the study applied to. Comparable criteria have been used before for the same purposes [7, 13], but there have also been some different criteria included in this paper. The three main criteria and the five sub-criteria have been considered within the scope of this research. The criteria for examination in this study are summarized in Table 1(B).

Table 1. Data source and criteria for examination in this study

(A) Data source	
Database:	Web of Science
Search topic:	Learning analytics
Search category:	Education educational research
Search time-span:	2011–2015 (five years)
Search result:	51 pieces of literature in total (including two reviews, 47 articles, and two editorials)
(B) Criteria for the examination of the articles used	
(1) The **research question** or **objective** of the studies	
— Monitoring and analysis; prediction and intervention; assessment and feedback;adaptation; personalization and recommendation; and reflection	
(2) The **methodology** used in the studies	
(2.1) **Data source**: Where did the educational data come from?	
— Closed/Protected, e.g. a learning management system vs open/distributed, e.g. personal learning environment	
(2.2) **Stakeholder**: Who is/are the participant(s)?	
— Student; teacher; educational institution; researcher; and system designer	
(2.3) **Study group**: What is/are the characteristic(s) of the participant(s)?	
— Primary school; secondary school; higher education	
(2.4) **Instrument**: What is/are the technique(s) used to perform the analysis of the collected data?	
— Survey/questionnaires; statistics; non-statistics; information visualization; data mining; social network analysis; content analysis; natural language processing; machine learning; group concept mapping; pattern information analysis; and ethnographic analysis	
(2.5) **Course or field of study**: To which area does the study apply?	
— Education technology; science, technology, engineering and mathematics; geographical education; health and physical education; educational research; computer science; education publications; humanities; media literacy education; medical education and digital image processing	
(3) The **key findings** of the studies	
— Learning outcomes (measured as positive, negative and neutral)	

4 Results

LA has a huge potential for supporting learning, teaching and education, and the number of publications on LA research has grown rapidly in the last few years. In this paper, the selected literature on LA for the research has been analysed for three main criteria and five sub-criteria as described above in Table 1(B), and the results can be summarized as follows.

4.1 Distribution of the Research Question or Objectives

There are many objectives in the selected literature and they have been examined one by one. Similar topics have been combined, which include monitoring and analysis, prediction and intervention, assessment and feedback, adaptation, personalization and recommendation, and reflection. The distribution of the studies on research questions or objectives is summarized in Table 2.

Table 2. Distribution of literature by research questions or objectives

Research question/Objective	Frequency (%)
Monitoring and analysis	10 (19.6 %)
Prediction and intervention	6 (11.8 %)
Assessment and feedback	8 (15.7 %)
Adaptation	9 (17.6 %)
Personalization and recommendation	3 (5.9 %)
Reflection	15 (29.4 %)

Table 2 shows that the most frequent objectives in the selected literature are on reflection (29.4 %), and monitoring and analysis (19.6 %). Fewer objectives aim for adaptation (17.6 %), assessment and feedback (15.7 %), prediction and intervention (11.8 %), and personalization and recommendation (5.9 %). This answers our research question 1 — 'What kinds of educational research have been conducted using an LA approach?'— by research question or objective.

4.2 Distribution of Data Source

The LA tools that have been proposed in the literature selected use different data sources. We classified the data sources into closed/protected [e.g. learning management system (LMS)] and open/distributed [e.g. personal learning environment (PLE)]. The distribution of the studies on where the educational data came from is summarized in Table 3.

Table 3. Reviewed literature by distribution of data source

Data source	Frequency (%)
Closed/Protected, e.g. LMS	23 (45.1 %)
Open/Distributed, e.g. PLE	28 (54.9 %)

Table 3 illustrates that studies from the chosen literature are 54.9 % from open or distributed sources and 45.1 % from closed or protected sources. The open or distributed sources include literature; Elgg®, the social networking engine; computer-supported collaborative learning (CSCL); web-based systems (such as wikis, learning and content management systems, forums, academic portals, repositories); and massive open online courses (MOOC). The closed or protected data sources include Equella; computer-assisted curriculum analysis; design and evaluation (CASCADE); virtual field trip (VFT); and QuesTInSitu — the Game, LOCO-Analyst and Blackboard. This answers our research question 2 — 'What kinds of data have been used for educational research using an LA approach?'— by the distribution of data source.

4.3 Distribution of Stakeholders

The stakeholders who participated in studies in the selected literature include students, teachers, educational institutions, researchers and system designers. The distribution of the studies on the participants is summarized in Table 4.

Table 4. Reviewed literature by distribution of stakeholders

Participant	Frequency (%)
Students	17 (23.6 %)
Teachers	21 (29.2 %)
Educational institutions	19 (26.4 %)
Researchers	12 (16.7 %)
Systems designers	3 (4.2 %)

Table 4 shows that most of the studies have targeted teachers (29.2 %), educational institutions (26.4 %) and students (23.6 %). Fewer studies have involved researchers (16.7 %) and system designers (4.2 %). This also answers our research question 2 — 'What kinds of data are used for educational research using an LA approach?' — according to the participants in the studies.

4.4 Distribution of Study Group

The studies selected have been classified by study group according to the participants' characteristics, which include primary school, secondary school, and higher education.

The distribution of the studies on study group according to participants' characteristics is summarized in Table 5.

Table 5. Reviewed literature by distribution of participants' characteristics

Study group	Frequency (%)
Primary school	0 (0 %)
Secondary school	6 (17.1 %)
Higher education	29 (82.9 %)

Table 5 illustrates that the study groups in the studies are concentrated heavily in higher education (82.9 %). There are fewer studies at the level of secondary schools (17.1 %) and none at the primary school level (0 %). This also answers our research question 2 — 'What kinds of data have been used for educational research using an LA approach?' — by study group according to participants' characteristics in the studies.

4.5 Distribution of Instruments

The selected studies have been classified according to the instruments used, which include surveys/questionnaires, statistics, non-statistics, information visualization (IV), data-mining (DM), SNA, content analysis, natural language processing (NLP), machine learning, group concept mapping, pattern information analysis and ethnographic analysis. Note that some studies applied a variety of methods and can therefore be found in multiple categories. The distribution of the studies on instruments used is summarized in Table 6.

Table 6. Reviewed literature by distribution of instruments

Technique or software tool	Frequency (%)
Surveys/Questionnaires	9 (14.3 %)
Statistics	3 (4.8 %)
Non-statistics	18 (28.6 %)
Data mining	8 (12.7 %)
Machine learning	3 (4.8 %)
Information visualization	9 (14.3 %)
Social network analysis	6 (9.5 %)
Content analysis	3 (4.8 %)
Natural language processing	1 (1.6 %)
Group concept mapping	1 (1.6 %)
Pattern information analysis	1 (1.6 %)
Ethnographic analysis	1 (1.6 %)

As can be seen in Table 6, the most used LA techniques in the literature reviewed take advantages of information retrieval technologies with classical tools, such as non-statistics (28.6 %), surveys or questionnaires (14.3 %), IV (14.3 %), DM (12.7 %), machine learning (12.7 %) and statistics (4.8 %). Other techniques, such as SNA (9.5 %), content analysis (4.8 %), NLP (1.6 %), group concept mapping (1.6 %), pattern information analysis (1.6 %) and ethnographic analysis (1.6 %) are also employed in the studies. This answers our research question 3 — 'What kinds of techniques/software tools are available for educational research using an LA approach?' — on the instruments used.

4.6 Distribution of Course of Research or Field of Study

The studies chosen have been classified according to application courses and their fields, which include education technology, science, technology, engineering and mathematics (STEM), geographical education, health and physical education, educational research, computer science, education publications, humanities, media literacy education, medical education and digital image processing. The distribution of the studies on the course of research or field of study is summarized in Table 7.

Table 7. Reviewed literature by distribution of course or field of study

Course/Field of study	Frequency (%)
Education technology	21 (38.2 %)
Science, technology, engineering and mathematics (STEM)	10 (18.2 %)
Geographical education	1 (1.8 %)
Health and physical education	1 (1.8 %)
Educational research	11 (20.0 %)
Computer science	5 (9.1 %)
Education publications	1 (1.8 %)
Humanities	1 (1.8 %)
Media literacy education	1 (1.8 %)
Medical education	2 (3.6 %)
Digital image processing	1 (1.8 %)

Table 7 shows that studies in the selected literature focus on education technology (38.2 %) and educational research (20.0 %) on LA. The effectiveness studies oriented to different courses are mainly on STEM (18.2 %), computer science (9.1 %) and medical education (3.6 %). Fewer studies are concerned with courses such as geographical education (1.8 %), health and physical education (1.8 %), education publications (1.8 %), humanities (1.8 %), media literacy education (1.8 %) and digital image processing (1.8 %). Again, this answers our research question 2 — 'What kinds of data have been used for educational research using an LA approach?' — by the courses or fields of the studies.

4.7 Distribution of the Key Findings

The studies chosen have been classified according to positive, negative and neutral learning outcomes, the distribution of which is summarized in Table 8.

Table 8. Reviewed literature by distribution of learning outcomes

Learning outcome	Frequency (%)
Positive	45 (88.2 %)
Negative	2 (3.9 %)
Neutral	4 (7.8 %)

In Table 8, it can be seen that the majority of the studies have a positive learning outcome (88.2 %) within the scope of the research. Meanwhile, the learning outcomes in two studies are negative (3.9 %), and in another four they are neutral (7.8 %). This answers our research question 4 — 'What kinds of key findings are observed for educational research using an LA approach?' — by learning outcomes.

5 Discussion and Conclusion

The literature analysed in this study has been chosen from the Web of Science which is an online subscription-based scientific citation indexing service. It provides a comprehensive citation search by accessing multiple databases that reference cross-disciplinary research and allows an in-depth exploration of specialized sub-fields within an academic or scientific discipline. Therefore, the selected literature on the topic LA in the field of 'educational education research' in this study is highly relevant and comes from journals with an impact factor ranging from 0.35 to 3.26. This is already evidence that LA, which involves large amounts of data in combination with information retrieval technologies, has substantial potential for use in education [14]. The novel information retrieved from LA can support individual learning as well as organizational knowledge management [15]. Research on the application of LA in education has been increasing since 2011 and this has been sustained up to the present.

The advantages of LA are that it reveals and translates the educational data from unknown to meaningful information and prepares it for students, teachers and educational institutions [13]. The objective which is applied most in the literature reviewed in this study is reflection (29.4 %) which has been distinguished as a fundamental objective in LA since 2009 [16]. Reflection is a process involving quantifying oneself from one's own performance for better learning outcomes. The second most common objective applied in the selected literature is monitoring and analysis (19.6 %) which, by comparing information on and interactions with students, can offer new perceptions of both learners and organizations in terms of effectiveness and efficiency. The third most frequent applied objective in the literature reviewed is adaptation (17.6 %), which adaptively articulates learners to the next move by consolidating learning resources and instructional activities according to individual learner's needs [7].

As there is a shift in focus from centralized learning systems to open learning environments, the use of closed/protected data sources as a dominant trend has changed. Our findings show that more open/distributed data sources (54.9 %) have been used in the studies in the selected literature, as compared to closed/protected data sources (45.1 %). The closed/protected data sources, such as LMS, have been dominant since the emergence of LA, while open/distributed data sources, such as PLE, have grown considerably in recent years; and the use of closed/protected and open/distributed data sources have become fairly balanced.

LA studies of pedagogical issues undoubtedly involve students and teachers as stakeholders. Traditionally, the investigation of students' behaviours and activities has been one of the main focuses in LA research. These studies emphasize the generation of student-centred feedback by tracking users' data from learning systems, but much less research was concerned with educator-centred feedback. However, recently, there has been a tendency for much more stress to be put on stakeholders other than students. Our findings have shown that the majority of the studies in the literature chosen have targeted teachers (29.2 %), educational institutions (26.4 %) and students (23.6 %), suggesting that educator-centred studies have been increasing. The involvement of stakeholders, such as researchers and system designers, has provided a more comprehensive view of information using LA.

The study group in the LA research in the literature reviewed has been focused on the level of higher education (82.9 %), with fewer studies at the secondary school level (17.1 %) and none on the primary school level. This phenomenon may be due to the fact that the research subjects are generally those within the age range for higher education who can take advantages of the technology by having adequate learning skills. Stakeholders, such as students at university level, fit these criteria well and are perfect subjects for researchers who are most likely to also be working in higher education institutions.

Different techniques or software tools can be applied in the development of education applications that support the objectives of educational stakeholders. LA takes advantage of information retrieval technologies that can contribute tailored information support systems to the stakeholders on demand, and can be applied to a vast variety of field of study [14]. It is clear from our findings that the techniques or software tools used range from classical LA tools to the latest advanced technological tools, such as the study conducted through mobile applications by Melero et al. [17]. In this sense, there would be no boundary for the application courses or fields of those studies, as shown in our findings on a wide variety of courses, ranging from humanities and medical to STEM. Nonetheless, education technology courses were the major field as technological advances play a critical role in the development of LA research.

The key findings on LA examined in terms of learning outcomes within the scope of research were mostly constructive. More than 80 % of the studies indicated positive learning outcomes, suggesting that LA as a field has strengthened learning, teaching and pedagogical decision-making. However, two studies showed that, regardless of how powerful and promising LA is as a technological advance in guiding and appraising the educational progress, technologies alone are not enough for seeing the whole picture [18, 19]. It is sensible to take into consideration human beings who are properly trained, determined, and dedicated to education — such as teachers, system designers, policy administrators and maybe parents — in order to complete the picture as a whole.

Research in the field of LA has been booming in the last five year, but LA is still at the infant stage in its development. Universities should take careful note of its advances and potential for use, together with conventional methods of student support, to achieve substantial improvements in the practice of higher education. This active research area will continue to contribute valuable pieces of work to the development of powerful and mostly accurate learning services for both learners and teachers.

References

1. Siemens, G., Long, P.: Penetrating the fog: analytics in learning and education. EDUCAUSE Rev. **46**(5), 30–40 (2011)
2. Learning Analytics: Definitions, Processes and Potential. http://learninganalytics.net/LearningAnalyticsDefinitionsProcessesPotential.pdf
3. van Barneveld, A., Arnold, K.E., Campbell, J.P.: Analytics in higher education: establishing a common language. EDUCAUSE Learn. Initiative. **1**, 1–11 (2012)
4. Papamitsiou, Z., Economides, A.: Learning analytics and educational data mining in practice: a systematic literature review of empirical evidence. Educ. Tech. Soc. **17**(4), 49–64 (2014)
5. Romero, C., Ventura, A.: Data mining in education. WIREs Data Min. Knowl. Disc. **3**, 12–27 (2013)
6. Proceedings of the 1st International Conference on Learning Analytics and Knowledge. https://tekri.athabascau.ca/analytics/
7. Chatti, M.A., Dyckhoff, A.L., Schroeder, U., Thüs, H.: A reference model for learning analytics. Int. J. Technol. Enhanced Learn. **4**(5–6), 318–333 (2012)
8. Siemens, G., Baker, R.: Learning analytics and educational data mining: towards communication and collaboration. In: Buckingham Shum, S., Gasevic, D., Ferguson, R. (eds.) 2nd International Conference on Learning Analytics and Knowledge, pp. 252–254. ACM, New York (2012)
9. Clow, D.: An overview of learning analytics. Teach. High. Educ. **18**(6), 683–695 (2013)
10. Bauer, M.W.: Classical content analysis: a review. In: Bauer, M.W., Gaskell, G. (eds.) Qualitative Researching with Text, Image and Sound, pp. 131–151. Sage Publication, London (2003)
11. Çepni, S.: Araştırma ve proje çalışmalarına giriş (3. Baskı), Methods and classifications used in educational research. Celepler Publisher, Trabzon (2007)
12. Karasar, N.: Bilimsel araştırma yöntemi [Research Methods], 11. Nobel Publisher, Ankara (2002)
13. Greller, W., Drachsler, H.: Translating learning into numbers: a generic framework for learning analytics. Educ. Tech. Soc. **15**(3), 42–57 (2012)
14. Johnson, L., Smith, R., Willis, H., Levine, A., Haywood, K.: The 2011 Horizon Report. The New Media Consortium, Austin (2011)
15. Butler, D.L., Winne, P.H.: Feedback and self-regulated learning: a theoretical synthesis. Rev. Educ. Res. **65**, 245–281 (1995)

16. Know Thyself: Tracking Every Facet of Life, from Sleep to Mood to Pain. Wired Magazine. http://www.wired.com/medtech/health/magazine/17–07/lbnp_knowthyself?currentPage=all
17. Melero, J., Hernández-Leo, D., Sun, J., Santos, P., Blat, J.: How Was the Activity? A Visualization Support for a Case of Location-Based Learning Design. Br. J. Educ. Technol. **46**(2), 317–329 (2015)
18. Macfadyen, L.P., Dawson, S.: Numbers Are Not Enough. Why E-learning Analytics Failed to Inform an Institutional Strategic Plan. Educ. Technol. Soc. **15**(3), 149–163 (2012)
19. Spector, J.M.: Emerging educational technologies and research directions. Educ. Technol. Soc. **16**(2), 21–30 (2013)

A Preliminary Study on the Impact of Availability of e-Resources on Part-time Teachers' Job Satisfaction in Hong Kong Self-finance Institutions

Kwan Keung Ng(✉), Ching Hong Luk, and Wai Ming Lam

School of Business and Hospitality Management, Caritas Institute of Higher Education, 18 Chui Ling Road, Tseung Kwan O, New Territories, Hong Kong SAR, China
{sng,eluk,plam}@cihe.edu.hk

Abstract. Improving efficiencies in the education sector via the sharing of electronic resources is important for enhancing teachers' job satisfaction. As the demand for higher education rises, together with budgetary pressures on the education sector, advances that improve teaching efficiency have been sought. This paper reports on research investigating the impact of availability of e-resources on part time teachers' job satisfaction in Hong Kong self-finance institutions. The part time teachers' views on e-resources and their job satisfaction will be examined by conducting in-depth discussion. Furthermore, it was expected to find that there were differences in job satisfaction between different extents of availability of e-resources for part time teachers. In other words, the existence of causal relationships between the availability of e-resources and job satisfaction of part time teachers was also explored. Information on part time teachers' conceptions and approaches was collected through in-depth discussion and job satisfaction was used as an indicator to reflect the importance of e-resources in education.

Keywords: e-Resources · Part time teachers · Teaching quality · Teaching performance · Job satisfaction

1 Introduction

E-resources have improved both access to teaching and learning materials as well as the flexibility of education, but their development requires considerable investment [30]. The benefits are amplified when resources are shared so as to enhance job satisfaction [36] and wide ranges of educational resource sharing initiatives have been developed around the world. In addition, information and communication technology (ICT) is becoming more and more a central part of education in many countries. Internet tools and services are and will obviously be of the utmost importance to pass on and disseminate knowledge for both teachers and students [8]. They are already widely used in institutions and it becomes urgent to develop methods and tools that will be appropriate for storing, manipulating and managing teaching materials in order to make it shareable and easy to use or reuse. Moreover, easy handling and large access to the resources are features that must be optimized by basing these methods and tools on information and

J. Lam et al. (Eds.): ICTE 2015, CCIS 559, pp. 185–194, 2015.
DOI: 10.1007/978-3-662-48978-9_18

communication technology. Notwithstanding, the availability of e-resources for part time teachers is sometimes limited; it may perhaps adversely affect their teaching performance so as to job satisfaction. This paper is to investigate the causal relationship between the availability of e-resources and job satisfaction of part time teachers in Hong Kong self-finance institutions, with Caritas Institute of Higher Education as a case study. In order to examine the relationship, in-depth discussion with a focus group of part-time teachers who are currently teaching at self-finance institutions was conducted to collect the views on the availability of electronic resources from part time teachers and their job satisfaction and the job satisfaction instrument were measured [37].

2 Literature Review

Electronic resources have been becoming more common in higher education and the availability resources can positively help improve the quality of education and enhance teachers' job satisfaction. In the following paragraphs, quality of education, the decline of quality education, the importance and benefits of electronic resources and job satisfaction will be discussed.

2.1 Quality of Education

There is no universally accepted definition on quality of education [26, 42, 48]. It sometimes refers to schools, teacher/pupil ratio, availability of educational resources inputs, etc. [4]. In this way, most scholars understand quality of education in terms of resource inputs and performance of education system. In particular, Jimenez & Pinzon [22] defined quality of education as "a dynamic concept that focuses on capacity and performance of the education systems and of its schools". The term 'dynamic' connotes that quality of education is "constantly changing to adapt to a world whose societies are undergoing profound social and economic transformation" [46].

In the context of the changing world and its changing needs, Makwati, Audinos, & Lairez [35] contend that perceiving quality in education as being universally understood and defined, is no longer acceptable and valid. Quality of education, therefore, has become more "country or environment specific and related to the goals, expectations and aspirations of a given community, and these may change over time" [35]. Such changes create a situation whereby "access to technology, modern education and resources play a major role in the ability to contribute or adapt to change" For example, Unesco [46] is one of the few emerging themes that is relevant to the definition of education quality in all contexts. In other words, the available resources are deployed and the extent to which these resources inputs are efficiently and effectively used becomes substantially vital in determining quality of education [40, 44]. All these resources inputs may profoundly influence the kinds and quality of the educational services offered as being either of acceptable or unacceptable standards for all the citizens of a given country or country-specific context [12, 35, 48].

Therefore, the present study attempts to explore the challenge facing most institutions and studies whether it is better to strike a balance between the key components of educational quality: namely access, efficiency, and effectiveness. Given the current realization of the influence of unavoidably embedded, context specific issues, it would perhaps be not surprising that the quality of education is declining in most education systems, the issue addressed in the following section. There it probably shows that better resources will lead to better education quality proven by researchers.

2.2 Declining Quality of Education

The quality of a nation's education system is the foundation for its social and economic growth [31]. All stakeholders in the education are increasingly attaching greater value to the quality of education. Unfortunately, the diminishing national resources and the lack of critical resources undermine the quality of educational opportunities, particularly in developing countries [3, 4, 27, 41]. This declining quality of education has become a big concern to most governments of the world [10, 38]. Since quality education is fundamental in contributing to educational effectiveness and to the success of individuals, families, communities and nations.

Whether additional school resources, including electronic resources, make a difference to student performance remains controversial and unclear [29, 33, 51]. To investigate what kinds of school factors and resources actually account for school performance and contribute to the improvement of quality of education, researchers have used various performance indicators as proxies for quality of education [19, 29]. Typical performance indicators include such items as standardized test scores, school attendance rates, school dropout rates, stakeholders' participation, infrastructure, administration, teacher training, and expenditures per student [13, 18]. In this way, the education quality might have a declining trend worldwide and more attention should then be paid to them.

2.3 The Importance of e-Resources in Higher Education

Internet has been playing an increasingly important role in higher education [23]. Access to accurate information on the Internet is not an easy task, therefore, there are a great number of directories and search engines available in this new media [15]. The rise of information technology has shifted education landscape. As the demand for higher education rises, together with budgetary pressures on the education sector, advances that improve teaching efficiency have been sought. A wide range of educational resource-sharing initiatives have been developed around the world. Open resources provide learners worldwide with unrestricted access to learning resources [11, 21].

Traditionally, the teaching is performed through theoretical and practical classes, and the consultation material consists of books and scientific journals. Now with the availability of new technologies and opportunities to teachers and students are opened. The use of these new technologies, however, has been a target of ongoing debate [2]. A variety studies have acknowledged the benefits of using information technology as a teaching tool in various fields [9]. For example, in health related fields, studies involving the application of information technology have evaluated the impact of the use of computers and compared its use with traditional learning [47]. These students suggested that computer may be used to improve their learning. To the best of our knowledge, these new technologies seem to provide a variety of teaching opportunities [16].

The use of a multimedia online resource had a positive impact on students' learning. Increased motivation of the students, cost effectiveness and user preferences may be partial explanations for such better performance [45]. Even when no difference is found, students may still rather prefer to use the electronic resources and augmented motivation may favour improved students' scores [29]. In addition, tools that allow tutor-student interaction also seem to be important in improving learning [49].

The educational process has been a target of ongoing debate, as the need to develop new strategies that favour the improvement of teaching standards [24]. A major concern regarding the use of new technologies is the development of critical thinking, defined as the capacity to analyse, evaluate, question, investigate and experiment [14]. A number of studies have demonstrated that applying new technological tools to teaching promotes critical thinking [6, 32]. In the teaching-learning process, information technology and communication have a diversity of uses that go beyond the transfer of information through classes and from textbooks to students through distance learning [17].

Although technology can facilitate and enrich teaching and learning, it can create problems as well. Some people may not have access to broadband internet reported difficulties in viewing electronic resources. These technological issues must be solved with online support, supplied through a collaborative learning environment, where students and teachers could exchange information and discuss with the teachers and the technical assistance team. Some studies have suggested that similar technical problems, as well as social factors and poor skills in using technological resources are the major barriers encountered by students and teachers in using these technologies [50].

To conclude, information technology and electronic resources have been becoming common in education and various studies showed that the availability of information technology and electronic resources can enhance teaching and learning.

2.4 Job Satisfaction in Academics

Numerous studies have been conducted on job satisfaction of typical organizations' employees. However, only a limited number of studies have focused on academics' job satisfaction as a subject of study. Kalssen, Usher and Bong [25] identified promotion, pay, supervisory support, team cohesion, job requirements itself and availability of resources as the prime factors of job satisfaction. In addition, Maertz and Griffeth [34] in a theoretical exposition reported eight motivational factors for job satisfaction which comprises of salary, job autonomy, good supervision, and interpersonal relationships. In addition, some researchers identified organizational culture as another factor of job satisfaction [5]. Ssesanga and Garrett [43] employed nine determinants to measure academics' job satisfaction, including teaching, research, remuneration, supervision, opportunities for promotion, co-workers behaviour, working conditions, governance, and the job itself.

People must be equipped with knowledge, skills, and capabilities to be effective citizens in their national and global communities (Musa & Smadi, 2013). Allocating sufficient resources to education is one way to achieve this goal and help citizens to benefit from globalization [39]. As teaching is among the main professions that attract many young people, teacher motivation has become a critical issue in the international educational process, and it has recently received extensive attention. Alkhawaldeh's [1] investigation into the professional needs of teachers if English highlighted the necessity of in service training programs, instructional media and appropriate teaching methods, consideration of students' needs in designing a curriculum, teachers' involvement in curriculum evaluation, exposing students to English spoken by native speakers, and the use of autonomous and co-operative learning techniques.

In addition, teachers who are satisfied with their work typically display higher levels of motivated behaviour and performance as well as lower levels of stress, anxiety and burnout [7]. The satisfaction that teachers gain from their work may be experienced individually, but teaching is not practiced in a social or cultural vacuum. Job satisfaction and motivation are influenced by teachers' interactions by cultural milieu and cultural values [20].

To conclude, the above previous studies showed that school resources will affect teachers' sense of belonging to schools and so as to their job satisfaction. As a result, job satisfaction will affect their motivation and performance. This study is to evaluate the causal relationship between the availability of electronic resources and job satisfaction of part time teachers in Hong Kong self-finance institutions.

3 Methodology

The research method attempts to handle the relationship between the availability of e-resources and academic job satisfaction among scholars in Self-financed Institutions in Hong Kong, this study is no more than a preliminary study based on part-time teachers, but it would be extended to full-time teachers, including all classes such as associate professors in future study.

An in-depth discussion with eight part-time teachers who have been currently teaching at self-finance institutes had been conducted. Those who were chosen to be interviewed are mature, with their ages fall between 31 and 50 years old, experienced with their teaching duration ranging from 3 years to 15 years, and well familiar with the academic operation, being employed by self-finance institutes for over 3 years. The programmes which they are teaching range from diploma (QF Level 3), Higher Diploma (QF Level 4) to Bachelor (QF Level 5).

Topics of the in-depth discussion have been focused on the e-learning tool(s) which their institute adopts? Which e-Resources they are currently using and are they an important tools for their teaching? Are there any e-Resources which they believe important but not be available at his/her institute? Are they satisfied with the e-Resources which are currently available at their institute? Would these e-Resources enhance their teaching? After all, are they satisfied with their part-time job as a lecturer at the institute?

4 Findings and Discussions

The following are the summaries of the in-depth discussion with the captioned part-time teachers:

4.1 Adoption of e-Learning Tools

All the interviewed part-time teachers replied they are using Moodle[1] as the e-learning tool at their institutes; and they believe Moodle is a useful and an important e-learning tool for their teaching. Besides Moodle, the part-time teachers also replied LearnHub[2], and YouTube Edu[3] are effective e-learning tools as well.

4.2 Availability and Importance of e-Resources

The following e-resources are all available and are commented important in their teaching by all the interviewed part-time teachers:

- Email.
- Classroom videos to be shared online.
- Laboratories video to be shared online.
- Online discussion.
- Online video sharing.
- Online research.
- Online test.

4.3 Utilization of e-Resources on Teaching

However, not all e-resources are being available and adopted by part-time teachers. Researchers find that when the e-resources are available in the institutes and used by the part-time teachers, their comments on these e-resources are positive and they expressed the high importance of these e-resources to their teaching. However, if those e-resources are not available in the institutes, the part-time teachers' comments on those e-resources are negative and they expressed the low importance of these e-resources since they do not have experience of using those e-resources, for example,

- Digital stories.
- Instant messaging.

---

[1] Moodle is a learning platform designed to provide educators, administrators and learners with a single robust, secure and integrated system to create personalised learning environments. Moodle is built by the Moodle project which is led and coordinated by Moodle HQ, an Australian company of 30 developers which is financially supported by a network of over 60 Moodle Partner service companies worldwide.

[2] LearnHub is the world's largest online social learning network dedicat-ed exclusively to international education. Its mission is to empower students and educators from every corner of the globe to connect with one another and to establish meaningful relationships. To students, it offers a variety of innovative tools that empower research and help students enroll in programs to meet their dreams.

[3] YouTube EDU brings learners and educators together in a global video classroom. On YouTube EDU, students have access to a broad set of educational videos that range from academic lectures to inspirational speeches and everything in between.

- Online demonstration.
- Online games.
- Online simulations.
- Podcasting.

Therefore, it is important for self-finance institutes to provide up-to-date e-resources to part-time teachers for their adoption and enhancing their teaching quality.

4.4 Impact of e-Resources on Job Satisfaction

All the interviewed part-time teachers replied they are satisfied with the existing e-resources which are currently available in the institutions; and they are also satisfied with the existing support received from the administrative and academic colleagues in the institutions. Besides, they also agree that adequate and up-to-date e-resources would facilitate their teaching quality as well as enhance their job satisfaction.

5 Limitations and Future Research

Because of limited time and resources at present stage, this is a preliminary study on the impact of availability of e-resources on part time teachers' job satisfaction in Hong Kong self-finance institutions; researchers have conducted a literature review on the importance of e-resources in higher education and job satisfaction in academics. In addition, researchers have also conducted a focus group to identify how importantly e-resources would those part-time teachers who are teaching in self-finance institutions perceive, how e-resources facilitate their teaching, and how e-resources lead their job satisfaction. From this viewpoint, the sample size of this research is rather limited, and may not reflect the real situation on the part-time teachers on how they adopt the e-resources on the teaching and impact on their job satisfaction. Hence, researchers recommend conducting a more comprehensive survey on the part-time teachers' who are teaching in the self-finance institutions in the future.

6 Conclusion

This paper demonstrated a preliminary study on exploring the perception of part-time teachers on their job satisfaction about the availability of e-resources in the academic context, as well as exploring the importance of e-resources on the teaching quality and performance, which in turn affects their job satisfaction.

In conclusion, e-resources are an emerging media and tools in nowadays teaching and learning. Unfortunately, the availability of e-recourses for part-time teachers is limited sometimes; and it may adversely affect their teaching performance so as to job satisfaction as well. Thus, part-time teachers of self-finance institutes should be supported by comprehensive e-resources to enhance their teaching quality and job satisfaction since it shows that better e-resources will lead to better teaching quality as well as job satisfaction by the researchers.

References

1. Alkhawaldeh, A.: The professional needs of English language teachers at Amman 1st and 2nd directorates of education. College Student J. **45**(2), 1–22 (2011)
2. Allen, M., Bourhis, J., Burrell, N., Mabry, E.: Comparing student satisfaction with distance education to traditional classrooms in higher education: a meta-analysis. Am. J. Distance Educ. **16**(2), 83–97 (2002)
3. Anderson, S.E.: The double mirrors of school improvement: the aga khan foundation in East Africa. In: Anderson, S.E. (ed.) Improving Schools Through Teacher Development: Case Studies of the Aga Khan Foundation Projects in East Africa, pp. 1–19. Swets and Zeitlinger Publishers, Lisse (2002)
4. Atchoarena, D., Hite, S.J.: Lifelong Learning Policies in Low Development Context: An African Perspective. In: Aspin, D., Chapman, J., Hatton, M., Sawano, Y. (eds.) International Handbook of lifelong learning, pp. 201–228. Kluwer Academic Publishers, Dordrecht/Boston/London (2001)
5. Boerebach, B.C., Lombarts, K.M., Keijzer, C., Heineman, M.J., Arah, O.A.: The teacher, the physician and the person: how faculty's teaching performance influence their role modelling. PLoS ONE **7**, e32089 (2012)
6. Brahler, C.J., Quitadamo, I.J., Johnson, E.C.: Student critical thinking is enhanced by developing exercise prescriptions using online learning modules. Adv. Physiol. Educ. **26**(1–4), 210–221 (2002)
7. Brouwers, A., Tomic, W.: A longitudinal study of teacher burnout and perceived self-efficacy in classroom management. Teach. Teach. Educ. **16**, 239–253 (2000)
8. Brunetaud, J.M., Darmoni, S.J., Souf, N.: A resource server for medical teaching methods of information in medicine, **41**, 177–182 (2002)
9. Chamberlain, N.R., Yates, H.A.: Use of computer-assisted clinical case (CACC). SOAP note exercise to assess students' application of osteopathic principles and practice. J. Am. Osteopath. Assoc. **100**(7), 437–440 (2000)
10. Chapman, D.W., Mahlck, L.O.: Improving Educational Quality Through Better use of Information. Pergamon Press, Oxford (1993)
11. Charlesworth, A., Ferguson, N., Schmoller, S., Smith, N., Tice, R.: Sharing eLearning content – a synthesis and commentary (final report). Joint Information Systems Committee JISC2007 (2007)
12. Cleland, I.: Networking quality: the issue is quality improvement. In: Ribbins, P., Burridge, E. (eds.) Improving Education: Promoting Quality in Schools, pp. 170–184. Cassell, London (1994)
13. Creemers, B.: The goals of school effectiveness and school improvement. In: Reynolds, D., Bollen, R., Creemers, B., Hopkins, D., Stoll, L., Lagerweij, N. (eds.) Making Good Schools: Linking School Effectiveness and School Improvement, pp. 21–58. Routledge, London and New York (1996)
14. Facione, N.C., Facione, P.A.: Externalizing the critical thinking in knowledge development and clinical judgment. Nurs. Outlook **44**(3), 129–136 (1996)
15. Flannery, M.R.: Cataloging internet resources. Bull. Med. Libr. Assoc. **83**(Suppl. 2), 211–215 (1995)
16. Goldschalk, D.R., Lacey, L.: Learning at distance. technology impacts on planning education. J. Plann. Educ. Res. **20**(4), 476–489 (2001)
17. Guri-Rosenbli, S.: Distance education and e learning: not the same thing. High. Educ. **49**(4), 467–493 (2005)

18. Hanushek, E.A.: Interpreting recent research on schooling in developing countries. World Bank Res. Observer **10**(2), 227–246 (1995)
19. Herpen, M.V.: Conceptual models in use for education indicators. In: Bottani, N., Walberg, H.J. (eds.) The OECD International Education Indicators, pp. 25–51. OECD Publications, Paris (1992)
20. Huang, X., Van de Vliert, E.: Job levels and national culture as joint roots of job satisfaction. Appl. Psychol.: Int. Rev. **53**, 329–348 (2004)
21. Hylen, J.: Open Educational Resources: Opportunities and Challenges (Reports). OECD's Centre for Educational Research and Innovation, Paris (2006)
22. Jimenez, L.J.P., Pinzon, A.R.: School inputs in secondary education and their effects on academic achievement. A study in Colombia (LCSHD Paper Series 36). Human Development Department: The World Bank Latin America and the Caribbean Regional Office (1999)
23. Jones, S., Johnson-Yale, C., Millermaier, S., Perez, F.S.: Academic work, the internet and US college students. Internet High. Educ. **11**, 165–177 (2008)
24. Jones, L.E.: Introducing the ICF: the development of an online resource to support learning, teaching and curriculum design. Physiotherapy **97**(1), 55–58 (2011)
25. Kalssen, R.M., Usher, E.L., Bong, M.: Teachers' collective efficacy, job satisfaction, and job stress in cross-cultural context. J. Exp. Educ. **78**, 464–486 (2010)
26. Kellaghan, T., Greaney, V.: Using Assessment to Improve the Quality of Education. UNESCO/IIEP, Paris (2001)
27. Kellaghan, T., Greaney, V.: Using Examination to Improve Education: A Study in Fourteen African Countries. The World Bank, Washington (1992)
28. Kinney, P., Keskula, D.R., Perry, J.F.: The effect of a computer assisted instructional program on physical therapy students. J. Allied Health **26**(2), 57–61 (1997)
29. Lee, J.W., Barro, R.J.: Schooling Quality in a Cross Section of Countries. National Bureau of Economic Research, Cambridge (1997)
30. Littlejohn, A.: Reusing Online Resources: A Sustainable Approach to E'Learning. Kogan Page, London (2003)
31. Lockheed, M.E., Verspoor, A.M., Bloach, B., Englebert, P., Fuller, B., King, E., Middleton, J., Paqueo, V., Rodd, A., Romain, R., Welmond, M.: Improving Primary Education in Developing Countries. Oxford University Press (Published for the World Bank), Oxford (1991)
32. Loos, G., Diether, J.W.: Occupational safety and health training on the Internet. Developing Qual. Instr. AAOHN J. **49**(5), 231–234 (2001)
33. Ludwig, J., Bassi, L.J.: The puzzling case of school resources and student achievement. Educ. Eval. Policy Anal. **21**(4), 385–403 (1999)
34. Maertz, C.P., Griffeth, R.W.: Eight motivational forces and voluntary turnover: a theoretical synthesis with implications for research. J. Manage **30**, 667–683 (2004)
35. Makwati, G., Audinos, B., Lairez, T.: The role of statistics in improving the quality of basic education in Sub-Saharan Africa. Paper presented at the ADEA Biennial Meeting 2003, Grand, Baie, Mauritus, 3–6 December 2003
36. McGill L, Currier S, Duncan C, Douglas P.: Good intentions: improving the evidence base in support of sharing learning materials (report). Joint Information Syustems Committee (JISC) (2008)
37. Mertler, C.A.: Teacher motivation and job satisfaction of public school teachers. (Unpublished Master's thesis). Ohio State University, Columbus, OH (2002)
38. Mugimu, C.B., Hite, S.J.: Uganda needs quality educational research. Educ. Mag. J. Educ. **3**(2), 12–15 (2001)
39. Musa, J.N., Smadi, O.: Globalization and english teaching in Jordan. J. Educ. Prac. **4**(8) (2013)

40. Psacharopoulos, G.: Economics of education a la Euro. Eur. J. Educ. **35**(1), 81–96 (2000)
41. Rameckers, F.J.M.A.: Effective monitoring of the quality of education: towards a managerial and participatory approach. Paper presented at the Secondary Education in Africa: Strategies for Renewal, UNESCO/BREDA-World Bank Regional Workshop in Mauritius on the Renewal of African Secondary Education (2001)
42. Ross, K.N., Mahlck, L. (eds.): Planning the Quality of Education: The Collection and use of Data for Informed Decision-Making. Pergamon Press, Paris (1990)
43. Ssesanga, L., Garrett, R.M.: Job satisfaction of university academics: perspectives from Uganda. High. Educ. **50**, 33–56 (2005)
44. Stuart, N.: Quality in education. In: Ribbins, P., Burridge, E. (eds.) Improving Education: Promoting Quality in Schools, pp. 8–17. Cassell, London (1994)
45. Thomas, K.J., Denham, B.E., Dinolfo, J.D.: Perceptions among occupational and physical therapy students of a nontraditional methodology for teaching laboratory gross anatomy. Anat. Sci. Educ. **4**(2), 71–77 (2011)
46. UNESCO: Ministerial round table "On Quality Education". Paper presented at the General Conference 32nd Session, UNESCO Headquarters, Paris (2003)
47. Veneri, D.: The role and effectiveness of computer-assisted learning in physical therapy education: a systematic review. Physiother. Theory Prac. **27**(4), 287–298 (2011)
48. Welch, A.R.: Quality and equality in third world education. In: Welch, A.W. (ed.) Third World Education; Equality and Equity, pp. 3–28. Garland Publishing, New York (2000)
49. Wen, C.L., Silveira, P.S.P., Azevedo, R.S., Bohm, G.M.: Internet discussion lists as an educational tool. J. Telemed Telecare **4**(2), 71–77 (2000)
50. Williams, P.: The learning web: the development, implementation and evaluation of internet-based undergraduate materials for the teaching of key skills. Act. Learn. High. Educ. **3**(1), 40–53 (2002)
51. Wobmann, L.: Schooling Resources, Educational Institutions, and Student Performance: The International Evidence (Working Paper 983). Kiel Institute of World Economics, Kiel, Germany (2000)

The Impacts on Learning via Social Media: A Study on Post-secondary Students in Hong Kong

Jeff K.T. Tang[1,2(✉)], Ho-Nam Yau[2], Shue-Fung Wong[2], and Sin-Ki Wong[2]

[1] School of Computing and Information Sciences, Caritas Institute of Higher Education, 18 Chui Ling Road, Tseung Kwan O, New Territories, Hong Kong
jtang@cihe.edu.hk

[2] Department of Mathematics and Information Technology, The Hong Kong Institute of Education, 10 Lo Ping Road, Tai Po, Hong Kong
{s1106828, s1105017, s1106762}@s.ied.edu.hk

Abstract. Social media are the forms of electronic interaction or communication that enable people to create or share ideas in virtual communities or online networks. By using mobile devices and web-based technologies, people can easily get access to these highly interactive platforms. This paper explores the potential uses of social media for university teaching and learning activities. It also aims to find out how social media is applied at universities in Hong Kong, and their benefits or pitfalls when compared to other applications. Facebook and YouTube will be deeply discussed in this paper. A research was conducted with undergraduates from different universities in Hong Kong by using an online survey, in order to know how satisfactory of the undergraduates are feeling when applying social media for academic purposes. Results show that students might make uses of the sharing, discussing and searching functions from the social media. However, at the same time, students would be rather easily distracted by the entertaining and social functions from the social media. Further evaluation of our survey information will be included in detail, supported by findings and theories from different literatures.

Keywords: Social media · Teaching and learning · Human factor

1 Introduction

Nowadays many students like to use social media to share their everyday things and feelings. Students trended to use several applications of social media especially Facebook[1] and YouTube[2] [8]. Apart from sharing feelings themselves, students can also use social media to reach educational purpose that can be applied in learning and teaching. On Facebook, students can easily to be grouped in order to discuss any things

[1] https://www.facebook.com/.
[2] https://www.youtube.com.

J. Lam et al. (Eds.): ICTE 2015, CCIS 559, pp. 195–208, 2015.
DOI: 10.1007/978-3-662-48978-9_19

about their academic works. It is because “Facebook group”, as Fig. 1, can be created by any member. There is also a conversation application in Facebook called “Messenger”, as Fig. 2.

Students can also share their documents, pictures, video and others file about their academic works to public or other classmates. YouTube provided a platform for member to upload or watch video so teacher can upload videos for education. On YouTube, students can get information to learn especially students in studying science. Some experiments cannot be demonstrated in the lesson because of the safety problem. According to an article - YouTube, critical pedagogy, and media activism [5], ‘learning requires dialogical communications between students and teachers’ and Comment is available to be left by members. Member can reply the previous comment too. Dialogical conversation can be allowed on YouTube.

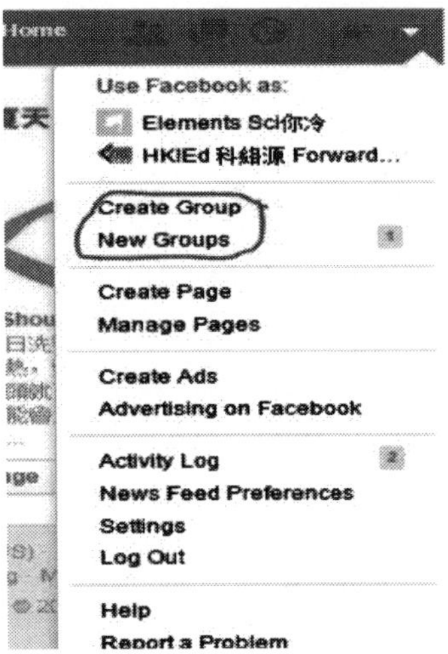

Fig. 1. The Facebook group.

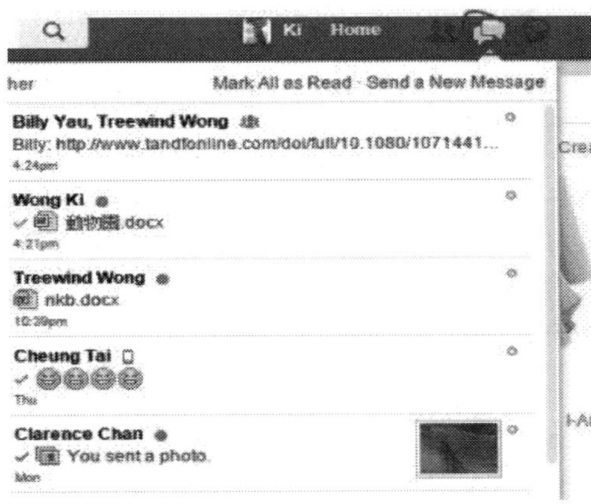

Fig. 2. The instant messenger on Facebook.

2 Related Work

In the book of “Learning, Teaching, and Scholarship in a Digital Age-Web 2.0 and Classroom Research: What Path Should We Take Now?” the author commented on both pros and cons about applying social media in learning [2]. Author mentioned that technology is bridge between learning and teaching. It can provide a platform for students to interact such as sending invitation, sharing their stances by voting, and receiving feedbacks from peer or instructor immediately and also increasing their reading and writing skills so students were expected to making progress of academic result. Books or literatures are free to download in some social scholar which is similar to library. It is obviously helping students to get knowledge. Finding books in library is not easy because there are many books in library. In online scholar, key words or book name were typed in search engine then books can be founded. Learning is no longer focusing on in-class lesson but students enjoy above benefits in any mobile devices.

Despite the pros of applying social media in learning, the public or private information on social media may not reliable. Author mentioned that data from social media is not promised to be hundred percent trustable by administrators of social media. Every member can post informative post on YouTube and Facebook without any permission. In fact, in the Digital Age-Web 2.0 learners can reach their academic score. Learners and teachers can use social media as the platform to learn and teach in everywhere. Especially, in the postsecondary level, students are mainly using computers to finish their assignments. The immediate interaction in the Internet is very important to exchange the academic information in the social media. Therefore, Facebook and YouTube are very useful tools for today's teaching and learning environment.

In the book of "Expanding the New Literacies Conversation", author thought that researchers were permitted to analysis literature on social media so it can provide richer understandings than school [6]. Author mentioned that several skills should be required when reading on the Internet. One of the skills is 'evaluate information critically'. It is really important to students because there are many magnanimity of information. Nowadays many people like to search information on Internet especially Wikipedia[3] however information from Wikipedia can be edited by anyone as Fig. 3. Students have to critically identify information in order to get the most reliable information. Students can choose some authority materials and websites to get information for example academic papers, books and government report. Unlike school, teacher is not supposed to educate students directly with standard text book or materials. In order to combine information from social media with formal teaching, students can ask for a consultation of information which is founded on social media with teacher. In the social media like Facebook and YouTube, most of the information is about entertainment and personal information. Therefore, students should have the critical thinking for selecting the information in social media to complete their homework or assignments.

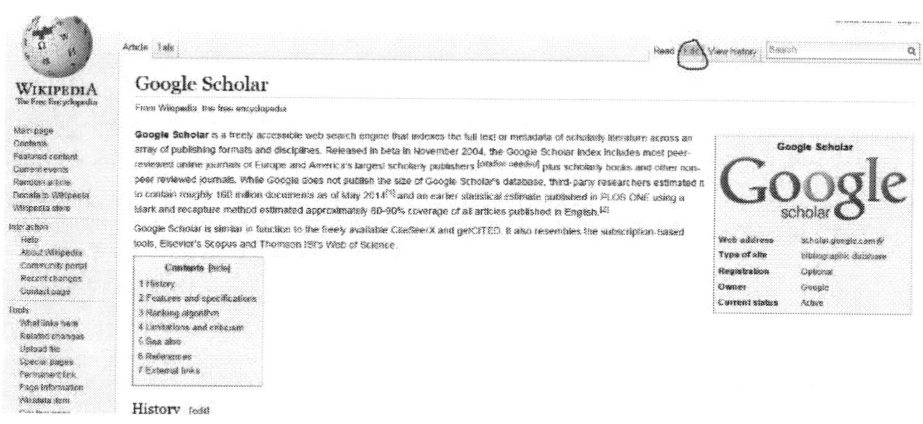

Fig. 3. The interface of Wikipedia.

[3] https://en.wikipedia.org/.

There is a journal written from Pierce [9] focusing on the teens commutation methods. The journal compared face-to-face communication versus technological communication among teens. The essay found out 280 high school students to fill in the questionnaire and the results discovered the situation of the usage of socially interactive technologies (SITs) in teenagers. There were a number of examples of SITs like online social sites, text messaging and instant messaging. About 35–40 % of students used online social sites like Facebook and Twitter, 1 to 4 h per day. The situation is more serious in females. The students general had the feature of social anxiety. For example, they were uncomfortable of taking with others face-to-face. The study also revealed that there was a positive relationship of the using hours of SITs and the social anxiety. The participants preferred using computers to make friend with other people but were afraid of making friend with others face-to-face. The females' participants spend more time to SITs to compare with males, therefore the girls felt more comfortable when they were using social media. Basic on this journal, the human relationship can be affected by the method of the communication. Even though people communicate with each other every day by the SITs, using Facebook to update others states and chatting with others in Skype, their social skills or the attitude towards reality communication may be decreased because the usage of social media.

This is about a special issue articles from Journal of Educational Technology and Society. This article pointed out mobile devices were being more useful and powerful in nowadays society [3]. The mobile devices played an important role in helping students to learn and teachers to teach. For example, they can read the safe copy version of their notes, edit the assignment and download the urgent document. The article claims that the mobile technology can assist the development of "situated classroom". Situated classroom means that learners can improve their knowledge in daily life. The development of mobile applications has the mobility, ubiquitous computing and portability. Learners can use their own devices to learn in everywhere in every time. In fact, the mobile applications include the social media application such as Facebook, Twitter and Google+. Students in the institute can use the mobile applications to improve their learning and teachers can create a situated classroom from the students to learn in formal or informal way.

It is no doubt that Facebook can be a potentially useful web technology for promoting effective academic practice. However, the prior application of Facebook is for social purposes more than for academic purposes. From the book "Facebook, social integration and informal learning at university: 'It is more for socialising and talking to friends about work than for actually doing work'", Madge, Mee, Wellens & Hooley [7] quoted a research that was conducted with first year undergraduates at a university in British by using an Internet survey for supporting the above idea. To start with, more than 73 % of the students agreed that Facebook had been very important in assisting them to form friendships at university. They would utilize this platform for searching and recognizing new friends by sending or accepting friend requests, keeping in touch with old friends by tagging or commenting, and planning social events by creating Facebook Group or Page, implying that Facebook literally provides a lot for social purposes. Indeed, by raising a statement of "Facebook is helpful to my academic life", more than half of the students chose "Disagree" or even "Strongly Disagree". Most of the students would only use its uploading and downloading function for learning purposes. This may reflect the truth that students make use of Facebook way more frequently for social rather than academic purposes. More to add, 25 % of the students felt that their academic work would often or usually be affected by the amount of time they spent on Facebook. This proves that Facebook may not be a suitable platform for academic purposes, but conversely distracting students from their formal studies. Furthermore, 41 % of the students chose "Agree" or "Strongly Agree" that they would not prefer teachers to contact them through Facebook for formal teaching purposes. Though the other 59 % of students supported the theory of using Facebook for formal teaching purposes, some of them suspected its effectiveness in practice. This explains that Facebook may not be the most appropriate place for formal teaching purposes.

YouTube is classified as a socially interactive technology that can be applied in classrooms. It involves many potential uses in teaching and learning. However, it is important to opt for appropriate teaching materials for students to learn well, since YouTube consists of too many types of videos. By referring the book "YouTube: Educational Potentials and Pitfalls", Jones and Cuthrell [4] analyzed and elaborated on the above idea. Firstly, YouTube videos can serve as guidelines for students to learn. The videos can be used for raising new concepts, visualizing abstract theories or highlighting crucial points. The video can be used as a model for classroom discussion or activities as well. These may facilitate interactions between teachers and students. Secondly, teachers can also search for creative lesson plans on YouTube. It includes video of model teachers presenting lectures which have been proven effective in classrooms. Even teachers can interact with the other teachers by sharing innovative ideas about teaching. Thirdly, students can share feedbacks to each other after viewing the videos, which peer reviews can be facilitated in the process. Nonetheless, the authors also stated that YouTube contains a vast number of junk videos that would not help students to learn. Teachers must ensure that the chosen videos have clear educational value, which are trustworthy, reasonable and accurate for students to refer and gain.

3 Proposed Method for Evaluating the Use of Social Media in Learning

The literature review showed there is a demand for evaluating the use of social media in learning of post-secondary students.

3.1 Our Findings

There are some pros and cons about learning and teaching through YouTube. YouTube is seen as a 'learning and teaching tool' beside in class learning. Firstly, members, no matter of teacher or student, are allowed to upload and watch video on YouTube. Some sessions cannot be demonstrated in class, for example video about dangerous experiment, so video should be used to replace experiment. Students did not miss any essential part of the topic and more practically to learn through YouTube. Live function is also a main function of YouTube because academic launch could be played instantly.

Some of teachers may use this function to provide their lesson so students can get information immediately. To compare with Jtv (Justin TV[4]) and Twich[5], YouTube live video can be saved as a regular video in member's channel. It can be saved as a record so that other students, who do not present at that time, can also watch that video. Chat room is providing an instant conversation between video uploader and watcher. Secondly, the function of comment provides a platform as 'dialogical communication' [5], students and teachers are allowed to start their conversation under a video. According to the above literature - "Learning, Teaching, and Scholarship in a Digital Age-Web 2.0 and Classroom Research: What Path Should We Take Now?", it is more effective for learning to receive feedbacks from teacher immediately. Students who have questions about the video should leave a comment so that video uploader can answer to solve their problems.

Although there are some pros about using YouTube for learning, cons and limitations are still existed. There is different information on YouTube but the realness of information cannot be ensured. Every member of YouTube can upload informative videos so audience may confuse about the realness of the video. Students must evaluate every video themselves critically which was suggested by the author of the book - "Expanding the New Literacies Conversation" to ensure the reliability of that informative video. Apart from asking teachers for the realness, so that it can be combined with the formal teaching, checking on the other reliable website or checking out more related videos to confirm it. Also there are many other videos on YouTube, that may not relevant to academic, but it may appear on the page of video. Students may be affected by that video especially some entertaining videos with attractive title. More to add, ethical issues such as copyright problems would happen when users re-quote videos without permission by owners. Besides, YouTube would collect Cookies from the user records. Personal privacy may be leaked to YouTube for business uses.

A number of pros and cons of using Facebook for academic purposes can be concluded from all the literature findings. When compared to the other non-social applications, Facebook provides spaces and functions for students to interact and communicate. Students can gather their classmates to share their views, voting for stances and upload their references on certain topics by creating Facebook Group or Page. Instant messages can be captured and sent in the Messenger box as well. Through giving and receiving feedbacks from each other, students can learn more from peer reviewing.

By comparing with Facebook and WordPress (other social media), both of them enable sharing of information. Yet, Facebook has more functions of facilitating social interaction and communication, while WordPress is more likely a publishing platform. Not only Facebook can raise our own ideas, but in additionally can explore and share contents created by other people. It can be said that WordPress emphasizes content creation, while Facebook focuses more on content curation, which students may gather, plan and discuss more on certain topics. As a result, student-student interaction can be eased and improved.

---

4 www.justin.tv/ (It is closed since 5th August, 2014).

5 www.twitch.tv/.

By comparing Facebook with Google drive (non-social media application), both of them can be used for sharing folders to the group-mates. Students can upload and download their needed documents as well. For functions such as message sending, immediate messages can be sent by utilizing Facebook Group, Page or Messenger box. Conversely, the communication of Google drive depends on email transferring. This means that users of Google drive cannot contact others in the same user interface (UI), which is less convenient than that of Facebook. However, the advantage of Google drive is that the file size of uploading and downloading has no limit. The maximum file size of Facebook is 25 MB (Fig. 4). Therefore, when students need to share bigger size files, Google Drive would be a better choice.

Fig. 4. The file size limitation of Facebook. (In English: the selected file is too big for upload. The upper limit is 25 MB.)

Moreover, Facebook can be browsed easily by using mobile devices. Documents stored in Facebook can be saved or downloaded in everywhere. Situated Classroom emphasizing gaining and improving knowledge in daily life can thus be fulfilled by its portability.

Every coin has two sides. Utilizing Facebook for academic purposes consists of some pitfalls as well. To begin with, Facebook consists of numerous functions for social and entertainment, which are the major selling points for attracting people to browse it. Though students can make use of Facebook for academic purposes, they would be more distracted by those interesting functions. Besides, Facebook may not be a suitable platform for formal teaching purposes. Not only teachers would find it difficult to interact with students but would in additionally feel hard to involve formal assessments for them. Furthermore, information spread in Facebook may not be completely trustworthy, as every member can share their own ideal answers easily in Facebook. Students have to be very cautious and critical when evaluating the information. More to add, since there is positive relationship of the using hours of SITs and the social anxiety, students who rely too much on Facebook for communication may feel anxious when having face-to-face interaction with the others in real life. Their social skills would be conversely worsened if they have been obsessed with Facebook.

3.2 The Experiment Design

In order to know more about the habits of using social media, especially Facebook and YouTube, for nowadays post-secondary school students, survey and a set of questionnaire is created. The target respondents are from Hong Kong post-secondary level institutions. Aims are going to be discussed by question. Question 1, 2 and 3 are going to know whether social media is famous for students to learn or get knowledge and also which media is the most famous media. Question 4 is aimed to know the level of reliability on such social media. Question 5 is set to count which function is the most useful and see they were concentrating on their works. About the purposes of question number 6–8, our group would like to understand whether social media negatively affect the learning process or not and the main content of the irrelevant information in social media. Question number 10 would like to determine the future development of learning and teaching is on mobile device.

4 Experiment and Results

In our survey about the usage of social media in The Hong Kong post-secondary level students in teaching and learning especially Facebook and YouTube, a questionnaire survey was created by our group. Using Google Forms to create the questionnaire and invited the related students through sending emails. The sample sides of the questionnaire were 23 people from different institutions. There are ten questions about the usage of social media for learning and teaching. The sample of the questionnaire will be attached in the annex.

According in to the results of questionnaire in question one, hundred percent of the respondents claimed that they had used social media before (Fig. 5). Therefore, the usage of social media is very common in Hong Kong.

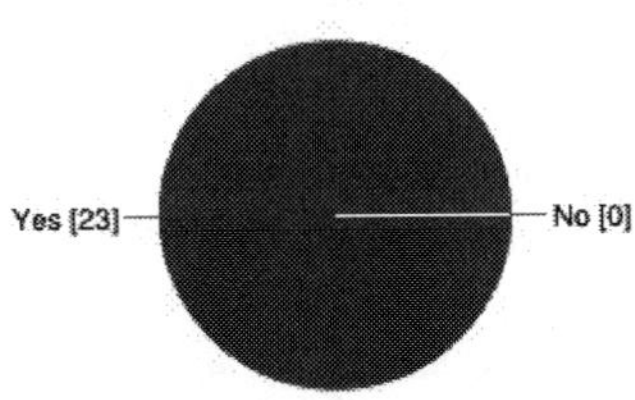

Yes	23	100%
No	0	0%

Fig. 5. The result of question 1.

In the second question, the results showed us that most of the people using Facebook that were about 95.7 % of students in the survey and 52.2 % of students have browsed on YouTube (Fig. 6). So that Facebook and YouTube are two of the famous social media for post-secondary students in Hong Kong.

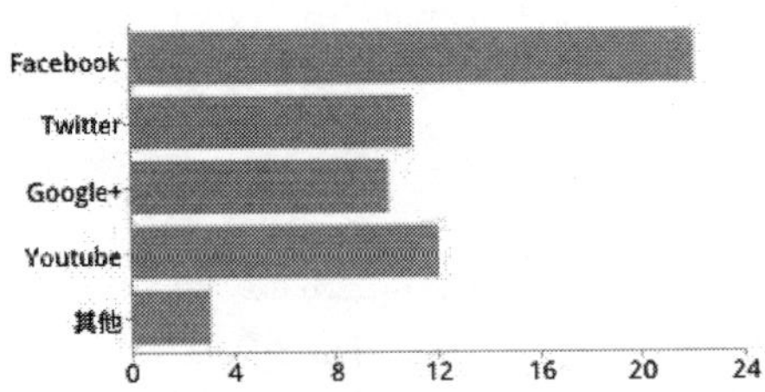

Facebook	22	95.7%
Twitter	11	47.8%
Google+	10	43.5%
Youtube	12	52.2%
其他	3	13%

Fig. 6. The result of question 2.

The question number three is about does the social media help learning and teaching for the students. There are 95.7 % students agree that the social media helping their academic needs (Fig. 7). To complex question number 2 and 3, most of the students used Facebook and YouTube as their social media and the social media can help learning and teaching. Therefore, most of the students think that Facebook and YouTube can help the learning and teaching in the scholar area.

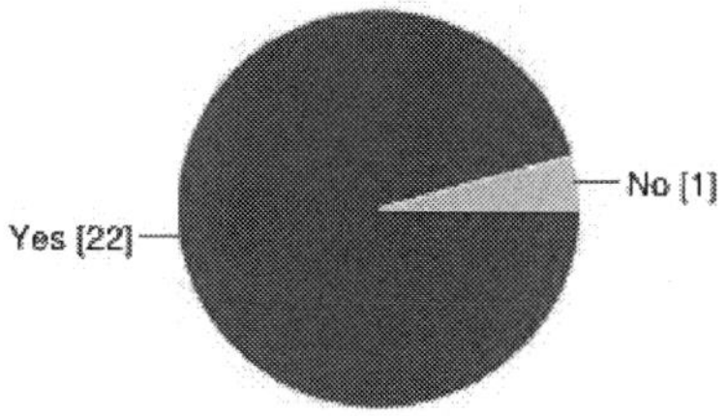

Yes	22	95.7%
No	1	4.3%

Fig. 7. The result of question 3.

About the habit of the usage of the social media, the major number of students (77.3 %) claimed that they use social media every day (Fig. 8). It can reflect that the social media applications are very poplar for Hong Kong post-secondary level students. They can use social media to update their friends' state, chat with their friends and also share information with other people. Thus, most of the respondents spend times in Facebook and YouTube every day.

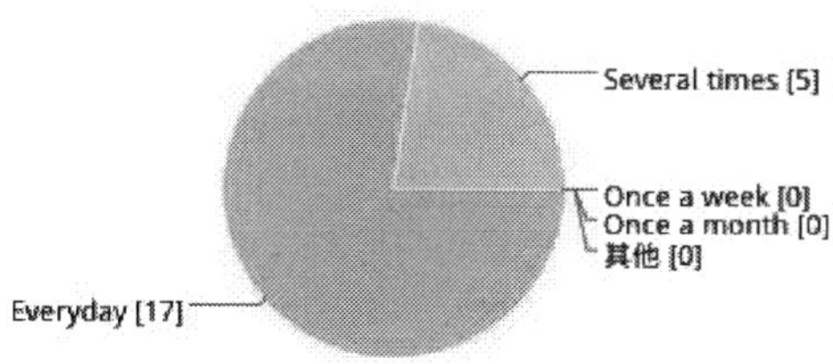

Everyday	17	77.3%
Several tmes a week	5	22.7%
Once a week	0	0%
Once a month	0	0%
其他	0	0%

Fig. 8. The result of question 4.

About the functions of social media for learning and teaching in the post-secondary level studies, there are 90.9 % of students tried the sharing folders function. Also, there are 50 % of students used the function of communication with group mates and 31.8 % of the respondents used social media to Searching information about the assignments (Fig. 9). One more thing need to look out is that there are serval number of students used social media to share photos and video to finish their assignments. This means that

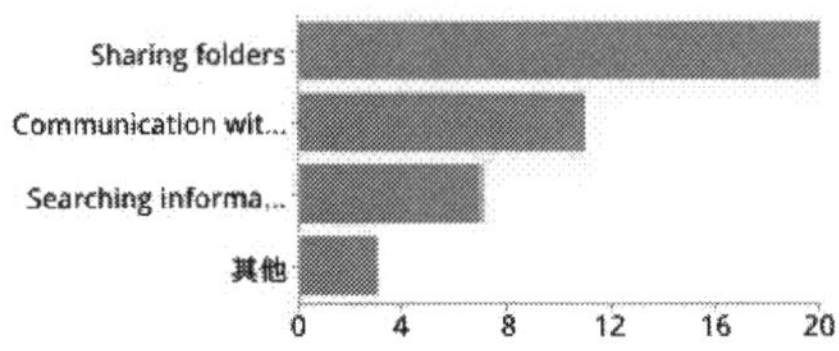

Sharing folders	20	90.9%
Communication with group mates	11	50%
Searching information about the assignments	7	31.8%
其他	3	13.6%

Fig. 9. The result of question 5.

the social media is very useful of the learning and teaching process in the post-secondary level. In other word, the teaching and learning is relied on the social media in Hong Kong.

It is no doubt that the social media can improve the teaching and learning for Hong Kong students. However, about the disturbing of social media when students doing homework, 100 % of students claimed that there are irrelevant information when they using social media for learning (Fig. 10). For the extent of the disturbing of social media, the major number of students claimed that they spend 25 % to 50 % of working hours on the irrelevant information of social media (Fig. 11). The irrelevant information is mainly about entertainment like jokes or video, such as YouTube video (Fig. 12). It may reflect that the social media contain a lot of irrelevant information for teaching and learning, teachers and students need to critical and carful to analyze the information from social media. On the other hand, learners need to hide the lure form the social media. In addition, when we focus on the specific case of the questionnaire, we discover that if the student uses more kinds of social media like using Facebook, YouTube, Twitter, Google+ and Instagram, the time of spending in the irrelevant information will be increase.

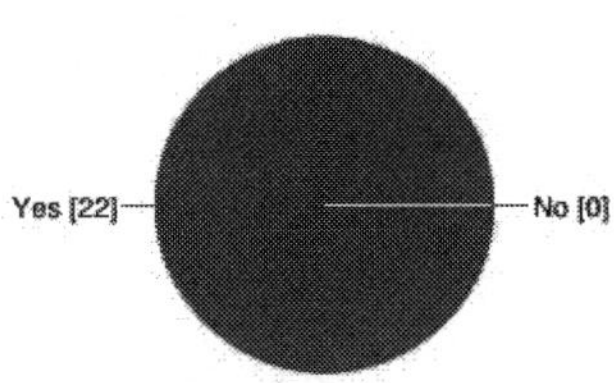

Yes	22	100%
No	0	0%

Fig. 10. The result of question 6.

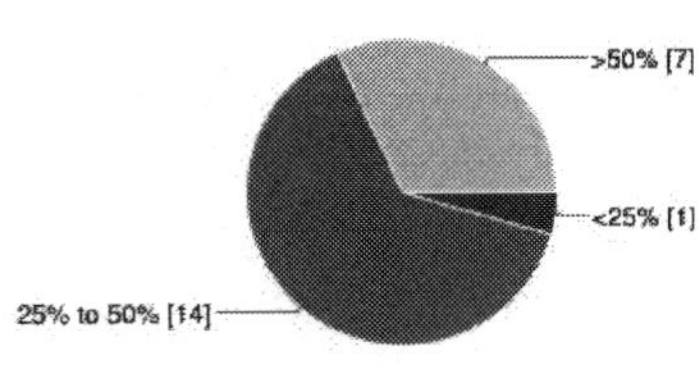

<25%	1	4.5%
25% to 50%	14	63.6%
>50%	7	31.8%

Fig. 11. The result of question 7.

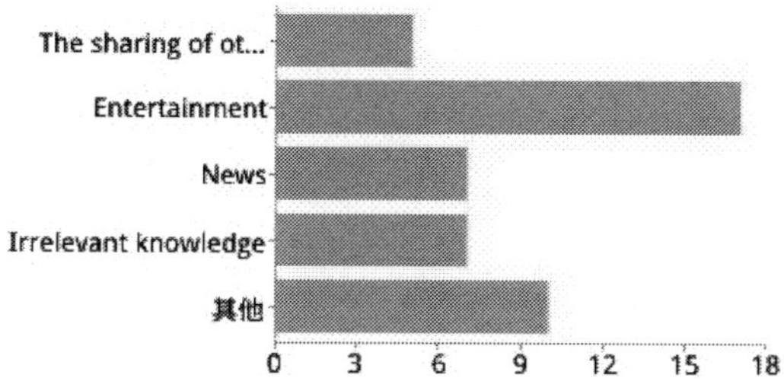

The sharing of other people	5	22.7%
Entertainment	17	77.3%
News	7	31.8%
Irrelevant knowledge	7	31.8%
其他	10	45.5%

Fig. 12. The result of question 8.

There are major number of respondents agree that the social media is the tools to improve their teaching and learning (Fig. 13). The results show that the Hong Kong post-secondary level students satisfy the functions of social media for learning and teaching and Facebook and YouTube are the tools for learning. On the other hand, 100 % of students used social media for teaching and learning in their mobile devices like smart phone and tablet no matter which OS like android, IOS or windows (Fig. 14). In fact, the mobile devices contain a lot of social media application like Facebook and YouTube. These applications are very popular. For example, the

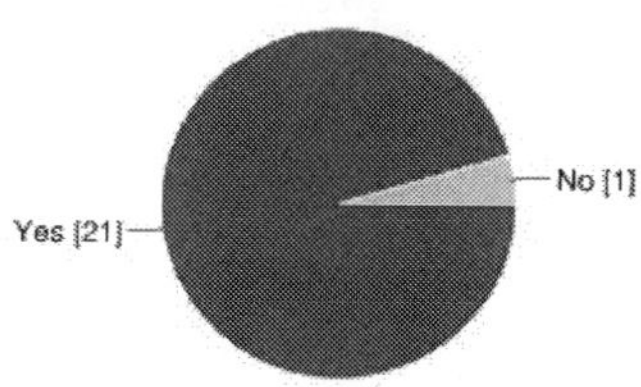

Yes	21	95.5%
No	1	4.5%

Fig. 13. The result of question 9.

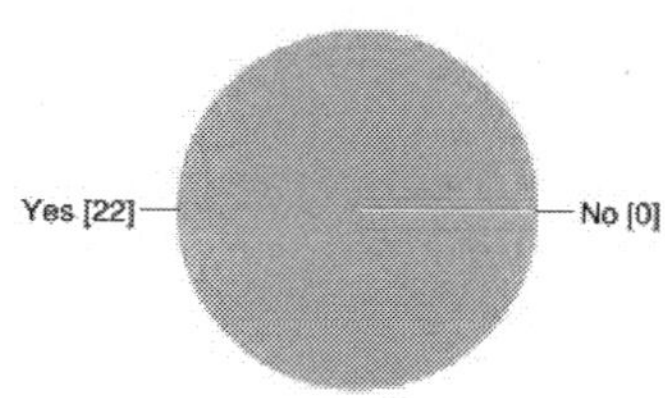

Yes	22	100%
No	0	0%

Fig. 14. The result of question 10.

installation rate of Facebook app in "Google play" is about 27,964,372 times [1]. In the results of these questions, the development of the social media is trended to mobile. Therefore, the learning and teaching process will become more convenience and portable in the foreseeable future. Students can learn in anywhere at any time.

5 Conclusion

In this paper, we focused are on the usage of social media for learning in Hong Kong. Facebook and YouTube are two of the famous social media for Hong Kong students studying in post-secondary level institution. The function of Facebook like sending message, sharing folders, collecting information and setting some election can be applied in the learning process. About the functions of YouTube, the major function is sharing video on the Internet. In the post-secondary learning, there are some assignments to require students creating video, especially for the communication major students. YouTube can provide a platform for students sharing video and also their minds and ideas to all around the world. Also, the previous part pointed out the comparison of the social media. Facebook compared with Wiki and YouTube compared with Justin TV and Twich. The comparison of the social media with other application can make a wider view for the usage of social media of students.

The survey done by our group through Google Forms questionnaire. The results can show that the habit of the usage of social media for the post-secondary level students in Hong Kong. Social media like Facebook and YouTube are very famous for them and they think that social media can improve their learning and teaching. However, social media like Facebook contain a lot of entertainment elements so that the focus of students may shift. Moreover, using mobile devices to browse the social media like Facebook and YouTube are the trend for learning in the future.

As future work, we will enhance e-learning platforms (such as MOOC that has high dropout rate) in order to attract students to continue learning, for example, incorporate with social media capabilities and entertainment elements. Also, the ethical impact of using social media will be studied in depth, in order to identify more potential harms the student may get during their learning on social network platforms.

Annex I. Questionnaire

Are social media improving learning or teaching?

1. Did you use any social media?

   ☐Yes ☐No

2. Which social media did you browse? (Can choose more than one option)

   ☐Facebook ☐Twitter ☐Google+ ☐Youtube ☐Other: ________

3. Did you use that social media to learn or teach?

   ☐Yes ☐No

4. How often do you use those social media?

   ☐Everyday ☐Several times a week ☐Once a week

   ☐Once a month ☐Other: ___________

5. Which functions do you always use for helping you learning? (Can choose more than one option)

   ☐Sharing folders ☐Communication with group mates

   ☐Searching information about the assignments ☐Other: ___________

6. Did you read/watch irrelevant information when you were using social media for learning?

   ☐Yes ☐No

7. If Yes, how many percentage of time did you spend in the irrelevant information when you were using social media for learning or teaching?

   ☐<25% ☐25% to 50% ☐>50%

8. The irrelevant information is about: (Can choose more than one option)

   ☐The sharing of other people ☐Entertainment ☐News

   ☐Irrelevant knowledge ☐Other: ___________

9. Did you think social media is the tool to help you in improving your learning or teaching?

   ☐Yes ☐No

10. Did you use social media for learning or teaching in your own mobile device?

    ☐Yes ☐No

References

1. Google play: Facebook, 23 April 2015. Accessed https://play.google.com/store/apps/details?id=com.facebook.katana
2. Greenhow, C., Robelia, B., Hughes, J.E.: Learning, teaching, and scholarship in a digital age web 2.0 and classroom research: what path should we take now? Educ. Researcher **38**(4), 246–259 (2009)
3. Jeng, Y.-L., Wu, T.-T., Huang, Y.-M., Tan, Q., Yang, S.J.H.: The add-on impact of mobile applications in learning strategies: a review study. Educ. Technol. Soc. **13**(3), 3–11 (2010)
4. Jones, T., Cuthrell, K.: YouTube: educational potentials and pitfalls. Comput. Sch. **28**(1), 75–85 (2011)
5. Kellner, D., Kim, G.: Youtube, critical pedagogy, and media activism (2010). Accessed http://www.tandfonline.com/doi/pdf/10.1080/10714410903482658
6. Leu, D.J., O'Byrne, W.I., Zawilinski, L., McVerry, J.G., Everett-Cacopardo, H.: Comments on Greenhow, Robelia, and Hughes: expanding the new literacies conversation. Educ. Researcher **38**(4), 264–269 (2009)
7. Madge, C., Meek, J., Wellens, J., Hooley, T.: Facebook, social integration and informal learning at university: 'It is more for socialising and talking to friends about work than for actually doing work'. Learn. Media Technol. **34**(2), 141–155 (2009)
8. Moran, M., Seaman, J., Hester, T.K.: Teaching, learning, and sharing: How today's higher education faculty use social media. Blogs, Wikis, Podcasts and Facebook: How Today's Higher Education Faculty Use Social Media, 2012, Pearson (2012)
9. Pierce, T.: Social anxiety and technology: face-to-face communication versus technological communication among teens. Comput. Hum. Behav. **25**(6), 1367–1372 (2009)

Comparative Study on Heterogeneous Profiling Sources for Second Language Learners

Di Zou[1], Haoran Xie[2(✉)], Fu Lee Wang[2], Tak-Lam Wong[3], Chung Keung Poon[2], and Wai-Shing Ho[2]

[1] English Language Centre, The Hong Kong Polytechnic University, Kowloon, Hong Kong SAR, China
daisyzou@poly.edu.hk

[2] Caritas Institute of Higher Education, New Territories, Hong Kong SAR, China
hrxie2@gmail.com, {pwang,ckpoon,wsho}@cihe.edu.hk

[3] Department of Mathematics and Information Technology, The Hong Kong Institute of Education, New Territories, Hong Kong SAR, China
tlwong@ied.edu.hk

Abstract. Stimulated by the arrival of the big data era, various and heterogeneous data sources such as data in social networks, mobile devices and sensor data for users have emerged, mirroring characteristics and preferences of data owners. These data sources are often used to construct user profiles so as to facilitate personalized services like recommendations or personalized data access. In the context of second language learning, learner data involve learning logs, standard test results, and individual learning preferences and styles. Given its attribute of reflecting the characteristics of learners, such data can be exploited to build the learner profiles. However, these data sources possibly include noises or bias, and hence influence the reliability of the correspondingly constructed learner profiles. Consequently, the inaccurate profiles may result in ineffective learning tasks that are generated by e-Learning systems. To tackle this issue, it is significant and critical to evaluate the accuracy of learner profiles. In a response to this call, we propose a novel metric named "profile mean square error" to examine the accuracy of learner profiles founded upon diverse sources. We also demonstrate how to construct various learner profiles though applying different data sources such as learning logs, standard test results, and personal learning preferences in e-Learning systems and pedagogical activities. Moreover, we conduct an experimental study among some second language learners, the results of which illustrate that the most accurate profiles are generated from multiple data sources if they are integrated in a rational way.

Keywords: Language learning · Learner profile · Evaluation · Profile accuracy

1 Introduction

Stimulated by the arrival of the big data era, various and heterogeneous data sources such as data in social networks, mobile devices and sensor data for users have emerged. These large volumes of data not only provide fruitful information and knowledge to

J. Lam et al. (Eds.): ICTE 2015, CCIS 559, pp. 209–218, 2015.
DOI: 10.1007/978-3-662-48978-9_20

users but also mirror characteristics and preferences of data owners. To facilitate understanding of behaviors and preferences of the data owners (users), the generated data are typically exploited for constructing user profiles so as to facilitate personalized services like recommendations [26] or personalized data access [23].

In the context of second language learning, learner data involve learning logs, standard test results, and individual learning preferences and styles [9]. Given its attribute of reflecting the characteristics of learners, such data can be exploited to build the learner profiles. For example, the historical learning vocabulary and vocabulary testing results can be used for constructing learner profile for language learners [30].

However, these data sources possibly include noises or bias, e.g., a vocabulary test with an unfamiliar topic to students and students are not interested to the topic in the test. However, the system may consider these students prefer this topic as the vocabulary test has been consolidated in their learner profiles. It is therefore that such noises and bias influence the reliability of the correspondingly constructed learner profiles. Consequently, the inaccurate profiles may result in ineffective learning tasks that are generated by e-Learning systems. In the above example, tasks with unfamiliar (or uninterested) topics to learners could be recommended if an unfamiliar topic has been included in their learner profiles.

To tackle this issue, it is significant and critical to evaluate the accuracy of learner profiles. In a response to this call, we propose a novel metric named "profile mean square error" to examine the accuracy of learner profiles founded upon diverse sources. The main contributions and organization of this article are listed as follows.

- Section 2 reviews related work about user/learner profiles in systems in e-Learning and other domains.
- In Sect. 3, we demonstrate how to construct various learner profiles though applying different data sources such as learning logs, standard test results, and personal learning preferences in e-Learning systems and pedagogical activities.
- Section 4 reports experimental study among some second language learners, the results of which illustrate that the most accurate profiles are generated from multiple data sources if they are integrated in a rational way.
- The research in this paper is summarized in Sect. 5.

2 Related Works

The research in user/learner profiles has been extensively studied in the areas of user modeling, recommender and personalized systems. In this section, we mainly review the related works about the user modeling techniques, e-Learning systems and the applications of these models in e-Learning area.

2.1 User Modeling Techniques

Without additional user efforts, Sugiyama et al. [21] proposed several approaches to adapting web search results achieved by constructing user profiles based on collaborative filtering. Yu et al. [27] presented three strategies for merging individual user profiles, and then recommended TV programs based on the consolidated profiles. Daoud et al. [7] adopted a session-based method to facilitate personalized search through using an ontological user profile. Raad et al. [19] proposed an approach to matching user profiles in various social networks so as to identify different profiles from the same real user.

More recent, tag-based and rating-based user profiles have been extensively studied in recommender and personalized systems [2, 23, 24], since the user-generated data like ratings or tags usually mirrors the user perceptions and opinions. User modeling techniques are often adapted to the characteristics of resources/items to be retrieved in the systems. Xie et al. [25] proposed a hybrid semantic item modeling approach according to the four distinct characteristics of recipe items, while Cai et al. [3] presented a tag-based resource modeling based on the vector space model (VSM). The corresponding user models in these researches are adapted and to be consistent with the item/resource models, the effectiveness of which have been further investigated in Cai et al. [4].

2.2 e-Learning Systems

With the development of Internet technology, e-Learning systems have been popular and widely adopted in decades [29]. Liu and Yang [15] proposed a the Adaptive & Personalized e-Learning System (APeLS) that provides dynamic learning content and an adaptive learning process for learners to enhance the quality of learning with a novel metric quality of learning (QoL). Pituch and Li [18] proposed and tested alternative models that seek to explain student intention to use an e-Learning system when the system is used as a supplementary learning tool within a traditional class or a stand-alone distance education method. Sun et al. [22] revealed that learner computer anxiety, instructor attitude toward e-Learning, e-Learning course flexibility, e-Learning course quality, perceived usefulness, perceived ease of use, and diversity in assessments are the critical factors affecting learners' perceived satisfaction.

Furthermore, Kumar et al. [13] discussed moodle architecture and comparisons between different virtual learning management systems. Cooper and Sahami [6] studied the education inflections on Stanford MOOCs (Massive Online Open Courses). Yuan and Powell [28] investigated how MOOCs can be integrated and used in traditional higher education. More recent studies focused on social and personalized e-Learning systems [20]. Ally and Prieto-Blázquez [1] studied and reviewed the trends for mobile e-Learning systems.

2.3 Language Learning Applications

The user modeling techniques has been also widely applied in language learning systems due to the fast development and popularity of web-based e-Learning systems [14]. To facilitate effective language learning, Chen et al. [5] presented a personalized intelligent mobile learning system which can appropriately recommend English news articles to learners based on the learners' reading abilities evaluated by the proposed fuzzy item response theory. Jung and Graf [12] designed a word association game to support the personalized vocabulary learning through modeling the individual learning needs.

Ogata et al. [17] presented a ubiquitous learning log system called SCROLL (System for Capturing and Reminding Of Learning Log) to build the learner profile based on what learners have learned in the daily life using ubiquitous technologies. In vocabulary learning systems, the learning preferences and test results are used for building learner profiles [9].

More recently, Hsu et al. [11] developed a mobile learning system based on the approach by providing a reading material recommendation mechanism for guiding EFL (English as Foreign Language) students to read articles that match their preferences and knowledge levels, and a reading annotation module that enables students to take notes of English vocabulary translations for the reading content in individual or shared annotation mode. Zou et al. [30] is the first piece of work to applied the involvement load hypothesis [10] from second language acquisition area for constructing load-based learner profiles, which are quite effective for recommending incidental word learning tasks. Lai [16] investigated and modeled the influence of teacher behaviors on learners' self-directed technology use.

3 Methodology

In this section, we firstly formalize our research problem by a mapping function. Secondly, we introduce how various input components can be obtained in the mapping function. Finally, we propose a metric for evaluating the accuracy of learner profiles constructed from heterogeneous sources.

3.1 Problem Formulation

The basic idea of profiling second language learners is to obtain their pre-knowledge on words from their historical learning activities such as tests or essays been taken. Formally, the idea can be represented by the mapping function θ as follows.

$$\theta : D \rightarrow P \tag{1}$$

where the mapping function θ maps each element d in a set of documents D to a learner profile p in a set of profiles P, d is a document used or generated in a learning activity (e.g., a learnt essay or a taken test), and p is a corresponding profile denoting the pre-knowledge on words learnt from the document.

3.2 Learner Profile Construction

According to the idea, the learn profile p should be a consisted and unified model to depict the pre-knowledge on words of learners. Formally, we define a learner profile p for a second language learner as follows.

Definition 1. Let $\{v_1, v_2, \ldots v_n\} \in V$ and $\{\mu_1^i, \mu_2^i, \ldots \mu_n^i\}$ be the vocabulary of all words and the degrees of pre-knowledge on each word for learner i, the learner profile p_i is represented by a vector:

$$p_i = (v_1, \mu_1^i; v_2, \mu_2^i; \ldots v_n, \mu_n^i)$$

where v_x is a word and μ_x^i is the degree of pre-knowledge on word v_x of learner i, and the degree of pre-knowledge is in the range [0,1]. The degrees of pre-knowledge on words can be obtained from the documents D in the above mapping function θ. In this research, we focus on three kinds of documents, which are reading essays (denoted by D^r), writing assignments (denoted by D^w) and testing papers (denoted by D^t) during the learning processes. We detail how to convert the three types of documents into the learner profile in the remaining parts of this subsection.

3.2.1 Reading Essays

For each learning essay $d^r \in D^r$, we can denote the essay by using a bag-of-words model. In other words, we represent the essay by a collection of words in this essay. We assume that the portion of a word in the essay reflects the degree of pre-knowledge on the word. For example, if a word 'science' frequently appeared in the essay, learners should be familiar with the word 'science' since the word is frequently appeared and learners encounter the word in different contexts. Therefore, we adopt the portion of words in an essay to denote the degree of pre-knowledge as follows.

$$\mu_x^i = f(v_x) / \sum\nolimits_{v_k \in d^r} f(v_k) \tag{2}$$

where $f(v_x)$ is the frequency of word v_x in the essay d^r, and the denominator is the total frequency of all words in the essay. Note that we do not eliminate the stop words from the essays as the high frequencies of stop words (e.g., 'the', 'a', 'is') actually reflects that learners have good pre-knowledge on these words.

3.2.2 Writing Assignments

Writing assignments are the typical word learning tasks for language learners to practice their productive knowledge about vocabulary. Similarly, we assume that the frequency of a word in a writing assignment mirrors how much pre-knowledge of a learner to the word. We employ the similar formula to Eq. (2) to calculate the degrees of pre-knowledge. The only difference is that d^r (a reading essay) is replaced by d^w (a writing assignment).

3.2.3 Testing Papers

Conducting a test is an important and essential way to examine how much word knowledge learners have on the target words. Instead of focusing on all words, we only focus on target words in a testing paper. We believe that testing papers (especially for word knowledge testing papers) have specific target words, while writing assignments and reading essays may not have. For the degree of pre-knowledge on these target words, we assume that the grade of testing papers can reflect them mainly. Therefore, the degree of pre-knowledge on a target word v_y in a testing paper is calculated as follows.

$$\mu_y^i = \frac{g(d^t)}{G^t} \times 100\% \;\; (v_y \in d^t) \tag{3}$$

where $g(d^t)$ is the grade of the testing paper d^t, G^t is the full grade in the marking system of the testing paper d^t (e.g., $G^t = 100$ if the full grade of d^t is 100), and v_y is a target word of the testing paper d^t. If a word is occurred in multiple testing papers, we take the average of Eq. (3) as the final degree of pre-knowledge on the word.

3.3 Profile Accuracy Measurement

To evaluate the goodness of learner profile, we propose a measurement called 'profile mean square error' in this paper. The idea is that the degree of pre-knowledge on a word of a learner can be regarded as the probability of answering correct meanings of the word in a test by the learner. In an extreme case, the learner should not give the correct meaning of a word if the degree of pre-knowledge level of the word in his/her learner profile is '0'. Inspired by this idea, we propose the following metric named 'profile mean square error' (PMSE) to evaluate the accuracy of a profiling method.

$$PMSE = \frac{1}{|L||T|} \sum\nolimits_{i \in L, t_x^i \in T} (t_x^i - \mu_x^i)^2 \tag{4}$$

where $|L|$ is the total number of learners, $|T|$ is the total number of target words in a word knowledge test T, t_x^i is the test score of word knowledge about the word v_x of learner i. The test score for a word is in a three-scale marking system, which contains '0', '0.5' and '1' as suggested in Folse's [8] Modified Vocabulary Knowledge Scale as shown in Table 1. The details of three scale of marking are:

- If the learner does not know the meaning of target words, '0' will be given;
- If the learner know the semantic meaning of the target word but he/she cannot use it in a sentence correctly, a partial score '0.5' will be given; and
- If the learner either knows or uses the word in a sentence correctly, a full score '1' will be given. The larger value of *PMSE* indicates less accuracy of the profiling method.

Table 1. Folse's (2006) Modified Vocabulary Knowledge Scale

1.	I don't know what this word means.
2.	I know this word. It means____________________. (provide an English synonym or a translation in your native language)
3.	I can use this word in a good example. Write your sentence here: ______________________________. (If you do #3, you must do #2 also.)

4 Experiments

In this section, we introduce the experimental settings and report the corresponding results. The experimental subjects and comparative methods are firstly reported. Secondly, the performance of the different profiling approaches and reported.

4.1 Subjects and Comparative Methods

Generally, we make the comparison among one three profiling methods (which only exploits the reading essays, the writing assignments and the testing papers respectively) and one hybrid profiling method taking the above three kinds of documents. We notate three profiling methods only using reading essays, writing assignments and testing papers as “RE, WA and TP” respectively. For the method using all three sources, we use abbreviation “HYB” to denote it.

For experimental subjects, we have invited 25 fresh undergraduates in a local university. We track their learning logs and collect totally 149 documents from their online learning system for a course. As some subjects absent several learning activities during the course, some methods (e.g., WA) do not all involve 25 subjects as shown in Table 2. For the HYB method, we select the subjects who involve all three learning activities, and obtain 107 documents from these 20 students.

Table 2. The descriptive statistical information about four profiling methods

Profiling Methods	Sources	No. of subjects	No. of documents
RE	Reading Essays	25	61
WA	Writing Assignments	21	42
TP	Testing Papers	24	46
HYB	All three sources	20	107

4.2 Performance on PMSE

Figure 1 shows the PMSE of all four methods. We can observe that the hybrid profiling method (HYB) achieves best performance (0.1656). A possible reason is that all three documents reflects pre-knowledge of learners to some extent, and more accurate and powerful profiles can be constructed if we integrate the sources in a rational way (e.g., we adopt mean to combine three kinds of documents in the HYB method).

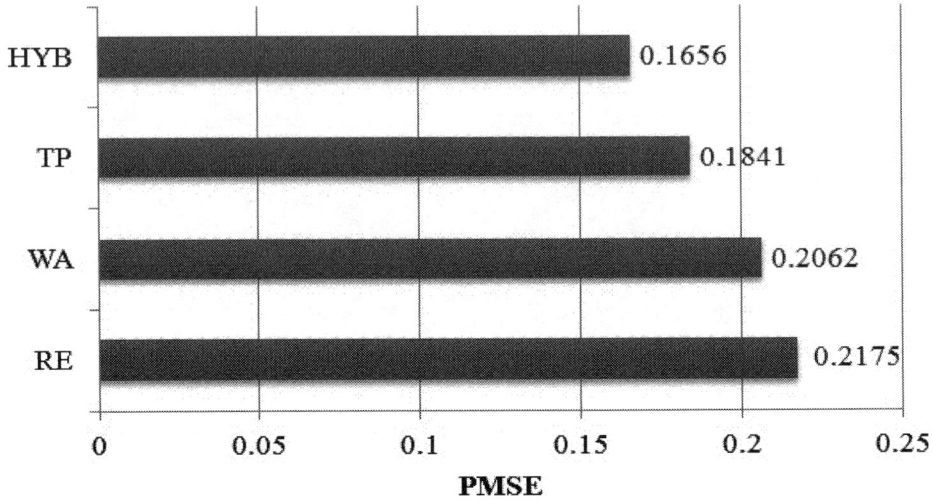

Fig. 1. PMSE of all four methods

Furthermore, the testing paper profiling (TP) method achieves the first runner-up in terms of PMSE (0.1841), which indicates that testing papers maybe the most accurate source to reflect the degrees of pre-knowledge on target words. However, the obvious trade-off here is that a testing paper often contains much less words than reading essays and writing assignments, so that we can collect the degrees of pre-knowledge from less learners.

5 Conclusion

In this paper, we propose a heterogeneous profiling method for modeling language learners. We also propose a novel metric named "profile mean square error" to examine the accuracy of learner profiles founded upon three sources. We have found that the testing papers are the most accurate source among all three kinds of documents. Moreover, the integration of all three sources can be more accurate and effective than the testing paper. For future research, we mainly continue our research in the following directions:

- We will compare other types of document sources for learner profiling;
- We will also try to find an approach to optimizing the parameters of weights among various sources as the linear combination is adopted currently;
- We will exploit the learner feedback and contextual information (e.g., location-based information) to improve the learning effectiveness.

Acknowledgement. The work described in this paper was fully supported by a grant from Research Grants Council of Hong Kong Special Administrative Region, China (UGC/FDS11/E06/14).

References

1. Ally, M., Prieto-Blázquez, J.: What is the future of mobile learning in education? RUSC Univ. Knowl. Soc. J. **11**(1), 142–151 (2014)
2. Choi, K., Yoo, D., Kim, G., Suh, Y.: A hybrid online-product recommendation system: combining implicit rating-based collaborative filtering and sequential pattern analysis. Electron. Commer. Res. Appl. **11**(4), 309–317 (2012)
3. Cai, Y., Li, Q., Xie, H., Yu, L.: Personalized resource search by tag-based user profile and resource profile. In: Chen, L., Triantafillou, P., Suel, T. (eds.) WISE 2010. LNCS, vol. 6488, pp. 510–523. Springer, Heidelberg (2010)
4. Cai, Y., Li, Q., Xie, H., Min, H.: Exploring personalized searches using tag-based user profiles and resource profiles in folksonomy. Neural Netw. **58**, 98–110 (2014)
5. Chen, C.M., Hsu, S.H., Li, Y.L., Peng, C.J.: Personalized intelligent m-learning system for supporting effective English learning. In: IEEE International Conference on Systems, Man and Cybernetics, SMC 2006, vol. 6, pp. 4898–4903. IEEE, October 2006
6. Cooper, S., Sahami, M.: Reflections on Stanford's MOOCs. Commun. ACM **56**(2), 28–30 (2013)
7. Daoud, M., Tamine-Lechani, L., Boughanem, M., Chebaro, B.: A session based personalized search using an ontological user profile. In: Proceedings of the 2009 ACM symposium on Applied Computing, pp. 1732–1736. ACM, March 2009
8. Folse, K.S.: The effect of type of written exercise on L2 vocabulary retention. Tesol Q. **40**(2), 273–293 (2006)
9. Huang, Y.M., Huang, Y.M., Huang, S.H., Lin, Y.T.: A ubiquitous English vocabulary learning system: evidence of active/passive attitudes vs. usefulness/ease-of-use. Comput. Educ. **58**(1), 273–282 (2012)
10. Hulstijn, J.H., Laufer, B.: Some empirical evidence for the involvement load hypothesis in vocabulary acquisition. Lang. Learn. **51**(3), 539–558 (2001)
11. Hsu, C.K., Hwang, G.J., Chang, C.K.: A personalized recommendation-based mobile learning approach to improving the reading performance of EFL students. Comput. Educ. **63**, 327–336 (2013)
12. Jung, J., Graf, S.: An approach for personalized web-based vocabulary learning through word association games. In: International Symposium on Applications and the Internet, SAINT 2008, pp. 325–328. IEEE, July 2008
13. Kumar, S., Gankotiya, A.K., Dutta, K.: A comparative study of moodle with other e-Learning systems. In: 2011 3rd International Conference on Electronics Computer Technology (ICECT), vol. 5, pp. 414–418. IEEE, April 2011
14. Li, Q., Lau, R.W., Wah, B.W., Ashman, H., Leung, E.W., Li, F., Lee, V.: Guest Editors' Introduction: Emerging Internet Technologies for E-Learning. IEEE Internet Comput. **13**(4), 11–17 (2009)
15. Liu, H.I., Yang, M.N.: QoL guaranteed adaptation and personalization in e-Learning systems. IEEE Trans. Educ. **48**(4), 676–687 (2005)
16. Lai, C.: Modeling teachers' influence on learners' self-directed use of technology for language learning outside the classroom. Comput. Educ. **82**, 74–83 (2015)
17. Ogata, H., Li, M., Hou, B., Uosaki, N., El-Bishouty, M.M., Yano, Y.: SCROLL: supporting to share and reuse ubiquitous learning log in the context of language learning. Res. Pract. Technol. Enhanced Learn. **6**(2), 69–82 (2011)
18. Pituch, K.A., Lee, Y.K.: The influence of system characteristics on e-Learning use. Comput. Educ. **47**(2), 222–244 (2006)

19. Raad, E., Chbeir, R., Dipanda, A.: User profile matching in social networks. In: Proceedings of the 2010 13th International Conference on Network-Based Information Systems, pp. 297–304. IEEE Computer Society, September 2010
20. Shi, L., Al Qudah, D., Qaffas, A., Cristea, A.I.: Topolor: a social personalized adaptive e-Learning system. In: Carberry, S., Weibelzahl, S., Micarelli, A., Semeraro, G. (eds.) UMAP 2013. LNCS, vol. 7899, pp. 338–340. Springer, Heidelberg (2013)
21. Sugiyama, K., Hatano, K., Yoshikawa, M.: Adaptive web search based on user profile constructed without any effort from users. In: Proceedings of the 13th International Conference on World Wide Web, pp. 675–684. ACM, May 2004
22. Sun, P.C., Tsai, R.J., Finger, G., Chen, Y.Y., Yeh, D.: What drives a successful e-Learning? An empirical investigation of the critical factors influencing learner satisfaction. Comput. Educ. **50**(4), 1183–1202 (2008)
23. Xie, H., Li, Q., Mao, X.: Context-aware personalized search based on user and resource profiles in folksonomies. In: Sheng, Q.Z., Wang, G., Jensen, C.S., Xu, G. (eds.) APWeb 2012. LNCS, vol. 7235, pp. 97–108. Springer, Heidelberg (2012)
24. Xie, H., Li, Q., Mao, X., Li, X., Cai, Y., Rao, Y.: Community-aware user profile enrichment in folksonomy. Neural Netw. **58**, 111–121 (2014)
25. Xie, H., Yu, L., Li, Q.: A Hybrid Semantic Item Model for Recipe Search by Example. In 2010 IEEE International Symposium on Multimedia (ISM), pp. 254–259. IEEE, December 2010
26. Yu, L., Li, Q., Xie, H., Cai, Y.: Exploring folksonomy and cooking procedures to boost cooking recipe recommendation. In: Du, X., Fan, W., Wang, J., Peng, Z., Sharaf, M.A. (eds.) APWeb 2011. LNCS, vol. 6612, pp. 119–130. Springer, Heidelberg (2011)
27. Yu, Z., Zhou, X., Hao, Y., Gu, J.: TV program recommendation for multiple viewers based on user profile merging. User Model. User-Adap. Inter. **16**(1), 63–82 (2006)
28. Yuan, L., Powell, S., Cetis, J.: MOOCs and open education: Implications for higher education (2013)
29. Zhang, D., Zhao, J.L., Zhou, L., Nunamaker Jr, J.F.: Can e-Learning replace classroom learning? Commun. ACM **47**(5), 75–79 (2004)
30. Zou, D., Xie, H., Li, Q., Wang, F.L., Chen, W.: The load-based learner profile for incidental word learning task generation. In: Popescu, E., Lau, R.W., Pata, K., Leung, H., Laanpere, M. (eds.) ICWL 2014. LNCS, vol. 8613, pp. 190–200. Springer, Heidelberg (2014)

A Comparative Analysis on National Quality Courses of Educational Technology

Chen Wu(✉) and Tian Yanfei

School of Educational Information Technology, South China Normal University, Guangzhou 510631, China
scnuhenwu@126.com, 672727020@qq.com

Abstract. Project of national quality courses was launched in 2003 which has 3904 national quality courses now. Among the national quality courses, there are 8 courses on educational technology from 7 universities. By reporting findings concerning the status of the 8 national quality courses on educational technology from the course website interface, course contents, course updates and interaction, this paper analyzes the experiences and problems of its effectiveness. Findings show that the course repetition, less resource types and updates, as well as interaction difficulty effect on the application of national quality courses.

Keywords: Comparative analysis · National quality courses · Educational technology

1 Introduction

For the quality of higher education in mainland China, Ministry of Education (MOE) launched the project of national quality courses from 2003 to 2010 and therefore provinces and cities got local quality course going. In the 9 years, universities and colleges developed thousands of courses for the national - level and provincial - level awards. These courses were requested being open to the society, providing opener and more convenient learning environments, and everyone including students and teachers can get learning resources from the quality courses. Until 2011, there are 3904 national quality courses covered laws, engineering, management, literature, pedagogy, economics, science, agriculture, medicine, history and military science.

Focusing on the national quality courses, many researches promoted suggestions and opinions around how to develop quality courses. A minority of researchers investigated the national quality courses, observing which status of development and application. The development process, current situation and application of national quality courses were investigated. There were 3904 national quality courses were approved by MOE in the 9 years [1], but most of the courses were used by the development groups themselves and then few updated [2]. Furthermore, compared with the request of national open video courses, the quality and quantities of national quality courses were to be perfected. More suggestions were proposed to improve the application of national quality courses. Rich resources, updated content and friendly

J. Lam et al. (Eds.): ICTE 2015, CCIS 559, pp. 219–229, 2015.
DOI: 10.1007/978-3-662-48978-9_21

interface were warmly welcomed by students [3]. And the development of national quality courses should resolve problems like how to use effectively, how to highlight the individual character of course, how to realize the idea of modern education [4]. National quality courses were also compared with open courses from USA, from management, application and demands [5].

National quality courses are important for the quality of higher education in mainland China. Teachers and students gain valuable resources and experience from online courses through national quality courses. Although the project was ended in 2010, we now inspect the national quality courses to find the problems in the project. Thus, this paper reports the problems and experiences of the development of national quality courses on educational technology based on the analysis and comparison, and hoping to give suggestions to the new project of course development.

2 Background

From 2003 to 2010, there were 3904 courses approved to be national quality courses. In 2001, document 4 from MOE put forward the request of multimedia application in required courses in the universities, so that the start of courses information. MOE launched the project of national quality courses in 2003, and proposed to develop 150 courses. In 2005, document 1 from MOE advanced the object of developing 1500 national quality courses, and promoted3 levels as university, province and nation level quality courses development, forming multi-discipline, multi-courses sharing platform online. Document 1 in 2007 from MOE proposed select 3000 courses to develop. By 2010, the project of national quality courses was completed. Among the selected courses, engineering courses make up 32 % of all courses, which are the most; Science courses accounts for 16.3 %, and medicine courses for 12 %. Philosophy courses are the smallest, only accounts for 1.1 %. But laws, pedagogy and economic courses are all below average. Table 1 shows the quantities of national quality courses in the 8 years.

Table 1. The statics of national quality courses from 2003–2010

Year / Amount / Level of academy	2003	2004	2005	2006	2007	2008	2009	2010
Undergraduate	126	249	247	262	411	400	400	438
Vocational-technical colleges	24	51	61	112	172	200	200	229
Online education					50	50	50	60
Military academies			5	16	7	19	29	36
	150	300	313	390	640	669	679	763

In the Network of National Quality Courses Resource (http://www.jingpinke.com), there are 56 courses belonging to educational courses. Among these 56 courses, 19 courses belonging to educational technology, accounting for near 34 % of the total educational courses. Education first-level discipline has 10 s-level disciplines as foundations of education, curriculum and teaching theory, history of education, comparative pedagogy, pre-primary education, higher pedagogy, Vocational-technical education, special pedagogy and educational technology. Obviously, educational technology courses had many advantages in the whole education courses to compete national quality courses, but inside educational technology there were few types of courses. Figure 1 shows the 19educational technology courses types and level of academy.

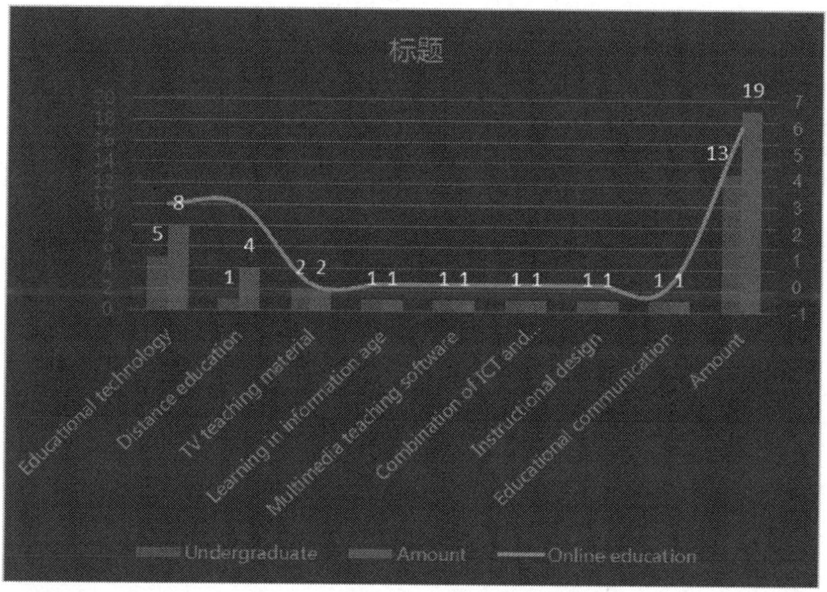

Fig. 1. Types and levels of academy of national quality courses on educational technology

For exploring the problems and experiences of the development of national quality courses on educational technology, we take these 8 courses as the analysis object. Table 2 shows the 8 courses name, university and approve time.

For the convenient statics and of the 8 courses, we give abbreviations to them using the course names, the master names and the approve year as Table 3.

Table 2. The 8 courses name, university and approve time.

No	Course Name	University	Master	Approve Time	Level of academy
1	Modern educational technology	Zhejiang normal university	Zhang Jian-ping	2004	Undergraduate
2	Modern educational technology foundation	Beijing normal university	HE Ke-kang	2006	Undergraduate
3	Modern educational technology	Shanxi normal university	FU Gang-shan	2006	Undergraduate
4	Introduction of educational technology	Beijing normal university	HUANG Rong-huai	2007	Undergraduate
5	Modern educational technology	Hebei university	ZHANG li-xin	2007	Undergraduate
6	Educational technology	Jiangnan university	Chen Ming-xuan	2009	Online education
7	Modern educational technology	Central China normal university	YANG Jiu-ming	2009	Online education
8	Modern educational technology	South China normal university	ZHANG Miao-hua	2010	Online education

Table 3. The abbreviations of 8 educational technology courses

No	Course name	Abbreviations
1	Modern Educational Technology	1MET(Z04)
2	Modern Educational Technology Foundation	2METF(H06)
3	Modern Educational Technology	3MET(F06)
4	Introduction of Educational Technology	4IET(H07)
5	Modern Educational Technology	5MET(Z07)
6	Educational Technology	6ET(C09)
7	Modern Educational Technology	7MET(Y09)
8	Modern Educational Technology	8EMT(Z10)

3 Process

To explore and compare online courses, courses website interfaces, contents, resources, updates and interactions are chosen for analysis purposes. And for the newest information from the 8 courses, we use information from course websites in masters' universities. But

2 courses could not enter in which are 2METF(H06) and 7MET(Y09), we use information from Network of National Quality Courses Resource.

3.1 Comparisons of Courses Website Interfaces

Comparing the website interfaces of selected courses, we find that every course has special interfaces and types of resources were different. There are 5 courses provided record videos of class and 6 courses provided PPT courseware online. From which we know that PPT and class records are the most convenient resources to provide. In the 8 courses, 1MET(Z04), 5MET(Z07), 6ET(C09) and 8MET(Z10) have more resources and resources types, as well as give more chances to students to interact. But almost all courses took courses as the declaration website, contents like teaching group, declarations and development objectives are provided too in the website. Table 4 is the comparison of courses website interfaces.

Table 4. Comparisons of courses website interfaces

Course	Teaching group	Resource	Experiment	Courses interactions
1MET (Z04)	Y	Courseware, videos, online test, References, students work	Virtual experiments	Intelligent answering, BBS, Moodle
2METF (H06)	Y	References, courseware, videos, Supporting test	Practice guidance	N/A
3MET (F06)	N/A	References, instructional material, students work, expand resources	N/A	BBS, message to teachers
4IET (H07)	Y	Videos, home works & exercises, tests	Introduction of students' practice	BBS
5MET (Z07)	Y	Expand resources, videos, courseware, tests, lectures, instructional material	Introduction of practice	BBS, blogs, online answering
6ET (C09)	N/A	Mind maps, videos, courseware, learning guidance, instructional material, references, expand resources, tests	Practice guidance	BBS, online answering, SMS
7MET (Y09)	Y	Courseware, instructional design, tests	Practice guidance	N/A
8EMT (Z10)	Y	videos, courseware, learning guidance, instructional material, references, expand resources, tests	Practice guidance and homework	BBS

3.2 Comparisons of Courses Contents

Obviously, the 8 courses we choose are so similar, and we try to analysis and compare their content in detail. From the amount of chapters, we find that 2METF(H06) has minimums number of chapters which is 4 and 5MET(Z07) has maximum number of chapters which is 14.

Course 2METF(H06) has 4 chapters as educational technology outline, educational media outline, routine media and instructional design. The course focuses on the exercise and practice in educational technology, and is benefit to people who like to learn educational technology fast. 5MET(Z07) has chapters as the nature of educational technology, technology in information age, history of educational technology, learning theory, teaching theory, communication theory, teaching media, teaching resources, teaching circumstances, analysis technology of teaching system, design of instructional strategies, technology of evaluation, ICT combined with disciplinary courses and modern distance education. 5MET(Z07) is suitable for the undergraduates who have no experience on teaching and using technology in education. Figure 2 shows the number of chapters of the 8 courses, and our recommendations.

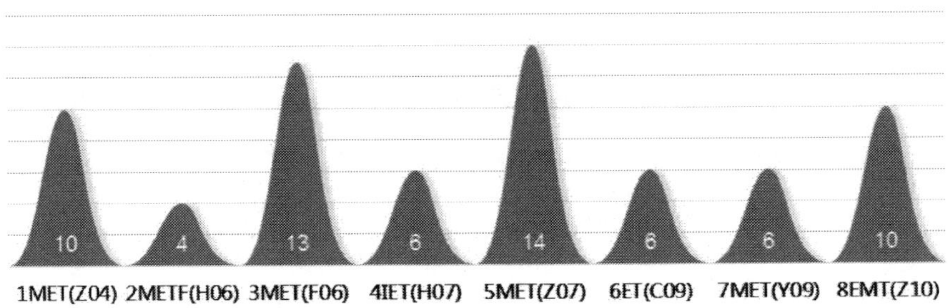

Fig. 2. Number of chapters of the 8 courses

Although the number of chapters are so different, due to the courses are the introductory courses of educational technology, they have large similarity in contents. Table 5 shows the contents similarity of the 8 courses.

Among the chapters, there are 7 courses having introduction to educational media and there are 6 courses have instructional design and educational resources or course development. About the educational media, all the 8 courses provide information media in text. Almost the courses provide such information in video, animation or picture. But videos about media providing by some courses are records of class, explaining theory of media, which is same with the information in text. In the 7 courses, only 1MET(Z04) provide virtual experiment to guide students in practice, 2 courses introduced new media like interactive whiteboard, electronic bag and touch-sensitive integrative machine etc. Therefore, the contents of 8 national quality courses in educational technology are certain similarity in detail and the knowledge of courses is inflexible with time. As the national quality courses, we should pay more attention on the resources sharing, and consider the diversity of contents. Educational technology has at

Table 5. Eight courses similar chapters

Contents in chapters	Courses
Educational technology outline	2METF(H06), 5MET(Z07), 6ET(C09)
History of educational technology	4IET(H07), 5MET(Z07), 8MET(Z10)
Educational technology theory	1MET(Z04), 3MET(F06), 4IET(H07), 5MET(Z07)
Audio-Visual Communication theory	1MET(Z04), 3MET(F06), 5MET(Z07), 8MET(Z10)
Modern educational media	1MET(Z04), 2METF(H06), 3MET(F06), 4IET(H07), 5MET (Z07), 6ET(C09), 8MET(Z10)
Instructional design	1MET(Z04), 3MET(F06), 4IET(H07), 5MET(Z07), 6ET (C09), 8MET(Z10)
Educational resources or course development	1MET(Z04), 3MET(F06), 5MET(Z07), 6ET(C09), 7MET (Y09), 8MET(Z10)
evaluation	3MET(F06), 5MET(Z07), 8MET(Z10)
ICT combined with disciplinary courses	4IET(H07), 5MET(Z07), 7MET(Y09), 8MET(Z10)
Online or distance learning	1MET(Z04), 4IET(H07), 5MET(Z07), 6ET(C09)8MET(Z10)

least 16 major courses, including educational technology, instructional design, the methodology of educational technology research, distance education, the basis of computer network, the design and development of multimedia courseware and etc. [6] However, educational technology now has 8 national quality courses, other major courses only have 1 or 2 national quality courses, some major courses even have no national quality courses. At this sense, national quality courses project should pay more attention to encouraging different courses to take part in evaluation.

Table 6. The contents of 6 courses in instructional design

Course	Contents	Practice stage	Cases
1MET (Z04),	instructional design, instructional evaluation	N/A	N/A
3MET (F06)	instructional design, instructional evaluation	N/A	N/A
4IET (H07)	design and development of education Software	N/A	N/A
5MET (Z07)	The design of teaching strategies, instructional evaluation technology	√	N/A
6ET(C09)	instructional design and evaluation	N/A	√
8MET (Z10)	instructional design and evaluation, Multimedia design and development	√	√

Instructional design is also the important content of educational technology, which need put theory into practice. The 6 courses having instructional design almost all introduce the theory and design process of instructional design, but few courses design training stages for students to practice or give effective case to guide students. By contrast, quality courses for online education are better than courses for undergraduate. 2 of 3 quality courses for online education provide instructional design practice guidance to students, defining courses for online education paying more attention on the ability of practice. Table 6 shows the comparison of the 6 courses in instructional design.

3.3 Comparisons of Resource Types

Resource types can give students more space to choose the learning method. Since MOE request courses applying national quality courses should provide 50 min class records, almost all 8 courses we choose provide videos on website. Besides the videos, we investigate other resource types in the 8 courses. In Table 7, we find in addition to videos and PPT, e-text is also the most popular resource type, but few courses can provide other types of resource. In videos, class records are in the majority, other types like micro-course, demonstrate videos are less. In nowadays, the forms of videos do not comply with the request of fragmentation learning. In addition, some videos need to a special plays or ought to download, some videos are not on the visuals, which affects the quality of courses.

Course 8EMT(Z10), the last course approved national quality course, provide most types of resource in the course. The course uses flash animations to explain contents

Table 7. Resource types of 8 courses

Course	Class records	Other vides	Pictures/animations	PPT	e-text	Virtual experiment	Resource tools
1MET (Z04)	N/A	N/A	√	√	√	√	N/A
2METF (H06)	√	N/A	N/A	√	√	N/A	N/A
3MET (F06)	N/A	N/A	N/A	N/A	√	N/A	√
4IET (H07)	√	N/A	N/A	N/A	√	N/A	√
5MET (Z07)	√	N/A	N/A	√	√	N/A	N/A
6ET (C09)	√	√	N/A	√	√	N/A	N/A
7MET (Y09)	√	N/A	N/A	N/A	√	N/A	N/A
8EMT (Z10)	√	√	√	√	√	N/A	√

like how the projector works; uses pictures to illustrate contents like how to use internet. Thus, course 1MET(Z04) is the only one providing virtual experiment to help students understand how to use equipment, in spite of approving in 2004. Furthermore, courses 3MET(F06), 4IET(H07) and 8EMT(Z10) provide resource tools to support student development.

3.4 Comparisons of Courses Updates

As the national quality courses, every courses get financial aid from MOE, and which could support the updates and maintenance for several years. Moreover, *the enforcement measures of national quality courses development* by MOE in 2003 also said national quality courses should update contents at least 10 % every year. Online courses update is also one of the most important methods to support sustainable development. We compared the update time and content of 6 courses having own website as Table 8.

Table 8. Update time and content of courses

Courses	Last update time	Contents updated
1MET(Z04)	2011.04.27	Unknown
2METF(H06)	2009.05.26	Unknown
3MET(F06)	2009.08.05	e-bag, Smart classroom, 3D printing technology
4IET(H07)	2010.06.21	videos, instructional resources
5MET(Z07)	2010.01.07	Theory, resource, media environment
6ET(C09)	2009.10.28	Unknown
7MET(Y09)	2009.10.28	Unknown
8EMT(Z10)	2010.06.21	Mobile learning

From Table 8, we find that among the 6 courses, the recent update time of course 2METF(H06) is May 2009, and course 1MET(Z04) is April 2011. After 2011, all the courses stopped update, because *the enforcement measures of quality resource sharing courses development* by MOE in 2012 requested all the national quality courses should upgrade to quality resource sharing courses. And yet, update of national quality courses was the biggest problem of the development of national quality courses. Many courses stopped update not long after being approved be national quality course. So, the latest developments of educational technology, like flipped classroom, micro-course and 3D print didn't appear in any of the 8 courses. And the content of courses cannot fully meet the requirements of the learning today, nor play an active role in demonstrating.

3.5 Comparisons of Course Interactions

National quality courses aiming at open, interaction provided by course is the important index of open. From Table 5, we find that except courses 2METF(H06) and 7MET

(Y09), other 6 courses having own website in university all provide various interaction ways to students. Courses 1MET(Z04) and 5MET(Z07) provided 3 interaction ways each as BBS, intelligent answering, real-time answering, blog and etc., giving larger spaces to students.

We logged in every interaction space to investigate the practical results and the findings as Table 9.

It is obviously, only 2 courses' interaction spaces can login outside their university, the other 4 courses interaction spaces all use intranets which means students from other universities can't ask questions or interact with other students on the courses website. Course 8EMT(Z10) can login outside the university, and a lot of comments by students and teachers were submitted on the BBS already, but the submitting only open to students registered. Course 3MET(F06) is the only course providing open interaction space, visitors from other universities also can use the test account to submit questions and comments freely.

Table 9. Investigation of level of open of course interactions

Course	Login outside university	Comments	Visitor comments
1MET(Z04)	N/A	N/A	N/A
3MET(F06)	Y	Y	Y
4IET(H07)	N/A	N/A	N/A
5MET(Z07)	N/A	N/A	N/A
6ET(C09)	N/A	N/A	N/A
8EMT(Z10)	Y	Y	N/A

4 Conclusions

It is undoubtedly that national quality courses project can facilitate learning and improve higher education quality nowadays; however, the enforcement process still need a more rational design and arrangement. The data implies that the national quality courses on educational technology have problems as the course repetition, less resource types and updates, as well as interaction difficulty. More work in the future we can do to improve the sharing of learning resources and develop the quality of higher education. We remarked that at the beginning of the project of national quality courses, the enforcement measures mentioned neither the evaluation criteria of national courses, nor the plan of evaluation. As one of important projects to improve quality of higher education, the uncomplicated enforcement measures couldn't give a clear direction to universities and teachers. On the other hand, for the sustainable development of national quality courses, a policy of routine inspection is lacked. Course update can not only keep the visit of the course, but also can develop the course itself. Routine inspection can effectively promote course update; thereby ensure the effective application of the course.

In the modern times, ICT takes more and more important role in the development of society. Education reform and development also inextricably link with technology.

The development direction of technology may change the learning method and circumstance; education should adapt to the change. It is our hope that our research can promote the development of long-term educational projects at the national level, having overall plans for the higher education developing.

References

1. Jun-jie, H., Gai-xue, Y., Jiang-min, W., Yong-liang, Y.: Revelations of national quality courses to open video quality courses—Thoughts on investigations on national quality courses from 2003 to 2010. Distance Educ. China **6**, 89–94 (2014)
2. Li-yan, S., Ai-jun, Z., Rong, D.: From national quality curriculum to the national quality open video class: Open education movement in China has entered a new period. Mod. Educ. Technol. **22**, 62–67 (2012)
3. Ling, Ma., Jiao, C., Yin, Q.: Empirical studies on factors of using intention of national quality courses website. Distance Educ. China **4**, 45–49 (2014)
4. Jia-nian, Z., Ling-yun, L., Zhen-xiang, S.: On the construction, application and evaluation of top-quality course in view of the performance. China Educ. Technol. **330**, 113–118 (2014)
5. Ai-hua, W., Qiong, W.: Study on sharing and application comparison of national quality courses to open courseware. Distance Education in China **6**, 16–21 (2010). 74
6. Zhong-xi, Y.: Analysis of main courses of a part of educational technology in teaching in mainland China. China Educational Technology & Equipment, p. 30 (2009). 国内部分教育技术学师范专业的主干课程分析
7. Ministry of Education, the enforcement measures of national quality courses development (2003)
8. Ministry of Education, the enforcement measures of quality resource sharing courses development (2012)

Learning Platforms and Advising Systems

An Experience Sharing on e-Learning Platform Upgrade

Janny C.C. Ng, Sze-Wing Leung(✉), Dickson T.S. Chan, Hades C.F. Tam, Benz C.L. Sze, and Ray K.C. Wong

School of Professional and Continuing Education, The University of Hong Kong, Hong Kong SAR, China
{janny.ng, swleung}@hkuspace.hku.hk

Abstract. Since the introduction of learning management system (LMS), the development of online learning has been changing rapidly in the past decades. With the advancement of information technology, numerous LMSs, such as WebCT, Blackboard and Moodle, had been developed. New features and advanced versions of LMSs are frequently released each year. HKU School of Professional and Continuing Education (HKU SPACE) adopted the first LMS, namely "SOUL", in order to enhance teaching and learning effectiveness since 1999. In view of enhancing the needs of a sophisticated online learning environment, SOUL was revamped based on Moodle, an open source system, and a new version named SOUL 2.0 was launched in 2011. After running for a few years, a system upgrade was taken place in 2014 to cope with the latest Moodle version 2.7, which mobile format is supported and improvements were made. With various customized features implemented to the SOUL 2.0, a set of coding standards was introduced by the development team to standardize the customization of source codes. This paper shares the barriers that the team faced during the upgrading process. It also illustrates how the coding standard and effective workflow were implemented at development phase, and the way to assure system coding and source data are migrated successfully.

Keywords: e-learning · Learning management system · Platform upgrade · Moodle

1 Introduction

HKU SPACE is committed to provide high quality educational opportunities for the communities since its establishment. Starting from 1999, the School adopted the advance from technologies to provide better learning and teaching experience for teachers and students by developing their in-house built learning management system, SOUL. It was a Web 1.0 platform which was mainly for students to download material and submit assignment files. The School started using an open source learning management system, Moodle version 2.1 to take the advantage of its Web 2.0 features of being a pedagogical driven, cost-effective and community supported learning management system (LMS) solution [9] since 2011.

J. Lam et al. (Eds.): ICTE 2015, CCIS 559, pp. 233–250, 2015.
DOI: 10.1007/978-3-662-48978-9_22

With the revolution bloom on Web 2.0 in recent decades, a variety of e-learning platforms have been introduced. In order to keep in pace with the technology and adapt different learning styles, each of those platforms could release several software updates and require frequent upgrading. While an e-learning platform always involves various stakeholders, previous studies have argued that the entire campus could have to suffer a disaster if an update procedure is not implemented with a thoughtful and thorough action plan [15].

According to Moodle.org, two versions would be published per year where major and minor updates would be applied to its LMS for adopting the updated technologies such as mobile-friendly features, improving the system performance, fixing security issues, etc. To take the advantages of the enhancements and new functions in latest versions, upgrading e-learning platform from older to newer become the only option for the higher educational institutes and is a challenge to the higher educational organization undergoing the adoption of the upgraded LMS [6].

This paper introduces a case study of the upgrade processes of our e-learning platform that comprise of complicated and huge amount of customization tasks and enhancements. It also discusses the challenges, which include schedule management, staff turnover, user involvement, launching preparations, etc., during the upgrade process. Last but not least, this paper shares good practices for developing and maintaining e-learning platforms. It is hoped that the case study and the experiences shared by the team could act as a reference for any party who prepares to update an e-learning platform, especially for major or critical updates.

2 Business Needs and Benefits on Platform Upgrade

Nah & Delgado [6] emphasized that 'Business Plan and Vision' and 'Top Management Support and Championship' are critical for a project while Petherbridge and Chapman [6] mentioned that planning on upgrading a LMS version to another requires sufficient resources. With the support from the School, the LMS upgrade project team kick-off the LMS upgrade by using the latest stable release of Moodle where many security issues were fixed, new functions were developed, performance were greatly improved and Moodle Mobile app was introduced after version 2.4. To upgrade a system, it means adding new features or installing more recent software patches to the existing LMS. It is definitely having many advantages to have a regularly upgrading on the existing LMS. For instance, users are able to get access to new features, the latest versions of software often has performance and functions improvement. Modern web access features like "drag and drop", refreshing part of the web page using AJAX and jQuery support, revamping the assignment module and logging methodology, supporting group assignment, adding book module into the core module, etc., are deployed on Moodle in the recent releases. These features also enhance user experience, in other words, improve the learning experience. In addition, we can save cost by updating system regularly as outdated system may no longer be supported by the LMS provider on bugs and security fixings.

Upgrades often include bug fixes and security patches. Therefore, staying on the upgrade path makes future upgrades easier. This reason for upgrading sounds not so compelling but the truth is, if we are sticking with a particular system, it's best to stay relatively current. Otherwise, a future upgrade can be nearly impossible or ridiculously expensive. Why? It is because most of the providers tend to stop providing support for older versions when they launch new ones. They only write scripts that let administrators upgrade system from the previous one or two versions. If it is over six or tens versions behind, there is no simple way to jump versions because the database or programming structure may have big changes. Upgrading LMS is the least we can do to keep pace and be proactive.

3 Planning for the LMS Upgrade in HKU SPACE

Open source system does not fit with standard models of software development [8]. With the nature of open source system, like Moodle, it provides a high flexibility for higher education institutions to customize the functions easily to meet the operational needs from their teachers and learners. We had hundreds of functions customized in most of the modules in Moodle version 2.1 platform in order to satisfy the needs of our stakeholders including students, teachers and programme staff. Due to the limited resources and tight project schedule for launching the SOUL 2.0 in 2011, there was lack of documentation on the code changes, hard to trace the coding due to the different coding style used by the developers and the high staff turnover rate in team. It becomes a big challenge for the project team to upgrade SOUL 2.0 to the latest version Moodle version 2.7.

Having a good upgrade plan and upgrade procedures are keys for the success of the project. To prepare a good upgrade plan for the system upgrade project, we have firstly studied the release notes to understand the changes in Moodle before we started planning the project and estimating the resource. Secondly, we had to design the development environment such as the hardware, operation system upgrade and other peripheral software upgrade. Then, we had to list all functions that we customized and estimate the resource for revamping the customized functions with updated methodology and merge them to the upgrade platform.

In addition to the estimation for the development work, a well-designed workflow for function testing and a clear procedure are also important for the upgrade process. Although Moodle has provided some scripts for migrating data from one release to later releases, we had made customizations not only on the functions but also on the database, data migration to the latest releases becomes another big issue. A well designed upgrade procedures and enough time for trial run exercise are musts for ensuring the data integrality after the platform is upgraded. During the trial run exercise, we identified different problems on data migration and developed customized scripts to enhance the efficiency and accuracy of upgrade process, such as altering fields in database, and updating the data content to be compatible with the updated platform.

When all work are ready, some efforts are needed before the upgraded system goes live, which is to backup data file, source code and database, and it can provide a fast fallback procedure when data is corrupted during migrating to production. At the project investigation and planning stage, the latest stable Moodle version was version

2.6, the resource estimation and design were based on this version. After migrating over 90 % of the customized functions from Moodle version 2.1 to version 2.6, the Moodle version 2.7.1 stable version was released. With the use of project management system, version control system and coding standard, we could easily further migrate the customized functions to Moodle version 2.7.1. Besides, from the experiences gained from trial run exercises and the well tested upgrade procedures, we migrated our customized LMS from version 2.1 to version 2.7 within the estimated duration and the upgraded system was successfully launched. In the following sections, we are going to share experiences on maintaining and upgrading a Moodle platform.

4 Good Practices Used for Maintaining and Upgrading a Moodle Platform

The development team of this project consists of one project manager, one main software engineer, three part-time software engineers and several part-time helpers who were employed for function testing. Within the limited time frame and hundreds of customized functions, we need a very good organization of the project development. One of the most important decisions to be made by the project manager is how to properly staff the project, her major goal is to maximize value creation for a given investment [1]. How to prioritize the function migration is the most important part. Use of project management system and introducing coding standard to ensure the functions handled by different developers reach the same standard, and also can be easily followed by different developers. Moreover, how to ensure the functions and data are migrated correctly, as well as how to get user involved during the upgrade process are another important elements. These elements will be discussed in this section.

4.1 Effectively Use of Project Management System for Recording and Tracking Progress of Tasks

Project management system is defined as a change management system and a collection of documented procedures that records how the deliverables and documentation of project were approved, changed and controlled. Project management system is also defined as a series of actions added to the process of getting tasks done on projects by working with project team members to achieve the project schedule, technical performance objectives and goals [3]. To achieve the project goals and objectives, we need to develop a project plan first. By complying with the project plan, we can identify the tasks and achieve the goals easily. Project management also includes managing the implementation of the definition, project planning, implementation, evaluation and maintenance.

In our LMS upgrade project, we adopted a web-based software project management tool, Trac. Trac is an issue tracking system for software development projects. It provides an interface to subversion, an integrated Wiki and convenient reporting facilities [12]. Trac allows wiki markup in issue descriptions and committed messages, creates links and seamless references between bugs, tasks, change sets, files and wiki pages. Also, the timeline showing all current and past project events in order makes the acquisition of an overview of the project and tracking progress very easy [2]; whilst the roadmap shows the road ahead, lists the upcoming milestones. Trac helps the project manager to keep close monitoring on each task and helps the developers to record the progress of each task in order to work collaboratively among developers as well as student helpers. It also allows the project manager to monitor the progress of the project via roadmap function in the Trac system. Figure 1 shows the roadmap for SOUL 2.0 project.

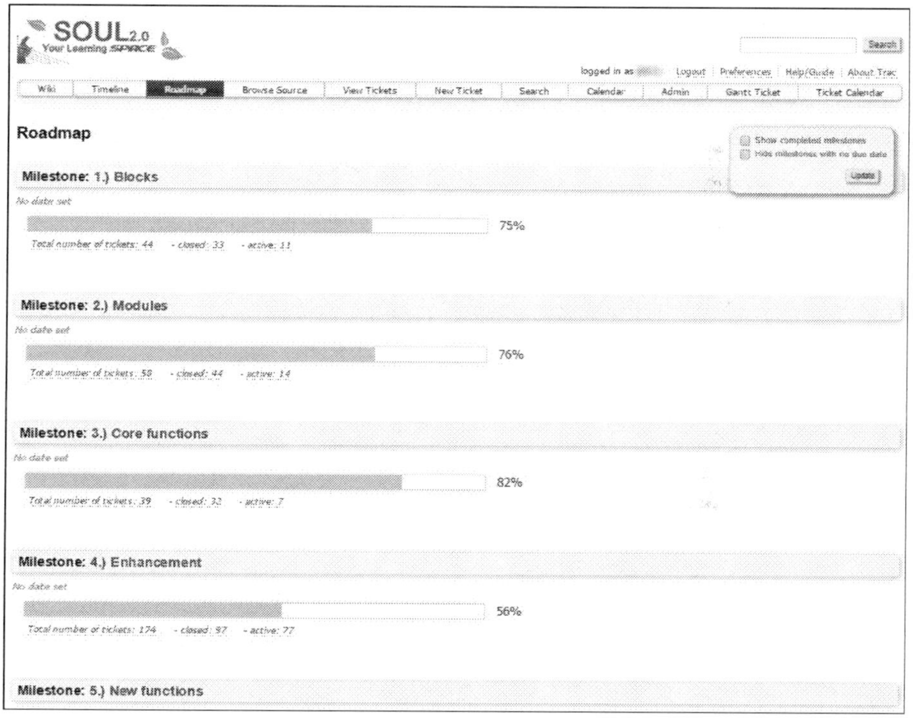

Fig. 1. The roadmap for SOUL 2.0 project

4.2 Improve Working Efficiency by Adopting a Version Control System

Crashing on coding development often happens in a collaboration project which has more than one developer. To avoid it, the project team used a software called Git to keep the version control of the source codes. Git is a distributed version control system, it supports distributed and non-linear workflows. Working directory of Git recorded complete history and full version tracking capabilities [14]. For example, there are a few developers who produce and develop the source code, they may change, extend, undo changes, and jump back to an older version, and they may need to modify the same files, the Git will keep track of the files and keep the history as version to indicate who made the change of the files.

A strict branching model designed around the project release is defined as the Git workflow. It does not add any new concepts and commands for the workflow, and it uses a central repository as the communication hub for all developers and engineers. In Git workflow, it is using historical branches structure of the project. Instead of the single master branch, it uses two branches, the master branch and the develop branch, to record the history or version of the project. The master branch saves or records the official release history while the develop branch serves as an integration branch for features.

Common conventions of Git workflow:

$$\text{Branch off (development)} \;=\; > \text{ Merge into : masterbranch} = > \text{ Release branch}$$

For example, at the beginning, there is a local repository as a clone of the Moodle 2.1 (from Moodle official site) repository and it may call the master branch, there are many other branches of the bug fix on the master branch. Figure 2 shows the relationship between master branch and other branches of the bug fix.

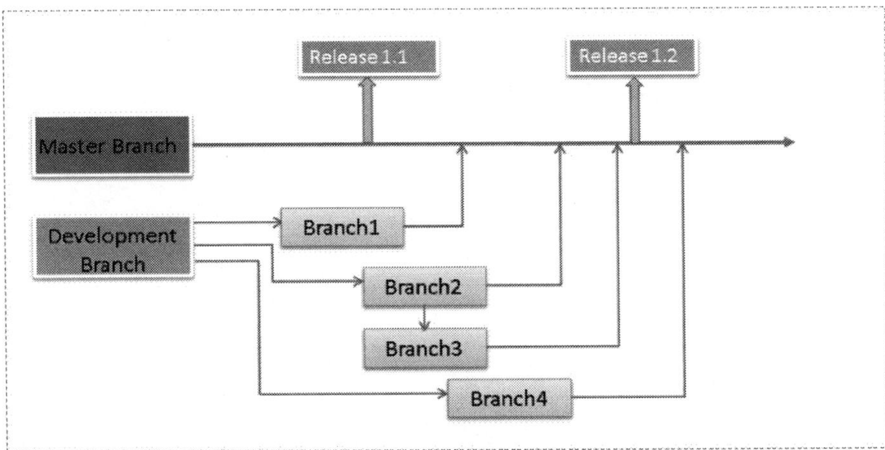

Fig. 2. The relationship between master branch, development branch and other branches

Figure 2 illustrates a simple relationship between branches. From the diagram, we know that Branch1, Branch2 and Branch4 are using the development branch. The Branch3 is basing from Branch2 because it requires some modifications from Branch2. And, once the Branch1, Branch2, Branch3 are completed and merged to master branch, a new release, named Release1.2, is launched to the production system. After that, another modification by Branch4 is performed and merged to the master branch. With using the version control system, we can easily identify the conflicts among thc branches and/or revert the merged branch(es) easily with several commands. It greatly improves the working efficiency of the team.

4.3 Use of Coding Standard Making Codes Handy and Traceable

In an open source collaborative project, we would face the problems such as the turnover of technical staff, tracking the previous issues long ago and different programmers may have different coding styles, etc. Therefore, the upgrade project team setup a coding standard for the developers to follow in order to prevent the problems. Veranga [13] pointed out that implementing a coding standard on a project can make the source code more comprehensive and easy for maintaining. Also, it can allow other developers to trace the code easily. Below are the examples:

A. **Modify a function or variable inside a class.** For any code modification happens inside a class, the following steps should apply:
   (1) Change the original class name with prefix “cold_”,
   (2) Create a new class to extend the class in step 1 just below the old class,
   (3) Override any variables or methods in the new class.

   Original code

```
<?php
  class USER {
            function get_user() {
                        return true;
            }
  }
```

   Modification code

```
<?php
//John Doe: SOUL2_00123 (23-Dec-2014) – echo message before return @Start@
  class cold_USER {
      function get_user() {
         return true;
         }
    }
  class USER extends cold_USER {
      function get_user() {
         echo “Hello World”
         return true;
         }
    }
  //John Doe: SOUL2_00123 (23-Dec-2014) – echo message before return @End@
```

B. **Modify a function not inside a class.** For any function modifications not inside a class, the following steps will apply:
   (1) Rename original function with prefix “fold_”,
   (2) Create a new function using the original function name with prefix of four spaces just below the old function.

Original code

```
<?php
function get_user() {
      return true;
}
```

Modification code

```
<?php
function fold_get_user() {
      return true;
}
//John Doe: SOUL2_00123 (23-Dec-2014) – echo message before return @Start@
function get_user() {
      echo "Hello World";
      return true;
}
//John Doe: SOUL2_00123 (23-Dec-2014) – echo message before return @End@
```

C. **Other modification handling.** For any modifications not inside a class or function, an inline modification will be used with comments.

Original code

```
<?php
  echo "Helo Wold";
```

Modification code

```
<?php
echo "Hello World"; //John Doe: SOUL2_00123 (23Dec-2014) – corrected typo words
```

4.4 Prioritize on the Function Migration to Fulfill the Needs of Majority of Users

There are over hundreds of customized features built in the system in the older version. With the lack of a well documentation on the customized modules and the staff turnover problem, it is nearly impossible to migrate all customization made in version 2.1 to the newer version within a few months. Prioritizing the customized functions migration by according to its importance therefore becomes an important task. It can allow the project team to see clearly the most important task to be handled first, and which can be on hold [4]. Besides the customizations made on the core libraries that we should migrate first, the project team also decided that all customizations made on the highly used functions would be migrated to the upgraded platform. To help understanding on the function usages among the active courses, a course function usage statistic was generated. Table 1 shows that the most popular function is uploading file resources to the course for student to download, followed by posting announcement for the latest news of the course. There were several modules not being used by any course, namely Lesson, Mindmap, Nanogong and Survey. These functions would not be enabled in the upgraded system at the beginning of the system launch until they are being well tested.

Table 1. Statistic on course usage of different module as at April 2013

Module name	No. of courses used
File resource	2175
Announcement	1697
Event calendar	1000
Folder resource	775
Label	567
Assignment	544
Turnitin assignment	490
URL	420
Grade book	203
Forum	89
Page	73
SCORM	57
Quiz	52
SWF	28
Questionnaire	24
VCLink	19
Choice	15
Glossary	14
Wiki	13
Workshop	12
Database	7
Group choice	3
Chat room	1
Lesson	0
Mindmap	0
Nanogong	0
Survey	0

4.5 A Clear Workflow for Development Deployment Can Improve Working Efficiency

A clear workflow for the development deployment can make the project run more effectively and efficiently. It helps complete the project in a timely manner, more consistently, safely and reliably. With adopting the Trac system, the project manager would issue tickets in the Trac system and assign them to developers. The developers would investigate and estimate the resource/time required for handling the assigned tasks. After the project manager accepts the estimated resources, the deadline for the development of those tasks would be set. The developers would first pull data from development repository to their local development environment to make sure the latest coding is being used. After handling the tasks and having well tested in local environment, the developers would push to development server. The code would be reviewed by a senior developer before merging to master branch, and then the functions were tested by the helpers and reviewed by the project manager. The branches would be deployed to a staging server periodically. The staging server is an environment which simulated the production environment. All branches would be deployed to the

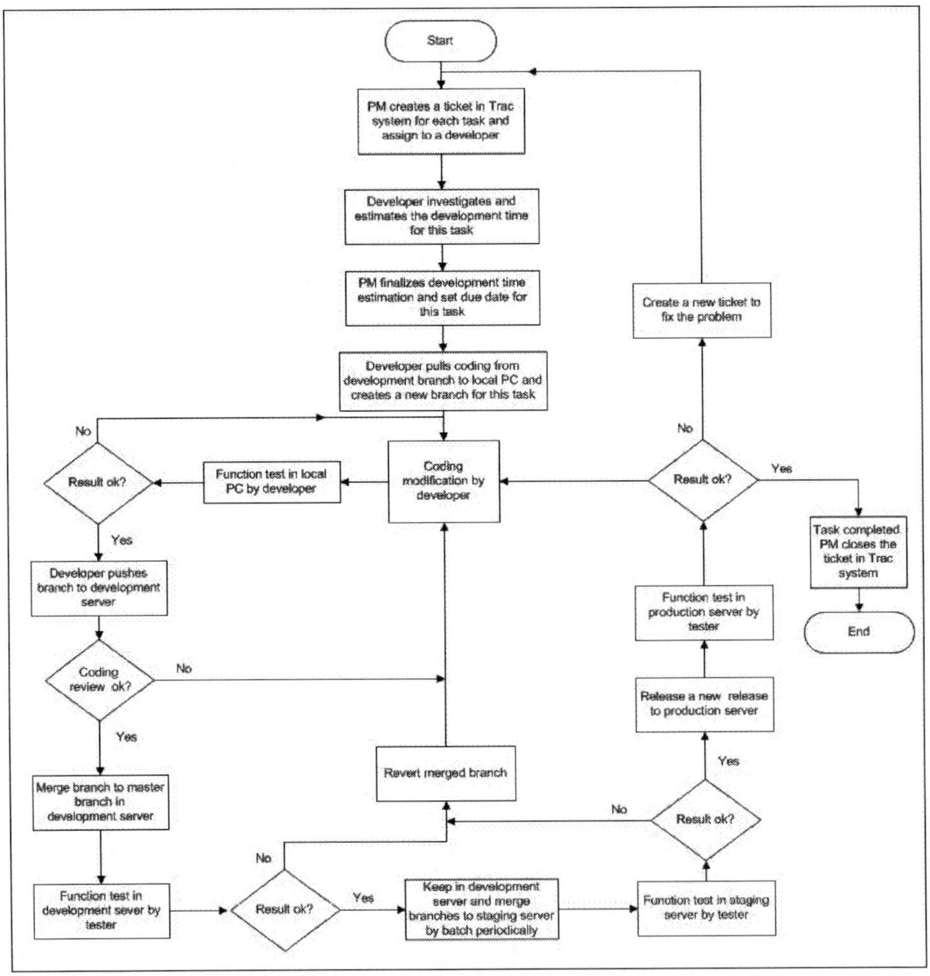

Fig. 3. Development deployment workflow

staging site for final confirmation. If there is any problem found in staging server, the merged braches would be reverted and the tickets would be assigned back to the developers for further investigation and fixing. These procedures are not only used during the system upgrade but also adopted in current system maintaining stage. The only difference is that, after the testing has successfully passed in staging server, it would launch to production site in a release. And, a final testing would be conducted in the production site. Figure 3 shows the workflow of the development deployment process.

4.6 Migration Planning to Reduce the Potential Risks of Error During Upgrade

A successful upgrade project requires a migration plan. The migration plan addresses issues associated with phasing out legacy systems and moving to the new system. These issues include user interface compatibility, database compatibility, transition support, system interface compatibility, and training. Also it involves tradeoffs between cost, schedule, risk, and resources. The migration plan should identify prototyping needs in system upgrade and which data are included in the migration process. Prototypes can effectively test the potential solution, especially in cases where current systems are complex and involve many users. The migration plan should identify prototyping needs. At the same time, it should address the extent to which migration considerations call for prototyping both to mitigate risks and to demonstrate proof-of-concept to users. A prototype can be completed in weeks as opposed to

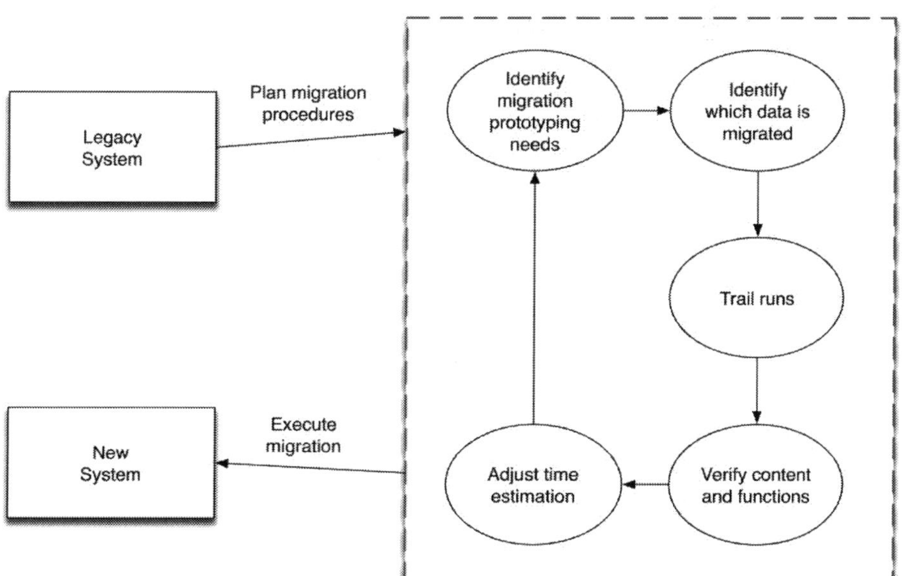

Fig. 4. Iterative migration cycle for system upgrade

months of laborious specification. An effective prototype can also be used for collecting comments from users on the new user interface and operational usage scenarios before system implementation decisions are made. In addition to identify the prototyping needs on system upgrade, it is also important to understand what types of data is migrated from the old system to the new one. Much of the data from the old server can be migrated automatically using the update tools but some are not. For those data are not convertible other tools or routine needs in order to achieve migration goals. Some of them must even be migrated manually. This may consume more time to complete task. Figure 4 shows the iterative migration cycle for upgrading a system.

4.7 Trial Run Migration Procedure to Reduce Risk and Simulate the Real Situation

In a LMS, it stores lots of information and materials in complex format. Before migration process begins, it is suggested to perform a pre-migration impact assessment to verify the cost and likely outcome of the migration. Throughout the pre-migration impact assessment, the procedures and potential risks can be identified. Besides, after several trial runs on the migration procedure, it can provide far more accurate analysis of resource requirements, the expected outage duration and help to refine the migration procedures.

During the trial run exercises, we identified over 20 issues of data and function migration problems. One of the critical issues was the server hardware requirement for performing the data migration in our upgrade process. It takes a long time to migrate the data, which have 10,000 courses and around 7,000 assignment submissions, with using a Virtual Machine server with 16G RAM and 8 vCPU. The whole process was improved by using a dedicated high performance server. Besides the hardware issue, some of the problems were due to the change of data fields in database during the function customizations in Moodle version 2.1. There were also some problems which were not handled by the migration tools provided by Moodle especially the assignment module and gradebook. Additional scripts were prepared for fixing those issues.

4.8 Time Estimation for the Upgrade Process to Ensure Accurate Estimations and Monitor Any Possible Failure at Early Stage

The amount of time taking for performing the migration or upgrade process varies based on how much data the LMS contains and how much customization LMS was configured in the old system. It helps identify the potential risks on the whole process of migration. Moreover, it allows us to obtain a more accurate time spent on each task especially for the major tasks such as installation, configurations of LMS and its plugins, customization of the new system, data migration, the upgrade process and any manual configuration tasks, testing, etc.

It is important to identify the most time consuming tasks, which makes us easier to determine whether the migration process is success or failure. For example, in trail run, migration of student assignments takes around four hours (80 % of total). However, in

Table 2. Upgraded procedures and the time estimation for each task

Task	Description	Estimated time completion		
		Hr	Min	Sec
Export database	Export database contexts from Legacy system	0	10	5
Compress database	Compress exported database	0	6	46
Transfer database	SCP compressed database to staging server	0	2	17
Decompress database	Decompress database and prepare for import	0	3	0
Import database	Import database to staging server	0	27	21
Fix data integrity problem	o Fix assignments data migration problem	0	0	20
	o Fix various database problems	0	0	9
	o Drop unused tables	0	0	2
	o Fix link problem on existing quiz	0	0	2
Git checkout to branch in stage 1	**Upgrade platform to MOODLE 2.2.11+**	**0**	**3**	**30**
Remove activities	Remove mindmap activity	0	1	30
Remove blocks	Remove customized blocks: SOUL2 block, cohort_control block, dndupload block, support_tools block, system reminder block	0	3	0
Git checkout to branch in stage 2	**Upgrade platform to MOODLE 2.6.4+**	**0**	**33**	**30**
Remove local plugin	Remove custlib, course_maintenance	0	1	40
Remove reports	Remove large scale log and report (email log, user tracking report)	0	1	30
Remove export method	Remove csv from grade export method	0	0	32
Backup database	**Backup the upgraded database as a staging backup**	**0**	**2**	**20**
Upgrade assignments	Upgrade all assignment (2.2) instance to assign instance	4	5	39
Restore database	Restore tables for customized plugins and blocks	0	2	0
Checkout DB_Stage3	**Upgrade platform to MOODLE 2.7.1**	**0**	**4**	**35**
Post upgrade DB fix	Add missing capabilities, load faq content, SCORM settings, convert course format	0	2	0
Final configuration	Enable CAS, edit CAS strings, mod enabler	0	3	0
Backup database	Backup database for production database server	0	2	20
	Total:	5	57	8

the migration it takes more than five hours, this gives administrator a signal that the migration process may be failure. Table 2 is an example of the time estimation process.

4.9 Use of Checklist for Data Migration Verification and Functional Test to Ensure Data and System Integrity During System Upgrade

A checklist with test cases was designed for verifying the data and functions migration. The checklist aimed to evaluate whether the expected outcomes have been achieved. During the trial run exercise, the data migrated was sampled checked and functions in the upgraded platform were tested by the development team. Outstanding issues were listed and fixings were applied to the upgrade scripts. Fine tune on the migration procedures and checklist were also performed during each round of trial run exercise. A sample of checklist used in the current task is shown in Fig. 5.

				Assignment										File				
Checked by	Test date	Course ID	Course code	Count in source	Count in upgraded platform	Checked URL	Submission type	Descriptions	Allow access period	Due date	submission inbox	Download all submission	Other remarks (if any)	Count in source	Count in upgraded platform	Checked URL	Description	Other remarks (if any)
example	5/30/14	101	SO 01-101-00 (31)	3	3	(randomly pick one assignment among the 3)	same	same	same	same	same	same	NA					
Tester1	8/23/14	38064	CC 88-768-12-01 (31)	4	4	http://10.21.x.xx/upgrade/mod/assign/view.php?id=355402	same	same	NA (not set)	NA (not set)	same	same	NA	47	47	[illegible]	same	NA
Tester1	8/23/14	41143	SE 01-118-04 (32)	0	0	NA	NA	NA	NA	NA	NA	NA	NA	0	0	NA	NA	NA
Tester1	8/23/14	42380	IT 06-133-12 (31)	2	2	http://10.21.x.xx/upgrade/mod/assign/view.php?	same	same	same	same	same	same	NA	14	14	[illegible]	same	NA
Tester1	8/23/14	41743	SE 35-805-06 (41)	1	1	http://10.21.x.xx/upgrade/mod/assign/	same	same	same	same	same	same	NA	5	5	[illegible]	same	NA

Fig. 5. An extract of a checklist for data migration verification and functional test

4.10 Get User Involved and Conduct User Training to Maximize User Capability and Experience on the New Platform

User involvement is one of the key factors of success of a computer system. Tait and Vessey [10] found that system complexity and resource constraints have strong effects on system success, either directly or indirectly through their influences on user involvement. Rossum [7] also pointed out that it is the best practice for coordinating the users during the migration process. A testing platform was setup for letting our users involve in verifying migrated data and testing the functions in the upgraded platform. The testing site was built with the final tested functions and the data was merged from the existing production platform. After the functional test and data verification were performed by the development team in the testing platform, users were invited to verify their course content in the testing site as well as try out the functions before the system launch.

A survey was conducted after the user verified the migrated data and functions used in their courses, 27 items related to data migration were asked for their checking and confirmation. We received the response on 21 courses, the result is presented in Table 3.

Table 3. Verify data after data migration in upgraded platform

Question		Yes (%)
I. Course materials		
1.	All Announcements are migrated correctly	87.50 %
2.	All File resources are migrated correctly	86.67 %
3.	All Folder resources are migrated correctly	93.33 %
4.	All Label resources are migrated correctly	93.33 %
5.	All Page resources are migrated correctly	90.00 %
6.	All URL resources are migrated correctly	87.50 %
7.	All VClink resources are migrated correctly	87.50 %
II. Course Activities		
8.	All Assignment and Turnitin Assignment activities are migrated correctly	90.91 %
9.	All Chat activities are migrated correctly	83.33 %
10.	All Choice activities are migrated correctly	85.71 %
11.	All Group Choice activities are migrated correctly	83.33 %
12.	All Database activities are migrated correctly	80.00 %
13.	All Forum activities are migrated correctly	80.00 %
14.	All Glossary activities are migrated correctly	80.00 %
15.	All Offline grade item activities are migrated correctly	83.33 %
16.	All Lesson activities migrated correctly	66.67 %
17.	All Mindmap activities are migrated correctly	80.00 %
18.	All Questionnaire activities are migrated correctly	83.33 %
19.	All Quiz activities are migrated correctly	83.33 %
20.	All SCORM package activities are migrated correctly	80.00 %
21.	All Wiki activities are migrated correctly	66.67 %
22.	All Workshop activities are migrated correctly	60.00 %
III. Others		
23.	All graded items are migrated correctly	80.00 %
24.	All Blocks are migrated correctly	83.33 %
25.	All course layout are migrated correctly	85.71 %
26.	All participants are migrated correctly	85.71 %
27.	All Calendar events are migrated correctly	85.71 %

From the result above, most of the data migrations of the modules had been confirmed with over 80 percent correctly of them migrated to the new platform, except Lesson, Wiki and Workshop activities. We found that user answered “No” in the survey due to the fact that the course enrollment to the user was missing in the testing site. Since no customizations were done on the Lesson, Wiki and Workshop and the utilization of the functions were very low, we assumed the migrations were correct as well.

We also asked the users to try the new platform in the testing site, feedback was collected afterwards. In Table 4 below, it was found that we received positive feedback on the upgrade platform, functions and new interface. The server performance improvement was not recognizable because of the scale of the testing site.

Table 4. Comments on functions in SOUL 2.0 upgraded platform

	New functions/enhancements	Agree (%)
(a) Enhancement on Assignment and Turnitin Assignment function		
1.	Allowing user to change from assignment submission type is useful	88.46 %
2.	Group assignment function is useful	78.85 %
3.	Improvement on the file upload by using drag and drop file uploading interface is useful	86.27 %
4.	The interface of Turnitin Assignment is improved	72.73 %
(b) Enhancement on interface		
5.	The interface is clear while the "Turn Editing On" function is on	88.46 %
6.	Allow user to edit the resources/activities name in the course main page is useful	84.91 %
7.	Combining the pull-down menu for Add a Resource and Add an Activity into one pull-down menu is a good improvement	77.36 %
8.	It is a good improvement and tidy interface by collapsing most of the common settings in setting page.	69.23 %
(c) Other enhancements		
9.	More help information on different functions is provided	72.00 %
10.	New types of access restriction settings is useful	66.67 %
11.	The server performance is improved	55.10 %
(d) New functions		
12.	I want to learn more about Rubric grading	50.00 %
13.	I want to learn more about Book recourse	50.00 %
14.	I want to learn more about Feedback activity	50.00 %
15.	I want to learn more about Badges function	38.30 %
16.	I want to learn more about Copy block function	46.81 %

From the survey results, we observed that users were not eager to learn the new functions. We discussed and decided to focus on the enhancement of the existing functions.

Torkzadeh & Van Dyke [11] examined the influence of training programs on Internet self-efficacy and user attitudes toward computers and the results suggested that training significantly influences Internet self-efficacy for individuals with 'high' or 'low' attitude towards computers. The team arranged a series of hands-on training workshops before and after the system was launched. A total 153 participants took part in the workshops. The workshops were recorded and uploaded to the platform for users to review it at any time. Although the user interface of the upgraded platform is similar to the original one, we believe sufficient training would help users adapt to the upgraded platform more quickly. Ongoing training workshop will be arranged to help new users to get familiar with the system, training on basic usage and specific functions will be arranged separately.

5 Conclusion

Implementation of a new learning management system is a rather easy task when compared with upgrading an existing one. However, upgrading a learning management system is an inevitable task in education institutes nowadays to strengthen their teaching and learning support services. After a system has run for several years, performing functions customization in the LMS and technical staff turnover are unavoidable. These make it hard for the new developers to maintain and support, or even upgrade the platform. In this paper, we shared good practices for maintaining the existing platform and highlighted the important strategies on implementing the system upgrade. This includes the use of project management system to keep tracing the task development history, adopting a version control system for both collaborating development work and storing versions, use of coding standard for improving not only the quality of source code but also make the code more traceable, and defining a clear development procedure. The preparation of migration plan, trial run of the migration procedures, getting user involvement and providing users training before and after a system go lives are also the key factors of success of a system upgrade project.

Our experience on SOUL 2.0 suggested that, implementing the project management system, version control system and the coding standard would not only help us monitor the changes on the functions easily, but also provide an easy way for system upgrade. This can be evidenced by our experience on further upgrade of the system from version 2.6 to version 2.7. We would conclude that the whole process of system upgrade was shortened by 70 % with the suggested measures and upgrading the system to the latest version should no longer be a panic task for the project team.

References

1. Boehm, B.W., Sullivan, K.J.: Software economics: a roadmap. In: Proceedings of the Conference on The future of Software Engineering, pp. 319–343. ACM, May 2000
2. Brookins, M.: Benefits of Using Project Management Software (2015). Accessed from http://smallbusiness.chron.com/benefits-using-project-management-software-2196.html
3. Ghioca, T.: Advantages and Benefits of Project Management Software, 8 February 2011. Accessed from http://www.rationalplan.com/projectmanagementblog/advantages-and-benefits-of-project-management-software/
4. Gosenheimer, C.: Project Prioritization. Office of Quality Improvement, University of Wisconsin (2012)
5. Nah, F.H., Delgado, S.: Critical success factors for enterprise resource planning implementation and upgrade. J. Comput. Inf. Syst. **46**(5), 99 (2006)
6. Petherbridge, D., Chapman, D.: Upgrading or replacing your learning management system: implications for student support. Online J. Distance Learn. Adm. **10**(1) (2007)
7. Rossum, P.: Best Practices in Data Migration. Research and Services The Data Warehousing Institute (2006)
8. Sandred, J.: Managing Open Source Projects: A Wiley Tech Brief, vol. 18. Wiley, New York (2002)

9. Sarker, M.O.F., Matthews, J., Gramp, J.: On optimal strategies for the development and operation of Moodle in Higher Education Institutions. In: Moodle Research Conference, pp. 5–13 (2013)
10. Tait, P., Vessey, I.: The effect of user involvement on system success: a contingency approach. MIS Q. **12**, 91–108 (1988)
11. Torkzadeh, G., Van Dyke, T.P.: Effects of training on Internet self-efficacy and computer user attitudes. Comput. Hum. Behav. **18**(5), 479–494 (2002)
12. Trac: Welcome to the Trac Project, 4 March 2015. Accessed from http://trac.edgewall.org/
13. Veranga, L.: 10 Benefits of Using Coding Standards to Software Development Team, 22 January 2008. Accessed from http://www.articlesbase.com/programming-articles/10-benefits-of-using-coding-standards-to-software-development-team-312610.html
14. Why Git? (2015). Accessed from http://www.git-tower.com/learn/git/ebook/command-line/appendix/why-git
15. Xu, H.: Learning management system transformation. In: MWAIS 2014 Proceedings. Paper 11 (2014)

Automated Grading of Short Literal Comprehension Questions

Andrew Kwok-Fai Lui(✉), Lap-Kei Lee, and Hiu-Wai Lau

School of Science and Technology, The Open University of Hong Kong, Ho Man Tin, Kowloon, Hong Kong SAR, China
{alui,lklee,s1098017}@ouhk.edu.hk

Abstract. This paper presents an algorithm for automated marking of natural language responses of literal comprehension questions. It highlights the crucial differences between the content and style of questions for assessing different levels of reading comprehension, and argues that the literal question type can be effectively handled by largely syntax and structural based algorithm. The efficient algorithm compares student answers with model answers along a token-based approach. The small semantic variations in student answers made the omission of corpus-based approaches more sensible. The algorithm was evaluated with real data obtained from a local secondary school, and the performance was found to be very promising.

Keywords: Automated grading · Reading comprehension · Part-of-speech tagging · Parsing · Natural language processing

1 Background

Reading comprehension, as an instructional tool, stimulates understanding of a text passage by quizzing students about its content, and thereby inviting students to read the passage thoroughly and critically. In addition to its formative purposes, comprehension questions are effective for assessment of reading skills. Many standardized tests, such as SDRT [14], WIAT-III [25] and WRMT-III [26], were developed for scientifically evaluating literacy ability and its constituent cognitive components [18].

The past few decades saw the sprouting of various theories of reading comprehension. Pearson [23] gave an excellent review of how teachers and researchers had changed their perspectives of reading due to advances in educational psychology, cognitive science, and social learning. Empirical findings have indicated that factors including word recognition, reasoning, oral comprehension, semantic awareness, syntax and fluency can predict comprehension [11, 13]. Word recognition, which involves symbol decoding, contextualization, and sense determination, is the most significant factor and the basis of higher reading skills [5]. The evidenced differentiation between levels of comprehension is a key consideration for both instruction and assessment. Kintsch [15] made distinction between two levels of reading comprehension: the lower level of comprehension is based on information explicitly found in text passages, and the upper

J. Lam et al. (Eds.): ICTE 2015, CCIS 559, pp. 251–262, 2015.
DOI: 10.1007/978-3-662-48978-9_23

level of comprehension requires integration of relevant information identified from several places in text passages, and possibly with previous knowledge to fill in gaps of understanding [3].

The aim of comprehension questions is to elicit responses that reflect the level of reading skills. Eason et al. [8] derived three question classes from the construction-integration model of reading comprehension [15]. *Initial understanding* or *literal* questions ask students to identify relevant information directly from the text. *Interpretation* questions, on the other hand, require information integration and utilization of background knowledge. The most challenging is *critical analysis* questions, which demand text reasoning and structural analysis. The coherence of the classification was validated by a large-scale study on the cognitive process in reading comprehension [9]. The expected format of responses to a question is determined by question style. Some question styles restrict the range of possible responses and grading can be objective and efficient. For examples, true-and-false and multiple-choice questions provide a set of options for answer selection. Other question styles expect a natural language response such as the so-called *5W1H* questions. The openness of a question determines the degree of convergence or divergence of the natural language response. Grading of open questions requires significantly greater effort to achieve objectivity and consistency. Finally, to inform teachers on how to properly design comprehension questions, there are guidelines available for selecting suitable question classes as well as the question styles. For example, Day and Park [6] suggested a grid for the organization of reading comprehension questions. The grid consists of five commonly used question styles, which are *yes/no*, *alternative*, *true/false*, *who/what/when/where/how/why*, and *multiple-choice*. It also consists of six comprehension classes, which are *literal*, *reorganization*, *inference*, *prediction*, *evaluation*, and *personal response*.

Grading comprehension questions with a natural language response achieves higher efficiency and objectivity if a computer marker is used. The aim of this paper is to present an algorithm for grading *literal* questions. Literal comprehension questions facilitate initial understanding by encouraging students to recognize key information in a text passage. It is highly relevant to drilling exercises designed for weak or beginner language learners. The observation that the openness of literal questions is relatively low, as the answers are literally found in the reading text, has allowed the algorithm to avoid time-consuming corpus-based operations. The algorithm can perform consistently across the *5W1H* question styles. Massively open online courses (MOOCS) [21] and intelligent tutoring systems [12] will benefit from this work. The rest of the paper will analyse the problem of automated grading of natural language answers, describe the algorithm, and report the findings of evaluation using real data collected from an English course in a local secondary school.

2 Related Work

There are three important aspects in the design of an automated grading system: (1) the *question* which determines the form of answer and the standard of assessment, (2) the *corpus* which defines the knowledge base for textual analysis of the answer, and (3) the *algorithm* which specifies the procedure of automated grading.

Automated grading of natural language answer or student response is studied in two related branches of research. Automated Essay Scoring (AES) systems are developed for grading text passages of at least a few paragraphs long. The questions tend to be open-ended, and therefore inviting students to express their ideas, build their arguments, and style their writing [4, 10]. AES is concerned with writing style rather than the accuracy of content. For example, e-rater V.2 extracts essay-construct features including organization, development, lexical complexity, and grammar [1]. It then gives a holistic score based on these features. AES has been used as a fast backup assessor in public tests such as GMAT and TOEFL [7].

Another branch of research is known as Automatic Short Answer Grading (ASAG). Burrows et al. [4] defined ASAG as "the task of assessing short natural language responses to objective questions". The questions tend to ask for specific responses of at most 1 to 2 sentences long. ASAG is concerned about the correctness of student responses with respect to a model answer. The model answer may be in the form of a manually created template for correctness matching. It may also be a string, which is then further processed for keyword matching, regular expression matching [2], or concept map matching [16].

However the applicability of ASAG techniques for grading comprehension questions is worth further consideration. ASAG systems that claimed to be suitable for reading comprehension did not factor in the levels of comprehension in their design [19]. Burrows et al. [4], in his excellent review paper, pointed out that reading comprehension should be considered as an exception from ASAG. The primary target of ASAG is testing knowledge recall but for reading comprehension it is recognizing answers in a text passage. Table 1 summarizes the properties that influence the design of automated grading for various question classes.

Automated grading needs various corpora as the knowledge base for text analysis. Plain text dictionaries, glossaries, and thesaurus could be handy sources for evaluating

Table 1. Various classes of questions asking for natural language responses

Question classes	Length	Skills to test	Focus	Openness
Essay	Paragraphs	Recall background knowledge and construct concepts and develop opinions	Writing skills and style	Open
Short answer	A phrase to a sentence	Recall background knowledge	Content	Closed
Literal comprehension	A phrase to a sentence	Recognize information from reading	Words	Fixed
Interpretation comprehension	Few sentences	Integrate information from reading and background knowledge	Content	Closed
Critical analysis comprehension	Few sentences	Analyze information from reading, recall background knowledge, and develop opinions	Content and writing skills	Open

word-to-word similarity or sense disambiguation. Wordnet [20] included various types of semantic relations between words in a digital form, which supports algorithm development for more accurate measurements. Wikipedia, the largest open-source online encyclopaedia, is perhaps the ultimate corpus for supporting accurate entity recognition, sense disambiguation, and semantic relation between words. Large corpora should normally give more accurate semantic measurement but pay a higher cost in the execution time.

From a student response to an ordinal grade usually takes several stages of processing in automated grading. Figure 1 illustrates the stages in typical automated grading algorithms. The *pre-processing* stage aims to remove word morphological features that are considered not relevant. Common filtering operations include case normalization, spelling correction, and inflection normalization (i.e. lemmatization). The filtered answer strings are then passed to the *feature extraction* stage, of which the objective is to extract items from the strings for comparison. The bag-of-words approach builds items from words and their n-grams. A student response is considered correct if its words and that of the model answer match. Semi-automated systems such as Auto-marking 2 use manually crafted regular expression to extract the items [24]. Assessment of higher reading skills however relies on recognizing the semantics of the words and between the words. Mohler et al. [22], for example, extracts dependency relations that would help bring concepts into grading. The support of annotated corpora is essential. In the *alignment and matching* stage, the extracted items from the student answer and the model answer are compared while tolerating paraphrasing and other variations in the choice of words. The items from the two are aligned to find the optimal pairing giving the highest similarity. The semantic meaning and similarity of pairs of items is obtained from various corpus-based methods based on Wordnet or Wikipedia. The final *grading* stage then converts the similarity measurements into an ordinal grade. The methods of conversion range from rule-based to machine learning approaches.

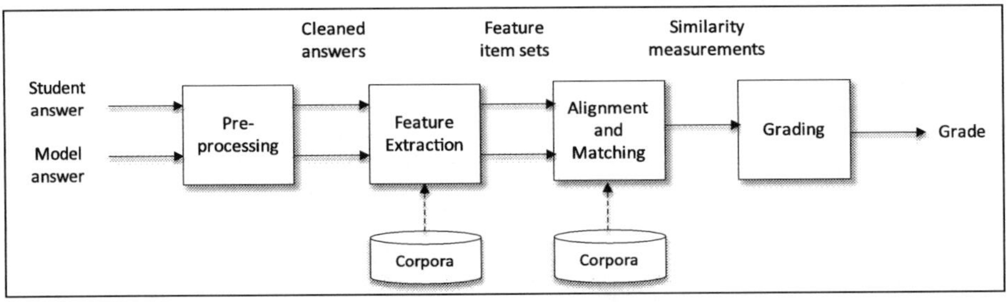

Fig. 1. The stages in typical automated grading algorithms

In summary, automated grading of responses of literal comprehension questions is found to be quite different from other automated grading tasks. The main challenge of such questions is to identify relevant information from the text passage, thus leaving little flexibility in the construction of answers. In a way, variations that are not of exactly the same meaning, such as making it more general or more specific, are discouraged. In addition, background knowledge does not play a role in grading, and therefore the computationally intensive corpus-based operations can normally be avoided. An efficient yet accurate automated grading method is to be introduced in the following section.

3 Method

The objectives of the proposed automated grading method include:

- Provide a similarity measurement for comparing student answer against model answer.
- Offer consistent performance of short literal questions across various question stems.
- Be computationally efficient.

In measuring the similarity between student answer and model answer, our method is built on three principles. First, the words in both the model answer and the student answer should come from the reading text. Using words and their n-grams as the items for comparison should be effective. Second, every answer should contain keywords that are essential, and other words that may be omitted. Some items should carry more weights in the similarity evaluation than other items. Third, the question stem specifies the information that students should recognize from reading text. It determines which items should carry more weights.

The above principles deal with acceptable variations in student answers. Clearly, the special case of exact match between student answer and model answer would pose no problem. However, for a model answer "*Mary was in the car*", whether "*Mary was in the vehicle*" as a student answer should be considered acceptable is dependent on the question stem. It should be acceptable if the question stem is "*who*" but less acceptable if the question stem is "*where*".

3.1 Design of the Automated Grading Algorithm

Figure 2 shows the design of our automated grading algorithm.

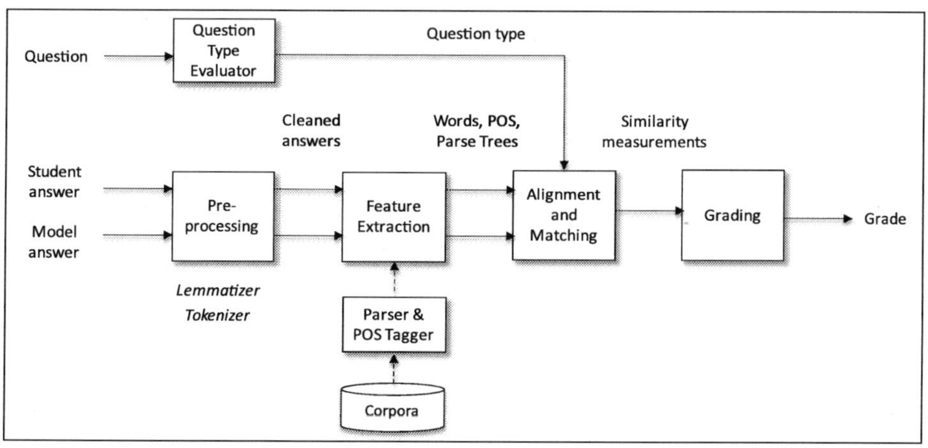

Fig. 2. The stages in our automated grading algorithms

The *Alignment and Matching* stage obtains the words, their part-of-speech (POS) and parse-trees of the student and model answers, and evaluates their similarities according to the question stem type. Different question stems consider different words as important. Table 2 lists the POS tags or the parse tree branches considered as important for each question stem type.

Table 2. Important features for different question stem types

Question stem types	Relevant POS tags or Parse-tree branches
What	Noun
Where	Noun, Preposition
When	Verb Phrase
Who	Noun Phrase
Which	Keyword (All words except Pronoun, Article and Conjunction)
Why	Noun Phrase, Verb Phrase
How	Phrase containing Cardinals
Do	Keyword ("Yes" or "No")
Would	Keyword ("Yes" or "No")

As described in Table 2, only the specific items with the relevant POS tags and those in the parse-tree branches will be involved in the comparison. Figure 3 illustrates the process with an example of a *what* question with two model answers. The reduction of items involved in the comparison has speeded up the execution and omitted unimportant variations.

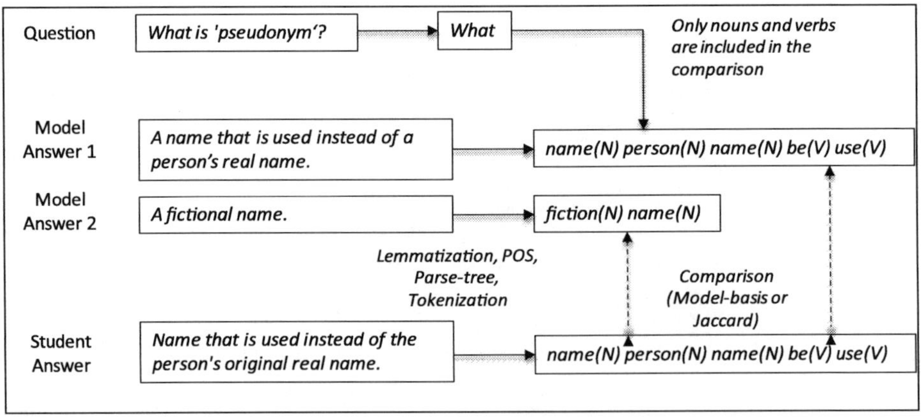

Fig. 3. An example illustrating the processing of the student answer and two model answers of a question

The simple set-theoretic comparison is suitable for literal comprehension questions. Student answers more likely contain words found in the text passages rather than constructing their own sentences. The pre-processing stage, which includes lemmatization, would have removed other undesirable variations. Therefore the more computationally expensive corpus-based approaches such as the Wordnet-based bipartite graph matching with the Hungarian algorithm would be overkill [22]. A number of comparison schemes may be applied, such as *model-answer basis* (i.e. percentage of items of model answers) or *Jaccard coefficient* (i.e. set similarity).

Examples of how several other question stem types are handled by the algorithm are listed in Table 3. For the *which* example, the student answer would get maximum grade

Table 3. Examples of the handling of which, how, and who questions

Which question: *A friend of yours wants to go out for dinner. She loves western food and loves to eat a lot but she does not want to pay too much for dinner. She also likes to sit outside. Based on the restaurant guide, which restaurant would you recommend?*	Items from model: alex bistro	Items from students: would recommend alex bistro
Model answer: *Alex Bistro*		
Student answer: *I would recommend Alex Bistro*		
How question: *According to the passage, how many people were killed in WWII?*	Items from model 1: 7000000 people (Cardinal Phrase)	Items from students: Seven trillion person (Cardinal Phrase)
Model answer 1: *7000000 people*	Items from model 1: Seven million people (Cardinal Phrase)	
Model answer 2: *Seven million people*		
Student answer: *Seven trillion person*		
Who question: *According to the passage, who is Obama?*	Items from model: President (Noun) United (Noun) States (Noun)	Items from students: President (Noun)
Model answer 1: *President of the United States*		
Student answer: *President*		

because it contains all the items of the model answer. For the *how* example, the student answer would be considered wrong. The two models answer are necessary because *7000000* and *seven million* are considered to be different to our algorithm. For the *who* question, the student answer would at best be a partially correct answer because the omission of "United States" was significant.

4 Evaluation and Discussion

A prototype implementation of the algorithm was developed using Java and the Stanford CoreNLP library [17].

An experiment was set up to evaluate the performance of the algorithm with reference to human markers. The grades given by the human markers were considered as the gold standard. We have not assumed that there is no error in the marking, as we will discuss this issue further in a later section. It is however significant that the performance is comparable to human markers, and it provides support for the use of automated grading in formative and summative situations.

Handwritten student answers of literal comprehension questions were collected from a local secondary school. An agreement of consent that ensures privacy and proper handling of the data was in place. The data set consists of 16 reading comprehension questions extracted from one examination and one in-class exercises, and for these questions there are a total of 887 student answers with a grade. Only three question stems were included in the study, which are *what*, *which*, and *why*. There were 5 teachers participated in marking. The data set also includes the question text and the model answers.

Some considerations were made to define the conditions of a match between the grades given by the algorithm and the teachers. The teachers' grades were on an ordinal scale but the maximum mark can be different from one question to another. The algorithm, on the other hand, generates a grade on an interval scale between 0.0 and 1.0. Table 4 shows the mapping between the teachers' grades and the algorithm's grades for questions with partial correct grade allowed. Table 5 shows the mapping for questions without partial correct grade. Note that the thresholds were arbitrarily set and no performance fine-tuning was carried out.

Table 4. Mapping for questions allowing partial correct grades

Teacher's grade	Grade descriptors	Algorithm's grade (Model)
Maximum	Correct	>0.75
Between 1 to Maximum - 1	Partial correct	Between 0.25 and 0.75
0	Wrong	<0.25

Table 5. Mapping for questions not allowing partial correct grades

Teacher's grade	Grade descriptors	Algorithm's grade (Model)
Maximum	Correct	>= 0.60
0	Wrong	<0.60

Among the 887 student answers, 118 of them belong to questions allowing partial correct, and the remaining 769 allow correct or wrong.

4.1 Results

The overall evaluation result is shown in Fig. 4. A total of 810 student answers were given the same grade as the human markers, representing an accuracy of 91.3 %.

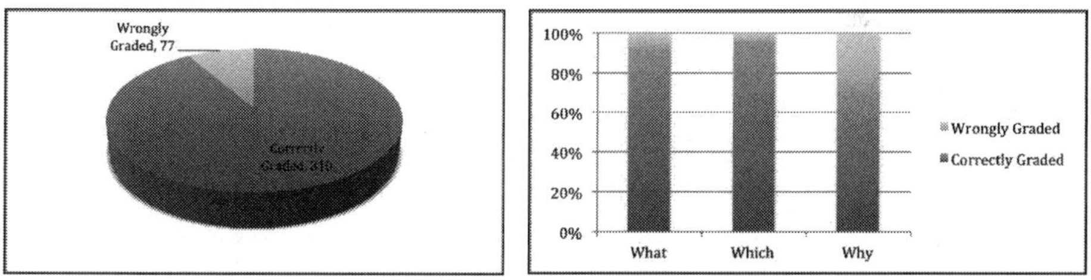

Fig. 4. Performance of the algorithm in the evaluation

The performance of the algorithms, as expected, differed according to the question stem. The wrongly graded cases were investigated and they were discussed in the following:

- One set of *what* questions was found to cause a lot of wrongly graded cases (nearly 50 %). The algorithm gave 0.0 but the teachers gave 1.0, which is the maximum. An interview with the teachers revealed that due to the poor performance of students, they decided to accept other answers. This issue of *sympathy marking* is to be discussed later.
- Most of the wrongly graded cases of *which* questions were found to be due to an implicit grading rule. The model answer of a couple of *which* questions contains a single word. The teacher markers rejected any answer with additional words, which is different from the algorithm.
- The algorithm actually performed equally well for the *why* question. The wrongly graded cases were due to a special character, which indicated the number of stars of a restaurant in the reading passage.

4.2 Limitations and Discussions

There are at least two shortcomings of the experiment. The first shortcoming is the insufficient number of data samples. The data set also does not include all the question stem types. The performance ratings could not be generalized. Clearly the experiment could have used an existing data set available from other studies, but unfortunately a public data set containing mainly literal comprehension questions could not be found. The second shortcoming is that the classification scheme for grade mapping was only *ad hoc*. One simple approach to resolve this issue is to remove the rule-based mapping and to replace it with a machine learning stage.

Data sets obtained from real sources have advantages and disadvantages. If the objective is to simulate a human marker, then real data sets can provide a good reference for evaluation. In our experiment, the data set was built from a rigorous grading process that involved grading meetings to discuss marking scheme and student performance. However, it was found that while the resulting data set should offer consistency, it did not necessarily agree with the advertised marking guidelines. The *sympathy marking* phenomenon mentioned in the previous section is one such example. There are often implicit marking guidelines that are unsuitable to be codified for evaluation.

Despite these data set problems, we carried out another evaluation based on synthesized data, hoping to discover issues for improvement of the algorithms. Table 6 below lists the issues discovered and suggestions of improving the algorithm.

Table 6. Findings from the evaluation based on a synthesized data set

Question stem types	Remarks
What	No other issue was discovered.
Which	Using POS tagger to identify the keywords did not improve the performance but increased significant execution time. A simple stop-word removal stage could provide comparable performance.
Why	No other issue was discovered.
Where	The tokenizer and the POS tagger failed to identify location strings such as Wan Chai. Similar to the case of which question, a simple stop-word removal stage could perform similarly to POS tagger.
When	The tokenizer and the POS tagger sometimes failed to extract verb phrase with all the relevant words (e.g. *arrived yesterday* instead of the correct *arrived yesterday morning*).
How	Phrases with cardinals could be extracted correctly. No other issue was discovered.

The time of executing the algorithm was reduced significantly when the Stanford POS tagger was not needed (for some question stem types). As a rule of thumb, marking 100 answers on a very ordinary laptop computer took less than half a minute. For question stem types requiring no POS tagger, the execution time dropped to less than 10 s. The reduction was mainly due to the loading time of a corpus for the tagger, which was a once off operation. This magnitude of running time should fit the performance requirement in giving immediate feedback in online comprehension exercises.

5 Conclusion

An algorithm for automated grading of natural language responses of literal question of reading comprehension was presented. Evaluation using real data obtained from a local secondary school showed that the performance was promising. The accuracy was found to be over 90 % and the computation time was sufficiently fast for quick feedback for e-learning systems. One major feature of the algorithm is the selection of items for comparison based on the question stem, recognizing that the question stem indicates the semantics to look for in the answers.

It is always tempting to integrate more advanced techniques for measuring semantic similarities between items. No doubt these techniques should improve accuracy in most circumstances. This paper should illustrate that through proper definition of problem, an effective algorithm could still be developed.

The findings of this research work indicated that future research on automated grading of short answers should differentiate reading comprehension tasks and knowledge recall tasks, and also make a distinction between different comprehension levels. Each of these situations would have very different requirements and trade-offs on the form of natural language processing. In particular, computationally fast yet accurate grading method for literal question types should exist, and its continued development should be very important for enhancement of future e-learning systems.

References

1. Attali, Y., Burstein, J.: Automated essay scoring with e-rater® V. 2. J. Technol. Learn. Assess. **4**(3), 3–30 (2006)
2. Bachman, L.F., Carr, N., Kamei, G., Kim, M., Pan, M.J., Salvador, C., Sawaki, Y.: A reliable approach to automatic assessment of short answer free responses. In: Proceedings of the 19th International Conference on Computational Linguistics, vol. 2, pp. 1–4. Association for Computational Linguistics (2002)
3. Best, R.M., Floyd, R.G., Mcnamara, D.S.: Differential competencies contributing to children's comprehension of narrative and expository texts. Read. Psychol. **29**(2), 137–164 (2008)
4. Burrows, S., Gurevych, I., Stein, B.: The eras and trends of automatic short answer grading. Int. J. Artif. Intell. Educ. **25**(1), 60–117 (2015)
5. Cutting, L.E., Scarborough, H.S.: Prediction of reading comprehension: relative contributions of word recognition, language proficiency, and other cognitive skills can depend on how comprehension is measured. Sci. Stud. Read. **10**(3), 277–299 (2006)
6. Day, R.R., Park, J.S.: Developing reading comprehension questions. Read. Foreign Lang. **17**(1), 60–73 (2005)
7. Deane, P.: On the relation between automated essay scoring and modern views of the writing construct. Assessing Writ. **18**(1), 7–24 (2013)

8. Eason, S.H., Goldberg, L.F., Young, K.M., Geist, M.C., Cutting, L.E.: Reader–text interactions: how differential text and question types influence cognitive skills needed for reading comprehension. J. Educ. Psychol. **104**(3), 515 (2012)
9. Eason, S.H., Sabatini, J., Goldberg, L., Bruce, K., Cutting, L.E.: Examining the relationship between word reading efficiency and oral reading rate in predicting comprehension among different types of readers. Sci. Stud. Read. **17**(3), 199–223 (2013)
10. Gomaa, W.H., Fahmy, A.A.: Tapping into the power of automatic scoring. In: Proceedings of the 11th International Conference on Language Engineering, Egyptian Society of Language Engineering (ESOLEC 2011) (2011)
11. Gough, P.B., Tunmer, W.E.: Decoding, reading, and reading disability. Remedial Spec. Educ. **7**(1), 6–10 (1986)
12. He, Y., Hui, S.C., Quan, T.T.: Automatic summary assessment for intelligent tutoring systems. Comput. Educ. **53**(3), 890–899 (2009)
13. Hoover, W.A., Gough, P.B.: The simple view of reading. Read. Writ. **2**(2), 127–160 (1990)
14. Karlsen, B., Gardner, E.F.: Stanford Diagnostic Reading Test, 4th edn. Psychological Corp., San Antonio (1995)
15. Kintsch, W.: Comprehension: A Paradigm for Cognition. Cambridge University Press, Cambridge (1998)
16. Leacock, C., Chodorow, M.: C-rater: Automated scoring of short-answer questions. Comput. Humanit. **37**(4), 389–405 (2003)
17. Manning, C.D., Surdeanu, M., Bauer, J., Finkel, J., Bethard, S.J., McClosky, D.: The stanford CoreNLP natural language processing toolkit. In: Proceedings of 52nd Annual Meeting of the Association for Computational Linguistics: System Demonstrations, pp. 55–60 (2014)
18. McArthur, G., Jones, K., Anandakumar, T., Larsen, L., Castles, A., Coltheart, M.: A test of everyday reading comprehension (TERC). Aust. J. Learn. Difficulties **18**(1), 35–85 (2013)
19. Meurers, D., Ziai, R., Ott, N., Bailey, S.M.: Integrating parallel analysis modules to evaluate the meaning of answers to reading comprehension questions. Int. J. Continuing Eng. Educ. Life Long Learn. **21**(4), 355–369 (2011)
20. Miller, G.A.: WordNet: a lexical database for English. Commun. ACM **38**(11), 39–41 (1995)
21. Mitros, P., Paruchuri, V., Rogosic, J., Huang, D.: An integrated framework for the grading of freeform responses. In: The Sixth Conference of MIT's Learning International Networks Consortium (2013)
22. Mohler, M., Bunescu, R., Mihalcea, R.: Learning to grade short answer questions using semantic similarity measures and dependency graph alignments. In: Proceedings of the 49th Annual Meeting of the Association for Computational Linguistics: Human Language Technologies, vol. 1, pp. 752–762. Association for Computational Linguistics (2011)
23. Pearson, P.D.: The roots of reading comprehension instruction. In: Comprehension Across the Curriculum: Perspectives and Practices in K-12, pp. 279–314 (2009)
24. Sukkarieh, J.Z., Pulman, S.G., Raikes, N.: Auto-marking 2: An Update on the UCLES-Oxford University Research into using Computational Linguistics to Score Short, Free Text Responses. International Association of Educational Assessment, Philadephia (2004)
25. Wechsler, D.: Wechsler Individual Achievement Test, 3rd edn. Psychological Corporation, San Antonio (2009)
26. Woodcock, R.W.: Woodcock Reading Mastery Tests, 3rd edn. Psychological Corporation, San Antonio (2011)

Applying the Semantic Graph Approach to Automatic Essay Scoring

Chak Shing Lo, Oliver Au(✉), and Bruce Kwong Bun Tong

School of Science and Technology, The Open University of Hong Kong, Good Shepherd Street, Ho Man Tin, Kowloon, Hong Kong SAR, China
chakshinglcs@gmail.com, {oau,kbtong}@ouhk.edu.hk

Abstract. Frequent quizzes are used to motivate students to study throughout the academic term instead of waiting until just before the examination. Teachers have been relying on the use of multiple-choice questions to reduce their grading effort. We have developed a tool that grades answers of essay questions automatically. The tool should be a welcome addition to a teacher's arsenal for quiz preparation.

The teacher will provide the model answer of an essay question. Incorporating some heuristics into the Stanford Parser, our tool recognizes the parts of speech of each word and creates a parse tree from each sentence. It builds a semantic graph from the sentences in the model answer. The graph uses nodes to represent words and phrases. A directed arc connects two nodes to represent a relation. Currently, four types of arcs are used: attribute, possession, classification and action.

In the same way, our tool determines the semantic graph of the student answer. Our tool compares the graph of the model answer with the graph of the student answer. It calculates a score to reflect their similarity. The relative weights of nodes and arcs are adjustable. WordNet helps us to identify synonyms so that the two answers need not be using the same wording to be considered similar.

Our tool has some limitations. First, our semantic graph cannot handle timing sequences, for example, "event A happens before event B". Second, our graph cannot handle conditional knowledge like "if X, then Y". In the future, we may be able to introduce new arc types to address these limitations. Our prototype is not yet ready to replace the grading performed by teachers in formal assessment. But it may be useful to allow students to check their understanding during their self-study.

Keywords: Semantic graph · Automatic essay scoring · Knowledge network · Text clustering

1 Introduction

Automatic Essay Scoring has great benefit for teachers and students. Teachers can save their time and effort in scoring student answers and students can get instant feedback after answering a question. Automatic Essay Scoring may also be useful in

J. Lam et al. (Eds.): ICTE 2015, CCIS 559, pp. 263–275, 2015.
DOI: 10.1007/978-3-662-48978-9_24

self-learning exercises (both online and offline) which have previously been limited to multiple-choice questions.

Teachers will provide a model answer for a question, and our tool can automatically grade student answers. A semantic graph will be built for each answer. After comparing the graphs of a student answer and the model answer, our tool calculates a score for the student answer. A key feature of our tool is allowing teachers to specify some alternative terms, and assign weightings to different parts of the model answer. Another feature is score adjusting. Teachers can assign scores to a few student answers with different degrees of similarity comparing to the model answer; our tool can adapt its scoring standard to match the teacher's standard.

2 Literature Review

2.1 Semantic Graph

Sowa [3] has pointed out 6 common types of semantic graphs, also called semantic networks, they are *Definitional networks*, *Assertional networks*, *Implicational networks*, *Executable networks*, *Learning networks* and *Hybrid networks*. The first three networks are usually used in knowledge representation, while remaining networks serve different purposes.

One of the well-known semantic graph types is the mind map. Nodes represent concepts; edges represent relations between two concepts. Words of a passage are linked in the semantic graph according to their meanings and relationship in the text and their meanings. These related words determine the ideas presented by the text [2]. Figure 1 is an example of our semantic graph representing the following passage. The details of the notation will be discussed in the methodology section later.

Passage: "Peter copied strings from different parts of the essay without changing any word. The strings are chunked and placed into various parts of the document. A checker can check plagiarism on literal-level easily."

The semantic graph is an *Assertional Network* which can hold the ideas presented by the essay. Our semantic graph contains a set of nodes representing all the non-stop words in the essay. Stop words are frequently used but not informative, for example: prepositions, "*the*", "*is*", "*am*", "*are*", and etc. If words are related semantically, they will be connected with arcs. As meanings are derived from individual words and their relations, ideas of a passage can be figured out by analyzing its graph [2].

2.2 Ambiguity

A sentence is ambiguous if it has multiple interpretations. This will interfere us from constructing a correct graph. Handling ambiguity is a challenge in natural language processing. The ambiguity problem is divided into three types according to the cause:

Lexical Ambiguity. It means a word/phrase in a sentence has more than one meaning to fit the sentence. Lexical ambiguity is a critical problem when trying to replace the

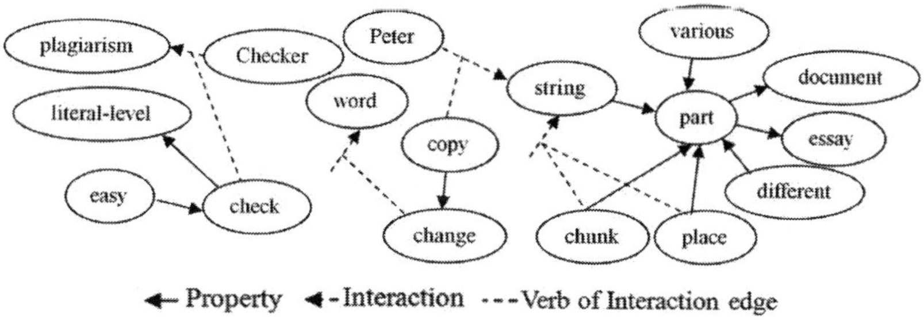

Fig. 1. Example of the semantic graph

synonym or antonym [1]. We usually replace antonym with negation, for example, replace "*false*" with "*not true*". Consider the following sentence.

"The teacher will mark it for you."

There are two different meanings for the word "mark", scoring or labeling. Both meanings can fit into the sentence. However, the meaning of the sentence is different if we replace "mark" with "score" or "label".

Syntactic Ambiguity. The complexity of grammar causes this ambiguity. Under different grammar rules, the sentence will have a different sentence structure. It affects the part-of-speech tagging and tree parsing process [1]. The following sentence is ambiguous. Zwith a word having the potential to be interpreted different parts of speech. The word "shocked" can be a verb or adjective.

"The man shot a boy shocked."

The following is another ambiguous sentence retrieved from the book, *Natural Language Processing with Python* [5].

"I shot an elephant in my pajamas."

In the above sentence, "pajamas" may belong to "I" or "elephant". It can mean "I wear my pajamas, and shot an elephant" or "An elephant wear my pajamas, and I shot the elephant".

Referring Ambiguity. This type of ambiguity arises when a pronoun can refer to multiple targets. A human being makes a judgment based on his or her common sense. However, a computer does not have such a common sense. The following sentence is an example. The pronoun "She" can refer to "Mary" or "Hong Kong". Human beings will judge that "She" refers to "Hong Kong" because they know Hong Kong is a city. However, a computer without this knowledge can judge differently.

"Mary told me that Hong Kong is good. She is a beautiful city."

3 Methodology

A teacher will provide the model answer and student answers. Our tool analyzes the sentences in the answers and determines the grammatical relations of the words. Based on the grammatical relation, the tool can build a semantic graph for each answer. The graphs of student answers are then compared against the graph of the model answer, and our tool returns a score for each student answer.

Teachers can provide alternative terms for the original terms used in the model answer. The alternative terms are considered the same as the original terms in score calculation. Teachers can also assign a weight to each part of the model answer. A part with a high weight value contributes more to the score. If a teacher marks a few student answers manually and provides their scores to our tool, our tool will adopt the same marking standard of the teacher for the remaining student answers.

3.1 Input and Output

Our tool reads input from two text files, one contains the model answer and one contains the student answers. Figure 2 is an example of the input files.

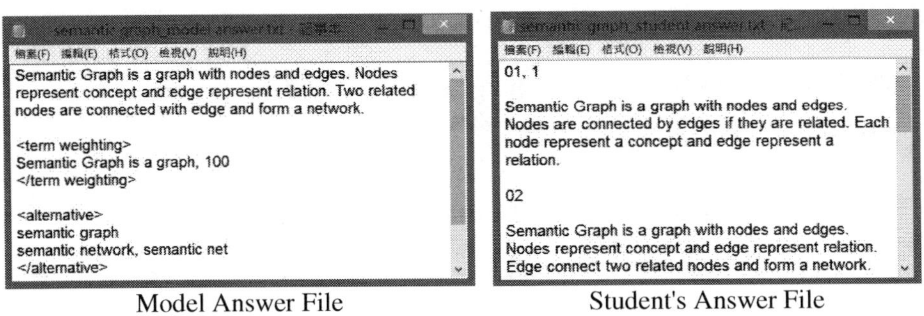

Fig. 2. Input files

The file on the left of Fig. 2 contains the model answer. Inside begin tag "< term weighting>" and end tag " </term weighting > ", each line contains a part taken from the model answer and an integer value as its weight delimited by a comma. In our example, "Semantic graph is a graph" weights 100 while other parts of the model answer each has the default weight of 1. Inside "< alternative >" and "</alternative >" tags, each input consists of two lines. The first line is the original term found in the model answer, and the second line contains the alternative terms. In our example, "semantic network" and "semantic net" are valid alternatives of "semantic graph". Our student answer file on the right of Fig. 2 has two student answers. The teacher assigns the score of 1 to the first answer and lets our tool to grade the second answer.

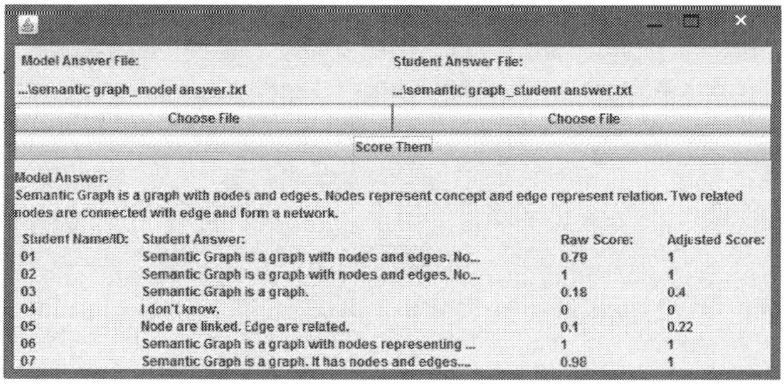

Fig. 3. UI and Output of Our Tool

Figure 3 shows our tool in action. Teachers choose the input files and start the automatic marking. The calculated scores are shown in the bottom half of the UI.

3.2 Finding Relations

The *Stanford NLP Group* provides a natural language processing API downloadable from their website. Our tools use the *LexicalizedParser* class to tag and parse sentences, and the *TypeDependency* class for finding the relationship between words and phrases.

Filtering Wrong Parse Tree. After processing a sentence, the *LexicalizedParser* returns several trees each with a negative score. The tree with a less negative score is more likely to be correct. Sometimes, the list of returned parse trees may contain some wrong trees. This is usually caused by the long length or complexity of the sentence. To determine whether a tree is wrong, we can re-parse all of its phrases. The following is our heuristic approach based on an assumption that the parser can parse shorter or simpler sentences more reliably. The heuristic is reasonable for two reasons. First, there would be fewer ways to structure shorter sentences. Second, if a sentence is parsed correctly and several phrases are recognized, the *LexicalizedParser* can always recognize and parse those phrases individually.

Let m be the number of phrases in the targeted sentence.
Let t_i be the parse tree of the phrases extracted from the sentence's parse tree for i = 1 to m.
Re-parsing the i-th phrase, the parser returns a set $P_{i,}$ where $P_i = \{t_{i,1}, t_{i,2}, \ldots, t_{i.n}\}$ where $t_{i,j}$ denotes one of the n parse trees returned for the i-th phrase.
If $\{t_j\} \cap P_i = \{\}$, using the heuristic stated above, we infer that the tree t_i is wrong. This mathematical notation asserts that after reparsing t_i, the returned parse trees in P_i do not include t_i itself. It means the tree t_i is not a correct parse tree for the phrase.

We tested the approach with 23 samples, most of the samples are selected from *Wikipedia*. In all samples, 87 % of the wrong parse trees are removed and no correct parse tree is mistakenly removed. 3 samples have wrong parse tree left after applying our approach.

3.3 Semantic Graph Notation

For each answer, a semantic graph can be built based on the grammatical relations determined by the *TypeDependency*. We designed some formats and rules for nodes and arcs in the semantic graph.

Nodes. Each node is assigned a unique ID. Words or terms with the same meaning should be represented by the same node. No node will store stop word in order to simplify the graph and comparison process. A term consists of inseparable words, for example: "Hong Kong", the meaning will be different if we separate them. Therefore, a node is created to represent the whole term.

Arcs. We use directed arcs in our semantic graphs; each arc stores the ID of nodes connected and the type of the arc. In our semantic graph, we have defined four types of arcs representing semantic relation. They are attribute, possession, classification and action. It is possible to define additional types if four types are insufficient. The arcs are defined below with examples:

Attribute:	"Peter is fat", which means "fat" is an attribute of "Peter".
Possession:	"Peter has an apple", which means one "apple" belongs to "Peter".
Classification:	"Red is a color", which means "red" is a subset of "color".
Action:	"Peter ate an apple quickly". The relation between "Peter" and "apple" is "eat", where "Peter" is the actor and "quickly" is describing the action "eat".

3.4 Constructing Semantic Graphs

When constructing a semantic graph, our tool will process the answers sentence by sentence. For each non-stop word or term, we will create a node to represent them. Since words or terms with the same meaning are represented by the same node, we have to identify synonyms. *WordNet* will be used for finding out synonyms of the targeted word. If a synonym node exists in the graph, that node will also represent the targeted word rather than constructing a new node.

Our tool builds arcs by analyzing the grammatical relations returned by the *TypeDependency*. According to the *Stanford Typed Dependencies Manual*, there are around 50 types of grammatical relationships [4]. We have grouped some of the relations that can be handled together and they are shown in the Table 1. For the rest of the relations, each should be handled independently according to their meaning.

Table 1. Group of grammatical relation can be handled together.

Group	Grammatical relation
Arcs Types	
Property	acomp(),amod(),appos(),cop(adjective,)
Belongs	poss(),possessive()
Subset	cop(noun,)
Interaction	agent(),dobj(),iobj(),nsubj(),nsubjpass(),pobj(),xsubj()
Other	
Conjunction	conj(),preconj()
Determiner	predet(),det(),num(),quantmod()
Term	nn(),goeswith(),mwe(),number(),prt()

3.5 Handling Syntactic Ambiguity

Our tool can only handle syntactic ambiguity. If a sentence is ambiguous, there should be multiple parse trees left even after removing all wrong trees. Any difference in the grammatical relations between the parse trees indicates more than one possible interpretation of the same sentence. Take the following sentence as an example.

"I shot an elephant in my pajamas".

There will be two parse trees left after filtering wrong interpretation and yield the following grammatical relations.

Interpretation A:	[nsubj(shot-2, I-1), root(ROOT-0, shot-2), det(elephant-4, an-3), dobj (shot-2, elephant-4), poss(pajamas-7, my-6),
	prep_in(shot-2, pajamas-7)]
Interpretation B:	[nsubj(shot-2, I-1), root(ROOT-0, shot-2), det(elephant-4, an-3), dobj (shot-2, elephant-4), poss(pajamas-7, my-6),
	prep_in(elephant-4, pajamas-7)]

The two interpretations differ in the boxed relations, prep_in(shot-2, pajamas-7) and prep_in(elephant-4, pajamas-7), which cause syntactic ambiguity. The boxed relation in Interpretation A means "I" wear the pajamas, while the one in Interpretation B means the elephant wears the pajamas.

When processing an ambiguous sentence, we will hold on to the ambiguous part while processing the rest. If other sentences in the same essay contain additional information to eliminate wrong interpretations of the sentence, our constructer component can choose the correct parse tree with the help of the graph just built. It repeats the process until no more disambiguation is possible. From the remaining trees, the constructor may choose the one with the highest score.

3.6 Retrieving the Identical Part of the Graph

After the semantic graphs are built completely, the same meaning presented in two essays can be determined by extracting the identical parts of the graphs. The extraction can be done by comparing the nodes and arcs of the graphs, then sets of identical nodes and arcs can be obtained with the formula (1).

$$\begin{aligned} \text{Set of identical nodes} &= \text{Set of nodes in A} \cap \text{Set of nodes in B} \\ \text{Set of identical arcs} &= \text{Set of arcs in A} \cap \text{Set of arcs in B} \end{aligned} \tag{1}$$

Our tool uses the following rules to detect identical nodes or arcs.

Nodes:	The words they are representing have the same meaning and part of speech.
Arcs:	1. The types of the arcs are same. 2. The directions of the arcs are same. 3. For action arcs, the nodes representing the verb are identical and the nodes representing subjects or objects are identical. 4. For the other arcs, all the nodes connected should be identical.

3.7 Calculating Score

With the two sets obtained from the formula (1), our tool can calculate the score for each student answer with 1 as the full mark.

Weighting. The default weighting of each node is 1. If the teacher has provided another weighting for a specified part of the model answer, our tool distributes the total weight to each node for the specified part evenly. The wordings used should be the same as the model answer. Here is an example.

Model Answer:	"Plagiarist copies string from different part of the essay without changing any word."
Specified Part:	"copies without changing any word"

There will be 8 nodes in the graph of the model answer, "string", "copy", "plagiarist", "part", "different", "essay", "change" and "word". If the teacher provides the weighting of the specified part is 30, the terms, "copy", "change" and "word" will each get the weight of 10.

Scoring Formula. The basic idea of the scoring is finding out the percentage of semantic relation in the model answer that the student answer contains.

Let w be the summed total weighting of the nodes in the nodes set obtained from (1). Let m be the summed total weighting of the nodes in the model answer.

$$\text{Score} = \frac{\text{w}}{\text{m}} * \frac{\text{Number of arcs in arcs set obtained from (1)}}{\text{Number of arcs in the graph of model answer}} \tag{2}$$

Adjusting Score. The raw score obtained from the formula (2) may be unsatisfactory. However, if the ranking of the student answers is correct, it is possible to adjust the score. Our tool will plot a graph with x-axis as raw score and y-axis as adjusted score. With the scored student answer provided by the teacher, several points can be plotted on the graph where x-coordinate is the score given by the tool and y-coordinate is the score given by the teacher. Our tool will simply draw lines to link the consecutive points and adjust scores base on the lines drawn.

4 Evaluation

An observational study is conducted. Due to the page limit, we will not show all the test samples, but for a better understanding, we will illustrate the result of a selected sample and the overall performance of all test samples will be shown.

4.1 Scoring

We will illustrate the result of the test samples in Table 2.

Tuning Weights. Under different weighting, our tool returns different scores. A poorly configured weighting lowers the accuracy in scoring. If the teacher assigns a heavy weight to a specified part, student answers missing the specified part will get a substantially lower score. A poor weighting also affects the ranking of student answers and interferes the tool from adjusting the scores in a latter process.

Table 2. The test sample

Question: "What is semantic graph?"	
Model Answer: "Semantic Graph is a graph with nodes and edges. Nodes represent concepts and edges represent relations. Two related nodes are connected with an edge and form a network."	
Student Answer:	
ID	Answer
01	"Semantic Graph is a graph with nodes and edges. Nodes are connected by edges if they are related. Each node represents a concept and edge represent a relation."
02	"Semantic Graph is a graph with nodes and edges. Nodes represent concepts and edges represent relations. Edge connects two related nodes and form a network."
03	"Semantic Graph is a graph."
04	"I don't know."
05	"Nodes are linked. Edges are related."
06	"Semantic Graph is a graph with nodes representing concept and edges representing relation. Two related nodes are connected with an edge and form a network."
07	"Semantic Graph is a graph. It has nodes and edges. Nodes represent concepts. Edges represent relations and connect two related nodes."

Table 3. Raw score returned by our tool under different weighting

Weighting\Student answer ID		01	02	03	04	05	06	07
a	Default (All Node weight for 1)	0.68	1	0.06	0	0.09	1	0.85
bi.	"Nodes represent concepts and edge represent relation." weight for 50	0.77	1	0.04	0	0.08	1	0.97
bii.	"Nodes represent concepts and edge represent relation." weight for 100	0.79	1	0.04	0	0.08	1	0.98
ci.	"related nodes" weight for 50	0.46	1	0.01	0	0.02	1	0.97
cii.	"related nodes" weight for 100	0.43	1	0.01	0	0.01	1	0.98
di.	"graph" weight for 50	0.77	1	0.17	0	0.02	1	0.97
dii.	"graph" weight for 100	0.79	1	0.18	0	0.01	1	0.98
e.	"Semantic Graph has nodes and edges" weight for 100	0.36	0.82	0.01	0	0.01	0.65	0.45
f	"Semantic Graph is a graph" weight for 100	0.79	1	0.18	0	0.1	1	0.98

From Table 3, we can see how the weighting affects scoring. In case (c), our tool considers the specified term, "related nodes", necessary for answers to get a high score. Student answer 01 expresses the term "related nodes" in another way, therefore, this term does not appear in the answer and score is deducted. In case (e), the teacher uses a sentence "Semantic Graph has nodes and edges", to refer the phrase "graph with nodes and edges" in the model answer. Our tool does not distribute the total weight to the nodes correctly and thus lowers the accuracy in scoring.

Adjusting Score. Our tool adjusts scores according to the teacher's scoring. Table 4 has the score for some student answers given by teacher and Table 5 has the adjusted scores corresponding to Table 3's raw scores.

Table 4. Score given by teacher

Student ID	Score
01	1
03	0.4

Table 5. Adjusted score

Weighting\Student Answer ID	01	02	03	04	05	06	07
a	1	1	0.4	0	0.3	1	1
bi.	1	1	0.4	0	0.43	1	1
bii.	1	1	0.4	0	0.43	1	1
ci.	1	1	0.4	0	0.41	1	1
cii.	1	1	0.4	0	0.41	1	1
di.	1	1	0.4	0	0.05	1	1
dii.	1	1	0.4	0	0.02	1	1
e	1	1	0.4	0	0.41	1	1
f	1	1	0.4	0	0.22	1	1

The adjusted score is correct for answer 01, 02, 06 and 07. They all get full mark. For answer 05, the student did not state what is a semantic graph, and therefore should get a zero mark. The adjusted score for answer 05 in case (d) is nearly zero which is satisfactory. Scores in other cases are incorrect due to the poor choice of weighting.

Overall Result. We tested our tool with 30 student answers and 4 model answers under different weightings and different answer-score pairs for adjusting score. The results are evaluated by comparing the score returned by our tool and the actual score given by the teacher. The returned scores of 77 % of the cases differ from the score given by the teacher for less than 0.05. The root mean square error of the rest is 0.31.

4.2 Special Cases

During evaluation, we discover some special cases that our tool does not handle well. They can be solved by providing alternative terms or specifying the weighting.

Rewrite the Phrase with the Same Meaning. If a phrase is completely rewritten into another different phrase or sentence, our tool may not be able to score the answer correctly. For example, a verb phrase is rewritten into a noun phrase or a sentence.

The following is an example of rewriting a phrase.

Model Answer:	"We cannot hear the voice on the phone clearly, because the surrounding environment produces so many noises."
Student Answer:	"We cannot hear the voice on the phone clearly, because of the background noise."

Our tool returns a low score for failing to recognize the similarity between "because the surrounding environment produces so many noises" and "because of the background noise". We alleviate this by giving a high weight to the term "noise".

Shuffling Properties in a List. The following is an example of shuffling properties

Model Answer:	"Peter loves eating red apple, green tomato and white chocolate."
Student Answer:	"Peter loves eating white apple, red tomato and green chocolate."

Our tool will always recognize the common meaning presented by the above answer is "Peter loves eating apple, tomato and chocolate" and return a passing grade. However, the correct score for the student answer should be zero as the student mixed up all the colors. This problem can be resolved by assigning high weight values to "red apple", "green tomato" and "white chocolate".

4.3 Limitations

Several limitations are identified during the evaluation. To overcome the limitations, it requires improvement on the notation and comparison rules of the graph.

Inverted Sentences. Consider, “Here comes the teacher.”. Our tool did not recognize it as an inverted sentence and mistakenly inferred that the action “comes” is performed by “Here” but not by “teacher”. This is one of the limitations of the Stanford Parser.

Conditional Sentence. This sentence type is not supported. It requires a special notation in the graph. More investigation in comparing and judging the condition correctly is required. It is hard to decide whether a student answer is correct or not if the condition is not fulfilled. The following is an example.

Model Answer:	“If it is raining, then Peter will stay at home.”
Student Answer:	“If it is not raining, then Peter will stay at home.”

Our tool recognizes the common meaning presented by the above answer is “Peter will stay at home.” and returns a passing grade. However, the condition in the student answer, “if it is not raining”, is incorrect. Therefore, the whole statement in the student answer is wrong. The student should receive a failing grade.

Timing Sequences. The current notation of the semantic graph used in our tool is not enough for timing sequence. For example, “I ate an apple, then I threw the apple to the rubbish bin.” and “ I threw an apple to the rubbish bin, then I ate the apple.” The performing sequence of “ate” and “threw” are exactly opposite in the two sentences, but our tool would return the same graph for them.

Irrelevant Answer. Some students tend to write lengthy answers which contain irrelevant information. If students cannot distinguish what is relevant and what is not, their scores should be deducted accordingly. However, our tool does not have the required knowledge to make this judgment, and will always return a high score as long as everything in the model answer has been covered by the student answer regardless of the fact that the student answer also contains rubbish information.

5 Conclusion

In conclusion, our tool can score student essays by building and comparing their semantic graphs against the graph of the model answer. With the features of our tool, weighting and score adjustment, the returned scores are reasonably close to the scores and expectation of the teacher.

To further improve score accuracy, we can use a knowledge network that holds some real world knowledge not present in the model answer. The network can also be used for disambiguation and judging if a student answer includes irrelevant or harmful information. However, building a large enough knowledge network is a big challenge and a time consuming process. It may also lengthen the program execution.

It is important to set a comprehensive set of rules for the comparison process. The rules used in our prototype are simple. Although it returns an acceptable performance during our evaluation, a better rule set can allow our tool to compare graphs more effectively and intelligently.

References

1. MacDonald, M.C.: The lexical nature of syntactic ambiguity resolution. Psychol. Rev. **101**(4), 676 (1994)
2. Smith, A.E.: Evaluation of unsupervised semantic mapping of natural language with Leximancer concept mapping. Behav. Res. Methods **38**(2), 262–279 (2006)
3. Sowa, J.F.: Semantic networks. Encycl. Cogn. Sci. **6**, 291–330 (2006)
4. De Marneffe, M.C., Manning, C.D.: Stanford typed dependencies manual, pp. 338–345. Technical report, Stanford University (2008)
5. Bird, S., Klein, E., Loper, E.: Natural language processing with Python. O'Reilly Media, Inc., Sebastopol (2009)

Use of Instant Messaging Communication in Tutoring Undergraduate Students

Francis Yue(✉)

School of Continuing and Professional Education,
City University of Hong Kong, Kowloon, Hong Kong
cmfrayue@cityu.edu.hk

Abstract. Some undergraduate courses require students to submit individual essay assignments as the summative assessment. These students are required to work on their own topic and complete a written report with or without oral presentation. These students need to be guided and supported in completing the report. This paper aims to study the use of two teaching methods as well as the use of student support in form of electronic communication (instant messaging) for tutoring a group of undergraduate students. Some survey data and electronic communication made (between the students and their tutor) during the period are collected and analyzed in this study. The impact of using two tutoring methods and instant messaging on the student assessment marks is studied. It is found that the average assessment marks for the two tutoring methods used are not much different. Besides, the use of instant messaging can help some students to perform better in their assignment report.

Keywords: Proactive learning · Instant messaging · Teaching and learning

1 Introduction

Proactive learning is a desirable mode of studying in a course when the students take an initiative to learn. It is widely accepted that university students should not expect the lecturers and tutors to teach all the concepts in details during class time. Instead, students should be motivated to learn themselves by looking for useful resource materials like books, journal, etc., available at the libraries or the Internet. Teachers can play an active role in encouraging students to learn proactively. This type of learning is related to Problem-based Learning (PBL). PBL focuses on deep learning rather than surface learning from the learners and promotes active participation from the latter.

With the popular use of smartphones among local undergraduate students together with the good Internet connection service, the use of instant messaging (IM) communication software tool plays an important role in enabling a better teaching and learning experience. The use of instant messaging enables the sending of customized feedback by teachers to students. There are some recent researches done on the use of such instant messaging communication tools on undergraduate dissertation and group project situations. Yue [14, 15] finds that students are very positive towards the use of IM and that female students are more active in exchanging instant messages in the undergraduate dissertation context only. This paper aims to study the use of two

J. Lam et al. (Eds.): ICTE 2015, CCIS 559, pp. 276–283, 2015.
DOI: 10.1007/978-3-662-48978-9_25

teaching methods in tutoring a large group of undergraduate students. The role of electronic communication (instant messaging) in facilitating the teaching is considered.

2 Literature Review

As defined by Boud and Feletti [3], PBL is a teaching approach that uses ill-defined real-life problems as the impetus for learning. In PBL, the learner is presented with a problem situation. He or she need to analyze the problem, formulates learning issues and questions, conducts an inquiry and research in order to find a solution [2]. The learners can acquire some discipline knowledge and problem-solving skills after tackling these problems [12].

Tan [11] points out that the goals of PBL include content learning, acquisition of process skills and problem-solving skills. In practice, in PBL, students are required to prepare the problem(s) before attending the tutorials. The students then undergo small-group discussions during the tutorials under the tutor's guidance. A representative of each group will share the group's answers with other students using an informal presentation. It is expected that students learn skills in how to work with others in solving problem(s) put forward to them.

There are fundamentally different pedagogical goals underlying conventional and PBL tutoring. In a conventional tutorial, the tutor's goal is to enable learners to reach a desirable level of understanding, while the primary objective of PBL tutorial is targeting at the deficiencies of learners. Marton and Saljo [7] consider two approaches to learning: surface approach and deep approach. Surface approach to learning refers to the situation that learners who just focus on memorizing what the teacher wrote, while deep approach considers learners who can understand the meaning of the content materials. In fact, the surface approach is characterized by a reproductive concept of learning, while deep approach is characterized by comprehending what is being said by the teacher. Hung, *et al.* [5] comments that studies have shown that PBL promotes in-depth understanding of the content but limits the breadth of content coverage.

Fox [4] considers face-to-face tutoring consists mainly of two activities: description and explanation of some domain by the tutor. PBL tutor should be less directly instructive than a conventional tutor. Savin-Baden [9] considers tutor as a facilitator in PBL. Later, Savin-Baden [10] suggests that PBL tutor can provide formative feedback to learners using IT such as online discussion boards. Wolcott [13] points out that learner-centered teachers encourage students' personal growth and that timely feedback can enhance interaction between the students and teacher. Repman and Logan [8] emphasize that interactions play a very important role in learning situation.

Tan [11] points out that PBL learners are encouraged to hold discussions not just during tutorials but beyond them. In addition to face-to-face communication, the discussions can be made possible through online learning platforms such as learning management system (e.g. Blackboard). Some researchers examines the integration of technology in Problem-Based Learning (PBL). Uribe *et al.*, [12] and Arts, *et al.* [1] reported findings that using IT in a collaborative learning environment that enables students to higher level of achievement and reasoning by increasing their ability to generate ideas and solutions. Lim [6] illustrates how IT is used in the PBL process and improves teaching and learning. There are four processes: (1) induction programme; (2) problem presentation and fact inquiry; (3) hypothesize, research, discuss and consensus; (4) solution presentation. The integration of IT is useful to PBL so that students develop ability in collaborative inquiry and self-directed learning.

3 Methodology

The target participants of this study are final-year Accounting students studying for a course on information systems (IS). The teaching involves a 15-h lecture followed by 6 weekly tutorial classes each lasting for 1.5 h. There are altogether 11 tutorial groups of 243 students involved in this study. All students are supposed to prepare the tutorial exercise questions in advance before attending the tutorials. The tutorial questions of each week include a case study on business information systems plus some theory questions. The questions especially those related to a business case are useful to students preparing for their written assignment. That assignment accounts for 100 % of the overall assessment and is the only assessment in the course. The deadline of assignment report for all students is about three weeks after the last tutorial class was held.

Two different methods of tutoring were separately administered to two classes of students enrolled in the same course in one semester. Method A corresponds to the conventional case that the tutor plays an active role by presenting answers to the tutorial questions with some class discussion. For Method B, the students in each tutorial group are divided into six teams with 3–4 students in each team. Each team of students will prepare the answers to the given tutorial questions in advance. This team of students will present the answers to the other students in the same tutorial group during the tutorials. This is followed by the tutor's comments. Method B involves students playing an active role during tutorial classes similar to that in PBL context. Method B requires some proactive learning from the students before attending tutorial classes. All students involved in the study are encouraged to communicate via electronic mail and/or instant messaging outside class hours with their tutor throughout the course period.

The students are required to select one of the three given topics and undertake independent research of theory (e.g. books, journal articles, the Internet) and practice (e.g. examples and case studies). Students need to select one business organization and its information system(s) for illustration purpose. A questionnaire survey was carried out at the last tutorial for each of the 11 groups of students. The students are asked to rate the seven statements listed in the questionnaire regarding the tutorial teaching. The response to each statement is measured on a 5-point Likert scale. Choice 1 corresponds to strongly disagree while choice 5 corresponds to strong agree.

4 Results

About 75 % of the students completed the survey questionnaire. A total of 183 (out of 243 students) completed the paper questionnaires were collected. The collected data were coded in electronic form and analyzed using the statistical software IBM SPSS.

Table 1. Average score values for 7 questions (Q1–Q7) grouped under teaching method adopted.

Questions	Average score		
	Method A (Tutor-centered)	Method B (Student-centered)	Overall
Q1. The tutor alone should present answers to the tutorial questions during the whole tutorial class.	3.99 (84)	3.65 (97)	3.81 (181)
Q2. Some students should prepare before class and present their answers during class followed by the tutor's comments and answers.	3.18 (84)	3.53 (97)	3.36 (181)
Q3. Students should not be required to prepare answers to tutorial questions before tutorial class.	2.80 (86)	2.83 (96)	2.82 (182)
Q4. Printed hardcopy of answers to questions should be made available to students during class time.	4.24 (86)	4.55 (97)	4.40 (183)
Q5. Answers to questions should only be made available at the Blackboard website one week after the tutorial class.	3.62 (86)	3.54 (96)	3.58 (182)
Q6. The present format of tutorial class is useful for me to complete the coming assignment.	3.99 (82)	3.55 (97)	3.75 (179)
Q7. I am happy with the present format of conducting tutorial classes.	4.06 (83)	3.61 (97)	3.82 (180)

The response to the seven statements is listed in Table 1. The number inside the brackets refers to the number of respondents involved.

It can be seen from Table 1 that the mean scores for all seven statements (except Q3) are above the middle value of 3. For Q1, the average score for Method A (3.99) is higher than that for Method B (3.65). The high average scores for Q1, Q6 and Q7 indicate that the students under Method A prefer to be taught with the tutor playing an active role in the tutorials. The low score of 2.80 and 2.83 (below mid-value of 3 on the scale) for Q3 irrespective of teaching methods indicates that the students are likely be aware of the advantage of preparing answers to tutorial questions before attending tutorials. The very high average scores of 4.24 and 4.55 for Q4 indicate that the students prefer to have some "confirmed" answers and comments on what have been discussed in class.

There are some comments written down in the questionnaires completed by respondents. The major ones are listed out as follows.

Method A (tutor-centered method)

- *"Can more focus on assignment"*
- *"Clear instruction. Good."*
- *"Tutorial time not enough, cannot cover all topics"*
- *"Class time is short. Our class of students are very passive, tutor is good enough not forcing us to answer questions."*

Method B (student-centered method)

- *"Only 6 tutorials, too short and rush"*
- *"The answers should be made available immediately not after"*
- *"It is helpful to improve the presentation skills; Accounting students are lack of experience in presentation"*
- *"Better to ask students questions from students after they prepared them at home"*
- *"The presentation by some students are not good"*
- *"Better to put the answers at the Blackboard earlier"*
- *"Should increase requirement of student presentation"*
- *"Overall the class was clearly understood, but the presentation time might be too long for class time."*
- *"More used to listen teacher's answers rather than those of classmates"*

The students under study do not contact the tutor via instant messaging during the 6-week tutorial period, though there are some face-to-face queries made by some students on the assignment during the tutorials. The exchange of instant messages started around the end of the 6-week tutorial period. About 18 % of students (44 students out of 243 students) contacted the tutor using WhatsApp before the assignment submission deadline on 29 September 2014. These messages relate to: (1) choice of essay topics; (2) choice of appropriate business organization and its information system; (3) content requirement of various sections in the assignment report; (4) assignment submission arrangements, etc. The details of instant messages exchanged are recorded. Relevant statistics for the two tutoring methods are collected and listed in Table 2.

It can be seen from Table 2 that the average number of issues (each issue involves a number of IM exchanges) raised in the IM exchanges for each student ranges from 1 to 10 and the average is 2.52. The average number of days that such IM exchanges for a student is 6.77 days. The average number of days that students first started to exchange instant messages with their tutor is 14.86 days before the assignment submission deadline. The average attendance rate of students for the two teaching methods, namely, 4.77 and 4.68 are similar. The average attendance rate of female students is better than male students for the corresponding two tutoring methods. Regarding the variation of attendance rate, Method A has a lower standard deviation than Method B. The standard deviation of attendance rate of male students is much higher than female students irrespective of teaching methods. Regarding assessment marks, the average value for the two teaching methods, namely, 56.07 and 54.18 are also similar. The average assessment marks for Method A (56.07) is slightly higher than Method B

Table 2. A table showing assessment marks obtained under different combinations of teaching method and use of IM.

	Overall	Method-IM Combination					
		Method A (Tutor-centered)			Method B (Student-centered)		
		WhatsApp (YES) (1)	WhatsApp (NO) (2)	Sub-total	WhatsApp (YES) (3)	WhatsApp (NO) (4)	Sub-total
Number of students	243	21	92 43 (M)	113 47 (M)	23 6 (M)	107 52 (M)	130 58 (M)
	105 (M)	4 (M)					
	138 (F)	17 (F)	49 (F)	66 (F)	17 (F)	55 (F)	72 (F)
Average attendance	4.72	5.62	4.58	4.77	5.17	4.57	4.68
	4.30 (M)	5.75 (M)	4.12 (M)	4.26 (M)	5.67 (M)	4.19 (M)	4.34 (M)
	5.04 (F)	5.59 (F)	4.98 (F)	5.14 (F)	5.00 (F)	4.93 (F)	4.94 (F)
Average assessment marks	55.06	60.00	55.17	56.07	52.52	54.53	54.18
	53.89 (M)	59.25 (M)	52.88 (M)	53.43 (M)	51.83 (M)	54.54 (M)	54.26 (M)
	55.95 (F)	60.18 (F)	57.18 (F)	57.95 (F)	52.76 (F)	54.53 (F)	54.11 (F)
Standard deviation of attendance	1.620	0.669	1.619	1.541	1.072	1.781	1.690
	1.866 (M)	0.500 (M)	1.749 (M)	1.738 (M)	0.516 (M)	2.030 (M)	1.978 (M)
	1.326 (F)	0.712 (F)	1.392(F)	1.276 (F)	1.173 (F)	1.438 (F)	1.373 (F)
Standard deviation of assessment marks	5.515	5.630	5.293	5.655	5.230	5.217	5.255
	5.120 (M)	1.893 (M)	4.807 (M)	4.955 (M)	4.119 (M)	0.741 (M)	5.263 (M)
	5.655 (F)	6.227 (F)	4.906(F)	5.391 (F)	5.663 (F)	5.145 (F)	5.285 (F)
Average number of IM issues exchanged	2.52	2.95	NA	NA	2.13	NA	NA
	2.90 (M)	4.25 (M)			2.00 (M)		
	2.41 (F)	2.65 (F)			2.18 (F)		
Average number of days with IM exchanges	6.77	8.05	NA	NA	5.61	NA	NA
	8.50 (M)	8.75 (M)			8.33 (M)		
	6.26 (F)	7.88 (F)			4.65 (F)		
Average number of days of first IM with tutor before deadline	14.86	16.00	NA	NA	13.83	NA	NA
	14.50 (M)	16.75 (M)			13.00 (M)		
	14.97 (F)	15.82 (F)			14.12 (F)		

Note: M stands for male students and F stands for female students; NA stands for Not Apply.

(54.18). Regarding the standard deviation of the assessment marks, Method A has a greater standard deviation than Method B.

5 Conclusion

In the present study, the average assessment marks under the two methods are similar. The use of PBL-type of tutoring method (Method B) does not lead to big difference of assessment marks when compared with Method A (tutor-centered method). It is gratifying that the use of PBL format of conducting the tutorials does not differ much from the traditional tutoring method. In fact, the efficacy of using PBL-like method might not be apparent in this study given that there are only six tutorials involved and the essay assignment is not a lengthy one. According to the comments received in the questionnaire survey, some students taught under Method B appreciate somehow the PBL-type of approach. In the present study, the students are working on their individual assignment report. It is reasonable to expect that some students will discuss the assignment with their classmates especially with those taught under Method B as students need to form teams to present their answers to tutorial questions. PBL emphasizes on team work so that students can learn from other team members. The fact that there is a smaller variation in the average marks obtained by students taught under Method B reflects that aspect.

On the other hand, the percentage of students who have exchanged instant messages with their tutor under Method A and Method B are quite similar. For those students under Method A who have exchanged instant messages with their tutor, the average assessment marks is much higher than those who have not done so. The feedback obtained by the tutor might have a positive effect on those students who have exchanged instant messages with their tutor. In the PBL context, the tutor plays an important role in being a facilitator during face-to-face tutorial class discussions and students are expected to develop better collaborative skills with their team members. According to the results obtained in this study, the role of tutor beyond tutorials seems to have an effect on student achievement results. Further research can be done in this area.

References

1. Arts, J., Gijselaers, W., Segers, M.: Cognitive effects of an authentic computer-supported problem-based learning environment. Instr. Sci. **30**, 465–495 (2002)
2. Barrows, H.S., Tamblyn, R.M.: Problem Based Learning: an Approach to Medical Education. Springer Publishing Company, New York (1980)
3. Boud, D., Feletti, G.: The Challenge of Problem-based Learning. Kogan Page, London (1997)
4. Fox, B.: The Human Tutorial Dialogue Project. Lawrence Erlbaum Associates, New Jersey (1993)

5. Hung, W., Bailey, J.H., Jonassen, D.H.: Exploring the tensions of problem-based learning: insights from research. In: Knowlton, D.S., Sharp, D.C. (eds.) Problem-Based Learning in the Information Age. Jossey Bass, San Francisco (2003)
6. Lim, C.: Integration of information technology in the problem-based learning process. In: Tan, K., Lee, M., Mok, J., Ravindran, R. (eds.) Problem-Based Learning: New Directions and Approaches. Learning Academy, Singapore (2005)
7. Marton, F., Saljo, R.: Approaches to learning. In: Marton, F., Hounsell, D., Entwistle, N. (eds.) The Experience of Learning. Scottish Academic Press, Edinburgh (1984)
8. Repman, J., Logan, S.: Interactions at a distance: possible barriers and collaborative solutions. Techtrends **41**(6), 35–38 (1996)
9. Savin-Baden, M.: Facilitating Problem-Based Learning. SRHE and Open University Press, England (2003)
10. Savin-Baden, M., Wilkie, K.: Problem-Based Learning Online. Open University Press, England (2006)
11. Tan, O.: Problem-based learning Innovation: Using Problems to Power Learning in the 21st Century. Thomson Learning, Singapore (2003)
12. Uribe, D., Klein, J.D., Sullivan, H.: The effect of computer-mediated collaborative learning on solving ill-defined problems. Educ. Technol. Res. Dev. **51**(1), 5–19 (2003)
13. Wolcott, L.L.: Distant, but not distanced: a learner-centered approach to distance education. Techtrends **41**(5), 23–27 (1996)
14. Yue, F.: Use of instant messaging communication in teaching and learning. In: Proceedings of the Inaugural International Conference on Open and Flexible Education, 16–17 January 2014
15. Yue, F.: Student engagement in the use of instant messaging communication in flexible education. In: Proceedings of the Inaugural International Conference on Technology in Education, 2–4 July 2014

A Teachers' Survey on the Effectiveness of e-Learning Platform in a Higher Education Institution

Wai-Shing Ho(✉), Anna Ng, Kat Leung, Fu Lee Wang, and Leung-Pun Wong

Caritas Institute of Higher Education, 18 Chui Ling Road, New Territories, Hong Kong
{wsho, hnng, kleung, pwang, lpwong}@cihe.edu.hk

Abstract. Technology plays an important role in many parts of education. Our institution has adopted an e-Learning platform and this platform provided many useful tools for teachers and students to use to enhance the teaching and learning experiences. However, not every teacher and student knows the tools and uses the tools properly as they are not familiar with the system. Teachers may have their own teaching and learning approaches that are useful for many years and might be further enhanced by the proper use of the e-Learning platform.

In this paper we would capture the current usage status of the e-Learning platform in our institution using a survey and identify the most desirable features that may help the teachers most. From the feedback from our teachers, we can analyse how the tools on the e-Learning platform can help the teaching and learning process and promote the use of the platform to all the teachers.

Keywords: E-learning platform · Teacher support · Teaching and learning strategy

1 Introduction

With the advancement of information technologies, e-Learning is becoming an integral part of our education. The popularity of digital technology drives the use of digital resources and communication tools for learning in school education [6]. Learners would use suitable e-Learning tools to select and process useful and reliable information from varying sources; and they would use communication tools share with their peers the information and collaborate to complete specific tasks. Thus, a tool that helps learners accomplishing all the tasks is important to their study.

E-learning platforms, such as Moodle[1], Blackboard[2], etc., provide an all-in-one support to teachers' and learners' e-Learning activities. Caritas Institute of Higher Education and her sister college, Caritas Bianchi College of Career, introduced Moodle as their e-Learning platform with the support of the QEGS fund by HKSAR Government 4 years ago. Currently, all the courses offered in both institutions have their corresponding

1 https://moodle.org/.

2 http://www.blackboard.com/.

J. Lam et al. (Eds.): ICTE 2015, CCIS 559, pp. 284–291, 2015.
DOI: 10.1007/978-3-662-48978-9_26

entries on Moodle and students are enrolled to those courses automatically. Teachers can provide lesson-related information very easily online, and students can also communicate with teachers or peers through the platform. Many teaching and learning activities such as assessments, discussions, etc., can be conducted online.

Although the Moodle platform provides a lot of different functionalities for various teaching and learning modes, not all teaching staff are familiar enough to the platform and can apply suitable functions to their teaching. Our colleges conducted an evaluation of the effectiveness of the Moodle platform. We aimed to check the current status of the platform usage (e.g., "How did our staff use the Moodle platform? What part did they like the most?", etc.) and locate the motivators and barriers to the effective usage of the platforms from the teachers' perspective. Through analysing the survey, we note that our colleagues mostly use Moodle as a distributer of teaching materials and a platform for broadcasting group message for students. In general, our colleagues' attitude to Moodle is positive and barriers to the use of Moodle are not strong. However, other useful functionalities are underutilized, as they are not familiar with the platform and do not know how to use those functions properly.

The paper is organized as follows. Section 2 will introduce the methodologies used in conducting the survey. Key observations will be discussed in Sect. 3. Related work will be presented in Sect. 4, and conclusions drawn from observations will be discussed in Sect. 5.

2 Methodology

A questionnaire was constructed to collect the teachers' opinions on the current status of the e-Learning platform usage and the motivators and barriers to the extensive use of e-Learning platform. The questionnaire had 4 components. First, we asked about the personal data of the teaching staff, so that we could analyse the relationship between their backgrounds and their attitudes towards the e-Learning platforms. Second, we consulted the teachers' views on various functionalities of Moodle, our e-Learning platform. Third, we listed out a number of motivators which may encourage them to use Moodle and a number of barriers which may hinder their interest in using Moodle in their teaching. Finally, we included 3 free-text questions to gather their suggestions to how to use Moodle more effectively in teaching.

On various functionalities of Moodle, we list some commonly used ones and asked the teachers to rate how often they use those functionalities in their teaching. The teachers can rate in one of the following six levels:

i. I don't know Moodle can do this.
ii. I know Moodle can do this, but never tried.
iii. I tried this on Moodle, but I did not use it in my courses.
iv. I seldom use this in my courses.
v. I sometimes use it in my courses.
vi. I usually use it in my courses.

These levels do not only tell us how frequently the teachers use those functionalities, but also tell us whether they know how to use those functionalities. This can give us the insight on the teachers' use of Moodle.

On the motivators and barriers to the use of Moodle, we listed out the factors as discussed in previous studies [8]. We asked the participants to rate the strengths of those factors in a 5-point Likert scale. The results could give us which motivating policies would be more useful to promoting the use of Moodle and which helps would lower the most significant usage barriers.

Finally, the questionnaire asked three free-text questions to get important suggestions not being covered by the previous parts of the questionnaire.

3 Observations and Discussions

Twenty faculties from all five schools in our institute have participated in the survey. Their views on the Moodle system will be discussed in this section.

3.1 Background Information

All participants have the experience in using Moodle, because it is the official e-Learning platform in our institute. They also had some experiences in using other platforms when they taught or studied in other institutions. The second most popular e-Learning platforms among our teaching staff are Blackboard and WebCT; 35 % of our staff had experiences in using them. More background information is shown in Table 1.

Table 1. Background information of our teaching staff participated in the survey

Demographic data	Percentage
Experiences in using common e-platforms	
Moodle	100 %
Blackboard	35 %
WebCT	35 %
eClass	15 %
piazza	5 %
Years of teaching experiences	
0–2 years	10 %
3–5 years	50 %
6–10 years	15 %
11–20 years	25 %

Table 2. Teachers' experiences in teaching-related functionalities on Moodle

Teaching activities	(i)[a]	(ii)	(iii)	(iv)	(v)	(vi)
Use Moodle to distribute lecture materials	0 %	0 %	0 %	0 %	10 %	90 %
Use Moodle to collect student assessments	20 %	25 %	10 %	20 %	15 %	10 %
Use Moodle to mark student assessments	30 %	30 %	10 %	15 %	10 %	5 %
Use Moodle to give assessment feedbacks to students	30 %	20 %	5 %	15 %	25 %	5 %
Use Moodle to release assessment scores to students	25 %	30 %	5 %	20 %	15 %	5 %
Use Moodle to conduct online quizzes	30 %	30 %	15 %	25 %	0 %	0 %
Use Moodle to conduct in-class quick surveys	40 %	20 %	15 %	20 %	5 %	0 %

[a] Please refer to Sect. 2 for the meaning of the six levels of responses.

3.2 Moodle Usage Experiences

All our faculties have used Moodle before. According to the survey, 90 % of our Moodle users used the platform to give lecture materials, including lecture notes, assignments, etc., to our students frequently. However, no course functionalities were being used by more than half of our colleagues in actual courses. For example, only 45 % of colleagues used Moodle to collect assignments from students, although 80 % of them knew that Moodle could do that. For advanced functions like maintaining question banks and conducting real-time online quizzes, only one-quarter of colleagues used them in their courses. Table 2 shows how the teachers evaluate the teaching-related functionalities of Moodle.

From the survey, we notice that most colleagues are still treating the Moodle platform as a "passive" way to give information to students, without utilising the full potential (e.g., interactive activities) provided by the e-Learning platforms to improve teaching and learning experiences.

Our Moodle administrator is responsible for setting up the system and performs the basic administrative tasks, such as managing users, creating courses and updating enrollments. Teachers treated Moodle as an alternative to the student information system and get students information for their management tasks. For example, 70 % colleagues have the experience of getting the email addresses of the students from Moodle for further communication. However, the utilization of the advance functions like score computation and backup/restore of courses over different academic years is still relatively low (Table 3).

From the survey, we can see that our colleagues were well-aware of the communication functions of Moodle system and actively used them as a formal way to communicate with the students. For examples, most course related announcements were made in forums or sent to students' message boxes. As shown in Table 4, 85 % of

Table 3. Teachers' experiences in administration-related functionalities on Moodle

Administrative functionalities	(i)	(ii)	(iii)	(iv)	(v)	(vi)
Getting the student list in a course	15 %	15 %	0 %	0 %	30 %	40 %
Enrolling students to your course	35 %	5 %	5 %	10 %	10 %	35 %
Getting the emails of the students	15 %	10 %	5 %	20 %	30 %	20 %
Computing the students' weighted scores	45 %	15 %	5 %	15 %	0 %	20 %
Backing up the materials inside an old course	40 %	0 %	0 %	30 %	20 %	10 %
Restoring previously backed up courses	50 %	0 %	5 %	20 %	25 %	0 %

Table 4. Teachers' experiences in communication-related functionalities on Moodle

On communicating with students	(i)	(ii)	(iii)	(iv)	(v)	(vi)
Posting notices in forums	0 %	10 %	5 %	5 %	50 %	30 %
Discussing course materials in forums	0 %	15 %	15 %	30 %	25 %	15 %
Sending personal message to a student	5 %	30 %	0 %	15 %	50 %	0 %
Sending group messages to all students in a course	5 %	5 %	5 %	5 %	40 %	40 %

colleagues used the Moodle system for announcements through forums or group messages.

Overall, we asked the teachers to rate Moodle in a scale between 0 and 5. 60 % of the colleagues gave the rating 4 or 5, which means that they were satisfied with the system.

3.3 Motivators and Barriers

Table 5 shows the top-5 motivators and the top-5 barriers to the use of Moodle system respectively. According to the studies on the barriers, our colleagues had the concern about the quality of the courses. They did not have the role model to follow, and did not know how to create good e-Learning courses. All these hindered their participation of the systems in teaching.

On the other hand, the top-3 motivators showed a strong attraction to Moodle if we could provide suitable support to our colleagues and reduce their workloads. These three motivators were much stronger than the others.

We noted that the general ratings of motivators were much higher than those of barriers. Therefore, providing suitable motivators should attract more colleagues to join Moodle as the barriers are not strong.

3.4 Suggestions

Our survey asked the teachers for the points they like most and the points they dislike most on Moodle. From the result, we noted that many colleagues liked the friendly

Table 5. Top-5 Motivators or Barriers to the use of Moodle system

Top-5 Motivators or Barriers	Average Rating
Motivators	
Improved infrastructure (hardware and software) deployment	3.72
Release time/Reduction in existing workload	3.67
Technical support	3.56
Personal interest to use technology	3.28
Better Internet bandwidth at workplace	3.17
Barriers	
No role models to follow	2.58
Lack of instructional design support for e-Learning	2.56
Concern about access to students	2.56
Concern about the quality of e-courses	2.47
Lack of training on the use of e-Learning platforms	2.42

interface provided by Moodle. Moreover, the "access from everywhere" web-based feature of Moodle was also welcomed by our colleagues. On the other hand, they did not like the speed of the system, especially in lessons in which a lot of students accessed Moodle at the same time. They also had concerns about the potential leakage of teaching materials and the fairness of online quizzes.

Most colleagues expressed that better training and support provided by the institute would be essential to the effective use of Moodle platform. More examples or role models on the use of various functionalities would also help. We also observed that from the colleagues suggestions like the ones listed in Table 6 actually came from some misunderstanding of the functionalities of Moodle. For example, real-time chat is provided by Moodle, and the combining of multiple courses can be done by the administrator. Thus, better training should unleash more power from the platform.

4 Related Work

e-Learning has been an important area in improving teaching and learning experiences. Bell and Federman [1] and Benta, Bologa, and Dzitac [2] analyzed the importance of online courses and its effectiveness in higher education institutions. The importance of e-Learning has been extensively studied [5, 6]. In this information age when every student has her own device, many e-Learning paradiagms are now the reality.

Table 6. Some comments from teachers on Moodle platform

• *If I teach two similar courses, can Moodle combine the two courses? Or does it support copy a whole class to another?*
• *Add an easier two-way communication channel between the teacher and the students. Add help messages when get stuck can make the teacher have more control over what they are doing, rather than give up on what they are doing.*
• *I would like to learn how I can input the scores on the moodle.*

Many e-Learning platforms are available. Some of them are proprietary, like Blackboard, while some are open, like Moodle. The application of Moodle in higher institutions are also analysed many studies [3, 4, 7]. In our study, we would like to share our own experience in using Moodle platform in e-Learning from the teachers' perspective.

How the platforms should be used in teaching and learning greatly affects the effectiveness of study. Various studies [9, 10] indicated that in additional to installing suitable e-Learning platforms, effectively using them to problem-based learning or other activities is the key to improve teaching and learning experiences. Our survey also studied how our colleagues improve the platform to fit their teaching needs.

5 Conclusions

Our institute has promoted the use of Moodle by putting all courses online and providing basic training on the use of the platform. However, from the results of this survey, we note that our colleagues require more training and role models to enhance the quality of the e-courses they create on Moodle. In order to improve the teaching and learning experience on Moodle, as suggested by the study of motivators and barriers, we could provide more training and better hardware. Moreover, mentorship programmes which provide role models to new colleagues would also help. Through the role model and trainings, we ensure that colleagues are aware of the Moodle functionalities that may be useful in their teaching, and are capable of using them.

In summary, online e-Learning platforms provide various useful functionalities to teachers to improve the teaching and learning experiences. Better training, e-Learning friendly policies can help promoting the use of e-Learning platforms.

References

1. Bell, B.S., Federman, J.E.: E-learning in postsecondary education. Future Child. **23**(1), 165–185 (2013). Accessed http://digitalcommons.ilr.cornell.edu/articles/928
2. Benta, D., Bologa, G., Dzitac, I.: E-learning platforms in higher education. case study. Procedia Comput. Sci. **31**, 1170–1176 (2014)
3. Cheng, G., Chui, H.L.: The Greater the online participation, the better the learning achievement? a study of integrating Moodle into learning. In: Li, K.C., Wong, T.-L., Cheung, S.K., Lam, J., Ng, K.K. (eds.) Technology in Education: Transforming Educational Practices with Technology, pp. 136–144. Springer, Hong Kong (2014)
4. Costa, C., Alvelos, H., Teixeira, L.: The use of moodle e-Learning platform: a study in a portuguese university. Procedia Technol. **5**, 334–343 (2012)
5. Garrison, D.R.: E-Learning in the 21st Century – A Framework for Research and Practice, 2nd edn. Routledge, New York (2011)
6. Kong, S.C., Chan, T.-W., Griffin, P., Hoppe, U., Huang, R., Kinshuk, Looi, C.K., Milrad, M., Norris, C., Nussbaum, M., Sharples, M., So, W.M.W., Soloway, E., Yu, S.: e-Learning in school education in the coming 10 years for developing 21st century skills: critical research issues and policy implications. J. Educ. Technol. Soc. **17**(1), 70–78 (2014)

7. Lui, R.W., Lo, K.K., Yiu, S.M.: Evaluating and adopting e-Learning platforms. Int. J. e-Educ., e-Bus. e-Manage. e-Learn. **3**(3), 229–233 (2013)
8. Panda, S., Mishra, S.: E-learning in a mega open university: faculty attitude, barriers and motivators. Educ. Media Int. **44**(4), 323–338 (2007)
9. Salmon, G.: E-tivities: The Key to Active Online Learning, 2nd edn. Routledge, New York (2013)
10. Uden, L., Beaumont, C.: Technology and Problem-Based Learning. Information Science Publishing, Hershey (2006)

Author Index

Made in the USA
Monee, IL
13 September 2026

62973750R00171